CONQUEST AND SURVIVAL IN COLONIAL GUATEMALA

Conquest and Survival in Colonial Guatemala

A Historical Geography of the Cuchumatán Highlands, 1500–1821

Fourth Edition

W. GEORGE LOVELL

McGill-Queen's University Press
Montreal & Kingston · London · Ithaca

© McGill-Queen's University Press 2015

ISBN 978-0-7735-4526-7 (cloth)
ISBN 978-0-7735-4527-4 (paper)
ISBN 978-0-7735-8365-8 (ePDF)
ISBN 978-0-7735-8367-2 (ePUB)

Legal deposit second quarter 2015
Bibliothèque nationale du Québec

First edition published in 1985
Second edition published in 1992
Third edition published in 2005

Printed in Canada on acid-free paper that is 100% ancient forest free
(100% post-consumer recycled), processed chlorine free

McGill-Queen's University Press acknowledges the support of the Canada
Council for the Arts for our publishing program. We also acknowledge
the financial support of the Government of Canada through the Canada
Book Fund for our publishing activities.

Library and Archives Canada Cataloguing in Publication

Lovell, W. George (William George), 1951–, author
 Conquest and survival in colonial Guatemala: a historical geography
 of the Cuchumatán Highlands, 1500–1821/W. George Lovell. –
 Fourth edition.

 Includes bibliographical references and index.
 Issued in print and electronic formats.
 ISBN 978-0-7735-4526-7 (bound). – ISBN 978-0-7735-4527-4 (pbk.). –
 ISBN 978-0-7735-8365-8 (ePDF). – ISBN 978-0-7735-8367-2 (ePUB)

 1. Indians of Central America – Guatemala – History. 2. Guatemala –
 History – To 1821. I. Title.

 F1466.4.L68 2015   911.7281   C2015-900320-2
                                     C2015-900321-0

This book was typeset by Interscript in 10.5/13 Sabon.

The cover illustration by Angelika Bauer, inspired by the iconography of the *Lienzo
de Quauhquechollan*, depicts a battle scene and place glyph for the Sierra de los
Cuchumatanes.

For Maureen and my parents,
and in fond memory of Oscar H. Horst (1924–2010)

Contents

Figures   ix

Preface   xi

Plates   xx

1 Introduction: Geography and the Past   3

PART ONE: THE REGIONAL SETTING

2 Physical and Human Geography   11

PART TWO: CONTACT AND CONQUEST, 1500–1541

3 Land and Life on the Eve of Spanish Conquest   31

4 Conquest and Subjugation by Imperial Spain   53

5 The Native Population at Spanish Contact   75

PART THREE: THE COLONIAL EXPERIENCE, 1541–1821

6 In Pursuit of Order: *Congregación* and the Administration of
  Empire   83

7 Economic Demands and Ethnic Relations: Spanish Control of the
  Native Population   108

8 Working the Land: Landholding Patterns and the Agricultural
  Economy   133

9 Collapse and Recovery: Demographic Change in the Native
   Population   157

10 Conclusion: Refuge in the Mountains   187

   Epilogue   191

   Glossary   211

   Appendix: Tables   221

   Bibliography   257

   Index   295

Figures

1 The Cuchumatán Highlands of Guatemala: Regional Setting and Principal Settlements 10

2 The *corregimiento* of Totonicapán and Huehuetenango 13

3 The *partido* of Huehuetenango 14

4 Archaeological Sites of the Cuchumatán Highlands 37

5 The Fortress of Zaculeu 62

6 Ecclesiastical Administration of the Cuchumatán Highlands 106

7 Proposed Division of Indian Landholding at Sacapulas in the Late Eighteenth Century 151

8 The Population of the Cuchumatán Highlands, 1520–1825 167

9 Smallpox in the Cuchumatán Highlands, 1780–81 168

10 Smallpox Mortality by Family Category, 1780–81 170

11 Estimated Mortality by *pueblo de indios* Caused by the Smallpox Outbreak of 1780–81 171

Preface

This book, the fourth edition of a work first published in 1985, is the outcome of events and circumstances dating back to my years as a graduate student. It seems appropriate at the outset to say something about how it all began, and how it all evolved. Keeping track of the past is seldom without challenge – we humans change as much as our interpretations of what we relay and relate to – but some aspects of life are indelibly wrought, their details amenable to fond recall.

Early on the morning of 25 June 1974, I left the Mexican city of San Cristóbal de las Casas and travelled for the first time to Guatemala. Having been in Mexico to conduct field research for my master's thesis, I had planned to spend only a few days before starting the long overland trip back to Canada. I stayed almost a month, absorbed and captivated by what I experienced.

At the border town of La Mesilla, two casual passport checks allowed me to walk from one country into another. I was struck immediately by the splendour of the scene. Colossal and imposing, the lush, green mountains that loomed ahead were a pleasant change after the gaunt look of much of central Mexico. Compared especially with the gutted, eroded terrain of the Mixteca Alta – I had spent a good deal of the summer in the highlands of Oaxaca – the land here seemed much more inviting. Not at all sure what to expect, I felt myself drawn in.

I bought a soft drink from a roadside vendor and climbed onto a waiting bus already chock-full of passengers. A stiffer libation would have prepared me better for the antics of the daredevil driver, revving up and honking his horn. We zoomed off just as a deafening peal of thunder roared across the heavens. I gaped out the window.

The features of landscape assumed an elemental, shifting guise: trees glimpsed, then engulfed by mist; a grape-dark, menacing sky; a torrential downpour of rain; a wan burst of sun; all around, a kaleidoscopic play of shadow and light. Steep patchworks of fields and forests towered above the valley that followed the course of the Río Selegua, its raging waters threatening to flood the road at every hairpin turn. The bus screeched to a halt mile after mile, dropping people off, picking people up, all of them carrying some item or other – a steel machete, a basket laden with fruit, a bundle of firewood, an armful of flowers, a chicken or a rooster, even a small pig. For the most part my fellow travellers were of indigenous Maya stock – men, women, and children wrapped up not just in startlingly colourful clothes but in exchanges beyond my ability to comprehend, for their conversations were conducted in an idiom my Spanish could not access. I reached my destination mesmerized.

In Huehuetenango's central plaza, a three-dimensional relief map forty-four paces in circumference informed me that the mountains I had skirted were the Sierra de los Cuchumatanes, home to dozens of communities identified by the names of Catholic saints painted on tiny metal flags stuck atop the map's surface like candles on a birthday cake. The virtual topography someone had toiled hard to render was littered with broken glass, plastic bags, cigarette ends, and dog shit. But there it was in front of me, framed by the curve of a low iron fence that toddlers ran around and sweethearts cuddled against, the semblance of an idea. As I was about to turn in for the night – a bed at the Hotel Central then went for one quetzal, the equivalent of one US dollar, fleas and roommates included – the idea insinuated itself and wouldn't let go: why not write about the Sierra de los Cuchumatanes and the Maya peoples who inhabit it? That was the beginning of my relationship with Guatemala, one that now spans four decades.

Three years later, in 1977, after a period of focused reading and a more scholarly formulation of ideas, my investigations began in earnest. The geography of the Cuchumatán highlands, I learned after perusing Franz Termer's seminal article "Observaciones geográficas en los Altos Cuchumatanes" (1927), lent itself to a multitude of options. The one that I chose was to piece together what happened to the land and its native peoples under Spanish rule. Such an orientation called for me to dedicate myself to archival research, so I spent much of 1977 and 1978 gathering material in the Archivo General de Centro América in Guatemala City and across the Atlantic in the Archivo General de Indias in Seville, Spain. After three lengthy sojourns in these archives, I then set off, by bus and on foot, on a trip through parts of the Cuchumatanes I had never visited before, bringing episodes I had read about in the documents freshly to life in my imagination. Having sacrificed the field for the archive for so long, it was exhilarating to walk once again over the hills and through the corn, even though the civil war that was to cause such destruction and loss of life between 1978 and 1983 was about to explode.

In December 1979 I defended the study I had written during the previous fifteen months as a doctoral dissertation. Since then I have had ample opportunity to continue working in Guatemalan and Spanish archives and to visit the Cuchumatanes time and again. Though these later forays have been undertaken with different research ends in mind, I have always kept a close watch for Cuchumatán data I had overlooked or did not know about before. While the material I gathered as a graduate student remains the foundation, the book in its present form incorporates findings from not only my own subsequent inquiries but also those of colleagues in related fields.

Despite considerable advances since my initial inquiries in the 1970s, the historiography of Spain in America continues to emphasize Mexico and Peru, to the detriment of our knowledge about other regions of that vast Indo-Euro-Afro world. This state of affairs is hardly surprising. It merely reflects the fact that the thrust of modern scholarship parallels closely the political and economic realities of colonial times: resource-rich "cores" such as Mexico and Peru were of far more significance to imperial Spain than resource-deficient "peripheries" such as Central America. The destiny of the isthmus has been vividly captured by William B. Taylor, who refers to Central America, situated "between the great mining centers and Indian populations of the Andes and Mexico," as "a rainbow of Spanish illusions and frenzied activity between the two pots of gold."[1]

Taylor's depiction remains as pertinent as ever. In the Mesoamerican context, ongoing research seeks to redress the epistemic bias of core over periphery, with more and more scholars moving south and

---

1 Taylor's words come from his review of Sherman (1979) and appear in the *Hispanic American Historical Review* 60, no. 2 (1980): 325. His characterization is based on a reading of Góngora (1962).

east from central Mexico to conduct studies on Oaxaca, Chiapas, Guatemala, and Yucatán.² What emerges most from these investigations is that we can no longer assume that the colonial experiences of a Mesoamerican periphery are but a simplified variant, retarded in time and marginal in space, of conditions that prevailed in the central Mexican core. This book examines the vicissitudes of life in a region certainly of peripheral status in the Spanish scheme of empire, one that (as at least one researcher suggests) might more precisely be considered a "periphery of a periphery."³ Before dismissing such a focus as being of minimal import to an understanding of Spain in America, we do well to remember that poor rural backwaters are where most Hispanic Americans, prior to the juggernaut of twenty-first century globalization, lived, worked, and died. For every Zacatecas or Potosí, for every Lima or Mexico City, there were (and are still) scores if not thousands of Huehuetenangos, modest provincial hubs related in myriad functional ways to smaller, less prosperous, more inward-looking communities in the surrounding countryside.

The findings on which the book are based, first and foremost, were made possible by my being awarded an Izaak Walton Killam Memorial Scholarship, which I held as a doctoral student from 1975 to 1978 at the University of Alberta in Edmonton. Postdoctoral funding from the Killam Program of the Canada Council (1981–82) enabled me to rework my dissertation into a series of articles, book chapters, and essays. Fellowships from Plumsock Mesoamerican Studies and the Social Sciences and Humanities Research Council of Canada then allowed me to consolidate my endeavours and, in 1985, to publish *Conquest and Survival in Colonial Guatemala* with McGill-Queen's University Press. That first edition was followed in 1992 by a second, and in 2005 by a third. A Spanish-language edition appeared in 1990,

---

2   For advances in our knowledge of these parts of Mesoamerica, see the volumes edited by MacLeod and Wasserstrom (1983) and by Adams and MacLeod (2000).

3   See Carol A. Smith (1978, 583–7). Farriss (1983, 33) considers Yucatán also to have been "a periphery of a periphery." Such marginal status means that, as with the Sierra de los Cuchumatanes, Yucatán "is no more likely to replicate the exact processes of change in central Mexico than central Mexico is likely to follow the same path as western Europe." It should be pointed out, however, that evidence from linguistics and plant domestication – see chapter 2 – places the Cuchumatanes at the very heart of where Maya culture and civilization are now thought to have originated.

and another in 2015. In preparing this fourth English-language edition, supported once again by the Killam Program of the Canada Council, I have made substantial changes to every chapter, reconfiguring the text and adding new data. I have also furnished readers with a new preface, a new epilogue, and a new set of maps and tables. The tables, some of which took years to compile in their present form, are now gathered together in an appendix.

Little did I imagine on that June evening in Huehuetenango four decades ago what would result from my contemplation of that funky relief map. For their belief in a book that keeps evolving, given a new lease of life by their loyalty and encouragement, I thank Don Akenson and Philip Cercone, whose labours on behalf of McGill-Queen's University Press are without parallel in Canadian publishing, and much to be applauded.

In both Guatemala City and Seville, the staff of the archives proved patient and helpful in guiding me through the customary growing pains of how to locate and request the necessary documents. The paleographic expertise of Carlos Estrada Lemus, Manuel Fuentes Mairena, Wendy Kramer, and Leonel Sarazúa solved many a problem. After my research in the archives, the work of numerous scholars provided a crucial framework for interpreting the Cuchumatán material, but it is important to single out the publications of the Berkeley School and the unrivalled contribution of Murdo MacLeod. During the dissertation stage of the study, I profited not only from the discreet supervision of John F. Bergmann – I turned out to be his one and only doctoral charge – but also from the guidance of Olive P. Dickason, Ruth Gruhn, Oscar H. Horst, and David C. Johnson.

Looking back to acknowledge my debts, both personal and professional, affords me mixed sentiments, for several of the individuals who influenced my thinking or who shaped who I am have passed on. Anyone I fail to mention by name I trust will forgive the oversight and remember instead the times we shared.

Bjarne Tokerud, whom I met while enrolled in my first seminar in anthropology, talked about Guatemala in a way that made me want to go there, which I did after I got my Mesoamerican bearings in Mexico. Tomislav Milinusic knew first-hand about other parts of Latin America, and his instincts set me straight. After I had ventured alone on a trip to South America, one that Tomislav and I had planned to undertake together, I was better prepared to return to Guatemala and get on with the job I knew by then awaited me.

In Guatemala, bumping into William R. Swezey in Don Pancho's *tienda* in Antigua opened up a universe and created an everlasting bond. Swezey introduced me to Christopher H. Lutz, whose trail I had come across in the archives and whom I was most curious to meet. Chris and Swezey were busy dreaming up the unique research institute that is the Centro de Investigaciones Regionales de Mesoamérica (CIRMA). The three of us struck up a partnership, which Chris and I invest in still, through our continued involvement with CIRMA and as collaborators in projects that fuel our desire to know more about Guatemala's alluring but tragic past.

I enjoy a similar working relationship with Noble David Cook, one that began when Henry F. Dobyns brought us together at the Newberry Library in Chicago. David and his wife, Sasha, are my Seville soul mates, two aficionados of a city that is now a cherished home base for part of the year. There, at the Escuela de Estudios Hispano-Americanos, the Universidad Pablo de Olavide, and the Universidad de Sevilla, I mix with colleagues and students who constitute a stimulating Spanish equivalent to their counterparts at Queen's University in Canada. Having been hired at Queen's in 1979 on a one-year, non-renewable contract, things (or so I like to believe) have worked out well. I trust that *mi querido jefe pelón*, Brian S. Osborne, a source of sage counsel always, concurs. John Walker stood resolutely behind me from the start, and has been there ever since. The wise words of Peter Goheen I also benefited from.

Before I embarked on a tenure-track position at Queen's, I spent a term as visiting scholar in the Department of Geography at the University of California at Berkeley. The great Carl Sauer had been dead a decade, but his legacy lived on. That spell at Berkeley, like that first trip to Guatemala, changed my life. I relish still conversations I had with Woodrow Borah, Bernard Q. Nietschmann, James J. Parsons, Dan Stanislawski, and John H. Rowe, all now deceased. Through them I forged close relationships, enduring as well as endearing, with Wayne Bernhardson, Susan E. Davis, and María Laura Massolo – ¡qué familia somos, todavía! Hanging out at UCB with the likes of Dave Larson, Bob Rice, Paul Starrs, and Jack Wright made for a lot of fun, too. Fellow geographers whose interests also lie in Latin America, and whose company I enjoy and from whom I learn much, include Stephen A. Bell, Elisabeth and Karl Butzer, David Carr, Oliver Coomes, William V. Davidson, William M. Denevan, Bill Doolittle, Daniel W. Gade, Susanna Hecht, Victoria L.

Henderson, Curt Holder, Leah A. Huff, Peter Herlihy, Taylor Mack, Kent Mathewson, Linda A. Newson, Catherine Nolin, Karl H. Offen, Alexandra Pedersen, Marie Price, David J. Robinson, Michael Steinberg, Matthew Taylor, Giselle Valarezo, Tom Whitmore, and Bill "Black Earth" Woods.

Among my writer friends, Eduardo Galeano, Tom Pow, Alastair Reid, and Ronald Wright keep me focused on what matters most, a trait they share with Antonio Acosta, Rolena Adorno, Armando J. Alfonzo, Christophe Belaubre, José Cal, Laura Cameron, Paul Chaput, Mary Ellen Davis, Alvis Dunn, Jordana Dym, Ted Fischer, Bill Fowler, Juan Gil, Mike González, Linda Green, Jim Handy, José Hernández Palomo, John M. Kirk, Wendy Kramer, Ken Mills, Jorge Luján Muñoz, Juan Marchena Fernández, David Parker, Tony Pasinski, José Manuel Peña Girón, Tristan Platt, Barbara Potthast, Matthew Restall, Alasdair Robertson, Oliver Rogers, Joan Schwartz, Nancy Van Deusen, Consuelo Varela, Eduardo Velásquez Carrera, John M. Watanabe, Stephen A. Webre, and Elías Zamora. Sandy Davis, Andy Gibb, Victor Perera, and Jan de Vos look down from above, in the esteemed company of Jack Bruce: there "isn't much time, and it's gathering darkness" – how true. Seldom do I agree with the visceral opinions of Michael Shawcross, O B E, but his eagle-eyed inspections of previous editions of this book have allowed me to tighten things up from beginning to end. Mike's assessment of my work is what matters, not (mercifully) what he thinks of me. Sharon Mohammed and Guisela Asensio Lueg extended me their myriad editorial skills, and Jennifer Grek Martin her cartographic prowess. Maureen McCallum Garvie, in Barriefield and beyond, is a partner and editor beyond compare. Never did I dream of meeting any individual or collective whose passion about life north of Huehuetenango could match my own, but Krystyna Deuss, Ruth Piedrasanta, Concepción Sáenz, and the staff of the Centro de Estudios y Documentación de la Frontera Occidental de Guatemala (C E D F O G) proved me wrong. For all those whose lives and lot I write about, Maya Indians especially, I dedicate this retelling of their struggle for survival, which is far from over.

I close my record of thanks with a few words about my parents. Like many of her inter-war generation, my mother had to leave school early to earn a wage that would help make family ends meet. She longed for me to get the education she herself was denied, and urged me to see the world as she never did. "Enjoy it for both of us, son." Her words are with me always. So, too, are the stories my father told me as a boy, of the years he sailed the Spanish Main – not as a latter-day conquistador (the music of Procol Harum resounds in my ears) but as a merchant seaman employed by Royal Dutch Shell, working aboard oil tankers that steamed in and out of Aruba, Cuba, Curaçao, and Venezuela after World War II.

Leaving Scotland to study in Canada, I soon realized, was only the beginning of the journey. Glasgow to Guatemala may seem an odd trajectory to some. Not, however, for me.

WGL, Autumn 2014

And what you thought you came for
Is only a shell, a husk of meaning
From which the purpose breaks only when it is fulfilled
If at all. Either you had no purpose
Or the purpose is beyond the end you figured
And is altered in fulfilment.

T.S. Eliot, *Little Gidding* (1942)

Photographs 1–8, 10–14, and 20 were taken by the author while conducting fieldwork in the region between 1975 and 1978.

1 Southern edge of the Cuchumatán highlands, viewed from the outskirts of Huehuetenango.

2 View of the Cuchumatán *páramo* near Chancol (elevation 3,000 m).

3 Corn in the *tierra fría* near Nebaj (elevation 2,000 m).

4 View of the *región andina*, looking toward the still-occupied remains of Hacienda Chancol (elevation 3,000 m).

5 Boys from the Mam community of Todos Santos Cuchumatán.

6 Boys from the Chuj community of San Mateo Ixtatán.

7 Mother and children, Todos Santos Cuchumatán.

8 Girl fetching water, Todos Santos Cuchumatán.

9 The *cabecera* of Santiago Chimaltenango, a "town-nucleus" *municipio* (courtesy of John M. Watanabe).

10 The *cabecera* of Todos Santos Cuchumatán, a "vacant-town" *municipio*.

11 Salt works on the Río Negro floodplain near Sacapulas.

12 One of the three salt wells at San Mateo Ixtatán (the crosses in front are the site of Indian *costumbre* activities).

13 The pre-conquest Mam capital of Zaculeu, looking north.

14 The Q'anjob'al community of Santa Eulalia, situated in the northern reaches of the Cuchumatán highlands.

15 Restoration drawing of Chalchitán, as rendered by Tatiana Proskouriakoff, looking south at the ball court group (courtesy of the Carnegie Institution of Washington).

16 Unexcavated temples in the west group at Chaculá. The photograph, probably taken about 1895–97, may be found with others of the same period in Seler's *Die Alten Ansiedlungen von Chaculá* (1901).

17 Restoration drawing of Chutixtiox, as rendered by Tatiana Proskouriakoff, looking north to the front ranges of the Cuchumatanes (courtesy of the Carnegie Institution of Washington).

18 Restoration drawing of Xolchun (Quiché), as rendered by Tatiana Proskouriakoff, looking south to the hilltop fortress of Pacot (courtesy of the Carnegie Institution of Washington).

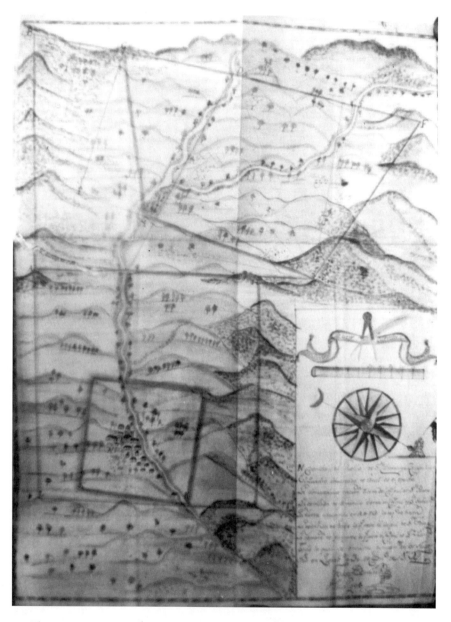

19 The *congregación* and environs of Sacapulas (for source and explanation, see chapter 6, footnote 32). Reproduced by kind permission of the Archivo General de Centro América.

20 Detail from a mural in the parish church at Chiantla, in which a robust-looking Spaniard (possibly meant to be the *encomendero* Juan de Espinar) oversees the labours of Indian miners.

21 The parish of Chiantla, showing *haciendas* Chancol and El Rosario and nearby *congregaciones* (for source and explanation, see chapter 8, footnote 27). Reproduced by kind permission of the Archivo General de Indias.

22 Land under dispute at Sacapulas in the late eighteenth century (for source and explanation, see chapter 8, footnote 61). Reproduced by kind permission of the Archivo General de Centro América.

23 Indian *congregaciones* and Spanish *haciendas* of Malacatán parish (for source and explanation, see chapter 8, footnote 66). Reproduced by kind permission of the Archivo General de Indias.

CONQUEST AND SURVIVAL IN COLONIAL GUATEMALA

I

Introduction: Geography and the Past

Geography and history fill up the entire circumference of our perceptions:
geography that of space, history that of time.

Immanuel Kant (1724–1804)

Geography, the study of place and space, of land-life relations, is a
diverse field of learning. Because of the discipline's expansive scope,
geographers are seldom in agreement about what the principal goals
of geographical inquiry should be. The diversity of geography is the
discipline's nemesis as well as its greatest asset, for too much of it
results in common ground being difficult to establish, and thus com-
promises exposure to a broader, more enriching range of knowledge.

There has been animated debate over the years about the rele-
vance to geography of what David Harvey termed historical, genetic,
or temporal modes of explanation.[1] In his vintage appraisal, *The
Nature of Geography* (1939), Richard Hartshorne noted that "some
geographers insist that in order to maintain the essential point of
view of geography – the consideration of phenomena in their spatial
relations – any consideration of time relations must be secondary
and merely supplementary."[2] Hartshorne was of the opinion that
"while the interpretation of individual features in the geography of
a region will often require the student to reach back into the geography of past periods, it is not necessary that the geography of a region
be studied in terms of historical development."[3]

Such a view of geography was not shared by one of Hartshorne's
contemporaries, Carl Ortwin Sauer. The year following the publication of Hartshorne's treatise, Sauer, in a presidential address to the
Association of American Geographers, asserted that "geography, in

[1] Harvey (1969, 407).
[2] Hartshorne (1939, 183).
[3] Ibid.

any of its branches, must be a genetic science; that is, must account for origins and processes."[4] Criticizing Hartshorne for not grasping fully the ideas of the German geographer Alfred Hettner, whom he much admired, Sauer continued:

> The geographer cannot study houses and towns, fields and factories, as to their where and why without asking himself about their origins. He cannot treat the localization of activities without knowing the functioning of the culture, the process of living together of the group; and he cannot do this except by historical reconstruction. If the object is to define and understand human associations as areal growths, we must find out how they ... came to be what they are ... The quality of understanding sought is that of analysis of origins and processes. The all-inclusive objective is spatial differentiation of culture. Dealing with man and being genetic in its analysis, the subject is of necessity concerned with sequences in time.[5]

Since that address, which Sauer regarded as "a confession of the faith that has stood behind [my] work,"[6] geography has found creative ways to embrace historical issues and move forward. In 1953, H.C. Darby claimed that "all geography is historical geography, either actual or potential."[7] Subsequent work by Andrew Clark in 1954, Clifford Smith in 1965, and David Harvey in 1967 also argued for the need to have historical analysis figure prominently in geographical inquiry.[8] In 1969, Alan Baker and three of his British colleagues stressed the "utility of historical geography" by stating categorically that "the geographical mosaic can only be understood with reference to the past,"[9] a way of thinking about geography long endorsed by Sauer.

In retrospect, we continue to be well served by how Harvey dealt with the issue in his *Explanation in Geography* (1969), written before he abandoned liberal, positivist ideas in favour of more radical,

4   Sauer (1941) in Leighly (1963, 352).
5   Ibid., 360.
6   Ibid., 361.
7   Darby (1953, 6).
8   Clark (1954, 70–105); Clifford T. Smith (1965, 118–43); and Harvey (1967, 549–608).
9   Baker et al. (1969, 48).

Marxist ones. After outlining what Hartshorne and Sauer had to say, Harvey concludes that "temporal modes of explanation (usually called genetic or historical explanations in geography) are important in geography and provide a useful but not exclusive mode of approach, given objectives appropriate for such modes."[10] Though a far cry from his later embrace of historical materialism, Harvey's words make eminent practical sense and transcend ideological preference: depending on the nature of the question being asked, historical perspectives may or may not be suitable for illuminating it. The backward glance of historical geography, in which more than a few tenets of Marxist thought may be deployed to good effect, is simply an instructive way of looking at the world in order to understand how it came to be.

HISTORICAL GEOGRAPHY AND THE CULTURAL LANDSCAPE

Central to the study of historical geography is the concept of the cultural landscape, as theorized and developed by Sauer. He held that "historical geography may be considered as the series of changes [that] cultural landscapes have undergone." The practice of historical geography, above all, entailed "the reconstruction of past cultural landscapes."[11] According to Sauer, cultural landscapes are shaped from natural landscapes by culture groups in a continuous, dialectic process:

> Culture is the agent, the natural area is the medium, the cultural landscape the result. Under the influence of a given culture, itself changing through time, the landscape undergoes development, passing through phases and probably reaching ultimately the end of its cycle of development. With the introduction of a different – that is, an alien – culture, a rejuvenation of the cultural landscape sets in, or a new landscape is superimposed on remnants of an older one.[12]

10 Harvey (1969, 418–19). Arguably today the geographer whose name and work is most recognized beyond the confines of the discipline, Harvey lays out his *volte-face* chapter by chapter in his *Social Justice and the City* ([1973] 2009).

11 Sauer (1925) in Leighly (1963, 344).

12 Ibid., 343.

The cultural landscape, in which human activity is given both formal and informal expression, is therefore dynamic in nature and must be viewed as a temporal as well as a spatial construct. Sauer claims: "We cannot form the idea of landscape except in terms of its time relations as well as of its space relations."[13] Aspects of time – evolution, change, continuity, sequence, succession – are key criteria in landscape analysis, and are the bedrock of historical geography.

HISTORICAL GEOGRAPHY IN A LATIN AMERICAN REGIONAL CONTEXT

Latin America has long attracted the scholarly attention of historical geographers, including distinguished contributions by Sauer himself as well as many of his Berkeley associates.[14] Research on the historical geography of the region, in conjunction with work undertaken by anthropologists, historians, and other social scientists, indicates a healthy multidisciplinary initiative, most notably in the field of Mesoamerican studies.[15] Despite considerable progress, however, gaps in our knowledge abound. The deficiency is especially marked

13 Ibid., 333.

14 Sauer's magnum opus is *The Early Spanish Main* (1963), a model of incisive research and artful exposition. His role in creating what French social scientists were the first to call the Berkeley School is showcased in the volume edited by Mathewson and Kenzer (2004). Another volume edited by Denevan and Mathewson (2009) features not only commentaries on Sauer's work but extracts from some of his lesser-known contributions. The great scholar is now the subject of an illuminating biography (Williams, with Lowenthal and Denevan, 2014). How historical geography has developed in a Latin American regional context may be charted by examining Denevan (1971); Robinson (1972, 1979); Davidson and Parsons (1980); Martinson (1992); and Knapp (2002). Since it began publication in 2002, replacing the *Yearbook of the Conference of Latin Americanist Geographers*, the *Journal of Latin American Geography* has assiduously logged developments in the field.

15 Taking stock of Mesoamerican research has for decades been the mission of the University of Texas Press's *Handbook of Middle American Indians*, a series begun in 1964 that now has more than twenty volumes. *Mesoamérica*, a journal published in Spanish since 1980, offers another means of appraisal; its *Índice general* (2008) surveys the contents of the journal's first fifty issues. In terms of English-language historiography, two projects stand out as benchmark assessments. The first is the three-volume *Oxford Encyclopedia of Mesoamerican Cultures*, for which David Carrasco (2001) served as editor-in-chief; the second is the three-volume *Cambridge History of the Native Peoples of the Americas*, volume 2 of which, edited by Richard E.W. Adams and Murdo J. MacLeod (2000), focuses on Mesoamerica. For a critique of the former, see Lovell (2004); for critiques of the latter, see Gruzinski (2002) and Patch (2002). Other pertinent literature is reviewed in the epilogue.

in the case of Guatemala, a country whose colonial past has left an enduring trace on its cultural landscape, but a country that remains little studied in the overall scheme of Mesoamerican research.

Seven decades ago, three respected archaeologists indicated that what was most lacking in studies of Guatemala were reconstructions of contact and colonial-period culture.[16] This same view was later articulated by ethnohistorian Henry B. Nicholson, who believed that scholarship would best be advanced by conducting what he called "reconstructive syntheses" of late pre-Hispanic and colonial times.[17] The need for such studies is underlined by anthropologist Robert M. Carmack, who asserts that "Guatemala is particularly rich in documentary source materials" yet remains "abjectly poor in bibliographic organization and reconstructive syntheses."[18]

One part of Guatemala in need of such reconstructive synthesis is the Sierra de los Cuchumatanes: hitherto, the contact and colonial experiences of this remote, isolated region have been largely unknown or the subject of speculation. What follows is an attempt to reconstruct aspects of the historical geography of the Cuchumatanes from the late fifteenth to the early nineteenth century. The book focuses on the changing nature of land-life relations and on the evolution of the Cuchumatán cultural landscape; the human factor is represented most of all in the myriad dealings between indigenous Mayas and Spaniards, the latter's criollo descendants, and mixed bloods known in Guatemala as Ladinos. The book's ultimate goal is to portray, as comprehensively as available sources permit, the major land-related features of the historical geography of the region between the years 1500 and 1821. Although discussion of the Cuchumatán evidence dominates the narrative, wherever possible I endeavour to interpret and situate those regional findings in a broader Mesoamerican context.

16 Kidder, Jennings, and Shook (1946, 259–60).
17 Nicholson (1975, 498).
18 Carmack (1973, 5).

PART ONE

The Regional Setting

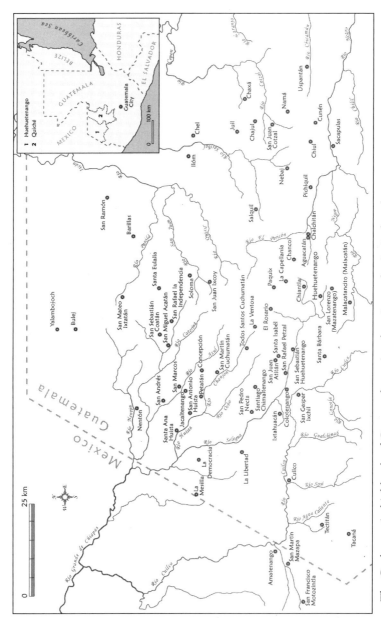

1 The Cuchumatán highlands of Guatemala: regional setting and principal settlements.

2

Physical and Human Geography

All that country was so beautiful it hurt.
        Oliver La Farge and Douglas Byers, *The Year Bearer's People* (1931)

The Sierra de los Cuchumatanes (plate 1) is the most massive and spectacular non-volcanic region of all Central America. Lying to the north of the Río Cuilco, and to the north and west of the Río Negro or Chixoy, the Cuchumatanes form a well-defined unit bordered on the north by the tropical lowlands of the Usumacinta basin and on the west by the hilly Comitán country of the Mexican state of Chiapas. With elevations ranging from 500 to almost 3,900 metres, the region straddles the Guatemalan departments of Huehuetenango and Quiché, constituting some 15 per cent (approximately 16,350 square kilometres) of the national territory (figure 1).

During the first two centuries of Spanish rule in Guatemala, Cuchumatán country formed part of an administrative division known as the Corregimiento or Alcaldía Mayor de Totonicapán y Huehuetenango (figure 2).[1] The jurisdiction included all of the

---

1 Figure 2 shows the "Corregimiento de Totonicapán y Huehuetenango," as rendered in the late seventeenth century by Francisco Antonio de Fuentes y Guzmán in his *Recordación florida* ([1690–99] 1969–72, vol. 3, 40–1). Most important Cuchumatán settlements are represented. Huehuetenango (Hueguetenango) is located in the centre of Fuentes y Guzmán's schema, at the headwaters of the Río Cuilco (Quilco). Distortion and fanciful configuration are most conspicuous in the bottom right or northeast corner, across the river from the land designated "Tierra de Chol y El Lacandón, Yndios Ynfieles." While working at the Archivo General de Centro América (AGCA) in August 2014, I had the opportunity to consult Fuentes y Guzmán's original version of the *Recordación florida*, which to my delight has the "Corregimiento de Totonicapán y Huehuetenango" drafted in colour. His attention to detail, more so than in his other cartographic representations, is surely related to fact that Fuentes y Guzmán knew Cuchumatán country intimately, by virtue of his serving there for many years as its district governor or *corregidor*.

present-day Department of Totonicapán, most of Huehuetenango, the northern half of Quiché, parts of Quetzaltenango, and the Motozintla area of the Mexican state of Chiapas. Toward the end of the colonial period, the jurisdiction was made a *provincia* composed of two units: the Partido de Totonicapán and the Partido de Huehuetenango. The unit referred to as the Partido de Huehuetenango corresponds in approximate territorial extent to the region here designated the Cuchumatán highlands (see figure 3).

Derived from the compounding of the Mam words *cuchuj* (to join or unite) and *matán* (superior strength), the name "Cuchumatán," or "Cuchumatlán," may be rendered as "that which was brought together by great force." Another possible derivation, however, could be related to the Náhuatl or Mexican term *kochmatlán*, meaning "place of the parrot hunters."[2] Regardless of origin, the term "Cuchumatán" appears to be an ancient one, and though more specifically associated with the communities of Todos Santos and San Martín in the heart of the mountains, the name broadly refers to the entire upland area of northwestern Guatemala. The look of the land is striking, and has moved to superlatives a number of writers, including Thomas Gage, John Lloyd Stephens, Franz Termer, and Oliver La Farge; its frontier feel, especially in the far north and west, is palpable.[3] Remote, isolated, and to this day difficult of access,

2 Instituto Geográfico Nacional (1961–62, vol. 1, 112); Arriola (1973, 103). See chapter 4 for discussion of a place glyph in the *Lienzo de Quauhquechollan* (Asselbergs 2004, 176; 2010, 282) that supports the latter derivation.

3 Gage ([1648] 1958, 160–7); Stephens ([1841]) 1949, 185–200); Termer (1927, 13; 1933, 160); and La Farge (1947, 1). See also Seler-Sachs (1900, 157–84 and 258–96); Blom and La Farge (1926–27, vol. 2, 439–48); Navarrete (1980, 7–19); Camus (2007, 18–27); and Piedrasanta (2009, 12–14). The keen eye and unique pen of Robert Burkitt (1930, 41–2) recorded the following:

> The southern front of the Cuchumatanes is a very definite line; and at any reasonable distance, it is a very distinct line to the eye. At a distance of twenty to thirty leagues, the effect of unity in the long mountain front is very striking. Riding from Quiché to Totonicapán, for instance, you see the Cuchumatanes as a great blue barrier on the north. The barrier seems to be penetrated here and there by black glens. But there is no rift or opening that you can see through. The general appearance is that of a solid, frowning rampart rising to a very even height and long stretched out. You wonder when you look at it what there might be behind.

The region is best delimited as a physical unit by Termer (1927, 7–13; 1933, 159–61), who was also awestruck by its compelling beauty: "a jewel beyond compare" (*joya inestimable*) is how he describes it, even though three woollen blankets were not enough to keep him from freezing there at night, his teeth chattering as he anxiously

2 The *corregimiento* of Totonicapán and Huehuetenango.

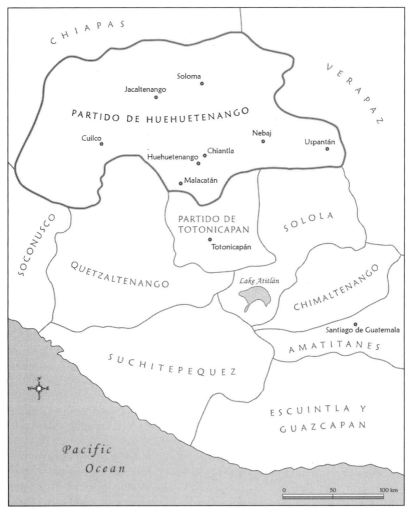

3 The *partido* of Huehuetenango.

though drug traffickers and peddlers of contraband goods pass through without too much inconvenience, the Cuchumatanes exude a spirit of place that is haunting, mournful, and difficult to convey in words. The lines of Guatemalan poet Juan Diéguez, however, composed in the mid-nineteenth century, evoke something of the region's ethereal splendour:

¡Oh cielo de mi Patria!
¡Oh caros horizontes!
¡Oh azules altos montes,
Oídme desde allí!
La alma mía os saluda,
Cumbres de la alta Sierra,
Murallas de esta tierra
Donde la luz yo vi!⁴

---

awaited dawn. Ricketson (1940, 349) is most evocative too, recalling being bombarded during a thunderstorm "by hailstones as large as pigeon eggs." Stephens ([1841] 1949, 196) awoke one bitterly cold morning, in the company of Frederick Catherwood, to find that "the ground was covered with a hoarfrost and water was frozen a quarter of an inch thick."

4 Juan Diéguez's poem, *A Los Cuchumatanes*, may be found in Recinos (1954, 30–3). In English translation, this stanza (the first of nine) runs:

Oh heaven of my homeland!
Oh precious horizons!
Oh high blue mountains,
Hear me from over yonder!
My soul salutes you,
Peaks of the high sierra,
Guardians of the land
Where my eyes first saw light!

The same lines are engraved on plaques at the *mirador* (lookout) some thirteen kilometres to the north of Chiantla near the top of the steep scarp slope of the southern Cuchumatanes. Early on a bright clear morning, the views can be stunning, from Volcán Tajumulco (4,220m) in the west to Volcán Agua (3,766m) in the east. The biting cold of high altitude life, however, leaves its mark on the local population, whose ruddy cheeks are chapped with frostbite, an appearance one usually associates with people who live in the upper reaches of the Andes. When I was at the *mirador* with my friend, colleague, and travelling companion, Eduardo Velasquéz Carrera, at the end of a trip we made across Cuchumatán country in December 2012, a group of children treated us to a recitation of Diéguez's poem "in situ," a memorable experience.

THE PHYSICAL SETTING

Viewed from the south, the "peaks of the high sierra" to which Diéguez refers indeed loom like "guardians of the land." The front ranges tower over 1,000 metres along a steep scarp slope, behind which lies an undulating plateau of breathtaking beauty. This lofty *páramo* (plate 2) or *altiplano* surface, known during colonial times as the Altos de Chiantla, is generally around 3,000 metres in elevation, but some locations lie upward of 3,800 metres. Such heights made it possible for an ice cap to form and glaciation to occur during late Pleistocene times some 10,000 to 25,000 years ago. Today the craggy surface of the *páramo* is riddled with sink holes and other karst features, which for the most part drain the plateau in subterranean fashion. East-flowing streams discharge into tributaries of the Río Chixoy, subsequently draining into the Río Usumacinta and the Gulf of Mexico. West-flowing streams drain into the Río Selegua, which runs along a deep canyon at the southern edge of the Cuchumatanes before joining with the Río Cuilco in Mexico to form the Río Grande de Chiapas.[5]

Away from the bleak, cold, windswept *páramo*, elevation decreases north and west to the humid rainforests of the Usumacinta basin. As holds true for all tropical highland areas, fluctuations in altitude result in extreme variations of climate, especially in temperature regimes. This variation, in turn, gives rise to myriad types of vegetation and a marked diversity in agricultural potential. Four altitudinal zones, each with its own distinctive environment, may be identified:[6]

1   *Tierra caliente* or "warm land." This zone lies below 800 metres in elevation and has mean annual temperatures of around 25°C. It is characterized by lush tropical growth and produces mahogany woods, bananas, cacao, and coffee.
2   *Tierra templada* or "temperate land." This zone ranges from 800 to around 1,500 metres in elevation and has mean annual temperatures of 18°C to 23°C. Coffee and sugar cane can be cultivated, and corn and wheat are grown in upper reaches.

5 Anderson (1969, 87); Anderson et al. (1973, 816); Steinberg and Taylor (2008, 256–8); Roy and Lachniet (2010, 1–7).
6 Stadelman (1940, 92–3); Recinos (1954, 85–8).

3 *Tierra fría* or "cold land." This zone (plate 3) ranges from 1,500 to slightly over 3,000 metres in elevation and has mean annual temperatures of 15°C to 17°C, with occasional sub-zero temperatures and resultant frosts. It is characterized by hardy species of pine, fir, oak, and cedar, and may be used to raise apples, potatoes, and wheat. Most land cultivated in *tierra fría* country, however, is farmed as *milpa*, which means that it is used to grow maize, *el santo maíz*, the holy corn. Indeed, corn may have first been domesticated in these environs, making the Cuchumatanes not only the hearth of Maya but of Mesoamerican culture writ large.[7]

4 *Región andina* or "Andean region." This zone is upward of 3,000 metres in elevation and has mean annual temperatures of below 10°C, with frequent sub-zero temperatures. Frosts are common, and there are occasional snow flurries during the cold season. For the most part uncultivated, though potatoes can be grown, and lightly settled in relative terms, the *región andina*, especially the Altos de Chiantla around La Capellanía and Chancol (plate 4), is utilized primarily as pastureland for sheep and was highly prized as such during the colonial period. Although a misnomer in strict geographical terms – the designation is that of Recinos – the *región andina* bears a striking resemblance to locales in the high Andes; hence the designation.

Two main seasons prevail: the rainy season and the dry season. The rainy season or *invierno* (winter) usually begins toward the middle or end of May and lasts until October. A normal six-month rainy season is interrupted at mid-season, sometime in July or August, by a *canícula*, or dry spell, which may last for a fortnight or more. During the rainy season, thunderstorms occur almost daily. Periods

---

7 Piedrasanta (2009, 102–6) reviews the hard scientific evidence judiciously, complementing her reading of it with observations culled from linguistics and studies of the mythic origins of maize. All point suggestively to locations in the Sierra de los Cuchumatanes. Over a century ago, Paul Schellhas ([1890] 1904), in Dieseldorff, Seler, and Förstemann (1904, 645), reached a similar conclusion, based on his interpretations of pictorial depictions in codices, pottery, and archaeological sites. He writes: "We must seek in that region, that is, in the interior of Chiapas and Guatemala, for the primal seat and origin of the ancient civilization of Central America." In terms of linguistic roots, Kaufman (1976) reckons that proto-Mayan, the precursor of all Maya languages, was spoken in the Sierra de los Cuchumatanes over four thousand years ago.

of heavy rain lasting days on end are also common. Such downpours, like the ones associated with Tropical Storm Agatha in May 2010, can cause loss of life as roads and trails wash out and mudslides bury everything in their path. Severe hailstorms are another threat. The yearly rains draw to a close in November, when the dry season or *verano* (summer) begins. Little rain then falls until May, when the cycle starts again.

From the chilly, blustery terrain of the *páramo* approaching La Ventosa, to the lush, temperate valleys of the Ixcán, to the dusty, scrubby environs around Sacapulas, the Sierra de los Cuchumatanes is a land of stark contrasts. A sense of its remarkable diversity has been nicely captured by Felix Webster McBryde:

> An immense fault block that rises over 1,000 metres above the trough of the Cuilco and Negro drainage basins, with a great escarpment forming the steep southern face, the Altos Cuchumatanes is the most elevated mountain region of its area in Central America. It is essentially a massif of dolomites and limestones in sharp contact with granite, presenting an extraordinarily rugged, deeply dissected surface.
>
> Above the thorny chaparral and cactus of the warm, dry canyon of the Río Negro, the higher reaches of the mountains are covered with pines and coarse grass. Still higher, the smooth, undulant summit area of the Cuchumatanes, foggy, cool, and moist the year round, is covered with scattered junipers, pines, and cypress, and with rolling meadows.[8]

The diversity of the physical geography of the Cuchumatanes is matched by an equal diversity in the human geography of the region.

THE HUMAN SETTING

According to the national census of 2002, Guatemala supported a population of 11.2 million, 41 per cent of whom were considered indigenous. Non-indigenous persons of mixed ancestry, referred to as Ladinos, made up the majority of the remainder. In the mountain areas north and west of the capital, Guatemala City, the indigenous communities predominate. Highland Guatemala, therefore, can in

8 McBryde (1947, 7).

large measure be considered Indian Guatemala, home to twenty-one Maya-language groups in all.

The 2002 census, the eleventh to be conducted at national level since 1778, recorded the total population of the Cuchumatanes at 1.05 million, of whom 742,284, or roughly three out of four, were indigenous (see appendix, table 1). While the total Cuchmatán population doubled in the thirty years after the 1973 census, the indigenous to non-indigenous ratio remained the same.[9] Native peoples in the Cuchumatanes (plates 5 to 8) belong to several closely related but distinct Maya-language groups, the most important of which are Akateko (Jakalteko), Awakateko, Chuj, Ixil, Q'anjob'al, Mam, K'iche', and Uspanteko.

Human settlement is spread unevenly over the region. Ladino communities predominate along the southern margins, most conspicuous in Chiantla, Cuilco, Huehuetenango, La Libertad, and Malacatancito; the Ladino presence is notable also in lower-lying parts of the north and west, in Barillas, Nentón, San Antonio, and Santa Ana Huista. Maya communities cling to the higher, more remote, and less productive terrain of central and eastern Cuchumatán country. Settlements and the land surrounding them are grouped together to form *municipios*, township divisions traditionally based on local ethnic affiliations. Anthropologists have considered these associations to be the most significant cultural groupings in highland Guatemala, for it was around the *municipio* that the classic form of what Eric Wolf termed the "closed corporate peasant community" gradually evolved.[10]

In the recent past, each *municipio* had its own structures of government, its own customs and traditions, its own dress and handmade clothing, and its own Roman Catholic patron saint, often less revered than pre-Hispanic deities paid homage to in mountain shrines by native shamans and soothsayers. Older native people often relate to their *municipio* with an almost mystical sense of belonging that is far stronger than the feeling of being part of the republic of Guatemala. Anthropologist Charles Wagley maintained

9 Instituto Nacional de Estadística (2003, 30-3 and 79-80). The total Cuchumatán population in 1973, the last official tally before the bloodshed and displacements of civil war, is recorded as 487,836, of whom 356,125 were considered indigenous. For the Department of Huehuetenango, Castañeda (1998, 44) calculates that, between the national census of 1950 and the one of 1994, "in those forty-four years population increased more than threefold."

10 Wolf (1957); Tax (1937); Carol A. Smith (1984, 198–200).

that this attachment stems from the *municipio* being "a continuation of the basic societal unit of pre-conquest society."[11] Wagley's view is supported by the findings of George Collier in Chiapas, where Tzotzil Maya communities "endured as ethnic entities through the colonial period to modern times, often with significant continuities in their internal organization."[12]

Such a view, however, has been challenged by Robert Wasserstrom, who claims (at least for central Chiapas) that indigenous communities acquired their individual identities relatively recently, that they "remained quite homogeneous in both their internal structure and their position within the colonial order. Only after independence, it seems, and in fact toward the end of the nineteenth century, did such towns acquire the distinct ethnic identities [that] later fired the imaginations of anthropologists."[13] The reasoning of La Farge, who knew the Cuchumatanes well, supports Wasserstrom's thesis that a good many features of Maya life derive as much, if not more, from the events and circumstances of the nineteenth century as from those of earlier times.[14]

All *municipios* have a *cabecera*, or township centre, which bears the same name as the *municipio* itself. The *cabecera* tends to be the hub of community life, whether the inhabitants of a *municipio* actually live there or in surrounding *aldeas* (villages) or *caseríos* (hamlets). Traditionally, two types of *municipio* could be distinguished: "town nucleus" (clustered settlement) *municipios* and "vacant town" (dispersed settlement) *municipios*. Most of the residents of "town nucleus" *municipios* lived in the *cabecera* itself and walked from their homes to outlying fields to perform agricultural chores. Santiago Chimaltenango, where Wagley's work in the late 1930s was elaborated upon by John Watanabe four decades later, once exhibited such a nucleated pattern of settlement (plate 9). In contrast, families

11 Wagley (1969, 55).
12 Collier (1975, 157).
13 Wasserstrom (1983a, 6; 1983b, 117–19).
14 La Farge (1940, 290–1; 1947, xi–xii). The issue here is one that scholars will debate for some time to come. Wolf (1957, 7) argued that "the closed corporate peasant configuration in Mesoamerica is a creature of the Spanish conquest," maintaining that "thoroughgoing changes divide the post-Hispanic community from its pre-conquest predecessor." For Jacaltenango, Collins (1980) makes a convincing case in support of Wolf's model, which Wolf himself ([1986] 2001) later modified. For an extensive critique, see Lovell and Swezey (1990) and Lovell and Lutz (2013, 96–119).

residing in "vacant town" *municipios* lived close to their fields, spending most of their time there and having occasion to visit the *cabecera* only infrequently. In such communities the township centre was often of modest proportion and boasted little else than a church, a plaza or market place, and a few Ladino-owned shops and some dwellings. Most Cuchumatán *municipios* belonged formerly to the "vacant-town" category, a classic example being Todos Santos, described memorably by Raymond Stadelman in 1940 as "a village within a maize field" (plate 10).[15] Given the accelerated transformations of the past quarter-century, Stadelman would be hard pressed to recognize the urbanized appearance of Todos Santos today.

With 80 per cent of the economically active population engaged in some form or other in agriculture, rural living in the region remains the norm, anchored around the cultivation of corn. In the 1930s, Stadelman recorded some 166 different varieties growing at altitudes ranging from 1,200 to 2,750 metres.[16] Corn lands above 2,000 metres are planted in February and March, usually before the first falls of rain. This planting is known as the *siembra de verano*, the dry-season planting. Corn lands below 2,000 metres are planted in April and May, shortly before or soon after the first rains. This planting is known as the *siembra de invierno*, the rainy-season planting. Higher fields planted during the *siembra de verano* grow more slowly and yield less than the lower fields planted during the *siembra de invierno*.[17] Corn yields fluctuate tremendously, with good land producing one hundred to two hundred pounds of shelled corn per *cuerda* (0.04 hectares); poorer, continuously worked fields, however, yield as little as eight to fifteen pounds per *cuerda*.[18] Beans and squash are cultivated along with corn, the three together constituting the age-old complex referred to by Wolf as "the Trinity of the American Indian."[19] Corn stalks serve as climbing support for

15 Stadelman (1940, 101). Todos Santos is immortalized in two books by Maud Oakes (1951a; 1951b), and its colourful but troubled past, as well as its globalized present, is captured on film in three documentary features by Olivia Carrescia (1982; 1989; 2011).

16 Stadelman (1940, 112).

17 Ibid., 13; Wagley (1969, 50).

18 Stadelman (1940, 117). To this day Stadelman's report, based on extensive fieldwork in the late 1930s and therefore conducted before the use of pesticides and chemical fertilizers raised yields significantly, remains the most thorough investigation of corn cultivation in Guatemala. See Watanabe (1981) for more recent data.

19 Wolf (1959, 63).

soil-enriching beans, while squash, a creeper with broad leaves, provides cover at ground level, preventing excessive erosion during the rainy season.

Specialization in certain grains, fruits, and vegetables is also notable at the township level. Wheat is an important cash crop in San Juan Ixcoy, Santa Eulalia, San Mateo Ixtatán, and Soloma, with the finest grain reputedly grown in San Miguel Acatán and San Sebastián Coatán. Aguacatán is noted for its garlic and onions, Huehuetenango for its peaches, and Todos Santos for its apples. Cuilco, Colotenango, and San Pedro Necta are famed for their oranges. The *tierra templada* around Barillas is coffee country.[20] Local specialties are taken to market, the proceeds used to buy basic provisions, particularly corn. Consumed mostly in the form of tortillas, corn is the mainstay of the indigenous diet.[21]

In addition to agriculture, two other land-related activities warrant mention: sheep raising and salt making. The Sierra de los Cuchumatanes has been involved with the raising of sheep since colonial times, when the first flocks were driven to Guatemala overland from Mexico.[22] Townships most associated with the practice include Concepción, San Miguel Acatán, San Juan Atitán, San Sebastián Coatán, Santa Eulalia, Soloma, and Todos Santos.[23] Indian sheep farmers usually operate on a small scale, with flocks of fifteen to twenty-five sheep.[24] In connection with sheep raising, McBryde recorded Aguacatán, Chiantla, Huehuetenango, and Santa Bárbara as important wool-weaving centres during the early 1940s, but noted that most of the Cuchumatán wool clip, then as now, was bought by itinerant merchants and transported to Momostenango, the principal wool-weaving centre of Guatemala.[25]

Salt making is carried out at Sacapulas and San Mateo Ixtatán. Production methods are primitive, involving simply the evaporation by sun and fire of briny water leached from nearby mineral springs. Only small amounts of salt are obtained from each evaporation.[26] Sacapulas salt in the form of round cakes is sold at the local market and is said to be an effective medicine against eye infections.

20 Recinos (1954, 192–3).
21 May and McLellan (1972, 94–104).
22 McBryde (1947, 38).
23 Recinos (1954, 205).
24 Aragón Cabrera and Ruíz Escobar (1975, 99).
25 McBryde (1947, 62–5).
26 Ibid., 58–60 and 73–4; Pettersen (1976, 55–66).

However, lacking the vital iodine component of the sea salt of the Pacific coast, it was for centuries the principal cause of the high incidence of goitre in the area.[27] Salt at Sacapulas comes from mineral springs scattered along the southern banks of the Río Negro or Chixoy (plate 11). Whenever the river floods, production is adversely affected.[28] At San Mateo Ixtatán, salt water is drawn from wells (plate 12) rented out by town authorities.[29] As in pre-Hispanic times salt is considered a key resource to have access to or to control; the existence of not one but two deposits is a major factor in explaining the antiquity of human settlement in the region.

Landholding in the Cuchumatanes must be viewed in the context of national patterns of ownership and distribution. Inequality is the defining, and deforming, characteristic. Nationally and regionally, substantial amounts of land are held by a privileged few, leaving an impoverished majority, much of it indigenous, to eke out an existence on the tiny percentage not in elite hands.[30] Deprived of the means to make ends meet, *municipios* throughout the Cuchumatanes, particularly those in the centre and north, exhibit some of the worst human development indices in all Guatemala. United Nations statistics for the Department of Huehuetenango as a whole indicate that 77.8 per cent of the population lives in a state of poverty. For San Mateo Ixtatán, however, the percentage is a damning 96 per cent, with Santa Eulalia (86.7 per cent) and San Juan Ixcoy (85.8 per cent) not far behind.[31] In rural societies such as these, shortage of land or

27 A condition of morbid enlargement of the thyroid gland, goitre often manifests as a large, pendulous swelling in the neck. It was the scourge of Sacapulas until government measures made it mandatory for iodine to be added to locally produced salt. When Thomas Gage ([1648] 1958, 166–7) passed through Sacapulas in the early seventeenth century, he was struck by how many of its inhabitants were afflicted by the disease.

28 Pettersen (1976, 55).

29 Stadelman (1940, 95). He writes: "The salt deposits consist of three wells, Shul, Nanal, and Almul, in which water with a high percentage of salt accumulates and is periodically removed to be boiled down by the Indians. These wells have been worked since before the Conquest, and the salt is famed throughout the Department as having medicinal purposes."

30 Universidad de San Carlos (1971, 122–5); Instituto de Agricultura, *Recursos Naturales y Ambiente* (2006, 55–7). Of the Department of Huehuetenango, Castañeda (1998, 51) observes: "The structure of land tenure is one of unequal proportions, with features that are truly appalling, in keeping with the country at large."

31 Tejeda Bouscayrol ([2002] 2010, 201–5) culls these statistics from UN sources dating to 2001.

lack of opportunity to work it in return for reasonable pay are the chief causes of widespread poverty.

The amount of land actually owned and operated as a family unit varies markedly from place to place and is often difficult to determine. In a study involving twenty-three Cuchumatán townships in 1940, Stadelman found that holdings ranged from 10.8 acres (4.5 hectares) in Santiago Chimaltenango to 2.7 acres (1.1 hectares) in San Antonio Huista. The most common size was between three and six acres (1.2 to 2.5 hectares).[32] Working with data generated forty years later, César Castañeda notes that "the greatest number of farm units, 238,892 or 94 per cent, are less than ten *manzanas* [seventeen acres] in area; of these, 111,456 or 44 per cent, are less than one *manzana*."[33] Today, families who own land work it as best they can, with little prospect of year-round employment from plots that diminish in extent generation after generation.[34] Thousands of Cuchumatán landholders, therefore, seek part-time employment as migrant labourers, moving to the Pacific coast to earn wages as hired hands on coffee, cotton, and sugar plantations.

At Nebaj in 1913, Robert Burkitt observed "an unceasing coming and going of labour contractors and plantation agents getting out gangs of Indians for the Pacific coast."[35] Some of Burkitt's remarks, phrased in his blunt but graphic style, are worth quoting at length. He writes:

> Years ago, when I first visited Nebaj, it was a different place from now ... I had struck the place at an especially bad moment. The plantation agents were at the height of their activity, scattering money, advance pay for work, and every Indian was able to buy rum. The rum business and the coffee business work

32 Stadelman (1940, 105).

33 Castañeda (1998, 51). A *manzana* is the equivalent of 1.7 acres. Castañeda's data pertain to the Department of Huehuetenango and do not include Quiché.

34 Higbee (1947, 180) reckoned that "about three arable hectares is the minimum necessary for independent family existence" in rural Guatemala. In local measures this translates into approximately seventy-five *cuerdas*, an amount that far exceeds what most families have access to. With only 12.2 per cent of the Department of Huehuetenango suitable for agriculture – see Castañeda (1998, 41, 52) – the problem of micro-units (*microfincas* or *minifundios*) is not only that "the land they encompass is of a very low productive capacity" but that the vast majority of plots are too small to be viable.

35 Burkitt (1930, 58-9).

together in this country, automatically. The plantation advances money to the Indian and the rum seller takes it away from him and the Indian has to go to work again. Work leads to rum and rum leads to work. I used to think that Chichicastenango was the drunkenest town in the country, but now I think it is Nebaj. My plans at Nebaj were upset by rum. There are two ruin places that I know of that are to be got at from Nebaj and I did nothing at either of them, and one of them I never even saw. The Indians I was going to take were never sober.[36]

What Burkitt witnessed in operation at Nebaj – a seasonal work-force procured from Maya communities in the highlands and channelled into plantation agriculture on the Pacific coast – was a venal system of debt peonage, devised and sanctioned by the national government. Exploitation of native labour is related to the plunder of native land that took place as a result of far-reaching reforms enacted by president Justo Rufino Barrios in the 1870s, which were then continued by his Liberal successors for a further half-century.[37] The imposition of Liberal Reform altered irrevocably the fabric of indigenous life throughout Guatemala; its impact on Ixil country in particular was notably destructive. Not only was the closed, corporate nature of community life broken down but temporary labour on a plantation often also marked the beginning of a process that led, ultimately, to permanent absence. The Nebaj area between 1894 and 1930 is estimated to have sent some six thousand workers each year to the coast. Many of them never made it home.[38]

36 Ibid., 58. La Farge (1947, 7) concurs with Burkitt, noting "when partway drunk, an Indian will sell his soul for more liquor; upon this the *finca* system is based."

37 Chester L. Jones (1940, 148–67); McCreery (1983, 735–59). For an overview of Liberal Reform, and an evaluation of the Cuchumatán data upon which much of the critique is based, see Lovell ([1995] 2010, 120–31). To the case studies documented by Watanabe (1990, 1992) for Santiago Chimaltenango; Lincoln (1945) and Stoll (1993) for Nebaj; Davis (1970, 1997) and Schwartzkopf (2008) for Santa Eulalia; and McCreery (1988) for San Juan Ixcoy may now be added the findings of Piedrasanta (2009) for Chuj communities in northernmost Huehuetenango, among them Bulej, Chaculá, Yalambojoch, and San Mateo Ixtatán. McCreery (1994) and Reeves (2006) frame the larger context within which Cuchumatán particulars can be thrown into even sharper relief. The epilogue furnishes further details about what I have termed (Lovell 1988) the "second cycle of conquest" – conquest by local and international capitalism.

38 Dessaint (1962, 340–1).

Stadelman noted in the 1930s that labour for coastal plantations was furnished by numerous Cuchumatán communities, including Concepción, Soloma, San Ildefonso Ixtahuacán, and Todos Santos.[39] A six-fold increase in population since the time of Stadelman's investigations, while lessening the need for coercive recruitment, has served only to further reliance on seasonal migration. For Guatemala as a whole, Lester Schmid reckoned that in the 1950s some 200,000 people were involved in the process; during the 1960s this number rose to over 300,000 and by the mid-1970s had reached an estimated 500,000.[40] Survival in the highlands, over time, had become increasingly dependent on economic demands in the lowlands. Though migration flows were disrupted when civil war intensified in the 1980s, by the end of the twentieth century national dynamics had assumed an international dimension as a result of migration from Guatemala to the United States and Canada.[41] Undertaken predominantly by younger men fleeing not just endemic poverty but chaotic violence that did not end when armed conflict drew to a close in the 1990s, this phenomenon is unprecedented. Remittances sent back to the Cuchumatanes by these resourceful migrants have had a dramatic effect on every aspect of community life, from what towns now look like and the services they offer to how changing values undermine long-established social mores and cultural conventions.[42]

39 Stadelman (1940, 95–103).
40 Schmid (1967, 1–2).
41 Tejeda Bouscayrol ([2002] 2010, 195–201).
42 Agencia Española de la Cooperación Internacional para el Desarrollo (2010). Though this study examines remittance impacts in Honduras and El Salvador as well as Guatemala, three Cuchumatán townships (San Juan Ixcoy, San Mateo Ixtatán, and Soloma) receive in-depth scrutiny. The AECID report (2010, 39) reveals that "some 4.5 million people in Guatemala receive remittances, of whom 47.7 per cent live in urban areas and 52.3 per cent in rural areas." Among the latter, the departments of Huehuetenango and San Marcos emerge as top recipients, with their agricultural work force benefiting considerably and their head towns spawning commercial ventures and a boom in house construction and the opening of hotels and restaurants. The *Prensa Libre* reported on 12 January 2007 that an estimated 1.3 million Guatemalans, many of them indigenous Mayas, live and work in the United States, sending or bringing back remittances valued at US$3.6 billion for the year 2006. As 2012 drew to a close, the *Prensa Libre* edition of 7 December reckoned that remittances that year would be closer to US$4.3 billion, with its edition of 10 November placing the number of "migrantes en EE.UU" at 1.5 million. Volumes edited or authored by Camus (2007, 2008) concentrate on transmigration and remittance flows in the Department of Huehuetenango. For a case study of Yalambojoch, see Falla and Yojcom (2012). With a national population currently

Deep-rooted attachments nonetheless endure, and an ever-evolving Maya culture is still to be found. Over the past five centuries, native communities have been subjected again and again to the onslaught of outside forces, forces that not only signalled change but at times threatened those communities with extinction. Against shattering odds, Indians and their ways remain a conspicuous element of the Cuchumatán scene.[43] The following pages undertake to reconstruct the cultural landscape of the region during the period of its critical evolution – from the eve of the Spanish conquest to the end of colonial rule in 1821 – and, in doing so, examine various land-related aspects of native life as they have developed through time.

---

estimated at 16 million, as many as one in ten Guatemalans may now live and work in the United States.

43 See Deuss (2007) and Piedrasanta (2009) for two recent studies that, like this one, document cultural continuity as well as cultural change being a palpable Cuchumatán dynamic.

PART TWO

Contact and Conquest, 1500–1541

3

Land and Life on the Eve of Spanish Conquest

The pre-Conquest history of the Cuchumatanes is still a matter for guesswork.

Oliver La Farge, *Santa Eulalia:*
The Religion of a Cuchumatán Indian Town (1947)

Written over six decades ago, but harking back to an even earlier period, the above words of La Farge have been voiced since, time and again, by numerous researchers.[1] Despite considerable advances in our knowledge of other parts of Guatemala before Spanish intrusion, few inquiries have focused on the Cuchumatán highlands. The reasons for this are not easy to discern but may be related to the region's lying off the beaten track and to the perception of there being a greater return on research conducted elsewhere. From an archaeological perspective, highland Guatemala has been worked much less than lowland Guatemala, due primarily to the greater size and complexity of settlement remains in the latter area. From an ethnohistorical perspective, the Maya peoples in Guatemala who attract most attention are K'iche'an-speaking, since it is chiefly for K'iche'an culture that native documentation relating to life in

---

1 Published in 1947, La Farge's study of Santa Eulalia was based on fieldwork he conducted there in the late 1920s and early 1930s. His assessment of how little was known then about pre-Columbian times, the pioneering work of Seler ([1901] 2003) notwithstanding, has been reiterated by Woodbury (1953, 9); Lischka (1979, 11); Navarrete (1980); Weeks (2003, xiii); and Piedrasanta (2009, 95). An exhibit featuring some striking Cuchumatán artifacts taken to Germany by Seler in the late nineteenth century, on display at the Ethnological Museum in Berlin in March 2013, noted that the region "even today is a remote destination, and interest in its archaeological record is not considered in the mainstream of Maya research."

pre-conquest times exists. The Sierra de los Cuchumatanes, predominantly a non-K'iche'an highland region, has been adversely affected by the lowland- and K'iche'an-oriented thrust of investigative endeavours to date.

A case may in fact be made that the Cuchumatanes have suffered undeservedly from scholarly neglect. While the ethnohistorical potential of the region is scant, the same cannot be said of its rich archaeological heritage. Apart from Woodbury and Trik's work at Zaculeu[2] (plate 13) and two projects carried out at Nebaj, one by an American team in the late 1940s,[3] another by a French group in the mid-1960s,[4] little in the way of systematic excavation has been done at other known sites. Some of these – Chaculá and Yalambojoch, for instance, to name but two – are quite remarkable, having been visited and commented on enthusiastically more than a century ago by none other than Eduard Seler, considered by Michael D. Coe "the greatest iconographer who ever lived."[5]

2 Woodbury and Trik (1953).
3 Smith and Kidder (1951). See also A.L. Smith (1955).
4 Becquelin (1969).
5 As quoted by Urschel (2009). During a field sojourn in Mexico and Guatemala from 1895 to 1897, Seler (1849–1922) was invited to Chaculá by his fellow countryman, Gustav Kanter, a German immigrant whose business interests involved cattle ranching. Kanter, whom Seler ([1901] 2003, 1) declared "rules here as a petty prince over a wide kingdom," was also an avid bibliophile and collector of local artifacts, making a library and a museum part of his living quarters at Hacienda Chaculá. Seler drew upon Kanter's collection to complement his archaeological survey of the region; descriptions of the collection may be found in Seler's classic work *Die Alten Ansiedlungen von Chaculá* (1901), not available in English translation until 2003. Seler's wife and soulmate, Caecilie, herself an astute observer and recorder of what the couple experienced and saw, published an account of their travels, *Auf alten Wegen in Mexiko und Guatemala*, a year before her husband did, but this has yet to be translated (Seler-Sachs 1900). Kanter took the Selers to the ruins that lay in the immediate vicinity of his hacienda, and also accompanied them to others at nearby Yalambojoch. Both sites made a striking impression on the visitors; Seler (1897, 68) recorded their prolonged stay at Chaculá as "the happiest and most rewarding of our entire trip," a view echoed by his wife (Seler-Sachs 1900, 261–92). The fate of Kanter and his noteworthy collection – "both destind to dizaster," as Burkitt (1925, 117) put it – are discussed by Navarrete (1979, 11–15) and Weeks (2003, 16–17), with the former admirably piecing together an account of what amounts to the appropriation, destruction, and salvage of national patrimony. To the challenges of conducting research of any sort in the Sierra de los Cuchumatanes, especially during the war years of the late 1970s and early 1980s, must now be added the risks of working there in an era of rampant drug trafficking.

Neglect of the archaeological record and the limitations of ethno-historical sources means therefore that any reconstruction of land-life relations in pre-Hispanic times must continue to be speculative. It is important, however, to sketch even the thinnest strands in order to establish some outline, hazy or indistinct though it may be, of the cultural landscape on the eve of Spanish conquest. To this end, this chapter follows four procedures. First, it lays out a frame of reference by chronological period and developmental stage, summarizing the state of archaeological thought. Second, it sets down the record that has been established for the Cuchumatanes so as to place the trajectory of the region in Mesoamerican context. Third, it identifies and comments upon ethnohistorical sources that pertain to the pre-conquest Cuchumatanes. And fourth, it offers a reconstructive synthesis with the goal of interpreting, from a fusion of archaeological and ethnohistorical data, the broad features of late pre-Hispanic life. Wherever possible, inferences are drawn from other better-excavated or better-documented areas close in time and space. The domain of the K'iche' Maya is of key importance in this respect, since rich K'iche'an sources complement the sparse Cuchumatán data and, used comparatively, can provide a clearer, more critical reconstruction.[6]

PRE-CONQUEST HIGHLAND GUATEMALA

Highland Guatemala, which forms part of the cultural realm identified by Paul Kirchoff in 1943 as Mesoamerica, has a long record of human settlement.[7] Excavation of an Early Man campsite

6 Carmack (1973, 1981) deals with the materials in question in masterly fashion. His views of K'iche'an cultural development, however, especially the influence upon it of Mexican, specifically Toltec, mores in the thirteenth century, has not gone unchallenged; see Gruhn and Bryan (1976) and Van Akkeren (2008, 65; 2012) for elaboration.

7 Kirchoff (1943). Mesoamerica has been reconceptualized since Kirchoff's first delineation of the region. Territorially, it is now considered to embrace Mexico south of the Lerma-Panuco watershed; all of present-day Guatemala and El Salvador; Belize, the former British Honduras, to which Guatemala still lays claim; and the westernmost parts of Honduras, Nicaragua, and Costa Rica. For a comprehensive discussion of research findings and critical thinking about Mesoamerican culture and civilization, see the substantive volumes edited by Carrasco (2001) and Adams and MacLeod (2000). Wolf (1959) remains an enduring classic. Cabezas (2005, 11–20, 181–5) furnishes a useful summary and developmental chronology. Arroyo and Salinas (2013) provide a comprehensive synthesis of archaeological research on Guatemala to date, concentrating on the advances made in the past two decades.

at Los Tapiales, in Totonicapán, indicates that the site was probably occupied around 9000 BC by a small group of hunters using fluted points, possibly to hunt big game.[8] At the other end of the time scale, a letter penned in 1524 by Pedro de Alvarado, as the Spanish conquest was underway, describes Guatemala as "well populated, with many strong towns."[9] This uninterrupted period of occupancy, stretching over at least ten thousand years, can be divided into four chronological-developmental stages – Paleo-Indian, Pre-classic, Classic, and Post-classic.

Paleo-Indian life dates back to humankind's first entry into the Guatemalan highlands, perhaps as early as 15,000 BC, and lasted roughly until 5000 BC.[10] This period was one of hunting and gathering, with wild foodstuffs such as grains, nuts, berries, seeds, and roots complementing fish and game around the campfire. Paleo-Indian bands were nomadic and small in number. After 5000 BC a gradual but fundamental shift occurred in subsistence patterns. Hunting and gathering were slowly abandoned in favour of a more settled agricultural life made possible by the successful domestication of certain food plants, the most important of which were maize, beans, squash, avocado, chili peppers, pumpkin, and tomato.[11] By about 1500 BC, sedentary village life was a cultural reality that contrasted sharply with the migrant camp life of earlier times.

The period designated as Pre-classic began around 1500 BC and continued until AD 300.[12] During this time the cultures of highland Guatemala underwent a profound transformation. Out of the simple, spatially confined, village style of life there emerged, by 500 BC, more stratified societies; within a few more centuries, the notion of statehood took hold. Socio-political change was accompanied by an intensification of agriculture and population growth. We can infer demographic increase from the greater number of settlements, their larger spatial extent, and indications of a marked socio-economic complexity within and among them.[13]

8 Gruhn and Bryan (1977, 258–9).

9 Pedro de Alvarado to Hernán Cortes, as rendered in Kelly (1932, 139). The words are from the first of Alvarado's two surviving letters to Cortés, dated 10 April 1524.

10 Borhegyi (1965, 6–7).

11 Sanders and Price (1968, 24).

12 Borhegyi (1965, 7–18).

13 Sanders and Price (1968, 29).

Classic culture in highland Guatemala emerged from pre-Classic ways by AD 300, flourishing throughout the region until about AD 1000.[14] The Classic was long regarded as a time of peace and prosperity, characterized by a theocratic, non-urban, non-imperialistic way of life. This view of the period has been reconceptualized; the Classic now appears peaceful and prosperous only in relation to the far more turbulent times that were to follow.[15] Although the peak of Classic civilization is most closely associated, in terms of architecture and artistic expression, with city states (among them Copán, Tikal, Palenque, and Piedras Negras) that evolved in the lowlands, Classic settlements also developed in the highlands. The most important of these was Kaminaljuyú, now engulfed by present-day Guatemala City. Around AD 400 Kaminaljuyú came under the influence of the great Mexican city of Teotihuacán. Locally there had already emerged a highly organized and stratified society; its theocratic bent can be inferred from temple mounds located around ceremonial plazas to form acropolis-like complexes.[16] Classic settlements in the highlands were built on open valley floors or hill slopes in close proximity to water, and were undefended but strongly nucleated centres. Sizable populations were supported by intensive agriculture employing terracing and irrigation on lands peripheral to the ceremonial complex.[17]

The Post-classic period opened around AD 1000 and closed with Spanish intrusion in 1524. As a chronological span, the Post-classic is generally divided into two units: the Early Post-classic (AD 1000 to 1200) and the Late Post-classic or Protohistoric (AD 1200 to 1524).[18] Life in Post-classic times is depicted as secular, militaristic, and volatile, especially when compared to the more stable era of the Classic. This depiction is substantiated by a move of populations away from unprotected valley bottoms or open land to fortified mountain slopes or hilltops. Locational change, when and where it did occur, may have been precipitated by internal strife and conflict, resulting possibly from a population climax or crisis.[19] According to Robert Carmack, the most important event of the Post-classic in

14 Borhegyi (1965, 19–41).
15 Sanders and Price (1968, 31).
16 Borhegyi (1965, 20).
17 Ibid., 19.
18 Ibid., 41–56.
19 Ibid., 41.

Guatemala was the arrival in the highlands, around AD 1250, of imperialistic Mexican migrants led by a Toltec military priesthood. Entering from the Gulf Coast by way of the Usumacinta and Chixoy rivers, these powerful and superbly organized invaders, the mythic founders of the K'iche' dynasty, established control over much of highland Guatemala in the course of some two hundred years.[20] By the end of the Post-classic, however, the hegemony of the K'iche' had greatly diminished. With their defeat in 1524, by forces led by Pedro de Alvarado, Spanish domination began.

THE ARCHAEOLOGICAL RECORD

The archaeological record reveals traces of occupation in the Cuchumatanes from the Late Pre-classic through the Classic to Late Post-classic times. As such, settlement remains span three of the four major Mesoamerican chronologies, and can therefore be dated back at least two thousand years, though humans were undoubtedly present long before.

The *Diccionario Geográfico de Guatemala*, the magnum opus of the late Francis Gall, records a total of 140 archaeological sites for the Cuchumatán region.[21] Table 2 lists fifty-six of these sites, those that have been most thoroughly studied, and figure 4 indicates their spatial distribution. Thirty-four of these sites (see table 3) may be placed, on the basis of ceramic evidence, in at least one major Mesoamerican chronological period.[22]

The pattern of cultural development that is revealed conforms to the broad features outlined for the Guatemalan highlands as a whole. The relative stability of Pre-classic and Classic times is

20 Carmack (1968, 59–64). See footnote 6, above, for sources that counter the views of Carmack.

21 Gall (1976–83). His tally is not definitive, nor was it meant to be, as many other sites exist that have yet to be formally recognized and named. Piedrasanta (2009, 95) alludes to a register of ninety-three archaeological sites compiled by the Instituto de Antropología e Historia for the Department of Huehuetenango, which she assiduously plots (Piedrasanta 2009, 99) as spanning the years from 2000 BC to AD 1524. Three other maps prepared by her (Piedrasanta 2009, 154 and 156) locate the northernmost sites and identify them by chronological period and developmental stage.

22 Tables 2 and 3 summarize archaeological data contained in Becquelin (1969); Burkitt (1930); Fox (1978); La Farge and Byers (1931); Lischka (1979); Navarrete (1979); Recinos (1954); Seler ([1901] 2003); A.L. Smith (1955); and Smith and Kidder (1951).

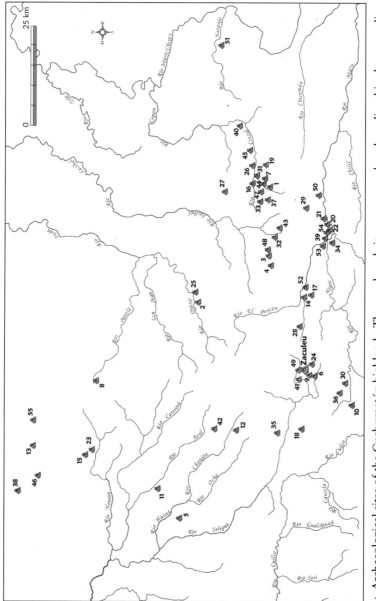

4 Archaeological sites of the Cuchumatán highlands. The numbered sites correspond to those listed in the appendix, table 2.

suggested by the undefended nature of such sites as Río Blanco, Cambote, and Chalchitán (plate 15), all situated without fortification in open valley floors. These and other Classic settlements functioned primarily as administrative-ceremonial centres for populations living and farming in surrounding areas. The Cuchumatán sites that attained the most refined Classical level in terms of art, architecture, and calendric expressions are those of Chaculá (plate 16), a sizable complex associated with nearby Quen Santo ("Sacred Stone"), Uaxac Canal ("Eight Stars"), and Yalambojoch. All four sites, according to Seler, would have had contact and dealings with the great city states to the north and east. He writes:

> The ancient inhabitants of Chaculá possessed elements of a highly developed civilization, the most magnificent creations of which excite our wonder in the monuments of Copán, Quiriguá, Palenque, and the ruins along the Usumacinta. Special forms of art and worship are expressed in the remains which we collected. That these races also knew and possessed the art, science, and civilization of the builders of the monuments at Copán and Quiriguá is demonstrated by two monuments [that] we found in Sacchaná, some distance from their original position, the ancient city of Quen Santo (*Cave of the Saints*) ... [The] population did not reside, as now, in compact communities covering a comparatively small area, but were widely scattered in the *barrancas* over the valleys and hills where the requirements of agriculture made it desirable. The center of the race, community, or society was marked by a sanctuary in which great regional festivals were celebrated ... [Most] indicative of a former large population in the region was the construction of level terraces by transverse rows of masonry, an arrangement made for the purpose of cultivating fields and to prevent the erosion of arable soil.[23]

23 Seler ([1901] 2003, 3 and 7). Weeks, in Seler ([1901] 2003, 19n64), identifies "Sacchaná or Sachán" as "an *aldea* of San Juan Ixcoy." Karl Sapper's 1899 map of the "Departement Huehuetenango der Republik Guatemala und angrenzenden Teile des Staates Chiapas," reproduced in Seler ([1901] 2003, 242–3), shows the site as being in neighbouring Chiapas, approximately twelve kilometres northwest of Quen Santo. Seler-Sachs (1900, 168) also furnishes a map with "Zacchaná" similarly located. The "two monuments" found there, Seler ([1901] 2003, 7) informs us, were "used as flagstones leading around the dwelling house" of a *finca* "near the road from Tepancuapam to Chaculá." When Seler ([1901] 2003, 13) examined the "stela fragments" in question, which he took pains to draw and later feature in his book,

The location and layout of Classic sites, low-lying and non-defensive, stand in marked contrast to the fortified morphology and elevated locations of the majority of Post-classic sites, particularly those of the Late Post-classic. During the Post-classic, open and undefended valley sites are thought to have been abandoned in favour of more readily defensible upper-slope or hilltop sites, many of which, including Pacot, Chutinamit, and Chutixtiox (plate 17), are surrounded by deep ravines or gullies. Although some valley sites indicate an unbroken sequence of occupation from Classic through to Post-classic times that is not accompanied by a move toward fortification, these sites were later protected by military outposts. Such was the case at Xolchun, established at the confluence of the Río Blanco and Río Negro and defended from the nearby hilltop site of Pacot (plate 18).[24] A similar arrangement was in place at the Mam capital of Zaculeu, located on an open plain but protected by the surrounding hilltop sites of Cerro Pueblo Viejo, El Caballero, and Tenam, as well as having defensive structures of its own.[25]

The archaeological evidence indicates warlike times for most of the Post-classic. Throughout Mesoamerican history, such situations have arisen from the uncertainties of life in areas that are densely settled, operating at the upper threshold of their carrying capacity. This period of flux and unrest was also characterized by a strong

---

he concluded that "one can recognize immediately that the same *katun* sign" (a glyph representing a count of 7,200 days) also occurs "on the stela at Copán and Quiriguá, the altar slabs of Palenque, and so forth," thus indicating cultural ties and connections. His wife, Caecilie (Seler-Sachs 1900, 158–9), discusses their trip to Sacchaná too; she also reproduces the "Hieroglyphensteine" they came across and affords us details of camp life during an archaeological dig at Uaxac Canal and Quen Santo (Seler-Sachs 1900, 273–82) that escaped her husband's attention. Falla (2011, 78–83) notes that Caecilie was at her observant best (Seler-Sachs 1900, 285–8) on the trip she took with "Don Eduardo" and Gustav Kanter to Yalambojoch. As with so many other Guatemalan artifacts – see Kramer, Lovell, and Lutz (2013, 2014) for elaboration – Seler saw fit to arrange for the shipment of the Sacchaná stela, along with stone idols from Quen Santo, back to Germany, where they form part of the holdings of the Ethnological Museum in Berlin, formerly the Museum für Völkerkunde. Plate 15, a restoration drawing of Chalchitán at its Classic zenith, as imagined by Tatiana Proskouriakoff, may be found in larger format in A.L. Smith (1955, 96).

24 Carmack (1965, 263). Van Akkeren (2008, 60–1) has an artistic reconstruction of the Sacapulas area, painted in watercolour by Víctor Manuel Aragón in a style reminiscent of Tatiana Proskouriakoff ([1946] 1963). Plate 17 (Chutixiox) and plate 18 (Xolchun and Pacot) are Proskouriakoff renderings, and may be found in larger format in A.L. Smith (1955, 100 and 105).

25 Fox (1978, 151).

and pervasive Mexican influence, indicated architecturally by the presence in many sites of such diagnostic features as altar shrines or platforms, double stairways, enclosed ball courts, round and long structures, and a centralized position in the ceremonial plaza of the main temple-pyramid complex.[26]

THE ETHNOHISTORICAL RECORD

Maya peoples who inhabited the Sierra de los Cuchumatanes have left behind a scant documentary record, which makes the task of historical reconstruction at best tentative. The most powerful autochthonous group of the region, the Mam, have but one document that we know of, the *Título Mam*, an account dealing primarily with land disputes between the Mam and the K'iche' in the Quetzaltenango area in the mid-sixteenth century.[27] Only for Sacapulas and environs does an important text exist, the *Título de los Señores de Sacapulas*.[28] The meagre Cuchumatán record, however, may be supplemented by several K'iche'an sources that touch briefly but significantly on aspects of pre-conquest history. These include the best-known Maya manuscript of all, the *Popol Vuh*, as well as the *Título C'oyoi*,[29] the *Títulos Nijaib*, the *Historia Quiché de Don Juan de Torres*, the *Testimonio de los Xpantsay*, the *Título de los indios de Santa Clara*,[30] and the *Rabinal Achí*.[31]

26 A.L. Smith (1955, 81–3) considers these features to be indicative of "Mexican influence."

27 Carmack (1973, 68) discusses the contents of the *Título Mam*.

28 Acuña (1968, 1–37); Van Akkeren (2008). See Carmack (1973, 37–9) for a critical analysis of the document's contents.

29 Carmack (1973, 39–41 and 265–345) offers a detailed study of the *Título C'oyoi*, including a transcription of the K'iche' text and an English translation of it. With James L. Mondloch, he reappraises the document and offers a Spanish translation (Carmack and Mondloch 2009).

30 The K'iche'an documents known as the *Títulos Nijaib*, the *Historia Quiché de Don Juan de Torres*, the *Testimonio de los Xpantsay*, and the *Título de los indios de Santa Clara* are transcribed in Recinos (1957). Carmack (2009) subjects the most important of the four *Títulos Nijaib* to critical reappraisal, as does Contreras (2008) for the *Historia de Don Juan de Torres*; Ivic de Monterroso (2008, 2009) for the *Testimonio de los Xpantsay*; and Van Akkeren (2009) for the *Título de los indios de Santa Clara*. See also Carmack (1973, 32–7; 43–4; and 50–3) for further discussion of, respectively, the *Títulos Nijaib*, the *Título de los indios de Santa Clara*, and the *Testimonio de los Xpantsay*.

31 Cardoza y Aragón ([1929] 1972) made a translation into Spanish of the *Rabinal Achí*, of which there have been several since, including those of Breton (1999) and Sacor Q. (2008). Tedlock (2003) renders the dance drama in English

K'iche'an Indians in pre-Hispanic times possessed written books and pictographic codices. We know, for instance, that versions of the *Popol Vuh* and the *Título de los Señores de Sacapulas* were in existence before the Spanish conquest. Some years later, around 1540, Bartolomé de las Casas records having seen such documents.[32] Unfortunately, no written or pictographic works that date back to pre-Hispanic times are at hand today, unlike those, for example, that have survived for the Mixtec region of Mexico.[33] After the conquest, Spanish priests taught their native charges to write in their own language using the Latin alphabet; in this way, important pre-conquest events were recorded. Francisco Ximénez, the parish priest of Santo Tomás Chichicastenango who in the early eighteenth century first found or was shown the *Popol Vuh*, puts it thus: "[The Indians] changed their way of writing their histories into our way of writing."[34] K'iche'an peoples were particularly assiduous in this regard and have left behind a rich assortment of data that, although written in post-conquest times, relates to life in Guatemala before the arrival of the Spaniards.

The purposes for which native documents were composed more often had to do with practical exigencies than a desire to record for the sake of posterity. Some documents are petitions for official titles to land; others solicit the right of elites to receive tribute and other rewards.[35] Regardless of the motives that first prompted indigenous scribes to write in the style of their conquerors, the documents

---

translation. See also Van Akkeren (2000a, 2000b). Carmack (1973, 44–6) once again has pertinent observations to make.

32 Carmack (1973, 11–13) and Acuña (1968). Las Casas does not mention either the *Popol Vuh* or the *Título de los Señores de Sacapulas* as being among the manuscripts he saw. The latter is still to be found in Guatemala, part of the holdings of the Archivo General de Centro América (A 1.18, leg. 6074, exp. 54886). A copy of the former, with Francisco Ximénez's transcription of the K'iche' text and his Spanish translation of it laid down neatly side by side in exquisite handwriting, forms part of the Ayer Special Collection (Ms 1515) of the Newberry Library in Chicago. Of the many editions of the *Popol Vuh* now available, the two undertaken by Recinos (1947, 1950), first into Spanish and then into in English, remain the best known and the most consulted. Carmack (1973, 25–6) considers the Recinos Spanish edition "probably the most accurate translation, a result of his exceptional knowledge of the classic Quichean languages. His elegant style more than any other translation captures the literary quality of the original Quiché account." Of the Recinos (1950) English edition, translated by Delia Goetz and Sylvanus G. Morley, Carmack (1973, 27) is equally complimentary, considering it "an excellent rendering of the Spanish."

33 See, for example, M.E. Smith (1973).

34 Ximénez, as rendered in Recinos (1950, 24).

35 Carmack (1973, 19–20).

that emerged from the practice contain important statements about land, settlement, tribute, and the political history of the late pre-conquest K'iche' state. Since many parts of the Cuchumatanes came under K'iche' control during Late Post-classic times (AD 1200–1524), K'iche'an documents that record this expansion may be consulted as useful sources of information.

We now integrate ethnohistorical data with the archaeological evidence summarized above to furnish an outline of land and life in the Sierra de los Cuchumatanes on the eve of Spanish conquest.

CONTACT SCENARIOS

The most important event in the late pre-conquest history of highland Guatemala was the rise to power throughout the region of the K'iche' Maya. According to K'iche' mythology, around AD 1250 Toltec migrants, possibly Chontal- or Nahua-speaking, moved from Tulán on the Gulf Coast of Mexico south and east into the Guatemalan highlands.[36] One migrant group established a base in the Chujuyub mountains, thereafter exerting control over the surrounding country and the indigenous Maya peoples, the Wukamak or Vuc Amag, who occupied it.[37] The invaders were absorbed linguistically by the much more numerous Wukamak; being exceptionally well organized, however, and led by an authoritarian military priesthood, the immigrants were able to subjugate the autochthonous inhabitants. From a fusion of two traditions – one Mexican, the other Mayan – the K'iche' dynasty was born.

Upon consolidating their grip over what was to become their homeland, the K'iche' founded Gumarcaah, the capital city later known as Utatlán. From Gumarcaah, they launched a series of expansionist campaigns, which resulted in much of highland Guatemala coming under K'iche' rule. The *Popol Vuh* states that this period of expansion began during "the fifth generation of men":

They came here to the town of Gumarcaah, as the Quiché named it, when Kings Cotuha and Gucumatz and all the lords came. There had then begun the fifth generation of men since the

36 Carmack (1968, 62–70).
37 Fox (1977, 83–5). The subjugation of the Wukamak or Vuc Amag is described in Recinos (1950, 192–204).

beginning of civilization and of the population, the beginning of the existence of the nation.

There, then, [at Gumarcaah] they built many houses and at the same time constructed the temple of God; in the center of the high part of the town they located it when they arrived and settled there.

Then their empire grew.[38]

Although Carmack has established that Gumarcaah was in fact founded during the eighth generation, around AD 1400,[39] it is possible, despite the chronological inconsistencies, to reconstruct the spatial evolution of the K'iche' state. Sometime between 1400 and 1475, under the leadership of "the marvellous kings" Gucumatz (1400–25) and his son Quicab (1425–75),[40] the K'iche' reached the zenith of their power. Military conquest and political expansion saw them move north into the Cuchumatanes, gaining hold of Sacapulas, Aguacatán, and Cunén, as well as parts of Mam and Ixil country, all of which (see figure 6) lay to the north of Gumarcaah.[41]

The most important settlement to fall was Zaculeu (plate 13), which has a record of continuous occupation from Early Classic times until the Spanish conquest.[42] Such continuity, lasting at least one thousand years, is not common in highland Guatemalan sites. A primary location "for the creation of political, social, economic, and sacred space" and a symbol of "cosmic, social, and moral order," Zaculeu exerted authority far beyond its immediate environs.[43] Communities aligned with Zaculeu included Cuilco and Ixtahuacán, which both sent forces to fight against the Spaniards when their troops attacked Zaculeu in 1525.[44] To the west, the sovereignty of Zaculeu extended along the Río Selegua toward Chiapas. Northward, its influence reached high into the Cuchumatanes, probably into the valley of Todos Santos and beyond, since it was from these

38 Recinos (1950, 215–17).
39 Carmack (1977, 5).
40 Recinos (1953, 228) and Carmack (1977, 6).
41 Fox (1977, 86).
42 The name "Zaculeu" (or "Zaculeuab" as it is written in the manuscript copy of the *Popol Vuh*) is a K'iche' word meaning "white earth"; see Carmack (1965, 242) and Arriola (1973, 166–7).
43 Woodbury and Trik (1953, vol. 1, 284). The description of Zaculeu's function as a traditional ceremonial centre comes from Wheatley (1971, 225–6).
44 Woodbury (1953, 16).

parts that warriors were also dispatched to assist the Mam ruler Caibil Balam in his struggle against the Spaniards.[45]

Though the nature of Zaculeu's relationship with surrounding Mam communities is as difficult to ascertain as the range of its spatial domination, it was certainly preeminent and presided over an extensive and populous hinterland. Its fall was a significant event, recorded in both the *Popol Vuh* and the *Título C'oyoi*:

> Here is the destruction and division of the fields and the towns of the neighboring nations, small and large. Among them was that which in olden times was the country of the Cakchiquel, the present Chuvilá, and the country of the people of Rabinal, Pamaca ... and the towns of the peoples of Zaculeu ... These [peoples] hated Quicab. He made war on them and certainly conquered and destroyed the fields and towns of the people of Rabinal, the Cakchiquel, and the people of Zaculeu. He came and conquered all the towns, and the soldiers of Quicab carried his arms to distant parts.[46]

> Our conquerors of the hamlets and fortified centers, they are the great warriors, our grandfathers and fathers ... Then the Mam of Zukiulew were driven out ... before their mountains and plains; there the mountains and plains [of Zaculeu] were taken. These were all their mountains and plains, their beautiful places, their structures. This was the succession of the lordship by Don Q'uikab ... Our grandfathers and fathers cast them out when they inserted themselves [among] the Mam of Zakiulew; indeed they were fierce warriors ... The fortified centers and settlements were brought down by them when they entered into the mountains and plains ... Their riches and wealth were fragmented, their structures and residences were torn into pieces, their precious stones and jewels, and black and golden stones were carried off.[47]

K'iche' domination of Zaculeu was accomplished at roughly the same times as the subjugation of Sacapulas and Aguacatán. The latter

45 Ibid., 17. See chapter 4 for details of the assault, siege, and surrender of Zaculeu.
46 Recinos (1950, 220–1).
47 Carmack (1973, 297).

campaigns are recorded in one of the *Xpantsay* documents and in the *Título de los Señores de Totonicapán*.[48] Another document relating to the Sacapulas area, the *Título de los Caniles*, states that people from Gumarcaah "came to take the rule. Thus all united at Mount Ramason, where [the K'iche'] took charge of the government."[49]

Sacapulas and Aguacatán were choice areas to dominate. Both were situated in *tierra templada* country that provided the K'iche' with a variety of foodstuffs not available in their *tierra fría* heartland. The areas also were associated with highly prized resources: Sacapulas was an important salt-producing centre, the closest such source to Gumarcaah, and Aguacatán furnished gems and precious metals.[50] Salt, a commodity that in pre-Columbian times served along with cacao and chili peppers as a medium of exchange,[51] was probably produced from the mineral springs at Sacapulas by the same rudimentary process of evaporation and leaching still employed today. The Spanish governor of Verapaz, Martín Alfonso Tovilla, who visited the area in the early seventeenth century, intimated that the K'iche' may have used the forced labour of prisoners of war in the exploitation of Sacapulas salt:

This town in ancient times served as a jail or prison, where the K'iche' kings, to whom these lands belonged, held captives from the wars they waged, because these K'iche' kings were very powerful. Each night they put the captives in a rock enclosure, which was very large, and by day they made them go to the salt factory, where they made much salt, of great importance. Because of this

48 Recinos (1957, 141–5); Recinos and Goetz (1953, 188).
49 *Título de los Caniles*, as rendered by Carmack (1965, 247).
50 Fox (1977, 87; 1978, 112). Recinos (1954, 54 and 76) mentions the mining of gold and silver at Pichiquil, which lies about twelve kilometres to the east of Aguacatán. Writing in the third quarter of the eighteenth century, Archbishop Pedro Cortés y Larraz ([1768–70] 1958, vol. 2, 41) also records gold mines operating in the vicinity of Sacapulas. Reference to gold and silver mining in the hilly land between Aguacatán and Sacapulas is made in a letter from a Spanish resident of Rabinal, José Joaquín González, addressed in 1808 to the *alcalde mayor* of Totonicapán and Huehuetenango. González writes that his brother, Tomás, a Dominican friar, encountered Indians working "a vein of gold and silver in a ravine near Pichiquil," then part of the *ejido* or common land belonging to Sacapulas; see AGCA, A 3.9, leg. 2899, exp. 43092. Chalchitán, which constitutes the eastern half of Aguacatán, means "place of emeralds."
51 Carmack (1965, 293).

production and the scarcity of salt, [the K'iche'] king was more powerful than his neighbors.[52]

Other territories conquered by the K'iche' included Cunén and Ixil country. Evidence is scant, but the *Rabinal Achí*, the dance drama first recorded by the French abbot Charles Étienne Brasseur de Bourbourg in the mid-nineteenth century and considered by Carmack to be a reliable source,[53] states that one of the protagonists, the K'iche' Achí, was "chief of the strangers of Cunén and the strangers of Chajul."[54] The *Rabinal Achí* gives no indication as to when K'iche' conquest took place, but it likely occurred around the same time as the subjugation of Zaculeu, Sacapulas, and Aguacatán, in the early fifteenth century. Cunén and Chajul lacked the resource significance of either Aguacatán or Sacapulas. Control over these two territories was exercised by immigrant lords who resided at Sacapulas and who pledged allegiance to Gumarcaah.[55]

Ethnohistorical evidence is corroborated by the findings of archaeology. Ceramic similarities between Gumarcaah and the sites of Chutixtiox, Chutinamit, Pacot, and Xolpacol indicate a close relationship.[56] Farther west, Zaculeu and the hilltop site of Xolchun (Huehuetenango) both exhibit settlement features characteristic of Gumarcaah, again suggesting K'iche' influence.[57] Available data may be slight, but point to K'iche' enclaves having been established in the principal centres of subjugated peoples. This inference is substantiated by lines from the *Título C'oyoi* that mention specifically the founding of a K'iche' enclave at Zaculeu:

The younger brother and sons of the lords were given instructions by the great lord, Don Q'uikab: "You valiant warriors, you conquerors of the fortified centers, you treaders of the land; go and be inhabitants of the lands at the fortified centers of the subject peoples so that they do not arrive there again. Conquer, you warriors, lancers; likewise go back and forth continually, make many land boundaries for us at each milpa in the canyons

52 Tovilla ([1635] 1960, 218).
53 Carmack (1973, 44–6).
54 Cardoza y Aragón ([1929] 1972, 35).
55 Carmack (1965, 247–78).
56 Fox (1977, 87; 1978, 17, 79, 82, and 85).
57 Fox (1977, 87).

of the fortified centers." [This] was said to them by the great lord, Don Q'uikab ... The inhabitants of the lands left [and went] before the Sakiulew peoples ... "Grab them by the armpits and sacrifice them, trample them, make yourselves valiant warriors, and watchful guardians."[58]

K'iche' conquest, therefore, in the words of Carmack, was "accompanied not only by the sacrifice of some of the captives, but also by a measure of political control, sub-administrators being placed in many of the conquered settlements."[59] These resident "sub-administrators" were charged with maintaining K'iche' authority, thereby ensuring that tribute was paid to Gumarcaah.

Campaigns of expansion, according to the *Popol Vuh*, were motivated by a desire for "the aggrandizement of the kingdom."[60] The K'iche' proved singularly successful in achieving this goal. At its maximum extent, attained under Quicab the Great in the mid-fifteenth century, the K'iche' state was sizable even by Post-classic Mesoamerican standards, stretching from Soconusco in the south and west to Verapaz in the north and east. Territorially, it embraced some 26,000 square kilometres and supported perhaps as many as one million people. It may have been the largest polity to have evolved in the history of highland Guatemala.[61]

Accounts that record the paying of tribute are contained in the *Popol Vuh* and one of the *Nijaib* documents:

The small towns and the large towns paid high ransoms; they brought precious stones and metals, they brought honey of the bees, bracelets, bracelets of emeralds and other stones, and brought garlands made of blue feathers, the tribute of all the towns.

   It was not little what [Gucumatz and Quicab] did, neither were few the tribes which they conquered. Many branches of the tribes came to pay tribute to the Quiché; full of sorrow they came [to Gumarcaah] to give it over.[62]

58 *Título C'oyoi*, in Carmack (1973, 298–9).
59 Carmack (1968, 77).
60 Recinos (1950, 228).
61 Carmack (1968, 77).
62 Recinos (1950, 228).

> The towns, as many as these chiefs [of Gumarcaah] had con-
> quered, came to pay tribute. They all came to leave it, without
> any of them failing to do so, because they were all subject to
> these chiefs, their conquerors.[63]

A levy was likely exacted every forty or eighty days, as Las Casas
records for Verapaz.[64] Items of tribute brought to Gumarcaah were
varied. A *Nijaib* document records cacao, *pataxte* (a pod similar to
cacao), fish, shrimp, turtles, iguanas, and cotton from the Pacific
coast.[65] The *Título de Santa Clara* mentions fish, crabs, and precious stones from Tz'utujil subjects living on the shores of Lake
Atitlán.[66] From the Sierra de los Cuchumatanes, Sacapulas would
have provided salt, copper, and small fish.[67] Aguacatán would have
paid tribute in *tierra templada* produce and likely also in precious
stones and metals.[68] Other communities would have paid tribute in
whatever item could be produced locally and was considered desirable – fruit, corn, lime (important in the preparation of corn tortillas), stone and timber for construction purposes, animal skins for
clothing, and numerous forest-derived products (dyes, tannin, kin-
dling, and torches).

By the mid-fifteenth century, our sources reveal most emphatically, the K'iche' had brought much of highland Guatemala under
the political and tributary jurisdiction of Gumarcaah. The precise
extent of K'iche' control, however, has yet to be determined. On the
basis of similarities between Cuchumatán sites and those of central
Quiché, Recinos speculates that domination of the Huehuetenango
area did not end with the conquest of Zaculeu and the establishment of a line of fortresses along the Cuilco and Selegua valleys.
Rather, he asserts, K'iche' hegemony reached into the heart of the
sierra, to the Mam-speaking communities of Todos Santos and San
Martín, and even farther to Jakalteko-speaking communities in the
Huista valley.[69]

63 As rendered by Carmack (1968, 77).
64 Las Casas, as cited by Carmack (1968, 77).
65 Recinos (1957, 78–9).
66 Ibid., 175.
67 Fox (1978, 111).
68 Ibid., 112.
69 Recinos (1954, 411 and 472–4).

This view is not shared by John Fox; he maintains that "the Jacalteca ... were beyond Quiché control and, seemingly, influence."[70] La Farge and Douglas Byers are more circumspect. "The high mountain barrier of the Cuchumatanes preserved its isolation," they write, "and like the various tribes immediately north and west it may have consisted of one or a number of petty provincial chiefdoms [where] there must have been a good many little towns, with a small semi-aristocracy, not very lofty, without stupendous monuments or striking riches, living out in a provincial way their simpler version of the general Mayan pattern of life."[71] They concede that K'iche' influence "did reach well in the Cuchumatanes," but acknowledge that "there must have been little here to attract them."[72]

Toward the end of the fifteenth century, K'iche' influence began to wane. Around 1475, after the death of the mighty Quicab, internal feuding resulted in one branch of the K'iche', the Kaqchikels, severing affiliation with Gumarcaah and striking out on their own; they migrated some thirty kilometres to the south and east where, in the vicinity of present-day Tecpán, the city of Yximché was founded, a stronghold from which to undertake their own campaigns of conquest.[73]

Kaqchikel secession precipitated a bitter war between Gumarcaah and Yximché, lasting some eleven years. By the end of hostilities, the Kaqchikels could do more than stand their ground, for on one occasion K'iche' warriors not only were routed but suffered the humiliation of seeing their rulers sacrificed to enemy gods.[74] War with the Kaqchikels led to a weakening of K'iche' control over occupied territories, among them those in the Sierra de los Cuchumatanes. By the early sixteenth century, at least three groups had shaken off the grip of Gumarcaah; the *Título de Santa Clara* records that the K'iche' were expelled from the lands of the Agaab people of Sacapulas, from the lands of the Balamiha people of Aguacatán, and from the lands of the Mam people of Zaculeu.[75]

---

70 Fox (1978, xi).

71 La Farge and Byers (1931, 7 and 195).

72 Ibid., 199.

73 See Luján Muñoz (2011, 54–9, especially map 27) for a summary of Kaqchikel dominion.

74 Fox (1978, 176).

75 Recinos (1957, 179) and Fox (1978, 106–7).

By the time the Spaniards arrived, a notable change had occurred in relations between Gumarcaah and territories over which it had once held sway. At the height of K'iche' rule, relations between Gumarcaah and conquered communities were similar to those of a feudal lord and his vassals. After widespread revolt, Carmack contends, relations more closely resembled "those of feudal lord to manorial lord."[76] The change is perhaps best exemplified by the state of affairs at Zaculeu: once subject to K'iche' authority, by the eve of Spanish conquest the Mam capital was once again autonomous, its rulers and their commoners considered allies as opposed to vassals. Indication of this status comes from none other than Pedro de Alvarado, who reported that the Mam ruler Caibil Balam was received with great ceremony and respect at Gumarcaah.[77]

The eclipse of K'iche' power resulted in even further fragmentation. Arriving in Guatemala in 1524, Spaniards encountered an unstable situation seething with local tensions and rivalries. Although, militarily, the Kaqchikels had gained the upper hand over other emerging nations, a vacuum of power prevailed throughout the region. There are strong indications that the vacuum would have been filled by the Aztecs of the Valley of Mexico had Spaniards not arrived before them and altered the course of Mesoamerican history.[78]

LAND, SETTLEMENT, AND SOCIETY

Late Post-classic or Protohistoric times, then, were beset by invasion and conflict, making the necessity of some kind of defence a consideration in occupying the land. This consideration is reflected in the location and layout of Cuchumatán settlements and in the social arrangements they infer. Most Protohistoric sites in the Cuchumatanes belong to one of three defence-oriented types. The first is those that lie on hilltops or spurs of land, like Xolchun (Huehuetenango), huddled at the end of a small plateau surrounded by deep ravines.[79] The second type includes settlements that may not be well situated defensively but boast man-made fortifications (bulwarks, causeways, walls, and ditches) or settlements that could be guarded from nearby

---

76 Carmack (1965, 310).
77 See Woodbury (1953, 10) and Fuentes y Guzmán ([1690–99] 1969–72, vol. 3, 56).
78 MacLeod ([1973] 2008, 37).
79 A.L. Smith (1955, 15).

hilltops, like Zaculeu.[80] To the third type belong sites that combine natural and devised elements, such as Chutixtiox (plate 17) and Chutinamit in the Sacapulas basin.[81] Of eighteen Cuchumatán locations that indicate Protohistoric occupation, twelve exhibit defensive or potentially defensive traits (see table 3).

The predominant settlement complex was that of the *tinamit-amag*, a "core-periphery" arrangement in which a social as well as a spatial distinction may be made. *Tinamit*, from the Nahua word meaning "walled or fortified town," were located on natural or artificially protected terrain. According to Carmack, *tinamit* were established under the wave of Mexican influence that swept through highland Guatemala after A D 1250. While some residential units lay outside the confines of the *tinamit*, as at Chutixtiox and Zaculeu, most were crammed inside, preventing any massive agglomeration. In this sense *tinamit*, though nucleated, were mostly non-urban or at best semi-urban entities, a far cry from such sophisticated and full-fledged cities as Teotihuacán or Tenochtitlán. *Tinamit* were, in essence, strongholds with religious and military functions, where priests and the aristocracy lived, and where commoners turned for spiritual guidance in times of peace and physical protection in times of war.[82]

Distinct both spatially and socially from *tinamit* were the *amag*. Derived from a K'iche' word meaning "vicinage or outlying district," these were dispersed forms of settlement indigenous to the region prior to its being affected by Mexican mores. *Amag* were where ordinary people lived. Writing in the early eighteenth century about pre-Hispanic times, Francisco Ximénez has left us with a memorable description of *tinamit-amag* characteristics. An "amag [is an] extended [place] like the legs of spiders," he states, "from which they take the similitude to give it this name, as if we were to say 'hamlet'. [The word is used] to differentiate [between] it [and] the 'cabecera' or towns, inhabited by lords and called *tinamit*, which means 'city or court.'"[83]

---

80 Fox (1978, 151).

81 A.L. Smith (1955, 16–21).

82 Carmack (1968, 81).

83 Ximénez, as rendered by Carmack (1968, 81). In the manuscript copy of his *Tesoro de las lenguas*, a trilingual dictionary housed in the Bancroft Library (M-M 445), the Ximénez entry for *amac* (*amag*) reads "el pueblo pequeño, que es como familia [o] como villa" (folio 7 verso). The entry for *tinamit* (folio 178 verso) reads "pueblo grande, como ciudad."

The fundamental differences between *amag* and *tinamit* reflect only a minute part of the social fabric on the eve of Spanish intrusion. Carmack contends, for instance, that the K'iche' of Gumarcaah lived in accordance with a structure that was "a complicated integration of rank, descent, territory, [and] hierarchy."[84] If similar norms prevailed in the Cuchumatanes, then the ruling elite would have concerned themselves with matters of politics and religion while their vassals laboured, provided, and fought for them. Lords were sacred, lived in comfortable abodes, received tribute (in goods and commodities, labour and wives) and dressed in fine woven cloths of coloured cotton. Their lowly subjects paid tribute, wore plain henequen clothes, and dwelt in rudimentary huts amidst their cornfields in the countryside. In between the lords and those they governed was a middle strata consisting of professional warriors, well-connected merchants, and skilled artists and artisans. At Gumarcaah there were also serfs and slaves, entirely beholden to their lords and rulers.[85] Social divisions existed within larger, subtle frameworks that involved a system of ranked lineages, noble and commoner alike. These operated, territorially, so as to combine together to form *chinamit*, estates that bore the name of the highest-ranking lineage. Several *chinamit* (plural *chinamitales*) would negotiate alliances and collectively constitute an even larger unit called a *calpul*, which the Spaniards termed *parcialidades*, some of considerable antiquity.[86]

When they arrived in the Cuchumatanes, Spaniards likely found there a socio-spatial order akin to that of K'iche'an lands to the south: parts of the region had been conquered by Gumarcaah in the course of the fifteenth century, its peoples governed thereafter by an implanted K'iche' cohort that (possibly in conjunction with co-opted local leaders) exercised political control in a strategic manner. Though K'iche' hegemony had long since ended by the time of Spanish intrusion, its influence and imprint lingered. It was left to Gonzalo de Alvarado, who initiated campaigns of Spanish conquest in 1525, to usher in an era of profound change far surpassing anything the Cuchumatán Maya had experienced or witnessed before.

84 Carmack (1977, 6). See also Zamora (1983b).
85 Carmack (1977, 6–9).
86 Ibid., 10–13.

4

Conquest and Subjugation
by Imperial Spain

Only dead bodies were to be seen, and a gift of pure gold that the *cacique*
[Caibil Balam] gave me. Thanks be to God that we were permitted to conquer those hosts of haughty Indians, so numerous and important.

> Gonzalo de Alvarado, on the surrender
> of Caibil Balam and the fall of Zaculeu (ca. 1526)

Wars waged for dominion over mutually desired lands and peoples
inevitably carry traumatic and far-reaching consequences, especially for defeated and vanquished factions. The Spanish conquest
of Guatemala was no exception. Subjugation by imperial Spain
(or "pacification," as the conquerors themselves glossed it) was a
harrowing experience for indigenous Mayas, all the more so because the devastation wrought by military engagements was reinforced for centuries thereafter by the imposition of Spanish values
that altered the very fabric of native life. Specific geographical
repercussions of conquest in the Sierra de los Cuchumatanes are
discussed at length in part 3 of this book. The present chapter reconstructs episodes of outside intrusion, and internal collusion, not
merely to furnish narrative details but, more importantly, to impart
a sense of spatial variation and logistical complexity in how conquest ran its uneven, erratic course: some areas were more difficult
to subjugate, and their inhabitants more militant in being brought
to heel, than others. Fundamental to this exercise is an apprecia-
tion of the extent of native resistance, a factor of vital importance
with respect to estimates (see chapter 5) of what the size of the
Cuchumatán population may have approximated at the time of
Spanish contact.

THE ARRIVAL AND IMPACT
OF PEDRO DE ALVARADO

"Only rarely," William L. Sherman contends, "has one individual dominated the society of his time and place in the way that [Pedro de] Alvarado did in Guatemala." To emphasize the point, he adds: "Perhaps no other conqueror left his personal imprint so clearly on a colony as the conqueror of Guatemala."[1] Though other actors, indigenous as well as Spanish, played important roles in the drama, as we will see, the conquistador has had an impact upon the country as enduring as that of conquest itself. Alvarado's determination to "strike terror into the land"[2] haunts Guatemala to this day.

The invasion began on 13 February 1524, when Alvarado entered what is now Guatemalan territory from neighbouring Mexico, to verify reports of "very rich and strange lands and many very different peoples"[3] that his commanding officer, Hernán Cortés, had learned of from trusted informants. Alvarado headed an army that included over four hundred Spanish combatants, 120 of whom were cavalry, and legions of "yndios amigos," native Mexican allies whose numbers were upward of 20,000 according to one source, possibly even more.[4] They encountered no appreciable resistance on the march – what a spectacle it must have been – along the Pacific coast. Only after their ascent up to the pass near Santa María de Jesús, "so rough that the horses could scarcely climb,"[5] did the invaders enter more densely settled parts of Guatemala. There they found K'iche' warriors awaiting them. A decisive confrontation took place on the plain where the city of Quetzaltenango (Xelahuh) now stands.

The K'iche' had failed in their efforts to forge an alliance with the Kaqchikels and the Tz'utujils, and so took on the enemy with a force drawn from their own ranks. Even then the invaders were outnumbered, but astute tactics and a superior military apparatus resulted in Spanish victory. The physical and psychological impact of cavalry on

1 Sherman (1983, 173).
2 Alvarado (1524), as rendered by Mackie (1924, 63). The conquistador's original Spanish is worded "atemorizar la tierra."
3 Cortés ([1524–26] 1963, 162). His precise words, in relation to Guatemala, are "muy ricas y extrañas tierras y de muchas y muy diferentes gentes."
4 Fuentes y Guzmán (1690–99), as cited by Woodbury (1953, 11), who adds, "Brasseur de Bourbourg lists 22,000."
5 Alvarado (1524), as rendered by Mackie (1924, 56).

adversaries who had never before seen a horse and its rider in action was as devastating as the material advantage of steel and firearms over the bow and arrow. After a fierce battle, during which it is said that Alvarado killed the native lord Tecún Umán in man-to-man combat, the K'iche's surrendered.[6]

After laying down arms, the surviving K'iche' lords invited Alvarado and his men to their capital, Utatlán (Gumarcaah), allegedly to discuss the terms of subjugation. At Utatlán, near the present-day city of Santa Cruz del Quiché, the lords made a last desperate effort to avoid defeat. A plot was devised whereby the Spaniards were to be lured into the fortress of the capital. Once they were inside, the causeway forming the main approach was to be destroyed, trapping Alvarado, his soldiers, and the much-feared horses inside. Both fortress and foe would then be set on fire.

Upon entering a half-deserted Utatlán, resembling more "a robber's stronghold than a city,"[7] the wary Alvarado sensed a conspiracy and ordered a retreat back across the causeway. His suspicions of ill intentions were confirmed when K'iche' warriors on the plain at the edge of the city renewed hostilities. Alvarado then instructed his troops to fall on the K'iche's without mercy. Their capital was laid to waste and the lords responsible for conspiring against the Spaniard were burned to death. In disarray, the K'iche' nation collapsed. A crucial gambit had resulted in Spanish victory. It proved, however, only to be the opening foray of a long and brutal war.

Following his defeat of the K'iche's, Alvarado soon realized (to reiterate the words of Cortés) that he indeed had "many different peoples" to deal with. Whereas the conquest of Mexico, relatively speaking, had been executed with prompt and ruthless efficiency, the reverse was the Spanish experience in Guatemala. Political fragmentation in post-Classic times meant that, unlike his commanding officer in Mexico, Alvarado had no single, dominant group to overpower. Rather, an array of small but tenacious groups had to be confronted one by one by one. Taking on the K'iche's was to be followed by a

6 Bricker (1981, 29–42). Carmack (2009, 109–10) and Carmack and Mondloch (2009, 53–6) transcribe native accounts of the death of Tecún Umán from, respectively, the *Título Nijaib* and the *Título K'oyoi*, which allude also to the K'iche' leader being savaged by killer dogs. Alvarado ([1524] 1924) makes no mention of Tecún Umán in his version of events.

7 Alvarado (1524), as rendered by Mackie (1924, 63).

series of hard-fought and exhausting campaigns, several of which Alvarado delegated to his followers – battles against the Poqomames, the Q'eqchi's, and the Ch'orti's, to name but three affiliations. The conquest of these and other Maya peoples continued throughout the 1520s into the 1530s, as did the rebellion of the Kaqchikels, initially Spanish allies who rose up after they could no longer tolerate how the invaders treated them.[8]

"The year 1525 found Pedro de Alvarado in control of almost all the provinces and cities of southern Guatemala," asserts Natalie Woodbury.[9] This state of affairs was, most emphatically, not the case. That very year, in a missive addressed to Charles V, Cortés observed:

> Pedro de Alvarado has never ceased making war upon them [the Indians of Guatemala] with upwards of 200 horses and 500 foot, all Spaniards, besides 5,000, and at other times even 10,000 Indians. [Yet] he has been unable to reduce them under Your Majesty's rule; on the contrary, they become stronger every day through the people who join them.[10]

A war of conquest may be said to have begun with Alvarado's arrival in 1524; it was still ongoing when he died in 1541, from wounds sustained in combat in Mexico. For much of this time – even after he was named "Adelantado," a title that bestowed on him executive royal authority – he was involved in exploits that took him away from Guatemala for months if not years on end. Pedro placed (among others) two of his brothers, Gonzalo and Jorge, in strategic charge during his lengthy absences, and both of their campaigns of conquest warrant our attention. It took the better part of two decades, therefore, in certain areas even longer, before Maya peoples in Guatemala fell under Spanish rule. During this period of prolonged combat, some groups not only held the European intruders at bay but, albeit briefly, actually inflicted defeat on them. Among indigenous Maya communities who staged dogged opposition to Spanish invasion were those of the Sierra de los Cuchumatanes.

---

8 For a detailed account of the conquest of Guatemala, and the Kaqchikel rebellion that perhaps best symbolizes prolonged Maya resistance to it, see Lovell and Lutz (2013, 3–74).
9 Woodbury (1953, 13).
10 Cortés (1525), as rendered by Mackie (1924, 20).

THE CONQUEST OF THE CUCHUMATÁN HIGHLANDS

Between the years 1525 and 1540, conquest in the region was directed against the Mam, Ixil, Uspanteko, Awakateko, and Q'anjob'al Maya, roughly in that order. Documentary sources indicate that a dozen or more armed confrontations took place. On one occasion, during the initial campaign against the Uspantekos in 1529, Spanish-led forces (always made up of a majority of *yndios amigos*) were resoundingly beaten back. Only after sustained resistance did the Cuchumatán Maya capitulate. A distillation of evidence, and reconstructions based upon it, now follows.

THE MAM

Moves to conquer the Mam began in 1525, a year or so after Pedro de Alvarado's gains in K'iche' country. Alvarado chose to delegate leadership of the campaign to his brother, Gonzalo. The counsel and command of a K'iche' lord, Sequechul, who had a personal score to settle, was pivotal: the plot to incinerate the Spaniards at Utatlán, he alleged, was suggested to his father, Chigna Huiucelut, by the Mam ruler Caibil Balam.[11] Sequechul wished to avenge what he considered the unjust execution of his father for being singled out as having engineered the plot. If Chigna Huiucelut had been burned at the stake for his role in the conspiracy, Sequechul maintained, punishment should be meted out also to Caibil Balam. With this end in mind, Sequechul offered to guide the Spaniards in an expedition against the Mam. To convince them of the desirability of conquest, he described Mam country as "great and rich," and assured them that "abundant treasure" would be among the spoils of victory.[12] His overtures were successful, and preparations were made to mount a major *entrada*.

11 Fuentes y Guzmán ([1690–99] 1969–72, vol. 3, 56) and Bancroft (1890, vol. 1, 695). Bancroft refers to the father of Sequechul not as Chigna Huiucelut but as Oxib Quieh.

12 Sequechul, as attributed by Fuentes y Guzmán ([1690–99] 1962–72, vol. 3, 56). The latter's precise words are "grande y rico" and "muchos tesoros" – which proved to be somewhat exaggerated.

Gonzalo de Alvarado wrote a detailed account of the conquest of the Mam, but his manuscript has yet to be found. It was in the safekeeping of Francisco Antonio de Fuentes y Guzmán in the 1690s when he was composing his sprawling chronicle, the *Recordación florida*; after that its whereabouts are unknown. In his translation of the work of Domingo Juarros, first published in Spanish (*Compendio de la Historia de la Ciudad de Guatemala*) in 1808 and in English (*A Statistical and Commercial History of the Kingdom of Guatemala*) fifteen years later, John Bailey states that Juarros had direct access to Gonzalo's manuscript, at that time "in the possession of Nicolás de Vides y Alvarado, one of his descendants."[13] Sedley J. Mackie, in his study of the conquest, also makes this claim.[14] Juarros, however, indicates that his information about what Gonzalo had to say comes not from the conquistador's manuscript but from Fuentes y Guzmán's cribbing of it. "One wishes that he had quoted [Gonzalo de] Alvarado's manuscript in full," Woodbury laments. "How much omission or elaboration has taken place in Fuentes [y Guzmán's] recounting we do not know, but since those parts of his *Historia* [the *Recordación florida*] which deal with campaigns covered in primary sources still available follow the original with fair fidelity, we can assume that the information is pretty much as Gonzalo gave it."[15] Woodbury too leans heavily on Fuentes y Guzmán for her rendering

13 Bailey, in Juarros (1823, 160).
14 Mackie (1924, 38).
15 Woodbury (1953, 19). Her assessment is not one that Bancroft (1890, vol. 1, 704) shared, as he held that Fuentes y Guzmán's *Recordación florida* "has many errors and is far from reliable." Carmack (1973, 96–7) is more inclined to Woodbury's point of view. He writes: "Fuentes y Guzmán claims that, shortly after 1526, Gonzalo de Alvarado, brother of Pedro, began writing a history of the conquest. His motive was to clear his name of accusations of cruelty against the Indians during the time he was in charge of the province while his brother was absent. Gonzalo's history has [also] been alluded to by [Bernal] Díaz del Castillo. Fuentes y Guzmán believed that the manuscript in his possession was only a 'notebook' (*cuaderno*) belonging to Gonzalo, and that the *History* had [already] been lost." Carmack continues: "I think it likely that he obtained Gonzalo's full account. Perhaps Fuentes y Guzmán expected too much because he had seen the impressive manuscript by Díaz del Castillo. From Fuentes y Guzmán's citations of the 'notebook,' it would seem that it contained an extensive account of the conquest, especially as it related to the fall of the Mam speakers in the Huehuetenango area. Because Gonzalo witnessed the conquest, his account is of considerable importance, even though we receive it secondhand through Fuentes y Guzmán. Of the probable distortions in the book, most appear to be in relation to the deeds of the conquistadores, who Gonzalo and then Fuentes y Guzmán attempted to vindicate and glorify."

of the conquest of the Mam. Although twice removed from the original source, Hubert Howe Bancroft preferred the filter of Juarros.

Gonzalo's troops departed from near Tecpán, then the Spaniards' base of operations, for Mam country early in July 1525. The party consisted of forty cavalry under the command of Alonso Gómez de Luarca; eighty infantry directed by Antonio de Salazar and Francisco de Arévalo; and two thousand Mexican and K'iche'an warriors coordinated by Jorge de Acuña, Pedro de Aragón, Bernardino de Oviedo, and Francisco de Verastegui. Another contingent of several hundred Indians acted as porters who could also be pressed into service as sappers, and were. The party first proceeded west to Totonicapán, which functioned as military and supply headquarters. After a brief encampment, allowing the recruitment of more *yndios amigos*, it headed north. Heavy rains made for slow transit; eight days passed before the invaders reached the Río Hondo, its raging waters proving tricky to cross. The trek continued until they reached a plain where the Mam town of Mazatenango stood, near the present-day San Lorenzo. Gonzalo wasted no time in ordering an attack. "Though the Mames offered a brave resistance," Bancroft writes, "they were routed with great slaughter."[16] The engagement is said to have lasted not even four hours.[17]

At dawn the following morning, Gonzalo and his men were about to march on Huehuetenango when they were diverted by a clamorous Mam army, reported as five thousand strong, from nearby Malacatán, now Malacatancito.[18] Charging to the sound of "timbrels, flutes, and conch horns,"[19] the Malacatecos advanced toward the enemy over an open plain. Gonzalo immediately called his cavalry into action. Those Indians not killed by Spanish lances or trampled to death beneath the horses' hooves were soon dispatched by the infantry, following in the cavalry's wake. The Malacatecos fought

16 Bancroft (1890, vol. 1, 697). See Fuentes y Guzmán ([1690–99] 1969–72, vol. 3, 56–7) and Bancroft (1890, 1, 696–7) for further details.

17 Fuentes y Guzmán, as attributed by Woodbury (1953, 14).

18 Woodbury (1953, 14) states that the Spaniards were attacked by "five hundred armed Indians," either a misprint or a misinterpretation. Fuentes y Guzmán ([1690–99] 1962–72, vol. 3, 58) clearly records the Mam forces to have numbered five thousand, not five hundred. His precise words, taken (so he says) from the manuscript of Gonzalo de Alvarado, are "reconocieren a acercárles por la llanura cinco mil indios armados que marchaban en regulada disciplina y militar disposición."

19 Gonzalo de Alvarado (1526), in Fuentes y Guzmán (1690–99), as rendered by Woodbury (1953, 14).

courageously, but when their leader, Canil Acab, "adorned with a great quetzal crest and carrying a golden shield and spear,"[20] fell to a blow from Gonzalo's lance, their spirits plummeted. Those who could fled the field of battle for the refuge of surrounding hills. With no further opposition, the invaders entered and laid claim to Malacatán, which had been left to the elderly and the infirm. Community leaders arrived later, bringing offerings of peace. Gonzalo accepted their unconditional surrender, declaring them henceforth subjects of the king of Spain. The campaign against the Mam was off to a promising start.[21]

After resting a few days, the Spaniards advanced on Huehuetenango, only to find it deserted. Hearing of their approach, Caibil Balam had opted to abandon the place and quarter his forces at nearby Zaculeu, a more fortified and defensible site. Gonzalo had Gaspar Aleman reconnoitre and take stock, during which a Mam captain, Sahquiab, fell into his hands. Via Sahquiab, Fuentes y Guzmán informs us, Gonzalo relayed to Caibil Balam the terms of the *Requerimiento*:

> You may tell your *cacique* that our coming [is] salutary for
> his people because [we bring] tidings of the true God and the
> Christian Religion, and that these tidings [are] sent by the Pope,
> the Vicar of Jesus Christ, God, and Man, and the Emperor King
> of Spain, in order that they might be converted to Christ of their
> own free will; but if they should not accept the peace offered
> them, that the death and destruction that may follow will be
> on their own [heads].[22]

20 Ibid., 15.

21 See Fuentes y Guzmán ([1690–99] 1969–72, vol. 3, 58–60) and Bancroft (1890, vol. 1, 697–9) for further details.

22 As rendered by Woodbury (1953, 15). The *Requerimiento* or Requirement was a document drawn up with the goal of placing the Spanish conquest on firm legal ground. Drafted on royal order by Juan López de Palacios, a juridical scholar, the *Requerimiento* was a summary of the history of Christianity from the creation of the world to the concessions granted imperial Spain by Pope Alexander VI. A copy of the *Requerimiento* was supposed to be carried by every leader of a conquering expedition, to be read aloud prior to the commencement of battle. The document called upon Indians to recognize the authority of the Catholic Church, the pope, and the monarch. By reading the *Requerimiento* before waging war, *conquistadores* considered themselves absolved from any responsibility of action, in effect believing their violent conduct to be undertaken in the guise of "just warfare." See Gibson (1966, 38–40) and Haring (1963, 7) for elaboration.

Sahquiab never came back to tell Gonzalo what Caibil Balam thought of this choice. The task of relaying the terms of the *Requerimiento*, three days after Sahquiab was dispatched to do so, then fell to a delegation of K'iche' intermediaries. They were not only refused an audience but were hailed with a shower of arrows as they approached Zaculeu. His patience at an end, Gonzalo readied his troops for battle.

Zaculeu had a formidable air. Though located on a plain, the Mam fortress was surrounded on all sides but one by ravines, and further protected by a man-made system of walls and ditches (figure 5).[23] Inside and adjacent to the stronghold, Caibil Balam had amassed an estimated six thousand warriors, who had come to defend Zaculeu from the immediate environs of Huehuetenango and as far afield as Cuilco and Ixtahuacán.[24] Horses and gunpowder may have represented a distinct material advantage, but the invaders and their *yndios amigos* were still outnumbered by more than two to one. Victory would not easily be attained.

Advancing on Zaculeu from the east, the Spaniards were met by a barrage of arrows and stones. Gonzalo, anticipating a siege, must

23 Figure 5 shows Zaculeu (Socoleo) as Fuentes y Guzmán depicted it in his *Recordación florida* (1690–99). The chronicler claimed to have visited the former fortress, most likely when he served as the *corregidor* (district governor) of Totonicapán and Huehuetenango in the late seventeenth century. Woodbury (1953, 17) considers his "map of the site" to have "more value as an attractive geometric design than it does an accurate record." While she concedes that "the location of the barrancas and the river is more or less in accord with the facts," the same cannot be said of "the disposition of the buildings," which "is purely imaginary." His flights of fancy aside, Fuentes y Guzmán clearly indicates that Zaculeu was protected against outside attack by an effective system (as borne out by the failure of Gonzalo de Alvarado's forces to capture the fortress) of walls, barricades, and ditches. The words that begin to the left of the northern entrance (bottom centre) and run clockwise around the drawing follow the course of a deep trench that surrounded the fortress almost completely, safeguarding it in much the same way as a moat would a medieval castle. For a full account of Zaculeu's archaeological excavation, and its controversial reconstruction with funds provided by the United Fruit Company, see Woodbury and Trik (1953) and Schávelzon (1990).

24 Fuentes y Guzmán ([1690–99] 1969–72, vol. 3, 63). His precise words are "un ejército de seis mil indios que estaba firme escoltando la puerta de aquella excelente defensa." Woodbury (1953, 16) writes: "It is doubtful whether such an army could even have been quartered within the confines of Zaculeu. More probably the total was no more than half the number given. Gonzalo de Alvarado would have considered it astute to present his encounters and siege in the best possible light and to credit himself with victory over an outnumbering enemy. We have no way of knowing what Fuentes [y Guzmán], one hundred and seventy years later, did to embellish the glory of Spain."

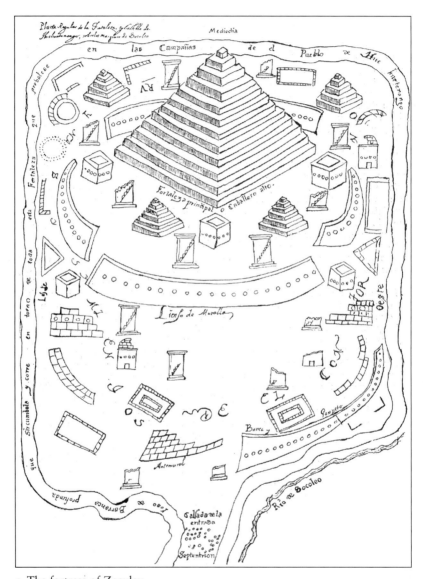

5 The fortress of Zaculeu.

have been surprised to find a Mam fighting force awaiting him and his men outside the fortress, guarding its least impregnable northern entrance. There and on the plain, the Mam stood their ground against the assaults of foot soldiers, but then succumbed to ensuing waves of cavalry. Even when reinforcements left Zaculeu to rejuvenate the Mam defence, the invaders pressed on. Soon the battlefield, in the words of Fuentes y Guzmán, was littered with "green crests covered in Mam blood," the chronicler adding for gory measure, "sometimes heads and bodies strewn in the way hindered the infantry and horses."[25] Realizing the futility of further combat, Caibil Balam ordered a retreat back inside the soon-barricaded fortress. Gonzalo, who had been wounded by a spear in the leg, positioned his troops on all sides of Zaculeu and prepared to lay siege.

No sooner had the siege begun when Gonzalo was forced to confront a massive Mam army descending from the mountains to the north. Recorded as eight thousand strong, this contingent had been rallied from the heart of the Cuchumatanes, the warriors drawn from towns aligned with Zaculeu.[26] San Martín, Todos Santos, Santiago Chimaltenango, and San Juan Atitán probably all furnished able-bodied men, who are described as having been covered "in war paint, wearing no clothes, unadorned with feather crests but armed with shields and lances [and with] both slingers and bowmen in the ranks."[27] Leaving a core of men under Antonio de Salazar to maintain the siege, Gonzalo turned to engage the fast-approaching Mam relief force. Once again the Mam were able to hold their own against the infantry but fell under the assault of the cavalry. Twice, Mam warriors inside Zaculeu attempted to break the siege and attack Gonzalo's forces from the rear. Salazar's men, however, stood firm. Corralled in his stronghold, unable to escape from it to lead the fray, Caibil Balam watched as disciplined and seasoned Spanish soldiers, backed by Mexican and K'iche'an auxiliaries, wiped out his followers. Gonzalo returned to the outskirts of Zaculeu, made camp, and hunkered down.[28]

The siege was begun in earnest in early September. Not until the middle of October did the Mam show any signs of capitulation.

25 Fuentes y Guzmán (1690–99), as rendered by Woodbury (1953, 16).

26 Fuentes y Guzmán ([1690–99] 1969–72, vol. 3, 66). His precise words are "un numeroso ejército de serranos … componíase de ocho mil hombres."

27 Fuentes y Guzmán (1690–99), as rendered by Woodbury (1953, 17).

28 Bancroft (1890, vol. 1, 700–1).

During this time very little food reached the fortress from surrounding communities, most of them already taken by the invaders. Lack of provisions and falling morale left the Mam weak, sick, and hungry. At one juncture, Spanish supplies too were in danger of running out. Native combatants resorted to eating the horses killed in battle, but this the Spaniards took no part in, celebrating joyfully when a shipment of food arrived from the lieutenant general of the Province of Quiché, Juan de León Cardona. A distraught Caibil Balam finally surrendered when his protectors reached the point of starvation. A huge stone at the northern entrance to Zaculeu was hauled to the side, and out stepped the disconsolate Mam ruler. Gonzalo is said to have greeted him with outstretched arms: "From the very first I wished to treat him as a friend; but when he saw that I treated him with affection his eyes filled with tears. His person showed the nobility of his blood and he appeared to be about forty years old."[29] No description is offered of what Zaculeu looked like, but (Gonzalo's being given "a present of pure gold" notwithstanding), it must have been a sorry sight.[30] The fate of Caibil Balam is unknown. Whether or not the warriors who surrendered with him were branded and subsequently dispersed as slaves of "just war" is also unknown, but this was likely the case.

After accepting Caibil Balam's surrender, Gonzalo ordered a reconnaissance of all towns hitherto subject to Zaculeu, and left a garrison in Huehuetenango under the command of Gonzalo de Solís. Satisfied that his four-month mission had been accomplished, and with minimal compromise to the Spanish cause, he returned to Tecpán with news of his victory.[31]

29 Gonzalo de Alvarado (1526), in Fuentes y Guzmán (1690–99), as rendered by Woodbury (1953, 19).

30 Fuentes y Guzmán ([1690–99] 1969–72, vol. 3, 70). "Un presente de buen oro" are the exact words the chronicler claims to have lifted from the manuscript of Gonzalo de Alvarado, who estimated at "mil y ocho cientos, que fueron los que murieron por defender la entrada que pretendían los castellanos" – "1,800 was the number of those who died defending the entrance from Spanish attack." The huge stone guarding the entrance to Zaculeu was ordered to be demolished.

31 Fuentes y Guzmán ([1690–99] 1969–72, vol. 3, 67–71). Huehuetenango – the name, "the old walled place," was given to it by Mexican auxiliaries who accompanied Gonzalo de Alvarado in his campaign of conquest – thereafter became the centre of Spanish control in the region. Its Mam name, Recinos (1952, 110) informs us, was Chinabjul. Arriola (1973, 166–7) renders the Mam name as "Chinabajul" or "Chinabahul," which translates as "in the hole of the shrewd and distrustful mole."

THE IXILES AND USPANTEKOS

With the fall of Zaculeu in October 1525, the western reaches of the Sierra de los Cuchumatanes came under Spanish domination. Two eastern enclaves, however, remained to be pacified: Ixil country and the lands adjoining it, those of their allies, the Uspantekos. For four years after the conquest of the Mam, these two areas, remote and isolated even by Cuchumatán standards, were deemed of little or no consequence. However, pesky harassment of Spanish forces, coupled with Uspanteko efforts to incite rebellion among the already vanquished K'iche', eventually convinced the Spaniards that an *entrada* into these parts was necessary.

Fuentes y Guzmán is again a key source of information, but unlike with his rendering of the conquest of the Mam, he had no firsthand account as substantive as Gonzalo de Alvarado's to lean on – at least none that he admits to and identifies. The materials at his disposal were mostly what chroniclers before him had left behind and the *Libros de cabildo* generated by the city council of Santiago de Guatemala, of which he was an active member in its capital prime.[32] Documents have since come to light, allowing us to furnish an alternate view of the conquest of the Ixiles and the Uspantekos to the one he provides. A summary of his depiction of events, as well as that of Bancroft, is followed by commentary based on these other sources.

The first *entrada* into the eastern Cuchumatanes, according to both Bancroft and Fuentes y Guzmán, consisted of sixty Spanish infantry and a mere three hundred *yndios amigos* under the command of

32 Carmack (1973, 98) notes, however, that Fuentes y Guzmán's account of the conquest of Uspantán "appears to have been based on a lost Spanish source, along with a native source, though he does not cite it. An official report of this conquest was registered in the *Libros de cabildo*, and Fuentes y Guzmán acknowledges it as the source for some of his information. [Antonio de] Herrera briefly described the conquest of Uspantán, and Fuentes y Guzmán was aware of that account." Spanish efforts to establish a capital from which to govern Guatemala, and by extension all of Central America, were plagued by misfortune. The city founded for such purposes in the Valley of Almolonga in 1527, today known as Ciudad Vieja, was destroyed in 1541 by a mudslide that engulfed it following a period of heavy rain. A new capital was founded six kilometres away in the Valley of Panchoy. That city, Santiago de Guatemala, today known as Antigua Guatemala, was at its civic height when Fuentes y Guzmán, born and raised in it, served on its municipal council in the late seventeenth century. Santiago de Guatemala was destroyed by a series of earthquakes in 1773, after which the capital was moved to its present location, Guatemala City.

Gaspar Arias, a member of the city council of Santiago de Guatemala.[33] Oddly, no cavalry were part of the dispatch: perhaps the terrain was deemed too mountainous for its deployment. Though small in number, the party was effective when it started out, bringing the Ixil towns of Nebaj and Chajul under Spanish control by the beginning of September 1529, albeit temporarily. It then marched farther east, toward Uspantán. Just before arriving there, Arias received word that he had been relieved of his position of council member by Francisco de Orduña, then acting governor of Guatemala. Arias returned immediately to Santiago to confront Orduña and demand reinstatement, leaving Pedro de Olmos in charge of completing the mission. Against the advice and counsel of his officers, Olmos decided to storm Uspantán in a full-scale frontal assault. His rash decision proved disastrous. The Spaniards had hardly begun their attack when two thousand Uspantekos ambushed them from the rear. Soon routed, the invaders suffered heavy losses. Those *yndios amigos* not killed in battle were rounded up and later sacrificed, "their hearts torn out," as an offering to the Uspanteko god, Exbalamquen. Survivors of the expedition, defeated and exhausted, fought their way back to Utatlán. There, "haggard and gaunt with famine,"[34] having suffered further casualties during an ambush between Sacapulas and Chichicastenango, they complained bitterly about Olmos's suicidal attack, considering themselves fortunate to be alive.[35]

About a year after this abortive *entrada*, the Spaniards mounted a second one. Under the command of Francisco de Castellanos, "a man of courage and brave spirit," according to Fuentes y Guzmán,[36] this expedition was notably stronger and better equipped than the first. Castellanos, who also served as government treasurer, left Santiago for the eastern Cuchumatanes with a party consisting of eight corporals, thirty-two cavalry, forty infantry, and a battalion of native

33 Bancroft (1890, vol. 2, 109) reports that Brasseur de Bourbourg, writing before him in the nineteenth century, recorded not three hundred but three thousand Indian auxiliaries having been conscripted to wage war on the side of the Spaniards. The latter would have been a more realistic number of warriors to amass, given the challenge at hand.

34 Bancroft (1890, vol. 2, 109). See also Fuentes y Guzmán ([1690–99] 1969–72, vol. 3, 18–19).

35 Fuentes y Guzmán ([1690–99] 1969–72, vol. 3, 18–20) and Bancroft (1890, 2, 108–10). Of Olmos, Kramer (1994, 91) writes, Orduña is said to have had "little faith in his abilities as leader, and his soldiers none."

36 Fuentes y Guzmán ([1690–99] 1969–72, vol. 3, 20). His precise words are "persona de valor y de gallardo espíritu."

auxiliaries. Following a brief stop at Chichicastenango, which provided an opportunity to recruit more indigenous fighters, the party trekked seven leagues north to Sacapulas. After a difficult crossing of the Río Negro, it began a slow ascent of the steep southern ranges of the sierra. On the upper slopes, Castellanos's troops came face to face with an army of between four and five thousand "rebellious and ferocious" warriors from Nebaj and neighbouring communities.[37]

As a "sharp and protracted struggle"[38] took place, Spanish cavalry managed to outflank the combative Ixiles, who withdrew to their stronghold at Nebaj, "protected on all sides by a deep ravine."[39] There they made a final stand. But their failure to be on maximum alert enabled several *yndios amigos* to scramble across the ravine, scale the stronghold's walls, and gain entry. Once inside, they set it on fire. In the ensuing chaos, the invaders broke through the main defence at the entrance to the fortress after many Ixiles left their positions to fight the fire. Castellanos and his men soon emerged victorious. Ixil warriors not killed in the fighting were rounded up, and the next day Castellanos ordered them branded "slaves of war" as punishment for their resistance. "Such was the effect of the fall of the fortress," Bancroft writes, "that the neighboring villages, as well as the large town of Chahúl [Chajul], surrendered without opposition."[40]

Following the capture of Nebaj and the capitulation of Chajul, Spanish forces, buoyed by victory and rested, marched east once again toward Uspantán. Castellanos arrived to find awaiting him an estimated ten thousand Indian warriors, drawn from not only from Uspantán but also Cunén, Cotzal, Sacapulas, and Verapaz. When the Uspantekos attacked, he barely had time to position his men. Although they were vastly outnumbered, Castellanos's savvy deployment of cavalry, plus the firearm superiority of his foot soldiers, won the day. Uspantán fell and, as at Nebaj, those warriors not slaughtered on the field of battle were taken prisoner and branded as slaves. After ensuring that towns allied with Uspantán also acknowledged Spanish hegemony, Castellanos returned triumphant to Santiago in Almolonga.[41]

37 Ibid., vol. 3, 21, and Bancroft (1890, vol. 2, 111–12).
38 Bancroft (1890, vol. 2, 112).
39 Fuentes y Guzmán ([1690–99] 1969–72, vol. 3, 21).
40 Bancroft (1890, vol. 2, 112).
41 Fuentes y Guzmán ([1690–99] 1969–72, vol. 3, 21–2) and Bancroft (1890, vol. 2, 112–13).

AN ALTERNATE VIEW

For the most part, Bancroft goes along with Fuentes y Guzmán's account of what took place in these two skirmishes, even though he cites his data as coming from sources other than the *Recordación florida*, the *Compendio* of Juarros in particular.[42] Recent archival findings call for critical reassessment. First, the part played by Gaspar Arias appears to be exaggerated. In a declaration drafted in 1541 of his "méritos y servicios," in which he recounts the deeds he carried out while serving the Crown, Arias himself makes no mention of having led an *entrada* to Uspantán. He states, however, that between April and August 1529 he led an expedition against the hostile Indians of Mazagua, in Escuintla.[43] Second, the actions of Francisco de Castellanos seem similarly inflated. In 1545, as Arias did four years before, the conquistador-cum-treasurer composed a record of services he rendered the Crown. While acknowledging that he fought at Uspantán, as well as providing men, horses, and arms for the campaign, nowhere in his statement does Castellanos claim that he acted as leader.[44] In fact, he attributes leadership of the second, successful campaign against Uspantán to Francisco de Orduña, as does another Spaniard, Gonzalo de Ovalle.[45] The research of Wendy Kramer reveals that Arias did fight alongside Orduña at Uspantán; it was there, in fact, and not in the capital, that they argued over Arias's membership in the city council of Santiago, Orduña at one point punching Arias in the face.[46] Sáenz de Santa María attributes Fuentes y Guzmán's unwillingness to credit Orduña with victory at Uspantán to his "not being interested in glorifying Don Francisco's memory," implying that the chronicler may have been a direct descendant of either Arias or Castellanos and so considered them more worthy of veneration.[47] Furthermore, evidence now at hand indicates that

42 References are made more often by Bancroft to the work of Fuentes y Guzmán when the conquest of the Mam is under discussion, far less so when the focus of attention is the conquest of the Ixiles and Uspantekos.

43 Archivo General de Indias (hereafter AGI), Guatemala 53, "Probanza de méritos y servicios de Gaspar Arias" (1541).

44 AGI, Guatemala 58, "Probanza de méritos y servicios de Francisco de Castellanos" (1545).

45 Ibid.

46 Kramer (1994, 91), citing Fuentes y Guzmán ([1690–99] 1969–72, vol. 1, 126 and vol. 3, 18–20); Bancroft (1890, vol. 2, 109).

47 Sáenz de Santa María (1969, lvii).

Jorge de Alvarado once led an expedition to Uspantán, about which Fuentes y Guzmán, Juarros, and Bancroft are mute.[48] Such disclosures may not radically alter our understanding of conquest history, but they do encourage caution when consulting the *Recordación florida*. They also raise fears, Woodbury's vote of confidence to the contrary, that Fuentes y Guzmán might have taken liberties when distilling Gonzalo de Alvarado's account of the conquest of the Mam.

What is clear, however, is that with the capitulation of Uspantán, whether to Castellanos or to Orduña, wars of conquest in most parts of the Sierra de los Cuchumatanes came to an end. Another matter entirely, of course, was native resentment at arrangements put in place afterwards. Diego de Rojas, the Spaniard rewarded with a twice-yearly payment of tribute from Uspanteko communities, warned in 1531 of lingering hostilities, declaring that what the Indians there needed was "a good hiding from time to time, in order to make them obedient and ensure that they stay at peace."[49] When native uprisings occurred in Guatemala, they were usually localized affairs put down quickly. While they lasted, however, there could be considerable violence, triggering fear and alarm on the part of the Spaniards. In 1534, four years after the fall of Uspantán, several of them were killed in disturbances involving the nearby communities of Aguacatán, Comitán, Ilom, and Serquil by Indians described as "mutinous and rebellious."[50] Slaves and servants working for the Spaniards also lost their lives. The fact that Jorge de Alvarado, then serving for the second time as governor of Guatemala, himself spearheaded forces that crushed this uprising gives some indication of the seriousness with which it was viewed. Writing from Aguacatán, Jorge expressed the opinion that the best way of dealing with the problem would be to burn the communities in question to the ground. He chose, instead, to make an example of those rebels most

48 AGI, Patronato 60-5-6, "Probanza de méritos y servicios de Francisco de Utiel" (1556).

49 AGI, AG 110, "Probanza hecha en nombre de la ciudad de Santiago" (1531). I thank Wendy Kramer for bringing this document to my attention, as well as to several others pertaining to the conquest of the Cuchumatanes. She translates the words of Rojas – see Kramer (1994, 55) – a bit differently than I do, adding that he also declared that Indians "need much punishment, and [have] to be brought to heel by the scruff of their neck."

50 AGI, Patronato 69-1-5, "Probanza de méritos y servicios de Rodrigo Ruiz" (1569). The Indians are described as "alzados y rebelados."

implicated, punishing them severely, "dogs that they are."[51] One Spaniard, Alonso Cabezas, testified that Jorge dealt with the Indians held responsible by "killing them, throwing them to the dogs, hanging them, and throwing them into pits."[52] In a letter to the Crown dated 14 May 1535, the city council of Santiago summarized the incident:

> The devil appeared before [the Indians] and told them that soon the Spaniards who lived in Santiago would perish, and that they should kill those other Spaniards who lived in towns outside the capital. Thus it was that in some of these towns upward of ten Spaniards were murdered and sacrificed, along with an even greater number of their slaves and servants. Although action was taken quickly, in order that matters would deteriorate no further, it was not possible to respond before much harm was done.[53]

Elsewhere in the Cuchumatanes, documents indicate that some time in the 1530s an *entrada* had to be organized to put down an uprising in the province of Puyumatlán, the name given to the area surrounding Santa Eulalia, where "towns at war" were said to exist.[54] To what extent Spanish hegemony was contested in other parts is difficult to say, but in 1539 there was official recognition of ongoing confrontation, Alonso de Maldonado informing the Crown on October 16 that "in this jurisdiction there is much territory yet to be pacified."[55]

AN INDIGENOUS PERSPECTIVE

A good deal of the effort that goes into determining what took place in Guatemala under Spanish rule calls for long hours of archival foraging, usually with modest return. Data emerge that are of genuine merit and worth, but seldom does one uncover a find of exceptional importance. Engaged in a routine doctoral grind in the city

51 As worded by Kramer (1994, 122), based on the contents of documents compiled by Arévalo (1857).
52 As worded by Kramer (1994, 122), based on evidence contained in AGI, Justicia 295, "Residencia de Pedro de Alvarado" (1535), folio 471.
53 AGI, Guatemala 41, "Cabildo de Santiago al Rey" (1535). Kramer (1994, 122) translates the words of the city council slightly differently.
54 Lehnhoff (1986, 81) and AGI, Patronato 66-1-3, "Probanza de méritos y servicios de Pedro González Nájera" (1564).
55 AGI, Guatemala 9A, "Alonso de Maldonado al Rey" (1539). His precise words are "en esta gobernación hay mucha tierra que está de guerra."

of Puebla in Mexico, Florine Asselbergs could not have anticipated that she would stumble across a remarkable early source that would break new scholarly ground. Housed in the Casa del Alfeñique, one of Puebla's venerable cultural institutions, the *Lienzo de Quauhquechollan* had been known to exist for some time, but prior to Asselbergs' sleuthing it was thought that the pictorial artifact referred to past episodes in the vicinity of San Martin Huaquechula, an indigenous community in the state of Puebla whose ancestors crafted the masterpiece in the sixteenth century. What Asselbergs found is that while the *Lienzo de Quauhquechollan*, an embroidered cotton cloth that measures 2.35 by 3.25 metres, does record information that relates to Mexico, for the most part it documents the role played by auxiliary forces from Quauhquechollan in the conquest of Guatemala.[56]

Accompanying Spanish expeditions in their military campaigns, Quauhquecholtecas not only fought alongside them but also settled in Guatemala after the worst years of conflict were over, as did many warriors from Tlaxcala. Much like the *Lienzo de Tlaxcala*, and in some regards even more so, the *Lienzo de Quauhquechollan* reveals an intricate involvement never before appreciated.[57] A veritable map of the subjugation of Guatemala, it records scene after scene of a second wave of conquest undertaken by Jorge de Alvarado between 1527 and 1529, when his brother, Pedro, had returned to Spain following the first wave of conquest from 1524 through 1527. Arriving in Guatemala from Mexico, bringing an estimated five to six thousand "Indian allies"[58] with him, Jorge did more than consolidate the gains of his brother; by penetrating areas Pedro had not, he brought Spanish might to bear on more territory than before. One such region entered and subdued was the Sierra de los Cuchumatanes.

56 Asselbergs has published several studies of the *Lienzo de Quauhquechollan*, which include two books in English (2004, 2008), one monograph in Spanish (2010), and two articles in Spanish (2002, 2009) that are synopses of her findings. With Matthew Restall (2007), she has also co-authored an account of the conquest of Guatemala in which indigenous agency besides that of Quauhquecholtecas figures prominently.

57 Cabezas Carcache (2009, 13) believes the "informative riches of the illustrations" of the *Lienzo de Quauhquechollan* to be "more comprehensive" than those of the *Lienzo de Tlaxcala*, the former showing, in addition to scenes of battle, "indigenous weaponry, Spanish soldiers, topographic glyphs, traps used by the Kaqchikeles [during their uprising], types of clothing, porters and human carriers, roads and trails, ball courts, markets, defeated Indians being hung or thrown to the dogs, ritual dances in honour of the fallen, and offerings to the gods as thanks for victory."

58 Asselbergs (2010, 121).

Asselbergs identifies four place glyphs she seeks to correlate with known Cuchumatán locations. The first depicts a deer (*maza*) above a walled fortress (*tenam*), signifying in Náhuatl (the language of the Aztecs that became a *lingua franca* throughout Guatemala in the wake of conquest) the name "Mazatenango."[59] We know from earlier discussion that Gonzalo de Alvarado, brother of Jorge and Pedro, conquered Mazatenango as part of his campaign against the Mam. Mazatenango's appearance in the *Lienzo de Quauhquechollan* is not rendered as a battle scene, so it may be that Quauhquecholtecas recorded the location simply to indicate it as part of the route they took with Jorge to wage war elsewhere.[60] A second place glyph shows a bird perched atop a mountain, which Asselbergs asserts "without any doubt is a reference to the Sierra de los Cuchumatanes,"[61] specifically "the region of Todos Santos Cuchumatán."[62] The bird, she states, can be construed to mean *cuchuma*, the Náhuatl word for a finch or warbler, or *cocho* (plural *cochome*), the Náhuatl word for parrot.[63] The glyph clearly depicts a scene of battle, with two Quauhquecholtecas to the right of the bird and mountain, one clad with a protective garment made of eagle feathers, in combat with three enemy warriors to the left. The third glyph shows a road ending in the mountains at a place represented by a walled fortess (*tenam*), which may refer to Huehuetenango, the word *huehue* meaning "old" in Náhuatl – hence "the old walled fortress." Asselbergs cautions, however, that this glyph, which shows two Quauhquecholtecas fighting against two adversaries, "is too damaged to know this for sure."[64] She is similarly hesitant about designating a Cuchumatán location to a fourth glyph, stating only that its battle scene "may possibly allude to the war of 1529–30 in Uspantlán, which at that time was part of Verapaz/Tecolotlán."[65] All four place glyphs are to be found on the uppermost left of the *lienzo*, corresponding to the far northwestern extent of Guatemala, precisely that part of the

59 Asselbergs (2010, 280).
60 From its placement in the *Lienzo de Quauhquechollan*, this Mazatenango may in fact be a different Mazatenango than the one conquered by Gonzalo de Alvarado.
61 Asselbergs (2009, 179).
62 Ibid., 176.
63 Asselbergs (2002, 48; 2009, 179; 2010, 282). A rendering of the place glyph by the artist Angelika Bauer adorns the cover of this book.
64 Asselbergs (2010, 282).
65 Ibid.

country traversed by the Sierra de los Cuchumatanes.[66] In an inspired flourish, akin to the narrative struck by Haniel Long in relation to the *Naufragios* (1541) of Álvar Núñez Cabeza de Vaca, Asselbergs concludes her reading of the *Lienzo de Quauhquechollan* by offering three narrative vignettes, the third rendering the Quauhquecholteca partnership thus:

> One of the campaigns of conquest executed from [Santiago in Almolonga] led to the north. [Headed] by our honoured captain Jorge de Alvarado, we entered the Verapaz area by way of Tequicistlán [Rabinal], and we waged another fierce battle at this site. We then conquered several other places in this area. We continued through the mountains, to the Cuchumatanes, where the people waited for us in ambush. They attacked us with the benefit of surprise. But our brave warriors defeated all of them.[67]

Quauhquecholteca participation in the conquest of the Cuchumatanes has now been firmly established. Their post-conquest presence in the region, however, as settlers who chose to stay behind rather than return home to Mexico, has yet to be determined. We have evidence of Tlaxcalan warriors doing so, putting down roots in the hope that privileges granted them as co-conquistadors would be respected. That proved not to be the case in at least two instances. "They treat us here like slaves," four Tlaxcalan leaders complained to the king in a letter they drafted in Huehuetenango on 10 January 1562. "Your Majesty's representatives are well aware of the wrongs they do us, of the laws they fail to enforce."[68] Five days later, writing

66 Despite her prudent caution, Asselbergs (2008, 179) concludes: "All this upper part of the *lienzo*, then, coincides with what we know about the military campaigns headed by Jorge de Alvarado in the Rabinal area (Tequicistlán) and in Verapaz (Tecolotlán); in the mountain region of Sacapulas and Uspantlán, in what is today the Department of Quiché; and in Aguacatán and Puyumatlán (now Santa Eulalia) in the Department of Huehuetenango." She also observes – see Asselbergs (2004, 181) – that "the distribution of the place glyphs depicted corresponds more or less to the distribution of those places on the ground. The document thus provides a geographical map that is quite accurate even by modern standards."

67 Asselbergs (2004, 177). While basing his account of "the marvellous adventure of Cabeza de Vaca" on historical fact, Long ([1939] 1987) opts to narrate what transpired – he calls it an "interlinear" – by resorting to tenets of creative non-fiction.

68 AGI, Guatemala 52, "Señores y principales de Huehuetenango al Rey" (1562). Their precise words are "estamos desfaborecidos como esclavos, nos hacen agravios por parte de los justicias asi del presidente como de los oidores, no guardan los mandamientos de V[uestra] M[agestad]."

to the king from Aguacatán, three other Tlaxcalan leaders echoed the complaint. "Instead of looking on us as their sons," they charged, "the president and his judges regard us as worthless. They consider us their slaves! Deprived and forgotten, we cry out in anguish and in grief."[69] In theory afforded all sorts of rights and concessions, among them grants of land, not having to pay tribute, and (at Sacapulas) access to prized salt deposits, in actual practice their reward for their military support could amount to naught.[70]

"It is common knowledge," wrote Diego de Manzanares on 30 June 1564, "that were it not for the friendly Indians who came from the provinces of Mexico with Pedro de Alvarado, it would not have been possible to conquer Guatemala."[71] The extent of the opposition to these campaigns of conquest throughout the Sierra de los Cuchumatanes – the ability to raise strong armies to resist intruders of many stripes – is an important indication that the region supported a sizable population at the time of Spanish contact.

69 Ibid., "Señores y principales de Aguacatán al Rey" (1562). Their precise words are "en lugar de hijos nos tienen en lugar de esclavos, estamos como cosa de nada del presidente y oidores y olvidados de los que pedimos porque pasamos grandes necesidades, quedamos llorando."

70 See Carmack (1973, 38) for more on the Tlaxcalan presence at Sacapulas, where ("possibly in 1551") a document was composed "by lords of the Canil and Toltecat ruling lines, primarily as a claim to the mineral springs located there."

71 Asselbergs (2010, 1), quoting Diego de Manzanares from AGI, Justicia 291, folio 127, recto (1564). His precise words are "fue publico e notorio que si los yndios amigos no vinyeron de las provinçias de mexico con el d[ic]ho adelantado [Pedro de Alvarado] no se pudiera conquistar la provincia de guatimala."

5

The Native Population at Spanish Contact

In ancient times the entire region was densely settled.
Eduard Seler, *Die Alten Ansiedlungen von Chaculá* (1901)

The size of indigenous populations in the New World prior to European intrusion continues to generate lively debate.[1] While some scholars have claimed that aboriginal inhabitants were few at the time of contact, others now maintain that their numbers must have been prodigious, at least in the culturally advanced regions of Mesoamerica and the Andes.[2] Related to the matter of population size is the issue of post-contact decline. Champions of sizable numbers at contact contend that there was a catastrophic loss of life in the aftermath of conquest; their critics, while acknowledging that depopulation took place, question its severity and extent.[3] The balance of scholarship now tilts in favour of higher than lower contact estimates, but the debate is far from resolved.[4]

Much remains to be done in this field of research in relation to Guatemala. A landmark study by Thomas Veblen, however, indicates that the Totonicapán area, which lies just to the south of the Sierra de los Cuchumatanes, was thickly peopled during late pre-Hispanic

1 Literature on the subject is now quite vast. Dobyns (1966) and Denevan ([1976] 1992) remain the best overviews, with Mann (2005) contextualizing adroitly why numbers matter. Surveys undertaken by Cook (1998), Alchon (2003), and Livi-Bacci ([2005] 2008) are also noteworthy endeavours.

2 On three occasions (Lovell 1992; 1998; 2006) I have attempted to take stock of the debate as comprehensively as possible.

3 David Henige (1998) is the most adversarial, and sceptical, of there having been sizable native populations at first contact, a view I have challenged (Lovell 2002) as much on moral as ideological grounds. See also Lovell and Lutz (2013, 173–83).

4 Denevan ([1976] 1992, 1) notes that "as the quality of the research improves, the trend is toward acceptance of higher numbers."

times and that its native inhabitants decreased dramatically in numbers thereafter.[5] Veblen, having analyzed the documentary evidence scrupulously, suggests that the contact population of Totonicapán may have been as large as that of the mid-twentieth century. He attributes demographic collapse in Totonicapán primarily to the impact of an array of Old World diseases on an immunologically defenseless population. Veblen's study of native decline is of considerable import, for it provides a pertinent frame of reference against which Cuchumatán data, scant and problematical, may better be appreciated. In a field of scholarship such as this, which involves no small amount of conjecture, any assessment can only benefit from valid comparative reckoning.

Veblen's estimate of the contact population of Totonicapán, based entirely on historical sources, calls into question the credibility of contemporary testimony, particularly sixteenth-century eyewitness accounts by Spanish conquerors. There is no better summary of the polemics of the issue than the following statement of Sherburne Cook and Woodrow Borah:

> Much of our information on Indian population in the years immediately preceding and following the Conquest comes from the conquerors themselves. Some information represents their efforts to determine the nature of the people and country they were entering. Other information arises incidentally from their reporting of what they did and of the hazards they overcame. Spanish reporting of the period of the Conquest has been impugned on two grounds: First, that the Europeans of the sixteenth century could not handle statistical operations or concepts of larger numbers; second, that all explorers and conquerors in a new land tend to exaggerate. If one reflects upon the complexity of European commercial and administrative techniques in the sixteenth century and upon the variety of motives and the rivalries among explorers and conquerors, a more defensible view would be that the Europeans could count and that a tendency to exaggerate in some would be balanced by a tendency to minimize in others. On the whole, we do better to receive gratefully the fragments that have come down to us and to apply the normal canons of textual examination and comparison.[6]

5 Veblen (1977, 484–99).
6 Cook and Borah (1971, 7).

Perhaps the most suspect data used to derive estimates of pre-Hispanic populations are reports of the size of Indian armies that confronted the Spaniards and their *yndios amigos* in the course of conquest. Some allege, for example, that Spanish conquistadors, in attempts to glorify their feats, exaggerated the magnitude of the forces they defeated in battle. This argument, however, fails to take into consideration the fact that these same conquerors, following "pacification," often became government officers charged with, among other duties, tribute assessment for both the Spanish Crown and privileged colonists. Since population size directly determined the levy of tribute, any conquistador with prospects of one day being responsible for assessing native tribute-paying capacity would tend to count with some measure of discretion, lest his failure to do so afterwards be discovered and cause him to run afoul of local administrators or higher authorities in Spain.[7]

Consistent with the view that favours taking contemporary testimony and subjecting it to scholarly scrutiny, Veblen has shown that Spanish estimates of Indian army sizes recorded for the Totonicapán area correspond reasonably well with data derived from other sources. Perhaps most significantly, Veblen claims that the work of the seventeenth-century chronicler Francisco Antonio de Fuentes y Guzmán, considered by some an unreliable source, in fact contains plausible figures for the size of Indian armies mustered by Totonicapán. Veblen explicitly states that "the data available on the size of the pre-Hispanic population of Totonicapán provide no basis for rejecting the demographic information contained in Fuentes y Guzmán."[8] This appraisal is noteworthy for one simple reason: reports of Indian army sizes, compiled by Fuentes y Guzmán as part of the *Recordación florida*, are among the few extant data that can be used to derive an estimate of the contact population of the Sierra de los Cuchumatanes.

Estimates of the size of Indian armies that resisted the Spaniards during *entradas* into the region, along with the names of towns supplying the warriors, are shown in table 4. Fuentes y Guzmán's source for the conquest of the Mam, we noted in chapter 4, was an account, alas now lost, written by the conquistador Gonzalo de Alvarado. In

7 Veblen (1977, 486–7).

8 Ibid., 497. Carmack (1973, 184) concurs: "It is my considered opinion that Fuentes y Guzmán was a better student of Indian culture than is usually recognized, and that his work is of inestimable importance."

his abridged version of what Gonzalo de Alvarado reported, Fuentes y Guzmán gives no indication of the size of the Indian army that defended Mazatenango (San Lorenzo), but he does state that the town "in those days was well-populated."[9] The chronicler's sources for the conquest of the Ixiles and Uspantekos include the *Libros de cabildo*, records of the municipal council of Santiago de Guatemala, and a collection of documents he calls the *Manuscrito Quiché*.

Between 1525 and 1530, the number of indigenous warriors that the Spaniards faced in battles in the Cuchumatanes is recorded by Fuentes y Guzmán as 34,000. For Totonicapán, Veblen uses a one-to-four ratio in correlating army size with total population; for the Tlaxcala region of central Mexico, Charles Gibson uses a warrior-to-total-population ratio of one to five.[10] A ratio of one to four, which Veblen considers conservative, generates a figure of 136,000; a ratio of one to five gives a total of 170,000. An average of the two produces an estimate of around 150,000.

In the years immediately preceding conquest, however, in all likelihood Cuchumatán communities were struck by the same lethal epidemic that in 1520 swept through other parts of Guatemala. This epidemic, possibly a combination of smallpox and pulmonary plague, entered Guatemala from Mexico and had a devastating impact. Old World in origin and consequently unknown in the Americas until the arrival of the Spaniards, it laid low the vulnerable native population and thus reduced both Indian numbers and resistance to military conquest.[11] The havoc and destruction wrought by the epidemic, a harbinger of even more catastrophic times to come, is recorded in a poignant passage in the *Annals of the Cakchiquels*:

> It happened that during the twenty-fifth year [1520] the plague began, oh, my sons! First they became ill of a cough, they suffered from nosebleeds and illness of the bladder. It was truly terrible, the number of dead there were in that period ... Little by little heavy shadows and black night enveloped our fathers and grandfathers and us also, oh, my sons!, when the plague raged ...

9 Fuentes y Guzmán ([1690–99] 1969–72, vol. 3, 57). His precise words are "entonces era de numeroso pueblo."

10 Veblen (1977, 487); Gibson (1952, 139). Dobyns (1983, 174–87) also employs a warrior-to-total-population ratio of one to five.

11 MacLeod ([1973] 2008, 39–40).

when the plague began to spread ... It was in truth terrible, the number of dead among the people. The people could not in any way control the sickness ... Great was the stench of the dead. After our fathers and grandfathers succumbed, half of the people fled to the fields. The dogs and the vultures devoured the bodies. The mortality was terrible. Your grandfathers died, and with them died the son of the king and his brothers and kinsmen. So it was that we became orphans, oh, my sons! So we became when we were young. All of us were thus. We were born to die![12]

In terms of assessing numerically such qualitative evidence, Murdo MacLeod claims that, given present-day knowledge of the impact of diseases such as smallpox or plague on human populations with no previous exposure to them, one-third to one-half of the population must have perished.[13] A Cuchumatán population that between 1525 and 1530 numbered around 150,000, therefore, may some five to ten years earlier have numbered 225,000 to 300,000. An average of these two figures produces an estimate for 1520 of around 260,000.

To place this figure in some kind of perspective, it is worth noting that the population of the region in 1950 was about 265,000 and in 1973 numbered around half a million.[14] This means that the contact population of the Sierra de los Cuchumatanes highlands may have been of the same magnitude as that of the mid-twentieth century. Though no more than a tentative estimate based on slim documentation, its credibility is supported by Veblen's estimate of the contact population of adjacent Totonicapán as being roughly the same size as its mid-twentieth-century count. The plausibility of the Cuchumatán estimate is enhanced when one considers that the demographic trajectories of three of Guatemala's Mesoamerican neighbours – Mexico, Honduras, and El Salvador – also indicate a long-term process of decline, recovery, and growth whereby human populations regain their contact magnitude some time toward the mid-twentieth century.[15]

12 Recinos and Goetz (1953, 115–16).
13 MacLeod ([1973] 2008, 18–20 and 41).
14 Morales Urrutia (1961, vol. 1, 432 and 644); *Octavo Censo de Población* (1975, vol. 1, 16–18).
15 Cumberland (1968, 367); Durham (1979, 23); Johannessen (1963, 34); and Lovell and Swezey (1982, 81–2).

An estimate of 260,000 must remain speculative until the discovery of documentary sources and archaeological excavation make possible a more reliable appraisal. There is little in existing records, however, to refute the notion of sizable populations at the time of first contact. Pedro de Alvarado, a veteran of Spanish campaigns against the populous groups of central Mexico, was clearly impressed with the density of settlement he found upon entering Guatemala. In his second letter to Cortés, written from the Spanish base near Tecpán on 24 July 1524, Alvarado states: "This land, so great and so thickly inhabited ... has more people than all the lands that Your Grace has governed up to now."[16] Even allowing for hyperbole, why dismiss the worth of such statements without having unimpeachable evidence for doing so?

By the end of 1530, Spanish domination over the Sierra de los Cuchumatanes had been effectively secured, albeit with a heavy-handedness that would reverberate long thereafter. Military campaigns continued in other parts of Guatemala throughout the 1530s, and beyond, with all the attendant chaos that warfare entails. It was not until a quarter century after the initial *entrada* of Pedro de Alvarado that conditions in Guatemala proved conducive to the establishment of any semblance of orderly government.[17] Only in the mid to late 1540s did imperial Spain begin to transform the lands of Maya peoples in Guatemala into a viable colony.

16 Alvarado (1524), as rendered by Mackie (1924, 86 and 88).
17 MacLeod ([1973] 2008, 44); Sherman 1983, 173.

PART THREE

The Colonial Experience, 1541–1821

6

In Pursuit of Order: *Congregación* and the Administration of Empire

We came here to serve God and the King, and also to get rich.

Bernal Díaz del Castillo (1492–1585)

When, writing first-hand of his experiences as a participant in the conquest of Mexico and Guatemala, Bernal Díaz del Castillo summed up matters so succinctly, he spoke for a good many besides himself.[1] Those words of his above evoke the three most powerful forces that, from the sixteenth century on, reshaped patterns of land and life throughout Spanish America: the Church, the state, and the ambition of individuals to attain and generate wealth.

Acting in unison, the Church, the state, and individual conquerors and colonists were responsible for the transfer, establishment, and cultivation of what anthropologist George Foster called simply "the Spanish way of life."[2] According to Foster, advancing "the Spanish way of life," in which an integrated philosophy about God, sovereign, state, and man dictated every action and deed, meant nothing less than the creation in the New World of a utopia modelled on Spanish tenets of religion, government, and culture. The failure to create such a utopia in the islands of the Caribbean, the scene of unmitigated disaster, served only to increase the appeal of the American mainland.[3] By the early 1540s Spain had already logged more than fifty

1 Díaz del Castillo, as rendered by Elliott (1976, 65). In his *Historia verdadera de la conquista de la Nueva España* ([1632] 1955, 1, 42), the conquistador turned chronicler also invokes the mantle of honour, wording things thus: "Siempre tuve celo de buen soldado, que era obligado a tener, así para servir a Dios y a nuestro rey y señor, y procurar de ganar honra, como los nobles varones deben buscar la vida, e ir de bien en mejor."

2 Foster (1960, 2).

3 Sauer (1966, 294) states that, by 1519, when Cortés was establishing a foothold for Spain on the American mainland and Charles V was setting up the Council

years' experience as an imperial power and in that time had made
two attempts to design codes of legislation aimed at efficient and effective administration of conquered territory. In both the Laws of
Burgos of 1512 and the New Laws of 1542, Spanish ideals of order,
unity, and just government were foremost.[4] All through the lands
that Spaniards erroneously called "las Indias" – the Indies – the policy of *congregación* (referred to also as *reducción*) proved a pivotal
initiative. Its geographical consequences were myriad and far flung.[5]

CONGREGACIÓN AND EMPIRE

As colonial policy, *congregación* involved gathering together dispersed native inhabitants, often no more than a dozen or so families,
into larger, more centralized towns and villages, which the Spaniards
called *pueblos de indios*. By "congregating" scattered households,
the aim was to expedite native instruction in Christianity by evangelizing missionaries. At the same time, however, civil administration
was promoted by making easier the organization of such arrangements as the enumeration of population, the payment of tribute, and
the control of labour. The spiritual thrust of *congregación* was incor-
porated into the Laws of Burgos, and later enshrined in the *Leyes de
las Indias*:

> With great care and particular attention we have always
> attempted to impose the most convenient means of instructing
> the Indians in the Holy Catholic Faith and the evangelical law,
> causing them to forget their ancient erroneous rites and cere-
> monies and to live in concert and order; and, so that this might
> be brought about, those of our Council of [the] Indies have met

of the Indies, much of the Caribbean was "a sorry shell. The natives, whom Columbus
belatedly knew to be the wealth of the land, were destroyed. The gold placers of the
islands were worked out. The gold treasures [that] the Indians of Castilla del Oro
had acquired had been looted. What most Spaniards wanted was to get out and seek
their fortunes in parts as yet untried and unknown." The fate of the Spanish Main
was but a prelude to similar devastation elsewhere in the New World.

4 Simpson (1966, 29–38 and 123–44) discusses the Laws of Burgos (1512) and
the New Laws (1542) respectively.

5 For contextual discussion of *congregación*, see MacLeod ([1973] 2008, 120–
42) and Martínez Peláez ([1970] 1975, 443–60 and 557–64). The relationship
between *congregación* and community is explored at length by Lovell and Lutz
(2013, 102–19). A review of pertinent literature is offered in Lovell (1990).

together several times with other religious persons ... and they, with the desire of promoting the service of God, and ours, resolved that the Indians should be reduced to villages and not be allowed to live divided and separated in the mountains and wildernesses, where they are deprived of all spiritual and temporal comforts, the aid of our ministers, and those other things which human necessities oblige men to give one to another; therefore ... the viceroys, presidents, and governors [are] charged and ordered to execute the reduction, settlement, and indoctrination of the Indians.[6]

As early as 1537, Francisco Marroquín advocated that *congregación* be carried out forthwith; the bishop's call, however, and two royal orders (*reales cédulas*) that followed it, were not acted upon until several years later.[7] In Guatemala, the main reason for the tardiness of *congregación* was the authoritarian hold exercised by the *adelantado* Pedro de Alvarado. The title of *adelantado*, conferred on Alvarado by King Charles V in 1527, gave its headstrong recipient a wide range of powers, none of which he was reluctant to use.[8] From the late 1520s until his death in 1541, still waging war at age fifty-six, Alvarado ruled and exploited Guatemala as if the country were his personal fief.[9] The conquistador and later governor of the province was preoccupied with wielding power and financing ambitious projects at the expense of fostering the growth of systematic and responsible government. Because of Alvarado's wanton behaviour, Sherman concludes, "the relationship of the Spanish Crown to the conquered peoples for the first quarter-century of colonization ... was

6 From Libro VI, Título III, *Recopilación de las leyes de las Indias*, as rendered by Simpson (1934, 43).

7 Van Oss (1986, 15). The *reales cédulas*, issued on 26 February 1538 and 10 June 1540, may be found in AGCA, A1, leg. 4575, folio 38 verso, and A1.22, leg. 1511, folio 10.

8 Elliott (1976, 59) defines *adelantado* as being "a hereditary title granted by medieval Castilian Kings and conferring upon its holder special military powers and the rights of government over a frontier province. The leader of an expedition would also expect to enjoy the spoils of conquest, in the shape of moveable property and captives, and to receive grants of land and a title of nobility." The entitlement, which Alvarado made rapacious use of, is also discussed in Haring (1963, 19–22).

9 See Lovell and Lutz (2013, 3–74) for an extended discussion of Alvarado's role in the conquest of Guatemala and his notorious tenure as its governor. His assets and how he came by them are examined in Sherman (1969).

one of malign neglect."[10] Not until after the *adelantado's* death, which occurred during the Mixtón uprising in Mexico in 1541, and the subsequent dismantling of his private estate, did Crown authorities in Guatemala consider it expedient to proceed with *congregación*.[11]

Toward the end of the 1540s, by order of the judge, or *licenciado*, Juan Rogel, *congregación* was finally embarked upon.[12] Orchestrated by Bishop Marroquín and scores of devout clergy, the campaign epitomized the "spiritual conquest" of the Indians. The first *congregaciones* were begun by missionaries approaching local leaders (*caciques* and *principales*) and encouraging them to approve the sites selected for new settlements. Engaging the native elite was a key factor in persuading the common majority to leave their old homes and take up residence in new ones. Some families departed willingly, heeding the insistence or entreaties of their leaders. Others left reluctantly, only after the threat of forceful eviction. Once assembled at a new location, Indians would plant the surrounding land as *milpa*. While the corn matured, a start was made on various tasks. A priority was always the erection of a church. After this, attention was turned to constructing a house for resident or visiting priests, to laying out a plaza in front of the church, and to allocating space around the plaza for such buildings as a town hall, a jail, and sleeping quarters where travellers might spend the night. Streets were laid out in a regular grid, running north to south and east to west.[13] Thus a semblance of order, so vital to the colonial mindset, was notably imposed. Conjured with Christian ends and economic gain foremost in mind, the logic of *congregación* stood in sharp contrast, in Spanish eyes, to the anarchy if not barbarism of pre-conquest times.[14]

A crucial consideration in the selection of sites was the nature of the physical setting. Pre-Hispanic settlements were often located on remote hilltops, surrounded by ravines and gullies, established more

10 Sherman (1983, 176).

11 García Añoveros (1987) reviews the sources upon which an evaluation of Alvarado's life and times can critically be made.

12 Recinos and Goetz (1953, 136). An extract from the *Annals of the Cakchiquels* runs: "In the fifth month of the sixth year after the beginning of our instruction in the Word of our Lord God [July 1548] the houses were grouped together by order of the lord Juan Roser [Rogel]. Then the people came from the caves and the ravines."

13 See Stanislawski (1947) for a discussion of the rationale behind town founding throughout Spanish America.

14 See Lovell and Lutz (2013, 96–119) for elaboration.

with a view to defence than to practical, day-to-day living. The civil and religious authorities responsible for *congregación*, on the other hand, favoured accessible valley locations, which entailed widespread population movement down from isolated mountains. If existing settlements showed site features compatible with Spanish criteria of open space, access to water, and proximity to agricultural land or enterprises requiring native labour, then *congregaciones* would be established in or close to them. In the Cuchumatanes, the settlement that Mexican combatants called Huehuetenango, for example, was built on the site of an earlier Mam one known as Chinabjul; and Chiantla, second only to Huehuetenango as a centre of regional importance during the colonial period, was founded near the Mam capital of Zaculeu. It was considered propitious to establish *congregaciones* in which a Catholic church was built on top of, or adjacent to, a native ceremonial complex, thus giving Spanish authority symbolic manifestation. Sometimes the stone of pagan temples was quarried and reworked to form a new edifice where those converted could worship the true Christian God. According to La Farge, this is likely what occurred in the founding of Jacaltenango, another important Cuchumatán location.[15]

From the outset, *congregación* created a dichotomy in the pattern of native landholding. As early as 1532, a *real cédula* declared that "Indians shall continue to possess their lands, both arable tracts and grazing lands, so that they do not lack what is necessary."[16] All *congregaciones*, by law, were entitled to an *ejido*, an area of communal land not cultivated but used for grazing, hunting, and a source of water and various products of the forest.[17] In addition to farming land in the vicinity of a *congregación*, Maya families continued to cultivate the land of their abandoned, but never forgotten, mountain homes.[18] The attachment of displaced residents to their ancestral terrain was ultimately to undermine and reconfigure Spanish objectives.

---

15 La Farge (1947, ix).

16 As rendered in Taylor (1972, 67), citing an extract from the New Laws of the Indies.

17 See Simpson (1934, 44).

18 For an informed eyewitness account, see the letter written to the Crown by the missionaries Tomás de Cárdenas and Juan de Torres, penned from the Dominican monastery at Sacapulas on 6 December 1555 (AGI, Guatemala 168).

CUCHUMATÁN SCENARIOS

In compliance with an order issued by Pedro Ramírez de Quiñones, one of the Crown's most experienced and intrepid judges, *congregación* was under way by the mid to late 1540s.[19] Rugged physical geography made effective resettlement a considerable challenge, but the Spanish authorities, led by Dominican missionaries, carried out Ramírez's instructions assiduously.

Most Cuchumatán settlements in existence today originated as *pueblos de indios* founded in the mid-sixteenth century. The historical record provides evidence of *congregación* having forged *pueblos de indios* at Aguacatán, Chajul, Chiantla, Cunén, Huehuetenango, Jacaltenango, Nebaj, Petatán, Sacapulas, San Antonio and Santa Ana Huista, San Juan Cotzal, San Martín, and Todos Santos Cuchumatán. Much of our information comes from the Dominican friar and chronicler Antonio de Remesal (1570–1619), who penned the first colonial history of Guatemala between 1615 and 1617, following a period of study and work in the colony.[20]

Some of Remesal's observations, detailed and nuanced, are worth examining at length. Of Aguacatán, for instance, he has this to say: "The town of Aguacatlán [Aguacatán] was congregated from a number of hamlets scattered all over the mountains by Friar Pedro de Angulo, Friar Juan de Torres, and others belonging to the Order of Santo Domingo who preached throughout these parts."[21] According to Remesal, Aguacatán and other *congregaciones* were founded by Dominican missionaries before ecclesiastical jurisdiction was passed to another order, the friars of Nuestra Señora de la Merced:

19 Sherman (1979, 141–3) has a vivid character sketch of Ramírez. A temperamental sort, Ramírez was nonetheless viewed by the Crown as one of its most capable and responsible officers. Besides more routine administrative duties, in 1559 he led the first expedition against the infidel Lacandones, organized by the Spaniards in a doomed attempt to halt the sacking of Christian towns in Chiapas and the Cuchumatanes. See also Recinos (1954, 382–3).

20 Antonio de Remesal, *Historia general de las Indias Occidentales y particular de la gobernación de Chiapa y Guatemala* ([1619] 1964–66). Several reservations aside, Carmack (1973, 178–80) considers Remesal "an important source on the early history and cultures of Guatemala." See MacLeod (1970) for an incisive look at the chronicler's life, his treatment at the hands of his adversaries, and their outrage at what he had to say, which hounded him to death.

21 Remesal [(1619) 1964–66, vol. 2, 259]. Aguacatán is today the *cabecera* of the *municipio* of the same name.

The Dominicans not only gave the Mercedarians jurisdiction over Indians in the city [of Guatemala]; they were also given jurisdiction over Indians outside [the capital] in the towns of Quiché and Zacapula [Sacapulas]. All that is nowadays [ca. 1615] administered by the [Mercedarian] monastery of Xacaltenango [Jacaltenango] was formerly under control of the Dominicans. Friar Pedro de Angulo and Friar Juan de Torres, along with other Dominicans, were responsible for the hard work of bringing together Indian families of many different tongues who lived in scattered, outlying hamlets ... The town of Yantla [Chiantla], which lies at the foot of the mountains, belonged to the [Dominican] Order ... The towns of these mountains, as far as Escuytenango in the district of Comitlán [Comitán], including Cuchumatlán [Todos Santos Cuchumatán], Güegüetenango [Huehuetenango], San Martín, Petatán, [and] Güista [San Antonio and Santa Ana Huista] ... were congregated by Dominican fathers who built in them houses and churches that are still standing today.[22]

Remesal recorded particularly minute detail for Ixil country, including the names of places that furnished populations for the "Indian towns" established at Chajul, Nebaj, and San Juan Cotzal. He writes:

To Chaul [Chajul] in the Sierra of Zacapulas were brought [the people] of Huyl, Boob, Ylom, Honcab, Chaxá, Aguazap, Huiz, and four other [locations], all of which were associated with smaller, dependent settlements. This was carried out at the request of the [Dominican] fathers who founded the monastery [of Sacapulas] and by order of Licenciado Pedro Ramírez de Quiñones ... To Aguacatlán [Aguacatán] and Nebá [Nebaj] were brought [the people] of Vacá, Chel, Zalchil, Cuchil, and many others, upward of twelve in number. To Cozal [San Juan Cotzal]

22 Ibid., vol. 1, 243–4). Chiantla, Huehuetenango, Jacaltenango, San Antonio and Santa Ana Huista, and Todos Santos Cuchumatán are today the *cabeceras* of their respective *municipios*. San Martín Cuchumatán is an *aldea* of the *municipio* of Todos Santos Cuchumatán. Collins (1980, 146–55) furnishes a slightly different version of missionary work than Remesal. She states that, by 1555, Mercedarians were already "carrying out missionary activities at the foot of the Cuchumatanes," which suggests that Remesal (a Dominican) may have been overly generous in recording the achievements of his order.

were brought together [the people of] Namá, Chicui, Temal, Caquilax, and many others ... Cunén was also formed by congregating there many smaller settlements.[23]

That Remesal recorded the names of outlying places from which people were moved is of special interest, not least because some of them continue to exist and are inhabited still.[24] Furthermore, though conceived as combining to form a new settlement, communities brought together often preserved their autochthonous identity by operating as individual units, which Spaniards called *parcialidades*, within a *congregación*. These were social and territorial units of great antiquity, and functioned as patrilineal clans or localized kin groups associated with particular tracts of land.[25]

Spaniards had great difficulty in distinguishing between the *parcialidades* and understanding the customs and conventions practised within them; Indians, however, were acutely aware of such differences. After being moved to a *congregación*, they continued to uphold age-old patterns of social discrimination. Far from being uniform and homogeneous, many a *congregación* was a mosaic of tiny groups that touched but did not interpenetrate, with families and kin keeping themselves to themselves. Dozens of *pueblos de indios* were organized internally along these lines, the displaced communities reconstituted within *congregaciones* as *parcialidades*. Thus Ylom (Ilom) and Honcab (Oncap or Onkap), settlements recorded by Remesal as forming part of Chajul, existed within the *congregación* as separate *parcialidades*. Similarly, Zalchil (Salquil) and Cuchil, recorded as

23 Remesal ([1619] 1964–66, vol. 2, 178–9. Cunén, Chajul, Nebaj, and San Juan Cotzal are today the *cabeceras* of their respective *municipios*. Ylom (now Ilom) and Chel are *aldeas* of Chajul; Huyl (now Juil) and Chaxá are two of Chajul's *caseríos*. Namá is a *caserío* of San Juan Cotzal. Zalchil (now Salquil) is an *aldea* of Nebaj. Colby and van den Berghe (1969, 43) state that Chaxá and Namá may no longer exist; in fact both do, listed as *caseríos* in Morales Urrutia (1961, vol. 1, 450 and 456). Chaxá is also marked on the 1: 50,000 topographic map of Tziajá published by the Instituto Geográfico Nacional; it lies about ten kilometres northeast of Chajul. Namá is also clearly marked on the 1: 50,000 topographic map of Nebaj; it lies about four kilometres southeast of San Juan Cotzal.

24 See Hill and Monaghan (1987, xv–xix and 76–89) for such a situation having unfolded at Sacapulas.

25 AGI, Contaduría 815, "Razón de las ciudades, villas, y vecindarios y tributarios de que se componen las provincias del distrito de esta Audiencia" (1683) lists 31 *parcialidades* for nine *pueblos de indios* in the province of Totonicapán alone.

forming part of Nebaj, also survived within that *congregación* as identifiable *parcialidades*.

During the second half of the seventeenth century, when assessing how much tribute should be levied on the Indians of Chajul and Nebaj, Spanish authorities arranged that payment be made not by town but by *parcialidad*. Ilom was assessed at 48 tribute payers, Oncap at 92, Salquil at 17, and Cuchil at 262.[26] Aguacatán, Cunén, Sacapulas, and San Juan Cotzal, all recorded by Remesal as having been formed by congregating several smaller settlements, likewise were assessed for tribute individually by *parcialidad*.[27] The fact that Spaniards allowed and accepted this practice suggests that it was simply the most convenient and efficient arrangement. It also indicates that, a century and more after *congregación* was implemented, the social groups that constituted a new settlement still retained a sense of their pre-conquest identity.

A good example of one such *congregación* is Sacapulas (plate 19). According to Captain Martín Alfonso Tovilla, the governor of Verapaz who passed through town in the early seventeenth century, Sacapulas had been formed by bringing together a half-dozen or so distinct Indian communities: "The town is divided into six *parcialidades*," he writes, "each of which comprises a unit known as a *calpul*, because when the missionaries [first] congregated them, as each had only a small population, they brought four or five to each town in order to make it larger. In this way each *parcialidad* maintained the name of the place it came from. And the lands that [the *parcialidades*] possessed [in the abandoned places] they still cultivate today, in order to grow corn and other bodily needs."[28]

Tovilla's testimony is confirmed a century and a half later by the parish priest of Sacapulas, Andrés Henríquez. Writing in 1786, he states that the *parcialidad* known as Magdalena, "like the other five of this town, was, and were, small settlements brought together by

---

26 AGCA, A3.16, leg. 1601, exp. 26391.
27 Ibid.
28 Tovilla ([1635] 1960, 218). His precise words are: "Está este pueblo de Sacapulas dividido en seis parcialidades, y en cada una de ellas hay una cabeza a que llaman calpul, porque cuando los padres los juntaron, como ellos tenían pequeñas poblaciones, traían cuatro o cinco a cada pueblo que hacían para que fuese grande, y así cada parcialidad de aquellas se quedó con el nombre del pueblo de donde vinieron. Y las tierras que tenían por suyas las gozan hoy y gozarán para hacer sus milpas y demás menesteres."

royal order to form the town of Sacapulas."²⁹ In a tribute list spanning the years from 1664 to 1678, five *parcialidades* are recorded,
three of them known by their indigenous names (Tulteca, Uchabaha,
and Aucanil) and two by their Spanish names (San Francisco and
Magdalena).³⁰ At the close of the eighteenth century, the *parcialidades* of Sacapulas still clung to their native identities but were all
known by Spanish names: Magdalena, San Sebastián, Santiago, San
Pedro, Santo Tomás, and San Francisco.³¹ The preservation of pre-
conquest identity within the *congregación* is also illustrated by the
fact that land in the Sacapulas area was held traditionally by *parcialidad* (plate 19).³² When a lengthy court case occurred toward the
end of the eighteenth century over land rights and boundaries, the
disputes were not contested between Indian and Spanish interests
but between rival *parcialidades*.³³

29 AGCA, A1, leg. 6037, exp. 53258. Henríquez states "como los otros cinco de
este pueblo fue, y fueron, pueblos pequeños, que por superior orden se juntaron a
constituir el pueblo de Sacapulas."

30 AGCA, A3.16, leg. 1601, exp. 26391. The "Razón de … vecindarios y tributarios" (see fn. 25) also records five *parcialidades* as discrete, tax-paying units. Four
are listed by their Indian names (Cutlán, Tulteca, Acunil, and Bechauazar) with
Magdalena the sole one identified by Spanish nomenclature. The *parcialidad* known
as Tulteca likely included descendants of Tlaxcalan auxiliaries who settled in
Sacapulas after the wars of conquest were over (see chapter 4). Relations between
them and Spaniards they once fought for were not always respectful, if the experiences of Tlaxcalan settlers in Aguacatán and Huehuetenango are anything to judge by.
There they filed complaints that their special status and rights were being violated, as
they were forced to work and to pay tribute, from which they were supposed to be
exempt. They also complained that they were being coerced into buying items of
merchandise, which they did not wish or need, at inflated prices from the local magistrate and priests. The Tlaxcalans considered their treatment unjust, since they had
already suffered great hardship and deprivation "in the service of Your Majesty"
under the command of Pedro de Alvarado. So disaffected were they that they requested to be transferred for administrative purposes to Mexico, where (at least so
they believed) they would be treated more appreciatively and with greater respect.

31 AGCA, A1, leg. 6037, exp. 53258 and A1, leg. 6040, exp. 53305. Carmack
(1973, 60 and 208) links *parcialidad* Santo Tomás with the Lamaquib lineage and
parcialidad Santiago with the Canil lineage. See also AGCA, A1, leg. 5979, exp. 52536.

32 Plate 19 is a reproduction of a map sketched in 1794 under the supervision of
Joseph Domingo Hidalgo. Land surrounding the town site of Sacapulas was owned
and operated by the various *parcialidades* that constituted the *congregación*. The map
records an ill-fated plan by Spanish authorities to redraw property boundaries in such
a way as to create an *ejido* out of land already laid claim to on the north and south
banks of the river in the immediate vicinity of the town site. The map, now missing,
once formed part of the documents contained in AGCA, leg. 6042, exp. 53327.

33 Carmack (1973, 206–9) has a summary of the conflict. For a detailed discussion, see Hill and Monaghan (1987, 90–132).

Autochthonous identity was maintained throughout the colonial period, therefore, by such practices as holding land and paying tribute by *parcialidad*. In the case of Aguacatán, deep-rooted social affiliations have persisted. Remesal's description of its founding by Dominican friars in the mid-sixteenth century has already been noted.[34] Most archival documentation relating to Aguacatán distinguishes between the *parcialidad* of Aguacatán and the neighbouring *parcialidad* of Chalchitán.[35] In Aguacatán today, a distinction can still be made between Aguacatecos living to the west of the town square and Chalchitecos living to the east of it, chiefly on the basis of language, styles of dress, and ceremonial rites.[36]

Despite marked survivals of pre-Columbian identity, though, *congregación* may be regarded as an operation that, judging by the number of settlements established and the compliance of Indian communities in furnishing tribute and labour, satisfactorily served important imperial objectives – at least on the surface. Like most colonial ventures, however, *congregación* was not without its failures, frustrations, and long-term modifications.

REGIONAL ADJUSTMENTS

A fraught experiment in *congregación* characterized the founding of Santa Eulalia, a town in the far reaches of the Cuchumatanes (plate 14). The first attempts had to be abandoned because Paiconop, the site originally chosen for the *congregación*, was too easily attacked by hostile Lacandones invading from Usumacinta country even further to the north. The settlement was moved to its present, more defensible site two kilometres to the southwest, but only after

34 Remesal ([1619] 1964–66, vol. 2, 259). His precise words are: "El pueblo de Aguacatlán ... era entonces muy grande, habíanle juntado el P.F. Pedro de Angulo, F. Juan de Torres y otros religiosos de la Orden, que predicaban en aquellas sierras de Cuchumatlán, de muchos caserías que estaban esparcidas por aquellos montes."

35 Aguacatán and Chalchitán, for example, were assessed separately for tribute purposes in both 1677 and 1683; see AGCA, A3.16, leg.1601, exp. 26391 and AGI, Contaduría 815. The latter source also records a *parcialidad* called Comitán, which then had only four tribute payers, as opposed to 64 for Aguacatán and 91 for Chalchitán.

36 Recinos (1954, 75) actually makes reference to "el doble pueblo de Aguacatán y Chalchitán," the "twin town" designation thus enshrined. See also McArthur and McArthur (1966, 140) and Brintnall (1979, 61–87).

a church and other structures had already been built at Paiconop.[37] Lacandón raids up into the *tierra fría* around Santa Eulalia, and also at San Mateo Ixtatán, took place throughout the colonial period, despite numerous attempts by the Spaniards to conquer and impose order on this especially troublesome group.[38] Toward the end of the seventeenth century, Fuentes y Guzmán declared that anyone making the trip from Santa Eulalia to San Mateo did so "with imminent risk from the Lacandón enemy, who invade the mountains to rob and harass our poor Indians."[39] In response to the situation, two peace-keeping forces were established, one at San Mateo and another at Santa Eulalia, to protect the Cuchumatán frontier to the west of the Río Ixcán. Not even regular policing, however, diminished the threat, and Lacandón incursions persisted for another century and more.[40]

Ixil *congregaciones* along the Cuchumatán frontier to the east of the Río Ixcán also suffered depredations at the hands of Lacandones. The area around Ilom was so vulnerable to attack that Ilom was ordered to be abandoned, even after a church had been erected there. Indians from Ilom were relocated to Chajul and Santa Eulalia, the former receiving the Ilom church altar, the latter the Ilom church bells.[41] Chajul was itself attacked many times, hostile Lacandones entering Ixil country by way of the Xaclbal valley. Unlike Ilom,

37 La Farge (1947, xi, 4, and 63). The name "Paiconop" in Q'anjob'al means "pueblo antiguo" or "old town." A settlement was founded and a church built there most likely because the site was an important ceremonial centre in pre-Columbian times.

38 AGI, Guatemala 168, "Fray Juan de Mansilla to the Crown" (30 January 1552). For a discussion of the expeditions mounted to pacify the Lacandones, see de Vos ([1980] 1993) and Stone (1932, 208–96). Efforts to congregate and Christianize them never had any lasting success, as Tozzer (1912) makes clear.

39 Fuentes y Guzmán ([1690–99] 1969–72, vol. 3, 39). His precise words are "con inminente riesgo del enemigo lacandón, que suele saltearle derraman con tropillas de pocos barbaros flecheros que se penetran por la montaña al robo de y la molestia de nuestros pobres indios."

40 La Farge (1947, 68) notes that Lacandones "committed depredations against Cuchumatán peoples" as late as "the early nineteenth century."

41 Colby and van den Berghe (1969, 40). Relocating Ixil-speaking Indians from Ilom in the Q'anjob'al-speaking community of Santa Eulalia made little practical sense, but is a good indication of how little Spanish authorities understood (or cared about) spoken ethnic affiliations. The distance from Ilom to Santa Eulalia is also about twice that of Ilom to Chajul. Indians from Ilom who were resettled at Chajul presumably formed there the *parcialidad* known as Ilom. That Ixil-speakers were moved from Ilom to Santa Eulaia is corroborated by Baltazar Valdivia, a missionary who worked throughout Ixil country in the mid-nineteenth century; see Elliott and Elliott (1966, 126–7) for elaboration.

however, Chajul was never given up on.[42] Ilom itself was eventually reinhabited, Ixiles from there preferring to return and risk being raided by Lacandones in terrain that was familiar to them rather than eking out an existence far from home – where the danger was no less real. Envisioned as offering if not safety in this world then salvation in the next, *congregación* in this case fell far short of its lofty goals.

A combination of other factors worked against the centripetal grip of *congregación*. Since many Indians were congregated involuntarily, Spanish authorities often had difficulty in keeping them tied to a new town site. In the seclusion of their old homes, they were free of such demands as paying tribute, providing labour, working on local roads or the parish church, and serving as human carriers. They also sought the refuge of the mountains when disease struck, as it did often, sometimes with dramatic impact.[43] Evangelizing missionaries believed that Indians would be better cared for in *congregaciones* at times of crisis, especially during outbreaks of disease. Herding people together to form *pueblos de indios*, however, likely had the opposite effect, as disease spread more virulently in areas of denser settlement than in the more scattered arrangements of pre-conquest times. Recurrent fugitivism, triggered and sustained by a complex interplay of cultural preference and existential circumstance, was at constant odds with Spanish notions of civilized residence epitomized, in theory, by *pueblos de indios*.

Geographical isolation and limited economic prospects likewise worked against effective *congregación*. Scarce native labour and scant commercial opportunity caused economic stagnation throughout Spanish Central America for much of the seventeenth century.[44]

42 Tovilla ([1635] 1960, 209); Ximénez ([1715–20] 1929–31, vol. 2, 221); and Termer (1957, 7–8). Ximénez writes: "In the year 1664, 'indios lacandones' reached the cornfields of the people of Chajul. In one [*milpa*] they came across an Indian mother breast-feeding her child. The mother ran for it, leaving her child behind, escaping to the safety of town and raising the alarm. Indians [from Chajul] took up arms and marched to the cornfields, some four leagues from town. When they arrived there, the Lacandones had already fled, but not before sacrificing the child, tearing open its chest and pulling out its heart."

43 See AGCA, A1, leg. 6118, exp. 56749, which concerns flight from Nebaj, and AGCA A3.16, leg. 249, exp. 5036, which concerns flight from Santa Eulalia. The phenomenon is dealt with at some length in chapter 9.

44 See MacLeod ([1973] 2009, 310–29), who builds the case for Central America on the foundation established for Mexico by Borah (1951). For alternative interpretations, see Bakewell (1970); Boyer (1977); Brading (1971, 1978); Brading and Cross (1977); and Israel (1975) for Mexico. Wortman (1982) debates the point

Even earlier, the exploitation of Guatemala's resources had seen materially minded Spaniards concentrate their attention either on the cacao-rich Pacific coast or on the fertile *tierra templada* to the south and east of the capital city of Santiago, where indigo dye could be made, cattle raised, and two or even three corn crops harvested each year. The highlands of the *tierra fría* to the north and west – remote, inhospitable, and of little market import – were considered much less attractive. A statement made in 1570 by the governor of Zapotitlán is revealing. "Neither in the highlands of Jacaltenango, nor in those of Huehuetenango is there any cacao," he informs us, "the land there being of poor and unfruitful quality, good only for raising corn and chickens."[45] Such appraisals, made by men more attuned to the potential windfalls of overseas trade than with more modest involvement in the local economy, had a notable geographical impact. Spanish interest in the Cuchumatanes after the region had been secured and *congregación* begun never was as intense as in better-endowed parts of Central America. This state of affairs prevailed during the stagnant or transitional years of the seventeenth century. It also seems to have continued to a lesser extent throughout the eighteenth and into the nineteenth century.

The consequences of this relative disinterest were far reaching. Native peoples to the north and west of Santiago were not so ignored that their communities became the breeding ground of overt rebellion, though outbreaks of violence did occur.[46] Indians instead nurtured cultural resistance to Spanish invaders by reverting, in the course of the seventeenth and eighteenth centuries, to many of their former ways. It was not a return to life as it was led before the conquest; such a reversal was impossible. Rather, it was a creative blend of elements of Hispanic culture that the Indians had accepted and elements of pre-Columbian culture they managed to maintain. Neither "Indian" nor "Spanish," this fusion of the old and the new produced

---

with respect to Central America. Gibson (1975) and Te Paske and Klein (1981) help reconcile the tension between opposing viewpoints.

45 AGI, Guatemala 52, "Diego de Garcés, *alcalde mayor* of Zapotitlán, to the Council of the Indies" (1560). His precise words are: "Ni en la sierra de Jacaltenango ni en la de Huehuetenango no hay cacao ninguno, porque toda ella es ... tierra pobre y estéril salvo de maíz y gallinas que hay en abundancia."

46 MacLeod ([1973] 2008, 326–7). Evidence from AGI, Patronato 69-1-5, indicates that a rebellion took place as early as 1534 involving Indians from Aguacatán, Ilom, and Serquil, in which several Spaniards were killed. For accounts of violent confrontation as Independence loomed, see Bricker (1981) and Pollack (2005).

a culture of refuge referred to by historian Murdo MacLeod as "conquest peasant."[47] In its outward forms and inner features, this cultural synthesis resembled the one shaped by neighbouring Maya communities in colonial Chiapas.[48]

The "conquest peasant" way of life led by Cuchumatán Indians during the seventeenth and eighteenth centuries developed several characteristics that conflicted with Spanish precepts of native well-being. One of these was the abandonment of *congregaciones* in favour of more dispersed forms of settlements – and a less beholden existence – as Spanish authority grew progressively weaker, particularly in areas far removed from central government in Santiago and isolated even from the watchful eye of local administrators in Totonicapán and Huehuetenango.[49] Another characteristic was the revival, or maintenance, of pre-Christian religious rites.[50]

One of the earliest references to *congregación* not being accomplished without frustration and risk of failure comes from Sacapulas soon after the policy was first implemented. Begun in the late 1540s, resettlement in these parts was given an added stimulus in 1553 when the Order of Santo Domingo received permission from President Alonso López de Cerrato to establish a monastery at Sacapulas.[51] The Dominicans chose to resettle various native groups around a site on the south bank of the Río Negro that had long been occupied, on account of the existence of important salt springs, by two communities later known as the *parcialidades* Santiago and San Sebastián.[52] Writing to King Charles V from their base in Sacapulas on 6 December 1555, Tomás de Cárdenas and Juan de Torres, two friars responsible for bringing dispersed populations together, speak of the obstacles to successful *congregación*. One was the extremely difficult terrain. "This part of the sierra," they state, "being so rugged and broken, caused us to encounter settlements comprising only

47 MacLeod ([1973] 2008, 328). See also La Farge (1940); Wolf (1957; 1959; and ([1986] 2001).

48 Wasserstrom (1983a, 69–106; 1983b, 118–19).

49 La Farge (1940, 282–91); MacLeod (1983, 202–3 and 206–7).

50 Gibson (1966, 75) considers that the missionary endeavours of the friars responsible for *congregación* succeeded not in converting Indians to orthodox Christianity but in creating a "syncretic" religion that was essentially "Catholic-Christian in its externals but non-Christian in some of its basic postulates or in its enveloping world view."

51 Fuentes y Guzmán ([1690–99] 1969–72, vol. 3, 15).

52 Carmack (1973, 206–8).

eight, six, or even four houses tucked and hidden away in gullies or ravines where, until our arrival, no other Spaniard had penetrated." The friars lament that in nearby mountains they had recently found "a very large quantity of idols, not in any way concealed but placed in full public view, as when before they were baptized." This comment suggests either the discovery by the missionaries of hitherto unknown places of abode or the return, at least temporarily, to former lands and old ways on the part of Indians who may have been congregated earlier. Cárdenas and Torres, with rare insight into the native mind, come closest to understanding visceral resistance to *congregación* when they remark that "among all these Indians there is not one who wishes to leave behind the hut passed on to him by his father, nor to abandon a pestilential ravine or desert some inaccessible craggy rocks, because that is where the bones of his forefathers rest." The friars add, "now that people have been brought together, they will have less opportunity to practice idolatry, and ourselves more opportunity to watch over them," meaning that Indians "can more readily be instructed not only in matters that concern our Holy Faith but also in proper human conduct."[53]

Cárdenas and Torres go on to suggest that the monarch should not listen to complaints lodged by Spaniards against Licenciado Alonso de Zorita, whose efforts to bring order and responsible government to Sacapulas and surrounding areas during his tour of inspection nine months earlier they praise and support.[54] False and malicious information, the Dominicans warn, was being spread in order to sabotage

53 AGI, Guatemala 168, "Tomás de Cárdenas and Juan de Torres to the Crown" (6 December 1555). According to Remesal ([1619] 1964–66, vol. 2, 432–3), Cárdenas "baptized more than two thousand Indians" after his arrival from Spain in 1553, the intrepid Dominican heading into the Cuchumatán sierra "like a mountain goat" and getting to know the rugged terrain "as if it were the streets of Seville." He is singled out as being "the father who worked hardest to save Indian souls, making one town out of four, erecting churches in them, and burning countless numbers of idols that the natives had hidden and surrendered to him of their own free will."

54 A reformist Crown official cast in the same mould as Alonso López de Cerrato, Zorita arrived in Guatemala in 1553 to help implement the New Laws of 1542. Keen, in Zorita ([1585] 1963), furnishes an account of the *oidor*'s experiences there. Zorita set out on his first *visita*, a tour of inspection, early in March 1555, arriving in Sacapulas later that same month. During the six months his *visita* lasted, Zorita travelled throughout Guatemala, making his way to remote mountain regions like the Cuchumatanes, which few senior bureaucrats had ever reached. A zealous destroyer of native idols, Zorita may have been esteemed by the Dominican friars of Sacapulas, but he was hated by secular Spaniards whose privileges as recipients of Indian labour and tribute he attempted to curtail. Nor was he a popular judge in the eyes of Franciscan friars. Successful lobbying by his enemies in Guatemala led to

Zorita's dedicated work. They single out in particular Spanish outrage at Zorita's recommendation that Indians be given a year's grace from paying tribute while they build new houses and plant new fields in and around the *congregaciones* they settle. Although Cárdenas and Torres insist that, at least to their knowledge, no excesses were being perpetrated by Spaniards against Indians in the Sacapulas region, they allege that uncontrolled exploitation motivated by "worldly interests" endangered the long-term success of *congregación* by causing natives to flee settlements to escape oppression.[55]

Two decades later, there are reports of families at Chajul living some distance from town and paying no attention to demands to return to the fold. Unlike their congregated kinfolk, these miscreants went uncounted and did not pay tribute. Tolerance of such fugitivism decreased Chajul's tax base. The district governor, Francisco Díaz del Castillo, was ordered by the Crown to conduct an inquiry and rectify the situation.[56] A century on, however, the situation here (and elsewhere) was far from rectified. Native families continued to drift away, deserting *pueblos de indios* for a freer life in their cornfields in the hills. Fuentes y Guzmán, for example, complained that "wild and uncivilized" Indians chose to make their homes in the mountains surrounding the town of San Juan Atitán rather than in town itself. This they did allegedly to be close to their *milpas*, but that was a mere pretext, he maintained, a ruse "to burn incense to their idols" in out of the way places.[57] At San Mateo Ixtatán, the chronicler reported, some forty families lived in the countryside at a place called Asantih, fourteen leagues distant from the *congregación*.[58]

Zorita being transferred for duties to the Audiencia of Mexico in 1556. See Vigil (1987) and Lovell (1990) for further discussion.

55 AGI, Guatemala 168, "Tomás de Cárdenas and Juan de Torres to the Crown" (6 December 1555). Their precise words are "intereses mundanos." The friars also make grim reference to reports about Indians in other parts of Guatemala who, according to Zorita, committed suicide by hurling themselves from hilltops in order to free themselves from abuse and exploitation once and for all.

56 Elliott and Elliott (1966, 126). The Elliotts cite as their source documents found inside the baptismal registry for Chajul for the years 1676–78.

57 Fuentes y Guzmán ([1690–99] 1969–72, vol. 3, 26). The chronicler calls them "indios agrestes y montaraces," their living out of town "pretexto e invención para incensar a los ídolos." Some of those committing sacrilegious acts were eventually apprehended and brought to justice in Huehuetenango. There, after a public flogging, they were forced to work for the parish church.

58 Fuentes y Guzmán ([1690–99] 1969–72, vol. 3, 40). He claims that, assisted by the parish priest of San Mateo, he personally went to Asantih, "tierra apartada del pueblo de Ystatlán," and oversaw the removal of forty families living there back into town. This was an extremely risky business, as Asantih lay only six leagues from

The parish priest of San Mateo, Alonso de León, put the number of fugitive families at twice that of Fuentes y Guzmán: "They do not figure on the tribute roll, a loss of revenue for His Majesty," he states. "Nor do they attend mass and take confession." Attempts on his part to deal with the situation brought him into conflict with Gaspar Jorge, a local leader who collected tribute as if the eighty families in question *were* on the tribute roll, apparently pocketing the proceeds and using them to indulge in all sorts of mischief. One of Jorge's pranks was to arrange for women to sneak into church at night, "not merely to whet his own villainy but so that their solicitations might tempt the father's honour." Another ploy was an attempt to frighten de León by witchcraft; the priest entered his quarters on one occasion to find, placed under his bed, "a brazier in which coals had been snuffed out with blood, and the stump of a tallow candle pierced with pine needles, also soaked in blood."[59] When he showed the brazier to an Indian and asked for an explanation, he was told that it had been put there to attract demon spirits that would kill him.

From his personal encounters, de León ventures candid opinions about native life in general. The relationship between father and son, he declares, is one in which "nothing is passed on save for how to take care of the cornfields and how to live all day long like savages in the hills." He feared that proper codes of behaviour would never take root, for the Indians of San Mateo "are at each other's throats, all year long." De León discloses that Jorge and his cronies had decided "to erect a shrine, on no authority but their own, some distance from town, at precisely the same spot where the sacrificial altar of pagan times used to be, on a hilltop between the remains of ancient temples, where on any given day may be found charcoal and incense and other signs of burnt offerings." The priest laments that "further transgressions against Holy Church include the sacrifice of turkeys, taken up to the hills to be dispatched with the blood of other animals." Driven by Satan, de León concludes, the Indians of San Mateo "with their nasty habits and evil ways have contaminated

Lacandón country. Asantih (see AGI, Guatemala 225) was where Spanish authorities suggested that Lacandones themselves be resettled in order to keep a closer eye on them. The measures taken by Fuentes y Guzmán had no lasting impact and set no enduring example.

59 AGI, Guatemala 159, "Testimonio sobre la perdición general de los indios" (1687).

the entire town in such a way that it remains Christian in name only."[60] So ineffective was Spanish control over the unruly *indios fugitivos* of San Mateo that some of them actually joined forces with the feared Lacandones for periodic raids on their Q'anjob'al neighbours to the south and west.[61]

A half-century later, Fray Sebastián de Aguirre, serving at San Miguel Acatán, reported serious backsliding there. The Indians, he claimed, resisted his attempts to hear confession, one of them being so bold as to strike him for being insistent in his demands. Aguirre's confrontation occurred after the central government in Santiago had earlier warned local officials not to be tolerant of religious non-conformity. Any native adult not regularly attending mass or ignorant of Catholic doctrine was to be given six to eight lashes and thrown in jail overnight.[62] In 1797, the district governor, Francisco Xavier de Aguirre, found and destroyed, two leagues distant from the town of Concepción, "the pagan shrine where the Indians go to offer sacrifices and prayers to the devil."[63] These observations, drawn from a considerable body of data, indicate that Catholicism as practised by Cuchumatán Indians was as unorthodox and syncretic as that recorded for other Maya groups.[64] Archbishop Pedro Cortés y Larraz, when he passed through the region in the late eighteenth century, dismissed the Christianity of his native flock as constituting "nothing more than appearance and hypocrisy."[65] "Because Indians are little more than fugitives in the mountains," he writes of Nebaj, "all sorts of wrongs occur, like going for two years without confessing or receiving the Holy Sacraments."[66] The situation was no better in Huehuetenango, "where not even one family in three resides in

60 Ibid.
61 La Farge (1947, x).
62 AGCA, A1.24, leg. 6035, exp. 55410.
63 AGCA, A3.16, leg. 225, exp. 5719.
64 Bricker (1981, 177–81); Wasserstrom (1983, 106–17).
65 Cortés y Larraz ([1768–70] 1958, vol. 2, 44). His precise words are that "su cristianismo no es más que apariencia e hipocresía."
66 Ibid., vol. 2, 48. Elliott and Elliott (1966, 127) record a Spanish priest who worked in Ixil country in the mid-nineteenth century as stating: "After 300 years of being evangelized, [the Indians] are today seen to be in a worse state than in the first century [of having been attended to], marching backwards toward their ancient barbarities, mixed with vices and vices and irreligion of other castes." For studies on the continuity of pre-Columbian systems of belief, see La Farge (1947); Oakes (1951a, 1951b); and Deuss (2007).

town."[67] As for Cuilco, "the people there normally live all alone, up in the hills, as is their wont."[68]

The Cuchumatán evidence, in short, points to an initial flurry of nucleation being followed, for a number of reasons, by a long period of dispersal. Attrition of the population base of *pueblos de indios* has been documented elsewhere. Nancy Farriss presents the process as a general proposition for colonial Yucatán, maintaining that "the Maya, like most people who practice labor-efficient forms of extensive agriculture, found (and still find) dispersed settlements most convenient for farming."[69] Her hypothesis – that "whenever the forces of integration weakened, the Maya would drift back into their preferred pattern of scattered settlement"[70] – is supported by the findings of several other scholars of Yucatán.[71] The drift there was so advanced by the late eighteenth century that, according to Peter Gerhard, "the settlement pattern was perhaps not greatly unlike that of pre-conquest times, with peasant houses scattered about and many *cabeceras* relatively deserted except during market days and religious festivals."[72] Rodney C. Watson and Robert Wasserstrom have noted a similar process for colonial Chiapas.[73] The Cuchumatán experience may simply conform to a southern Mesoamerican or Maya norm.

CIVIL AND RELIGIOUS ADMINISTRATION

The *congregaciones* or *pueblos de indios* formed in the mid-sixteenth century were but tiny components of a grand administrative scheme designed to facilitate all levels of government, from local affairs to issues of state. The complex, massive bureaucracy that ran the

---

67 Cortés y Larraz ([1768–70] 1958, vol. 2, 117). The archbishop's informant, Félix Fernando Rosel, "de edad como de cuarenta años," told him "que no existe en los pueblos aún la tercera parte de sus familias."

68 Ibid., vol. 2, 137. "Viven en los pueblos muy pocas familias," he records, "lo cual es conforme a la inclinación de los indios, que apetecen vivir en los montes y solo."

69 Farriss (1978, 216).

70 Ibid., 188.

71 See, for example, Cook and Borah (1974, vol. 2, 14–20); García Bernal (1978, 111); Grant Jones (1983, 64–88); Clendinnen (1987, 141–2); and Patch (1993, 45–66).

72 Gerhard (1979, 29–30).

73 Wasserstrom (1983a, 89–90); Watson (1990).

Spanish empire combined rather than separated responsibilities of office. However, two basic hierarchical structures – one political or judicial in nature, the other ecclesiastical – may be identified.

Politico-judicial jurisdiction was headed by the Crown, its authority absolute. The Crown was advised on matters pertaining to its New World colonies by the Council of the Indies, a body normally resident in Madrid, although for a short period it convened in Valladolid when the Spanish capital was located there. The Council of the Indies recommended broad lines of policy and nominated individuals to positions both high and low. It audited accounts, heard or received testimony, and reviewed the conduct and performance of those chosen for office. Executive charge overseas was in the hands of viceroys, usually well-connected Spaniards who ruled in the king's name and were responsible for attending to revenue, justice, and native welfare. Viceroys were assisted by advisory boards know as *audiencias*; geographically, where they sat provided an important focus for regional affiliation. The area presided over by an *audiencia* was divided into units called *corregimientos* or *alcaldías mayores*, each entrusted to the care of a *corregidor* or *alcalde mayor*, district governors cum magistrates whose job it was to coordinate tribute collection, organize work parties, and in general keep themselves informed of local events and circumstances. In Guatemala, *corregimientos* or *alcaldías mayores* were made up of varying numbers of *pueblos de indios* – Indian towns or *congregaciones* – governed (usually from a distance) by a *corregidor* or *alcalde mayor* represented in each community by native *alcaldes* (mayors) and *regidores* (councilors).[74]

Paralleling the civil, politico-judicial structure was the ecclesiastical one. The authority of the Crown over the Church was assured under the terms of the *Patronato Real*, a pact between Rome and the Spanish monarchy that guaranteed, by papal bulls issued in 1501 and 1508, that control over religious affairs would be placed in the hands of the royal court. Among these controls were the power of nomination and the management of church revenue. The largest unit of ecclesiastical geography was the archbishopric or archdiocese, to

---

74 Haring (1963, 161–2); Gibson (1966, 90–9); Cline (1972a, 24–6). The challenges of running such a vast empire in day-to-day practical terms, with reference to Guatemala in particular, are grappled with to dazzling effect by Sellers-García (2014).

which all component bishoprics or dioceses were subject. Each bishopric or diocese was internally composed of a number of curacies or parishes. To this episcopal organization belonged the secular clergy, so named because they "lived in the world" (Latin, *sæculum*). Such ecclesiastics were distinct from the regular clergy, who belonged to a specific religious order (Franciscan, Dominican, or Mercedarian) and were bound to certain vows or rules (Latin, *regula*). Initially, the regular clergy had exclusively a missionary mandate and thus committed themselves to providing for the spiritual welfare of the Indians. The secular clergy, by contrast, were more concerned with the spiritual needs of Spaniards, criollos, and mestizos.[75]

During the colonial period, most of the isthmus of Central America, with the exception of the area of present-day Panama, was civilly administered as the *audiencia* of Guatemala. Today, this same unit would comprise the Mexican state of Chiapas, the now fully autonomous Belize, and the independent republics of Guatemala, El Salvador, Honduras, Nicaragua, and Costa Rica.[76] Created in 1543, the *audiencia* of Guatemala, formally a subunit of the Viceroyalty of New Spain, was placed under the charge of a presiding officer, or *presidente*, who was subordinate to the viceroy in Mexico City.

Within the *audiencia* of Guatemala, the Cuchumatanes formed part of the administrative division known either as the *corregimiento* (1547–1678) or the *alcaldía mayor* (1678–1785) of Totonicapán and Huehuetenango (see figure 2).[77] This same area, after the imposition of the intendancy system in 1785–86, became the *provincia* of Totonicapán and Huehuetenango and was divided into two: the *partido* (district) of Totonicapán and the *partido* of Huehuetenango.[78] The latter jurisdiction corresponds in rough areal extent to the Cuchumatán highlands (see figure 3) and comprised some forty Indian

75 Haring (1963, 166–93); Gibson (1966, 68–78); Cline (1972a, 26–70).
76 Cline (1972a, 21); Gerhard (1972, 129); MacLeod ([1973] 2008, 23 and 400).
77 Gerhard (1972, 132).
78 Cline (1972b, 161); Juarros ([1808] 1981, 46–8). An integral part of the administrative overhaul known as the Bourbon Reforms, the intendancy system was introduced throughout Spanish America during the second half of the eighteenth century. It was designed, according to Gibson (1966, 170), "to centralize the colonial administration still further under the Crown, to eliminate the abuses of office holding, and to increase royal revenue." Wortman (1975; 1982, 129–56) examines the impact of the reforms in detail.

towns (see table 5) that emerged from the process of *congregación* in the mid-sixteenth century.

The *pueblos de indios* of the Cuchumatanes were divided for purposes of ecclesiastical administration into eight parishes, each having a *cabecera de doctrina*, the town where the local priest lived and from where he made his parish rounds (see figure 6 and table 5). The *cabecera de doctrina* gave its name to the entire parish. Priests were obliged to recognize the authority of the bishop of Guatemala, resident in the capital city of Santiago. It was not until 1745 that the bishopric of Guatemala was raised to archdiocesan status, a situation that meant that for the first two hundred years of Spanish rule, the bishopric of Guatemala came under the ecclesiastical jurisdiction of the archdiocese of Mexico.[79]

The task of converting Cuchumatán Indians to Christianity was initially granted to friars belonging to the Dominican order, and it was under their aegis that *congregación* was first carried out. At least one Franciscan, however, appears to have ventured into Dominican territory and left his trace. Writing in the late seventeenth century, Francisco Vázquez states that from 1545 on, Sacapulas and "many other" towns were founded by the Franciscan missionary Gonzalo Méndez.[80] Vázquez was himself a Franciscan and so would have been disposed toward portraying his order in the best possible light, which included encroaching on Dominican terrain to spread the Word of God. His statement, though, is corroborated by the eighteenth-century Dominican chronicler, Francisco Ximénez, who claims Méndez was responsible for "converting to the Catholic Faith" the *parcialidades* San Francisco and Santo Tomás, two groups that formed part of the *congregación* of Sacapulas.[81]

By the close of the sixteenth century, most parts of the Cuchumatanes had passed into the hands of the Mercedarian order, a more acceptable arrangement for Dominicans to stomach than allowing their Franciscan rivals to assume control. Alonso Ponce, a Franciscan friar, records Huehuetenango and Chiantla as being under Mercedarian supervision when he passed through on a trip from

79 Cline (1972a, 27).
80 Vázquez ([1688–95] 1937–44, vol. 2, 32).
81 Ximénez ([1715–20] 1929–31, vol. 1, 1910).

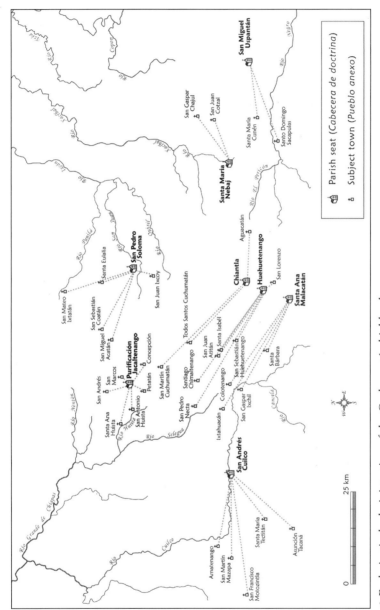

6 Ecclesiastical administration of the Cuchumatán highlands.

Guatemala to Mexico in 1586.[82] By the end of the seventeenth century, over thirty towns in the Cuchumatanes were under Mercedarian charge, with the Dominicans maintaining a presence in only six.[83] In 1754, a royal edict ordered all parishes to become secular, but by special permission it was possible for a member of the regular clergy to continue to serve as a parish priest. The Cuchumatán parishes of Jacaltenango, Malacatán, and Nebaj, for example, were still administered by regular clergy at the end of the colonial period.[84]

Both the politico-judicial and ecclesiastical arms of government in Spanish America were rigidly hierarchical. The dictates of those at the top were transferred, in theory if not always in practice, into action and fulfillment by those at the bottom. The state sought, by deed and decree, to extend and exert its control over every facet of colonial life. In the following chapter we focus our attention on the operation of certain institutional controls and the impact they had on land and life in the Cuchumatanes.

82 Ponce, San Juan, and Ciudad Real ([1586] 1966, 208–12); Remesal ([1619] 1964–66, vol. 1, 242–4). Collins (1980, 148), citing a source in the local archive, states that Mercedarian friars were present in Jacaltenango at least ten years before Ponce passed through the region. According to Remesal, members of the Mercedarian Order left Spain for spiritual work in the New World in 1537, arriving that same year in Mexico and entering Guatemala in 1538. They came to Guatemala, as did all the missionary orders, with royal sanction. In 1542, the Mercedarians were given land in the newly founded capital of Santiago (in Panchoy) and built an impressive monastery there. Remesal, a Dominican, claims that the first Mercedarians were not "missionary oriented" in the strict evangelical sense, restricting themselves to the spiritual welfare of Spaniards and criollos who had been born and raised as Christians. He asserts that only after the Dominicans had ceded parts of "Quiché and Sacapulas" to the Mercedarians did the latter spread north and west from Guatemala with any degree of missionary commitment. For a history of the order in the New World, see Nolasco Pérez (1966). The Mercedarians' arrival in Guatemala is commemorated in Zúñiga Corres (1968). For further discussion, see Collins (1980, 148–55) and van Oss (1986, 59–60).

83 Fuentes y Guzmán ([1690–99] 1969–72, vol. 3, 15–44).

84 Recinos (1954, 466); Cline (1972a, 27).

7

Economic Demands and Ethnic Relations: Spanish Control of the Native Population

Knowing how evil, incorrigible, and unruly the Indians of these parts are, especially those of Huehuetenango, it is no great sin to beat them, or to threaten to beat them. A strong grip must be kept on them always.

Juan de Espinar (1537–40)

Relentless exploitation of the native capacity to work formed the basis of the colonial economy and lay at the heart of any enrichment that accrued either to the Spanish Crown or to individual Spaniards over the course of Spain's three-century domination of the New World. While demands placed on the indigenous population were unending, the institutional forms that exaction took varied considerably, both temporally and spatially. At the local level, the manner in which goods and services were usurped differed according to a number of factors, including the structure and complexity of pre-conquest society, the size of the native workforce, regional economic potential, geographical location, relations between Spanish colonists and Crown authorities, and attitudes toward the treatment of the native population. In the Cuchumatán highlands, as elsewhere, imperial Spain exploited *pueblos de indios* through the operation of several coercive devices. The various means of accumulating surplus, controlling production, and manipulating consumption are reviewed below as comprehensively as sources permit, with an emphasis on the dynamics and tensions of colonial subordination.

THE *ENCOMIENDA*

The *encomienda* was a means by which privileged Spaniards enjoyed the right to exact tribute, and initially also labour, from a specified number of Indians in a designated town or group of *pueblos de indios*. Its history as an institution is complex. Grants of *encomienda* in the first half of the sixteenth century, assigned primarily to soldiers who had fought with distinction in battles of conquest, frequently involved the allocation of impressive amounts of goods and services. When *encomienda* was finally abolished during the more enlightened years of the eighteenth century, it represented little more than a system of awarding small pensions to favoured members of the criollo and peninsular Spanish elite.

Encomenderos, individuals who held and shared *encomiendas*, often wielded considerable power as recipients of native tribute and labour in the early period of Spanish rule. Thereafter, the Crown introduced legislation painstakingly devised to limit the economic and political power of the *encomienda*, and above all to prevent even the most energetic of *encomenderos* from becoming semi-autonomous feudal lords. Such measures as the curtailing of the labour component and the prohibition of inheritance beyond a certain number of "lives" did much to stifle the *encomienda*. Thus, in the course of the late sixteenth and seventeenth centuries, by a deliberate process of attrition, *encomiendas* either reverted to the Crown or were severely constrained as a source of private income. In this way, to use a characteristic phrase in the literature, the *encomienda* was "tamed." Of particular importance in this erosion of power in Guatemala were reforms carried out during the terms of office of President Alonso López de Cerrato (1548–55) and President Diego García de Valverde (1578–89). The privileges of *encomienda* originally granted by the Crown were thus gradually whittled down or completely removed by the subsequent implementation of restrictive legislation.[1]

---

1 The word *encomienda* is derived from the Spanish verb *encomendar*, meaning "to entrust." Being awarded title to an *encomienda* entailed the right to receive tribute; it was not a grant of land. The entitlement carried with it certain obligations, among them to ensure that Indians held in *encomienda* received instruction in the tenets of Christianity and the Catholic faith, an obligation little attended to, let alone fulfilled. The standard work in English on the subject is Simpson ([1950] 1966). See also Kirkpatrick (1939); Lockhart (1969); and Zavala (1935, 1940). A splendid analysis of *encomienda*, focusing on central Mexico, may be found in Gibson (1964, 58–81 and 413–34). For Guatemala, the study of the institution by Rodríguez Becerra (1977) has now been superseded by that of Wendy Kramer (1994).

CUCHUMATÁN SCENARIOS

Although relatively scant and of limited reconstructive potential, extant archival documentation suggests that the history of *encomienda* in the Sierra de los Cuchumatanes conforms to the pattern outlined above. Titles to several Cuchumatán towns are recorded in the *tasaciones de tributos* (tribute assessments) prepared in 1549 by President Cerrato, a source long considered a definitive benchmark (see table 6). A much-needed corrective to understanding the pre-Cerrato history of *encomienda* is provided by Wendy Kramer, who concludes that, "far from being the starting point of the Guatemalan *encomienda*, or reflecting recent innovations wrought by the new president, Cerrato's tasación reflects the circumstances and allegiances of six different men, influenced by and responding to the vicissitudes of eleven different governments."[2] These six men and their eleven governments (see table 7) often assigned or exchanged, confirmed or removed *encomienda* privileges worth thousands of pesos annually. Table 8 summarizes Kramer's findings as they relate to the Cuchumatán highlands.

One notable feature of Kramer's findings is that rewards were formalized, as at Tecpán Puyumatlán (Santa Eulalia) and Uspantlán (Uspantán), long before any semblance of Spanish control materialized, suggesting that *encomienda* may have been manipulated as an incentive to conquer as well as a privilege granted thereafter. Another striking feature in the documents is the wealth that early *encomiendas* could generate, even in parts that lay, like much of the Sierra de los Cuchumatanes, off the beaten track. Some awards, such as those for Huehuetenango, Jacaltenango, and Sacapulas, even after Cerrato's adjustments, furnished enough tribute and labour to provide *encomenderos* with a comfortable living.[3] By the early seventeenth century, however, prohibitive legislation and a dwindling native population resulted in the failure of the *encomienda* system to support its recipients in the style of life to which they aspired. *Encomienda* privileges around the year 1610, as is evidenced by documentation for San Juan Ixcoy, San Mateo Ixtatán, Soloma, and Uspantán, resembled little more than a modest type of pension.[4] By the middle of

2 Kramer (1994, 236).
3 See AGI, Guatemala 128, "Tasaciones de los pueblos de los terminos y jurisdicción de la ciudad de Santiago de Guatemala" (1548–51).
4 AGCA, A1.39, leg, exp. 1751, ff. 78 verso, 81 verso and 211.

the seventeenth century, *encomienda* benefits were minimal and, at Aguacatán, Chajul, and Nebaj, were the equivalent of a very humble annuity.[5] In 1678, at the depth of the economic recession widespread throughout much of Central America, the *encomienda* income accruing to the holder of both Chiantla and Huehuetenango, along with the town of Guajiaquero in Honduras, amounted to only four hundred pesos a year.[6] By the end of the first quarter of the eighteenth century, holders of *encomienda* had completely lost interest in the institution and turned to other potentially more lucrative concerns. Most Cuchumatán *encomiendas* were then declared vacant and reverted to the Crown.[7] For the remainder of the colonial period, *pueblos de indios* paid tribute not to individuals but, via Crown officials, to the royal treasury.

THE *ENCOMIENDA* HISTORY OF HUEHUETENANGO

Documentation pertaining to Huehuetenango, perhaps not surprisingly given its size and importance, is the most detailed at hand for the Cuchumatanes. A Spaniard named Juan de Espinar is recorded as having been awarded title on 3 October 1525 by the Adelantado Pedro de Alvarado himself.[8] Since this date coincides with the last days of the month's-long siege of Zaculeu, Huehuetenango may have been given to Espinar for his involvement in the campaign, though no record has been uncovered of his having participated in it. Don Pedro's concession was confirmed on 26 March 1528 by his brother Jorge, who issued Espinar a second title to the town and its environs.[9] When the acting governor Francisco de Orduña passed through the region in December 1529 on his way to conquer Uspantán, he was incensed to learn that Espinar had shortly before ordered Indians to raze the homes where they lived and move closer to Huehuetenango. Espinar had convinced them to do this by alleging that such would be their fate in any case when Orduña and his war party arrived;

5 AGCA, A1.16, leg. 2808, exp. 40648.

6 AGCA, A1, leg. 1752, folio 17 verso.

7 AGCA, A3.16, leg. 2890, exp. 42579; A3.16, leg. 2890, exp. 42580; A3.16, leg. 2890, exp. 42581; and A3.16, leg. 2890, exp. 42587.

8 Kramer (1994, 52, 59, and 204), drawing on the contents of AGI, Justicia 1031, "Juan de Espinar con Pedro de Alvarado sobre el pueblo de Huehuetenango" (1537–40).

9 Kramer (1994, 75), drawing on the contents of AGI, Justicia 1031, "Juan de Espinar con Pedro de Alvarado sobre el pueblo de Huehuetenango" (1537–40).

relocating, which would have swelled Espinar's potential tributary population, may even have afforded those displaced some protection. In any event, Espinar's duplicity led to Orduña calling him, most unflatteringly, an "hijo de puta," the son of whore.[10] In August 1530, Pedro de Alvarado stripped Espinar of his *encomienda* and reassigned it to Francisco de Zurrilla, with whom he struck a deal that would see them exploit Huehuetenango as business partners.[11] A year later, however, after Espinar had fled imprisonment in Guatemala to plead his case in court, the Audiencia in Mexico City saw fit to rule that Huehuetenango be returned to him. Thereafter, until his death some thirty years later, a combination of astuteness, tenacity, and political savvy, coupled with a mean streak that drifted at times into downright cruelty, kept Espinar the master of Huehuetenango. He also had keen entrepreneurial instincts, controlling the sale of Indian tribute and developing an elaborate infrastructure of mining and agricultural activities in and around Huehuetenango. His mining operations were made possible by the discovery of silver at Chiantla (see plate 20) and gold placer deposits about ten kilometres to the south of Huehuetenango, along the course of the Río Malacatán.[12]

Good fortune for Espinar proved a curse for the Indians he controlled as *encomendero*. When Huehuetenango was in its heyday, Espinar enjoyed an income of some 9,000 pesos each year from his involvement in mining and another 3,000 pesos from his agricultural transactions. At the mines, a fellow Spaniard served as the technician concerned with extraction procedures, while a foreman (*mayordomo*) supervised the labour of native servants and slaves. A pig farm was established close to Huehuetenango, and Espinar laid claim to enough land to raise and store large quantities of corn and beans for consumption throughout the year. The foodstuffs paid to him as tribute he either fed to the Indians working his mines or sold to neighbouring Spaniards. By any standards, he was enterprising, dogged, and unyielding, determined to do well – and wealthy enough that,

10 AGI, Justicia 1031, "Juan de Espinar con Pedro de Alvarado sobre el pueblo de Huehuetenango" (1537–40).
11 Kramer (1994, 102), drawing on the contents of AGI Justicia 1031, "Juan de Espinar con Pedro de Alvarado sobre el pueblo de Huehuetenango" (1537–40).
12 Kramer (1994, 206 and 216), drawing on the contents of AGI, Justicia 1031, "Juan de Espinar con Pedro de Alvarado sobre el pueblo de Huehuetenango" (1537–40); AGCA, A3, leg. 2863, exp. 41698 and A3, leg. 2798, exp. 40470.

before their acrimonious falling-out, he could afford to lose a substantial sum of money playing cards with Pedro de Alvarado.[13]

Espinar lived long enough to see the population of Huehuetenango shrink to a fraction of what it had been when he was initially awarded the *encomienda* (see table 9). One factor affecting the population size was the loss of some surrounding towns, assigned to other Spaniards after 1530. Espinar's forfeit of Huehuetenango for one year to Zurrilla precipitated a lawsuit that records the bounty the latter briefly enjoyed (see table 10). Espinar's desire to retain Huehuetenango made perfect sense, for the loss was substantial: some of the commodities listed in the left-hand column of table 10 would have fetched a handsome return at market. In addition, labour at the gold operations alone represents between 43,200 and 72,000 workdays per year on the part of Indian men, and 10,800 workdays on the part of Indian women. The right-hand column of table 10 reflects the shrunken, "tamed" *encomienda* of Huehuetenango after Cerrato had wrestled with the beast. Even mid-century, however, Espinar could still console himself with having the eleventh-largest entrustment of Indians in all Guatemala, not including those *encomiendas* that paid tribute to the Crown.[14]

Why Espinar was awarded Huehuetenango in the first place remains unclear. The only explanation Don Pedro could offer, years after first awarding title, was to state that "as a result of continuous warfare in the region, the distribution of *encomiendas* [has] been irregular," adding "there [are] men like Espinar to whom the captains, in order to placate the appetites [of their soldiers], [have] given disproportionately large encomiendas, while others who deserve good *encomiendas* [have] ended up with very little."[15] He goes on to remark that "Espinar is a person of low standing and menial occupation, someone who has survived by plying his trade as a tailor. His Majesty orders that tradesmen of the mechanical arts should not be granted Indians but, rather, that they should practice their trades so that they benefit newly settled lands and kingdoms. Indians should

13 Sherman (1979, 388) puts the sum lost at the gambling table at "20,000 pesos de oro." Kramer (1994, 208), drawing on the contents of AGI, Justicia 295, "Residencia de Pedro de Alvarado" (1535), states that "Alvarado won two horses and, another time, 4,000 pesos from Espinar."

14 AGI, Guatemala 128, "Tasaciones de los pueblos de los términos y jurisdicción de la ciudad de Santiago de Guatemala" (1548–51).

15 AGI, Justicia 1031, "Juan de Espinar con Pedro de Alvarado sobre el pueblo de Huehuetenango" (1537–40).

be granted to members of the nobility and persons of status, not the likes of Espinar."[16]

Espinar himself sums up succinctly the reason he was able to start off and thereafter fare so well: "I have always sought to stay and reside here in the province of Guatemala without [wishing] to leave it for anywhere else." Alvarado could not have failed to consider the words a direct criticism, if not a barbed slight, of his own restless, peripatetic ways.[17]

In 1562, after Espinar's death, Huehuetenango was granted to Luis Manuel Pimentel, a Spanish resident of Santiago de Guatemala who was later awarded sizable agricultural holdings in the area.[18] When Pimentel died in 1575, the *encomienda* was left to his widow, Doña Juana de Guzmán.[19] Around 1580, at the time of the new province-wide *tasación* of President Valverde, Huehuetenango is recorded as having been held by the man Juana had married, one Francisco de la Fuente, who received a rather meagre amount of tribute from 367 tributaries:

> The town of Huehuetenango, held in *encomienda* by Francisco de la Fuente, a resident of Santiago de Guatemala, was formerly assessed at 570 tribute payers, one full tributary being the equivalent of two widowers or two single men, each one giving his *encomendero* a piece of cotton cloth measuring four *piernas*, a chicken, and half a *fanega* of corn [at regular intervals]. President Valverde and his judge, Dr Villanova, presently assess the town as having 367 tribute payers, each of whom delivers similar items of tribute.[20]

The downward adjustment of the tributary count by Valverde and Villanova was carried out after Cerrato had already reduced it significantly thirty years before, reflecting the two factors most responsible for the decline of the *encomienda* as a viable economic entity: the enforcement, by officers of the Crown, of legislation deliberately

16 Ibid.

17 Kramer (1994, 204), drawing on the contents of AGCA, A1.29, leg. 4678, exp. 40244.

18 AGCA, A3, leg. 2863, exp. 41698 and A3.16, leg. 2798, exp. 40470.

19 AGCA, A3.16, leg. 2808, exp. 40633.

20 AGI, Guatemala 10, "Razón de las tasaciones que se han hecho después que el presidente [Valverde] vino a esta audiencia, de pueblos de su distrito con lo que antes tributaban" (1582), folio 15.

designed to curb the power of *encomenderos*, and the diminution of a native workforce frequently stricken by wave after wave of epidemic disease (see chapter 9).

Almost a century after the Valverde *tasación*, the *encomienda* of Huehuetenango entailed a modest contribution from a mere 156.5 tributaries who paid their *encomendero*, José de Balcárcel, a small sum of cash along with (as in the times of Cerrato and Valverde) some corn, chickens, and cotton cloth.[21] In 1678 the *encomienda* was given to Doña Mariana de Alvarado y Velasco, a resident of Madrid, who derived from it an insubstantial pension. Soon thereafter the *encomienda* escheated, and the Crown became the sole recipient of the Indian tribute of Huehuetenango.[22]

Two developments in the *encomienda* history of Huehuetenango are of special interest. First, there was an early connection in the district between *encomienda* and landholding per se. Two sixteenth-century *encomenderos* of Huehuetenango, Juan de Espinar and Luis Manuel Pimentel, both owned land in the vicinity of the town; the latter in particular was assiduous in seeking formal title to land within the spatial limits of his *encomienda*.[23] Though scholars consider the history of the *encomienda* and that of the *hacienda*, or landed estate, as legally separate and distinct, there was frequently, as James Lockhart has pointed out, a close link "in the realm of actual practice" between the two institutions.[24] Such a link is apparent in the case of Huehuetenango, always the most lucrative *encomienda* in the Cuchumatán region. Second, there was a marked tendency toward absentee holding by the late seventeenth century as the Crown increasingly awarded *encomiendas* in Central America to powerful Mexican families or members of the peninsular Spanish nobility, much to the chagrin of Guatemalan criollos.[25] One of the last *encomenderos* of Huehuetenango was the *madrileña* Doña Mariana, who probably never set foot near her *encomienda*, and would likely have thought of it only when wondering why her pension from the royal treasury amounted to so little.[26]

21 AGCA, A3.16, leg. 1601, exp. 26391.
22 AGCA, A1, leg. 1752, folio 17 verso.
23 AGCA, A3, leg. 2863, exp. 41698.
24 Lockhart (1969, 416).
25 MacLeod ([1973] 2008, 293).
26 AGCA, A1, leg. 1752, folio 17 verso. For comparative purposes, with the *encomienda* history of one single Cuchumatán community in mind, see Collins (1980, 74–103) on Jacaltenango.

THE *TASACIÓN DE TRIBUTOS*
AND THE *SERVICIO DEL TOSTÓN*

Since *congregación* and the creation of *pueblos de indios* were undertaken with economic as well as spiritual considerations in mind, it is no coincidence that the reshaping of native settlement patterns coincided with attempts by the Crown to compile accurate lists of the number of Indians who could be expected to serve as suppliers of tribute. This routine procedure of assessing the tribute-paying capacity of *pueblos de indios* resulted in the periodic drafting of a basis for levy known as the *tasación de tributos*.

The *tasación de tributos* recorded the number of Indians in any given town from whom tribute could legally be exacted. Such people were designated *indios tributarios*. Although Spanish definition of the term varied during the turbulent years of subjugation, by the end of the sixteenth century and for the remainder of the colonial period (save for an attempt at change, in 1786, in the Ordinance of Intendants) a *tributario* was classified as a married Indian male between eighteen and fifty years of age, together with his wife and children. As a taxation category, a *tributario* was therefore a family head, and represented one domestic or household unit. Widows, widowers, and unmarried adult males and females were defined as half-tributaries. Exemption from paying tribute, a status referred to as *reservado*, was granted to native leaders and their eldest sons, to children, to the aged, to the sick and infirm, and to those Indians involved in some way with the work of the Church. A *tasación* usually stipulated the amount of tribute that a tributary or half-tributary was responsible for furnishing. The setting of uniform rates and quotas was designed to minimize abuse on the part either of *corregidores* collecting for the royal treasury or of *encomenderos* collecting for themselves.[27]

Depending on whether a town was assigned to an *encomendero* or held by the Crown, tribute accrued either principally to a private individual or wholly to the royal treasury. The operation of *encomienda* represented a decentralization of the tribute exaction and therefore conflicted with the desire of the state to monopolize all such relations with indigenous groups. It was because of the commitment of the Crown to establishing a centralized economic order under absolute

27 Cook and Borah (1971, vol. 1, 17–25); Haring (1963, 263–5).

state control that a policy purposely stifling the *encomienda* was ardently pursued. As *encomiendas* reverted to the Crown in the course of the seventeenth and eighteenth centuries, Indian tribute formed an increasing part of imperial finances. In Guatemala, the amount collected annually in the mid-sixteenth century was about 10,000 pesos; toward the end of the eighteenth century, around the time of the Bourbon Reforms, the state's share had increased to more than 120,000 pesos.[28]

As well as enlarging its portion of Indian tribute relative to that enjoyed by *encomenderos*, the state also exacted from every tributary, whether in Crown towns or private *encomiendas*, an annual *real servicio* of one-half peso, or one *tostón*. This additional tax, known as the *servicio del tostón*, was initially imposed in 1592 as a short-term measure to help the royal treasury pay for the Invincible Armada. It continued to be collected, however, well into the eighteenth century.[29] When first levied in the *corregimiento* of Totonicapán and Huehuetenango, the *real servicio* amounted to some 5,000 *tostones*, a figure that grew to about 6,500 *tostones* in 1683 and reached 7,500 *tostones* in 1710.[30]

Cuchumatán Indians, like all native groups, were required under colonial law to pay tribute twice each year, on the *tercio de San Juan* (June 24th) and on the *tercio de Navidad* (December 25th). Given what they had to deliver, neither the Feast Day of Saint John nor Christmas Day could have been much cause for indigenous celebration. Tribute was usually collected at the local level by Indian *alcaldes* and *regidores*, who were responsible either to *encomenderos* or to *corregidores* for the provision of the stipulated amount. Failure on the part of native representatives to collect the necessary quotas often resulted in their being thrown in jail.[31] Once collected, the tribute, if paid in kind, was usually sold at public auction. The

28 Archivo General de Simancas, leg. 6, número 53, "Sumario general de lo que valen todas las Indias a Su Magestad" (1558); Wortman 1982, 153. The former source is a financial summary compiled for the Crown's benefit using the latest fiscal accounts at hand. Although dated 1558, the figures for Guatemala pertain to the late 1540s, as the *tasaciones* carried out by Cerrato are cited as the source of information.

29 Cook and Borah (1971–79, vol. 1, 20); Haring (1963, 277).

30 AGCA, A3, leg. 2713, exp. 38919 (1593); AGI, Contaduría 969 (1595); AGI, Contaduría 815 (1683); and AGI, Contaduría 973 (1710).

31 Fuentes y Guzmán ([1690–99] 1969–72, vol. 3, 18) mentions that, as the seventeenth century drew to a close, failure on the part of six Indian *alcaldes* to collect tribute in Ixil country resulted in their imprisonment – for over two years. The chronicler himself considered the sentence "duro y miserable" – "severe and miserable." He

monetary proceeds were then commuted to the appropriate recipients, either in the colonies or the mother country.[32]

The earliest, most complete *tasación de tributos* for Cuchumatán *pueblos de indios* dates to the third quarter of the seventeenth century.[33] At that time most Cuchumatán towns, perhaps indicative of their minimal relative worth, were still held in private *encomienda*. Cash payments to the Crown in the form of the *servicio del tostón* amounted to a little over 2,000 pesos annually. *Encomenderos* were paid in kind with commodities such as beans, chickens, corn, cotton cloth, and palm or reed mats (*petates*). In 1768, a century later, tribute continued to be paid at least partly in kind, despite persistent demands by the Crown (then theoretically the sole recipient of tribute) that all payments be made in cash.[34] By 1788, after the imposition of the intendancy system had increased fiscal efficiency, the Cuchumatán *tasación* brought in roughly 8,000 pesos per year and constituted approximately one-twelfth of the Guatemalan total.[35]

The semi-annual furnishing of tribute, in normal years, must have been accepted by the Indian population as part of their servile lot, an individual and collective burden that somehow had to be met, not questioned or challenged. This was certainly the view held by Spanish officialdom, and indeed was the undisputed basis upon which colonial rule was predicated: to the Spaniards, tribute was regarded as "a just token of the vassalage owed by Natives to the Sovereign."[36] The hand of fate, however, from time to time prevented or retarded the payment of tribute: outbreaks of sickness; the ravages of drought, earthquake, and fire; and crop destruction due to locust invasions all took a toll.[37] Among such calamities, the disease factor was of

acknowledged that, among "gente tan agreste y montaraz," "people so uncouth and uncivilized," there would always be problems getting tribute paid on time.

32 MacLeod ([1973]) 2008, 113).

33 AGCA, A3.16, leg. 1601, exp. 26391.

34 AGCA, A3.16, leg. 501, exp. 10261 and A3.16, leg. 501, exp. 10263.

35 AGCA, A3.16, leg. 246, exp. 4912; Wortman (1975a, 222–38). According to Wortman (1975b, 277), total government revenue from Indian tribute payments in Guatemala by the early nineteenth century "averaged almost 100,000 pesos annually." Indian tribute was then one of the four major sources of Crown revenue, the other three being (1) income from government monopolies such as tobacco, liquor, and playing cards; (2) taxes on trade and commerce; and (3) the state's share of church tithes.

36 These words come from the *Libro mayor de contaduría general de tributos del cargo de su contador Don Juan José de Leuro*, as cited in Van Aken (1981, 431).

37 See, for example, AGCA, A1.11, leg. 6111, exp. 56055, dealing with a period of drought in Sacapulas; AGCA, A3.16, leg. 2901, exp. 43258, with respect to an earth tremor in Chiantla; AGCA, A3.16, leg. 2899, exp. 43061 and A3.16, leg. 2899,

the greatest consequence, judging by the profuse documentation in which numerous Cuchumatán communities request either a pardon or a reprieve, on the grounds of disease-related poverty, from their tributary obligations. The following plea by the Indian leaders of Santa Eulalia, made in the early nineteenth century during an outbreak of typhus, may be considered bleakly representative:

> Señor Alcalde Mayor: We, the *alcaldes* and *principales* of the town of Santa Eulalia, implore you to look on us as your sons. All in our town is lost. There are some who are homeless and others who are without food, it now being years since fields were planted and attended to. Many people are therefore without corn to eat and survive on. Before God we declare this to be no lie. Those who fled have yet to return, [seeking refuge from the epidemic] in the [towns of the] coast, in Jacaltenango, and in Soloma. We live in fear, dear sir, because our children continue to die. Before God we declare this to be no lie. Help us, and show us some mercy, by requesting of the President that he pardon us from paying tribute. There is no corn at all in town.[38]

Appeals such as this one, even when accompanied by letters from priests sympathetic to the desperate plight of their parish charges, rarely elicited more than characteristic indifference from authorities whose primary concern was that the stipulated levy, regardless of material circumstances, be punctually furnished.

THE *REPARTIMIENTO, SERVICIO PERSONAL,* AND DEBT PEONAGE

The term *repartimiento* refers loosely to an official allotment of Indians, theoretically hired out as wage workers, whose compulsory labour was used to further any number of Spanish ends.[39] Like the *encomienda,* the legal history of the institution is complex, but the essential principle behind its operation remained constant and clearly

---

exp. 43062, which relate to a fire that occurred in Santa Ana Huista; and AGCA, 3.16, leg. 2899, exp. 43064, pertaining to an invasion of locusts that was causing widespread concern.

38 AGCA, A3.16, leg. 249, exp. 5036.

39 *Repartimiento* is derived from the Spanish verb *repartir,* meaning "to allocate, distribute, or partition."

defined: Spanish exploitation of the native capacity to work, every-where and anywhere, whether on farms or in mines, as domestic help or in community service.

Under the terms of *repartimiento*, Spanish colonists petitioned the Crown for native workers and were assigned individuals or parties for stipulated lengths of time – days, weeks, or months – at predeter-mined wage rates. After the contract was fulfilled, Indians suppos-edly returned to their communities, to be replaced by other recruits. The *repartimiento* was considered necessary, indeed vital, for it was widely held by the Spanish authorities that unless forced to work under such arrangements, the natives, being inherently slothful, would lapse into corrupt vagabondage. *Repartimiento* labour, there-fore, prevented a return to "indolence and idolatry."[40] Participation in the system was ensured by compelling Indians to pay a variety of secular and religious taxes that could often best be met by engaging in wage labour.[41]

Data pertaining to *repartimiento* is even scarcer than that for the *encomienda*, the fragments at hand mostly pertaining to demands made by mining and ranching operations in the Chiantla area. Apart from the age-old problem of document survival, this deficiency may to some degree reflect spatial discrimination in how *repartimiento* operated. Generally, the closer an Indian town or village lay to a Spanish settlement or business interest, the more likely it was that the native inhabitants would be subjected to a *repartimiento* draft.[42] In this respect it may well be that indigenous communities in the remote Cuchumatanes, overall, were less exploited than more acces-sible communities elsewhere in highland Guatemala. By the same token, however, distance and isolation from the moderating hand of responsible Crown officials in Santiago de Guatemala might have prompted more brutal and ruthless excesses on the part of recipients of Indian work parties.

40 Sherman (1979, 194).

41 Simpson (1938) remains an important contribution to our understanding of *repartimiento*, as do Gibson (1966, 143–7) and Villamarín and Villamarín (1975, 16–19), though MacLeod ([1973] 2008, 207 and 295–6) and especially Sherman (1979, 191–207) now supersede them when dealing with how the intitution oper-ated in Spanish Central America.

42 MacLeod (1973) 2008, 294. Luján Muñoz (1988, 53–60) shows this to be emphatically the case in his study of native communities that lay close to the colonial capital, Santiago de Guatemala. For Chiantla, see AGCA, A3, leg. 244, exp. 4013; A3.12, leg. 226, exp. 4084.

The right to enjoy compulsory unpaid labour, known as *servicio personal*, or personal service, was initially part and privilege of the *encomienda* system; it is in this specific context that allotments of Indian work parties in the Cuchumatán region are first documented. In his lawsuit against Pedro de Alvarado in the 1530s, the *encomendero* of Huehuetenango, Juan de Espinar, stated that his *encomienda* privileges included the labour of two hundred to three hundred *indios de servicio*. All were put to work, alongside 250 Indian slaves, in Espinar's mines at Chiantla and Malacatán, from which the *encomendero* derived a handsome yearly income of more than 8,000 pesos. In addition to those who laboured in the mines, Espinar also had Indians who worked his land or tended his swine.[43]

The Indians of Sacapulas, as part of their *encomienda* stipulation, were required to provide their *encomenderos*, Cristóbal Salvatierra and the younger son of Juan Páez, with four *fanegas* (roughly 210 kilos) of salt each month. Prior to the reforms of President Cerrato in 1549, Indians were required to haul salt from Sacapulas almost one hundred kilometres over difficult terrain south to Santiago de Guatemala. *Servicio personal* was eventually replaced at Sacapulas by an annual levy of fourteen *xiquipiles* of cacao.[44] Since the closest source of this product was the cacao groves of Suchitepéquez in the *tierra caliente* far to the south, payment necessitated a migration at least as demanding as the one from Sacapulas to Santiago. Not everyone who made the trek to the south coast in search of cacao made it back alive to the highlands.[45]

Even after the Cerrato reforms, the service component of *encomienda*, although greatly reduced, did not entirely disappear. The towns of Aguacatán, Jacaltenango, Soloma, and Uspantán, for example, continued in the second half of the sixteenth century to provide

43 See notes 8 to 12 above concerning the gist of the lawsuit; for more detailed discussion of its ramifications for the Indians of Huehuetenango, see Lovell and Lutz (2013, 129–48).

44 AGI, Guatemala 128, "Tasaciones de los pueblos," folios 69 and 71. A *xiquipil* was a measure of 8,000 cacao beans. Three *xiquipiles* equalled about as much as a *tameme*, an Indian porter, could carry. It would therefore have taken the labour of five able-bodied men to carry the load of tribute from Suchitepéquez to Sacapulas, a distance of some one hundred kilometres. For elaboration see Bergmann (1969, 87–91).

45 MacLeod ([1973] 2008, 87). Correspondence relating to Indian migration for labour purposes may also be found in AGI, Guatemala 10, 39, and 40.

their *encomenderos* with *indios de servicio* who tended swine and flocks of sheep.[46]

Several distinctions were made, at least on paper, between labour coerced from Indians as *servicio personal* (which received no remuneration) and that allegedly rendered voluntarily (and which should have been paid for) as *repartimiento*. While, as Sherman points out, "the simultaneous operation of these two forms of forced labour invites confusion,"[47] far less ambiguous is the fact that whereas the *repartimiento* in New Spain, except in relation to mining and public works, was legally abolished in 1632,[48] the institution in Guatemala remained fully operational for the remainder of the colonial period.[49] Indians in the Cuchumatanes, for example, were frequently called upon "to contribute freely" toward the maintenance of roads and trails. As late as 1770 they were being forced to serve as human carriers, of wheat and flour, by the notorious Juan Bácaro, an *alcalde mayor* of Totonicapán and Huehuetenango, whose "violent extortions" prompted Archbishop Cortés y Larraz to describe him as "of atrocious reputation in the whole of the province of Guatemala."[50] Similarly, there were repeated requests for *repartimientos* of Indians to serve as shepherds on Cuchumatán sheep farms and to work in the silver and lead mines north of Chiantla.[51] And on at least three occasions, during the Lacandón *entradas* of 1685 and 1695, and in the expedition to quell the Tzeltal uprising in Chiapas in 1712, Cuchumatán Indians served as guides, pack bearers, and auxiliaries for Spanish military forces.[52]

Though the Crown was seldom, if ever, resolute in matters concerning indigenous welfare, by the early seventeenth century some measures had been taken to halt the most blatant forms of exploitation. By this time, however, many Spaniards who depended for a

---

46 AGI, Guatemala 128, "Tasaciones de los pueblos," folios 54, 57, and 93 verso.

47 Sherman (1979, 193).

48 Borah (1951, 39–40).

49 Webre (1980, 234–40).

50 AGCA, A1, leg. 1547, exp. 10201; A1.22, leg. 2891, exp. 26645; A1.21.8, leg. 190, exp. 3860; Cortés y Larraz (1768–70) 1958, vol. 2, 124–33). The archbishop's precise words invoke the "extorsiones violentas" of a man he considered "un monstruo inapeable." Patch (2013, 116–42) offers a more benign, revisionist view of Bácaro's dealings, especially with his business partner Juan Montes de Oca.

51 AGCA, A3.12, leg. 226, exp. 4084.

52 AGI, Guatemala 225, "Audiencia of Guatemala to the Crown (3 February 1714); AGCA, A1.12, leg. 6095, exp. 55413 and A1.22, leg. 3024, exp. 29157; and Recinos (1954, 385–9).

livelihood on native toil had moved from officially sanctioned coercion to a more individually contractual form of "free" labour: debt peonage. In peonage, a condition of indebtedness tied a worker, and often his offspring, to an employer whose primary objective was to hold onto labour by maintaining the state of indebtedness through loans representing an advance on wages. Employers would then insist that the debt be repaid through work.[53] Characteristically, this arrangement is often interpreted as a seventeenth-century phenomenon devised to optimize Spanish control of a diminishing native workforce: Indian labourers, so numerous during the first fifty years after conquest, were by the early seventeenth century a scarce resource worthy of protection. Debt peonage offered such protection.

In the Cuchumatanes, peonage was most prevalent on the large *haciendas* of the Altos de Chiantla, where various elements of physical geography combined to produce some of the finest pastureland in all of Central America, even if the alpine locale (cold, windswept, bleak, and isolated) was as inclement to humans as it was ideal for the raising of livestock, especially sheep (plates 2 and 4). A document relating to the Altos de Chiantla for the year 1689 mentions that "it has always been the custom to pay Indians who voluntarily work as shepherds twelve *reales* and four handouts of corn each month."[54] When one of the largest properties, Hacienda Chancol, was sold in 1749, the purchase included a debt of 270 pesos owed by Indian workers who were considered part and parcel of the transaction. In this way, their labour was secured by the new owner, Manuel Francisco de Fuenlabrada.[55]

After Fuenlabrada's death, Chancol and an adjoining *hacienda* called El Rosario were purchased by Francisco Ignacio de Barrutia, a resident of Santiago de Guatemala, whose ambition was to transform the Altos de Chiantla into one vast property, the Hacienda Moscoso. By the close of the eighteenth century, Barrutia's holdings amounted to an impressive five hundred *caballerías* (21,250 hectares) and constituted good cropland, prize grazing, plentiful water, and fine stands of timber, as well as producing high-quality grain,

53 Gibson (1966, 147).

54 AGCA, A3, leg. 2775, exp. 40090. The original wording is "ha estado siempre en costumbre [que] los indios voluntariamente quisieren pastorear los ganados ovejunos [y reciben] doce reales y cuatro cajas de maíz en cada un mes."

55 Recinos (1954, 201).

cheese, and livestock.[56] Living permanently on Hacienda Moscoso were numerous Indian families who had been there, Barrutia declared, "from time immemorial, voluntarily tending more than twenty thousand head of sheep." When an attempt was made by the Indian *alcaldes* of a nearby community to convince Spanish authorities that the families resident on Barrutia's property should be resettled in their native birthplace in order to help meet the tribute assessment, the *hacendado* protested bitterly, stating that the families in question lived where they did through choice and that, receiving payment for their services both in land and wages, they therefore had sufficient means "not only to support themselves and next-of-kin but also to honour punctually their tributary obligations."[57] The fact that Indian families involved in the dispute opted to stay put on Hacienda Moscoso rather than return to their home town may actually have been for them a more acceptable alternative. Borah, for instance, points out that if a native worker "was bound to an employer, he was at least reserved for the service of that employer and protected to a considerable measure from the extortions to which he had been subject as a member of the Indian community."[58] Likewise, MacLeod notes that "a surprising number of Indians seem to have been happy to leave the villages," adding that, while the *hacienda* "was no paradise," it nonetheless "offered some protection against the depredations of *corregidores*, petty merchants, parish priests, and Indian *alcaldes* and *regidores*."[59]

ADDITIONAL SECULAR AND RELIGIOUS DEMANDS

Despite the proclamation of laws and royal edicts calling for responsible supervision of native welfare, colonial reality was often radically different from administrative rhetoric. Among the Crown officials whose job it was to protect and defend Indians, few groups were more negligent of their posts, or more abusive of their charges,

56 AGCA, A I, leg. 6001, exp. 52831; Recinos (1954, 201–2).

57 AGCA, A I.24, leg. 6096, exp. 55491. Burrutia's precise words are "de inmemorial tiempo se han mantenido, mantienen voluntariamente, algunas familias de indios ascrípticos que sirven en el pastoreo, y cuidado de estos ganados que pasen de 20,000 cabezas, por cuyo trabajo se les paga el [sueldo] acostumbrado en tabla y mano propria. No sólo tienen para mantener sus familias y obligaciones sino también para satisfacer punctualmente sus tributos y derechos particulares."

58 Borah (1951, 42).

59 MacLeod (1983, 194).

than the high magistrates known as *alcaldes mayores* and ordinary magistrates called *corregidores*.[60] Entrusted to safeguard native investments like the *caja de comunidad*, or community fund, these officials invariably exploited such resources as private capital.[61] Moreover, by subjecting common Indians to all sorts of extra-legal exactions, from non-payment for personal services to excessive collection of tribute, *alcaldes mayores* and *corregidores*, sometimes operating in collusion with local priests and native leaders, increased their salaries significantly. One device resorted to in the Cuchumatanes, as in neighbouring Chiapas, was a mechanism of forced sale and compulsory acceptance known as the *repartimiento de mercancías* or *reparto de efectos*.[62]

Under this practice, *corregidores* and *alcaldes mayores* supplied Indians with various commodities, insisting that they be purchased at prices considerably favourable to the seller, regardless of whether or not the recipients wanted the merchandise in the first place. While there is evidence that the system operated in Huehuetenango as early as 1561, and was prevalent in the parish of Cuilco in 1641 and 1690, the *repartimiento de mercancías* seems to have been most prolific in the eighteenth century (see table 11). The most common item involved in these transactions was cotton, which Spanish officials distributed in raw, bulk form among Indian women, compelling them to spin it into thread and then weave it into *mantas*. The finished article

60 See Patch (2013, 42–78 and 116–42) for detailed discussion of the background and behaviour of these officials, including a case study of Huehuetenango and the dealings of the infamous Juan Bácaro.

61 See Haring (1963, 162) for a general discussion of the *caja de comunidad*. The pilfering of community funds in Cuchumatán *pueblos de indios* is highlighted in AGCA, A1.73, leg. 2805, exp. 24655 and A1.73, leg. 2805, exp. 24656, both files dating toward the end of colonial times.

62 MacLeod (1983) covers the topic broadly, as does Haring (1963, 132–3). Collins (1980, 127–30) offers local examples for Jacaltenango and Wasserstrom (1983, 43–9) in more regional terms for Chiapas. See also AGCA, A.1, leg. 2, exp. 23 and A1.24, leg. 4649, exp. 39688. Dated 1687, the former *expediente* includes documents charging that the *corregidor* of Totonicapán and Huehuetenango, Captain Joseph de Arría, caused the ruin of Indians through heavy taxation and the forced acceptance of unwanted goods, among other extortions. The case against Arría was spearheaded by the bishop of Guatemala. In the latter *expediente*, dated 1716, the Captain General of Chiapas, Pedro Gutiérrez de Mier y Terán, is requested to conduct an inquiry into multiple abuses of office levelled at the *alcalde mayor* of Totonicapán and Huehuetenango, Lucas Colomo. Allegations are made that Colomo, among other misdemeanours, embezzled funds, falsified tributary numbers, did not pay the going rate for goods supplied to him, and was overzealous in his collection of tribute.

fetched a handsome profit – for the entrepreneur, not the worker – when sold at market. Raw wool was also circulated among male weavers with the same end in mind. Other items peddled to Indians included axes, clothes, iron tools and implements, and (on occasion) money. Although native communities frequently petitioned against the *repartimiento de mercancías*, stating that the involuntary sales caused them to neglect their families and their fields, most directives from the *audiencia* ordering *corregidores* and *alcaldes mayores* to cease their odious commerce were ignored.[63]

Just as Indians were vulnerable to exploitation by secular officials, so also did they fall prey to the demands of the clergy. A government order issued in 1561 stipulated what goods and services priests could legitimately request of their native parishioners, but such theoretical regulations (like so many others) were seldom adhered to in practice.[64] Haring observes that "opportunity for exploitation was especially abundant in the more remote Indian parishes, to which the more worthless friars were frequently sent."[65] An isolated region like the Cuchumatanes certainly gave more materially minded clergy ample scope for self-enrichment. While parishes there were occasionally administered by honest and dedicated clergy, others concerned themselves more with personal gain than with Indian salvation. Abuses once again appear to have been most prevalent in the eighteenth century, with priests and friars accused of various transgressions, including failure to reimburse for personal services, selling Indian livestock without native consent, overzealous collection of funds to celebrate mass or hear confession, and embezzlement of church finances (see table 12). The last complaint was often lodged with

63 AGCA, A3.12, leg. 2897. exp, 43013; Cortés y Larraz ([1768–70] 1958, vol. 2, 124); and Recinos (1954, 214–17). Patch (2013, 122, 133, and 138) sees the operation of *repartimientos de mercancías* quite differently, viewing it as a means whereby "Huehuetenango was brought into the world economy as an industrial producer," its indigenous inhabitants afforded the opportunity to participate beneficially "in business" thanks to the dealings of a magistrate and a merchant whose revenues during a partnership that lasted four and a half years totalled "between 90,000 and 101,000 pesos."

64 AGCA, A1.2, leg. 2245, exp. 16190, folio 183 verso. The government order decreed that, "in order to avoid mistreatment of Indians," clergy could request no more than "two chickens each day and two dozen eggs each week, along with delivery [each week] of one *fanega* of corn." Also called upon to serve, covered by community funds, was an Indian woman "to make bread" and an Indian male "to gather enough fodder to feed a horse."

65 Haring (1963, 192).

respect to the clergy's use of assets belonging to *cofradías* (table 13), religious sodalities maintained in Indian villages to support specific fiestas and to commemorate certain Catholic holidays.[66]

ETHNIC RELATIONS

Relations between Spaniards and Indians were based on the former holding the latter in varying degrees of servitude. For most Spaniards, native submission was not an issue of polemic or debate; it was simply taken for granted, something that was accepted as a right of conquest, a natural fixture in the imperial enterprise. Coexistence under these terms could hardly foster compassion or respect. What it did breed was suspicion, distrust, hatred, and fear. Colonial subordination, the institutionalized exploitation of one culture by another, generated ethnic tensions in which the vanquished were often pushed to the limits of endurance and beyond.

One common response was flight, the abandonment of *congregaciones* for a fugitive life in the hills, where abusive authority did not reach and could not penetrate. Scores of families from San Mateo Ixtatán had opted for this solution by the late seventeenth century.[67] Some of these "indios diabólicos" actually went so far as to return to their *pueblo* and run the parish priest, Friar Alonso de León, out of town.[68] The rebellious Ixtatecos vented their anger in 1720 by robbing Spanish livestock, stealing some seventy-two sheep while flocks were being driven down from the Cuchumatanes into the city of Comitán in Chiapas.[69] The *hacendado* whose flocks were plundered, Juan Martínez de la Vega, suffered further losses nine years later at the hands of Indians from Chiantla, who invaded his property and made off with forty head of cattle and a number of horses.[70] Alarmed by these events, Martínez de la Vega, a prominent and powerful landowner, called for the imprisonment of the culprits and a strengthening of Spanish commitment to law and order.[71]

Most manifestations of Indian contempt or delinquency ended with a half dozen lashes and several days in jail, the routine punishment

---

66 Ibid. (192–3).
67 AGCA, A1, leg. 2, exp. 23.
68 Ibid.
69 AGCA, A1.1, leg. 6087, exp. 55071.
70 AGCA, A1.1, leg 6095, exp. 55425.
71 AGCA, A1.1, leg. 6087, exp. 55071.

for such misdemeanours as theft, religious unorthodoxy, lack of respect, and failure to pay taxes. Some Spaniards, however, took the law into their own hands, administering a more extreme form of justice.

A particularly nasty incident took place in the mining district of Chiantla in 1725. At a lead mine called Las Ánimas, to the north of Chiantla not far from the *camino real*, the owner, Pedro de Montoya, had a disagreement with an Indian worker, verbally berating and then physically assaulting him. The confrontation was witnessed by the native miner Juan López, who expressed his disgust at Montoya's behaviour by laying down his tools and starting to walk off the job. When Montoya ordered López to return to his post, the Indian ignored the commands and continued to walk away. Montoya, already agitated, became incensed and attacked the defenceless López with a pick, striking him four or five times in the chest and face. López fell to the ground, badly wounded. Several of his fellow miners, all from nearby Santa Bárbara, rushed to his assistance, having watched the assault in helpless terror. López, described by his companions as a robust worker of thirty to thirty-five years of age, was carried back to Santa Bárbara, blood spilling from his mouth. He died a few days later of his injuries. Though the Indian workers who had witnessed the assault brought criminal proceedings against Montoya, he was cleared of the charge a year later after serving a brief jail sentence in Santiago de Guatemala. A letter of exoneration stated that Montoya, a native of Tegucigalpa but at the time of the incident a wealthy Spanish resident of Huehuetenango, was a considerate employer, paying his native miners one *real* per day and never abusing them or treating them cruelly or disrespectfully.[72]

Few incidents, even ones as vicious as the above, saw Indians themselves resort to violence. Such a militant response occurred only rarely, notably during disputes involving property rights or irregularities in the collection of tribute. With respect to the latter, certain developments in the late colonial period triggered a brief but alarming native uprising in the Cuchumatanes, essentially a spillover of the Totonicapán rebellion of 1820.[73] Though the seditious Ixtatecos

72 Recinos (1954, 72). See also AGCA, A1.15, leg. 2893, exp. 26696; A1.15, leg. 4149, exp. 32864; A1.24, leg. 1585, exp. 10229; A3.9, leg. 2897, exp. 43005.

73 The Totonicapán rebellion has been researched and written about by, among others, Contreras (1951); Martínez Peláez (1985); Bricker (1981, 77–84); and

came close several times to staging a full-fledged insurrection, and there is evidence of native dissent during the early nineteenth century at San Martín Cuchumatán and in Ixil country, it was the Indians of Sacapulas whose revolt against Spanish authority provoked the most serious confrontation.[74]

The roots of the conflict, like so much else that determined indigenous fate, lay in the political dynamics of Europe, specifically the aftermath of the French invasion of Spain in 1808. Napoleon's overthrow and capture of King Ferdinand VII precipitated a national revolution during which a regency and parliament (Cortes) governed those parts of Spain not conquered by the French. Ruling in the king's name from the city of Cádiz, the Cortes drew up a constitution that was promulgated in March 1812, only to be repealed in May 1814 when the monarch was restored to the throne. Six more years of political crisis ended in March 1820 when King Ferdinand yielded to demands for a parliament and the reinstatement of the Constitution of 1812. Where these events, at first seemingly far removed from the day-to-day concerns of Cuchumatán Indians, affected native life directly was in relation to tribute. In keeping with its liberal predilection, the Cortes abolished Indian tribute throughout Spanish America on 13 March 1811, only to see it reintroduced on 10 January 1815 after King Ferdinand had returned to power. Attempts to resume the collection of tribute following a four-year period when, in theory at least, the obligation had been relaxed served only to cause confusion, then to spread unrest, and finally to prompt rebellion among a number of indigenous groups.[75]

McCreery (1989, 39–58). The most thorough treatment to date is that of Pollack (2005, 2008).

74 Evidence of unrest at San Mateo Ixtatán, specifically opposition to the payment of tribute in 1803, may be found in AGCA, A3.16, leg. 2899, exp. 43052. For dissent at San Martín Cuchumatán, see A1.1, leg. 6922, exp. 56945, which concerns an Indian called Manuel Paz, who allegedly spoke out against heavy-handed colonial rule in 1812. His anti-government sentiments were reported to the authorities by Fray Manuel Echevarría. The parish priest of Nebaj, Fray Domingo Dubón, reported widespread resistance to tribute collection in Ixil country in 1819, many Indians fleeing to the refuge of the mountains rather than remain in town and pay the tax. Other Indians left to hide out and work on the Pacific coast. See AGCA, A1.1, leg. 6118, exp. 56749, for full details.

75 Anna (1983, 64–114); Bricker (1981, 77–84); and Rodríguez (1978, 85) contextualize the issue nicely.

Native opposition to the restoration of tribute in Guatemala was particularly vehement in the Totonicapán area. Open revolt began there on 20 February 1820, when the Indians of Santa María Chiquimula rioted against efforts by their parish priest, José Patricio Villatoro, to collect taxes from them without proper authorization.[76] News of the Chiquimula affair spread quickly to other towns, including Sacapulas, some forty kilometres to the north.

A confrontation took place in Sacapulas on 20 March 1820 when the *alcalde mayor* of Totonicapán and Huehuetenango, Manuel José de Lara, arrived in town to collect tribute, which he claimed was considerably in arrears. Presented with the request for payment, the Indians told the *alcalde mayor* that word had reached them of tribute having been abolished, and of towns elsewhere, including Chiquimula, having refused to deliver. Lara consented to a temporary suspension of the tax while an Indian delegation went to the capital, Guatemala City, to find out whether or not tribute should still be furnished. A peaceful solution seemed assured until one Indian, apparently misunderstanding what had been discussed and agreed upon, began hurling abuse at the *alcalde mayor*. Lara ordered the unruly culprit to be seized and was about to punish him when the man's family and other Indians intervened. Tensions mounted when Lara drew a knife to defend himself. His action ignited a full-scale riot, from which he was fortunate to escape with his life. He fled, shaken but unharmed, to Huehuetenango, from where some four hundred troops, including reinforcements from Chiantla, were later dispatched to crush the uprising and reassert Spanish authority.[77]

The Sacapulas incident, coming only one year before Guatemalan independence from Spain, underscores the servile basis on which relations between Spaniards and Indians were founded and conducted throughout the colonial period. However, it would be simplistic and misleading to maintain that imposition of Spanish rule resulted in the enslavement of the native population. During the first quarter-century of Spanish hegemony, chattel slavery was certainly the miserable fate of any Indian unfortunate enough to be captured alive during military confrontation. Such luckless individuals, branded as

76 Bricker (1981, 80).
77 Ibid., 81. See also AGCA, A1.21, leg. 193, exp. 3944 and A1.21, leg. 194, exp. 4966.

esclavos de guerra (slaves of war), are recorded by Fuentes y Guzmán as having been rounded up in the Cuchumatán region after the battles of conquest lasting from 1525 to 1530.[78] Thereafter, few references to outright enslavement exist. A different matter entirely, of course, is the fate of natives pressed into yielding labour to Spaniards under circumstances that could be equally intolerable.

Through the operation of the institutions discussed above, a considerable and continual burden was placed on Indians by their Spanish masters. These devices, and others such as the *derrama* and the *salutación*, kept the native population in a condition of servitude.[79] The *encomienda* system, requiring specific towns to furnish privileged individuals with labour and tribute, set the institutional precedent upon which subsequent exploitation was based. *Encomenderos* put Indians to work at various tasks: they laboured in mines; they hauled heavy loads from one town to another; they tilled fields and tended flocks; they spun cotton and wove it into cloth; they served as domestic help in Spanish households. Some of the agricultural chores demanded of Indians introduced them to things they had never known, seen, or handled before: horses, cattle, sheep, goats, pigs, chickens, and the cultivation of wheat, the Spanish staple so different from the native corn. Twice yearly, Indian towns paid commodity tribute either to private *encomenderos* or to the Crown. Even in times of dire hardship – following a drought or an earthquake, after an invasion of locusts or an outbreak of disease – *pueblos de indios* received little sympathy or concession from officials intent on collecting tribute.[80] Although the Cuchumatanes were never of spectacular importance to the colonial regime, it is evident that the quality of Indian life under Spanish rule was characterized by "steady and unabated deterioration,"[81] as Wasserstrom has said in relation

78 Fuentes y Guzmán ([1690–99] 1969–72, vol. 3, 22–3).

79 Gibson (1964, 93) considers the term *derrama* to cover "extra or unauthorized tributes" in general. MacLeod ([1973] 2008, 316) defines the practice more specifically as one in whereby local officials bought goods cheaply and then sold them to Indians at greatly inflated prices. The *salutación* was an illegal payment Indians were forced to make to priests or bureaucrats who passed through their communities on official business; see AGCA, A1.22, leg. 2600, exp. 21351; Fuentes y Guzmán ([1690–99] 1969–72, vol. 3, 25); and MacLeod ([1973] 2008, 315; 1983, 192).

80 For details of time, place, and episode, see AGCA, A1.1, leg. 6111, exp. 56055; A3.16, leg. 2901, exp. 43256; A3.16, leg. 252, exp. 5161; A3.16, leg. 2899, exp. 43064; A3.16, leg. 2899, exp. 43044; A3.16, leg. 249, exp. 5036; and A1.14.7, leg. 386, exp. 8037.

81 Wasserstrom (1983a, 107).

to neighbouring Chiapas. Demands made of native communities may have been so excessive that entering into debt peonage with a Spanish landholder offered better prospects of survival than remaining a tributary of the Crown in a *pueblo de indios*.[82] It is within such dismal circumstances that native peoples in the Cuchumatán highlands endured their worldly lot, compelled to do so by masters unflinching in their belief that, having saved pagan souls by bringing them tidings of the Christian God, not *here* but *hereafter* was all that should concern them.

82 See AGCA, A1.24, leg. 6096, exp. 55491, for a case in point.

8

Working the Land: Landholding Patterns and the Agricultural Economy

Juan Martínez de la Vega has more than one hundred *caballerías* of land on which to raise his livestock, which is more than enough.

Testimony of the Indians of Todos Santos
and San Martín Cuchumatán (1737)

The key role played by the *hacienda*, or landed estate, in the economic, political, and social development of Spanish America has long been recognized.[1] In their classic contributions to the literature, Woodrow Borah and François Chevalier[2] both contend that in colonial Mexico the emergence of the *hacienda* coincided with a period of native population decline and economic downturn in the sixteenth and seventeenth centuries. Chevalier presents an image of rural patriarchs presiding over feudal domains worked by an impoverished and servile peasantry. Once created, the *hacienda* and the power that its wealthy owners symbolized cast a long, oppressive shadow. Borah, for instance, maintains that, by the end of the seventeenth century, an economy distinctly Mexican in character "was already organized on the basis of *latifundia* and debt peonage, the twin aspects of Mexican life [that] continued nearly to our day and [that] helped provoke the Revolution of 1910–17."[3]

Colonial Guatemala experienced a similar demographic and economic crisis, one that saw Spaniards turn to the land as never before.[4] According to Murdo MacLeod, however, Spanish interest in the acquisition of land was more intense to the south and east of Santiago

---

1 For a review of pertinent literature, see Mörner (1973, 183–216) and Van Young (1983, 5–61).

2 Borah (1951); Chevalier (1952).

3 Borah (1951, 44).

4 MacLeod ([1973] 2008).

de Guatemala because of the region's greater accessibility, fertility, and entrepreneurial potential compared to that of the north and west.[5] The consequences of the seventeenth-century economic depression, as in Mexico, were profound, because it was during this period, asserts MacLeod, that "the basis was laid for the modern political and economic divisions of the area, and for the cultural cleavage between Indian and Ladino [that] hampers Guatemalan nationhood to this day."[6]

As in any field informed by rigorous research, the views of Borah, Chevalier, and MacLeod have been modified or reinterpreted in the light of recent findings. In the Mexican context, the Borah-Chevalier thesis seems not to apply to the Valley of Mexico where, according to Charles Gibson, the evidence "suggests only a limited role for peonage," even though "with respect to land there can be no doubt that the *hacienda* came to be the dominant mode of control."[7] Farther south, the research of William B. Taylor on the Valley of Oaxaca indicates that though large Spanish estates, landless Indians, and debt peonage were certainly to be found, they were there neither common nor characteristic.[8] *Haciendas* owned and operated by Spaniards did emerge, but Indians still controlled two-thirds of the agricultural land of the region during the last century of colonial rule.[9] Taylor maintains that such a significant departure from the schema of Chevalier in particular merely reflects the deficiencies of an overgeneralized model that fails to take into account the nuances of time and place. An awareness of regional variation is all-important: "What holds for the Valley of Oaxaca in 1750," he declares, "is unlikely to hold for Colima in 1800."[10] Such a viewpoint, urging that spatial comparison be more measured and mindful, is similar to the one called for by Miles Wortman in relation to economic trends and fluctuations in seventeenth-century Central America.[11] On the basis of his familiarity with several parts of southern Mesoamerica, Taylor speculates that landholding in colonial Guatemala may approach a middle ground between the extremes represented by

5 Ibid., 230 and 308.
6 Ibid., 260.
7 Gibson (1964, 406–7).
8 Taylor (1972).
9 Ibid., 35–110.
10 Taylor (1974, 389).
11 Wortman (1982, 15–16 and 41–90).

the Chevalier or north Mexican model and the example of the Valley of Oaxaca.[12]

Like the two that precede it and the one that follows, this chapter is steeped in archival detail, reconstructing patterns of Spanish and Indian landholding in the Cuchumatán highlands throughout the colonial period to pierce together this vital aspect of the cultural landscape.

PATTERNS OF SPANISH LANDHOLDING

In his landmark work on Spanish Central America, MacLeod contends that the first Spanish conquerors and colonists in the region were not motivated primarily by feudal ambitions. Their frame of mind, he argues, was much more entrepreneurial and mercantilist in nature. Only when exploitation of the work of others proved less lucrative than initially anticipated did Spaniards focus attention on the land and concentrate on establishing private rural estates, ventures of less glittering aspiration. For much of the sixteenth century, then, control of labour was considered more important than control of land as a means of personal enrichment. Emphasis was thus placed during the initial period of Spanish rule on regulating the native workforce through such coercive devices as the *encomienda* and the *repartimiento*, geared toward the booming trade in cacao that dominated Central American commerce in the second half of the sixteenth century.[13]

Spanish interest in the Sierra de los Cuchumatanes parallels the pattern of exploitation and involvement developed by MacLeod. An early flurry of excitement with the realization that gold could be panned along the course of the Río Malacatán was not long maintained. The gold of Pichiquil and San Francisco Motozintla, the frustrated Spaniards found, was more mythic than real.[14] Gold and

12 Taylor (1974, 387–413).
13 MacLeod ([1973] 2008, 80–95, 235, and 374–89).
14 Recinos (1954, 54–5 and 75–8). According to Fuentes y Guzmán ([1690–99] 1969–72, vol. 3, 49–51), there was a gold mine near San Francisco Motozintla, the location of which local Indians wished to conceal from their Spanish masters. On one occasion, however, at the insistence of their parish priest, Fray Francisco Bravo, a delegation led the friar there blindfolded, allowing him to help himself to as much gold as he could carry. The dispensation was afforded Bravo, so Fuentes y Guzmán tells us, as a farewell gift on the priest's being ordered to return to Spain. Though sworn to secrecy, Bravo informed government officials of the mine's existence before

silver were plentiful enough to provide Juan de Espinar, the man who worked the local deposits most successfully, with a handsome return of 8,700 pesos in 1537, but even Espinar had to adjust his expectations.[15] During the colonial period, the mines of Chiantla produced notable quantities of silver, which decorated church altars throughout Guatemala. The scale and output of the operation, however, even when undertaken in conjunction with lead mining, was far less significant than that of central Honduras, and nothing at all like that of Guanajuato and Zacatecas in the Viceroyalty of New Spain or Potosí in the Viceroyalty or Peru.[16] By the close of the sixteenth century, the few Spaniards who decided to maintain an interest in the Cuchumatanes saw that greater security and better prospects lay in taking up land than in forcing a depleted native population to render labour in marginal mining enterprises.

Among the earliest titles to land in the region were four awards made between November 1563 and May 1564 to the *encomendero* of Huehuetenango, Luis Manuel Pimentel. The first award, for which Pimentel paid five hundred pesos, was for two *caballerías* near

---

heading home. A fact-finding party from Santiago de Guatemala, led by Licenciado Juan Maldonado de Paz, then arrived in Motozintla and demanded to be shown the mine's whereabouts. Despite imprisonment, torture, and the threat of hanging – the chronicler intimates that some Indians were indeed executed for remaining silent – the locals refused to yield to Spanish intimidation. After eleven months of fierce interrogation, Maldonado de Paz returned to Santiago empty-handed. Upon his arrival in Spain, Bravo is said to have used the gold of Motozintla to adorn an image of San Pedro Nolasco, founder of the Mercedarion order, in a church in Málaga. See also AGI, Patronato 66-1-3 and Martínez Peláez ([1970)] 1998, 184–8). Galeano ([1982] 1985, 212–13) offers readers of his epic trilogy *Memory of Fire* a masterful telling of the tale.

15 Sherman (1979, 71 and 92); Fuentes y Guzmán ([1690–99] 1969–72, vol. 3, 47–8). See also chapter 7.

16 Fuentes y Guzmán ([1690–90]) 1969–72, vol. 3, 44–51) and Recinos (1954, 53–79) contain valuable summaries of the mining operations carried out at Chiantla. For archival documentation, see AGCA, A1.24, leg. 6091, exp. 55307; A3, leg. 224, exp. 4013; A3.9, leg. 2899, exp. 43044; and A3.9, leg. 2900, exp. 43193. The famous image of the Virgin in the parish church, Nuestra Señora de Chiantla, was itself made from the silver of nearby mines. A mural to the right of the main altar (see plate 20) was badly damaged in the earthquake of 4 February 1976. Painted in the 1950s by Carlos Rigalt Anguiano (1901–77), the mural depicts the mining tradition of Chiantla. Another of Rigalt's murals, painted on the right-hand wall as one enters the former Banco de Guatemala premises in Huehuetenango, records the region's fame as a centre of livestock-raising. For a discussion of silver mining in neighbouring Honduras, see Newson (1982).

Huehuetenango, to be used to cultivate wheat.[17] The title also stipulated that the land had to be fully cultivated within two years, and that no sale of property could occur until four years had passed. A second title to two *caballerías*, in nearby Chiantla, was granted to Pimentel for land to grow corn, at the same cost and carrying similar restrictions regarding resale.[18] He was awarded two further titles for grazing land near Huehuetenango, to raise sheep, goats, cattle, horses, and mules.[19] All four titles state that the land was allocated "without injury" (*sin perjuicio*) to local Indians and that the grants did not conflict with the legal claims of any other party. In addition to landed property, Pimentel acquired ownership of a water mill in Huehuetenango that had formerly belonged to Juan de Espinar.[20]

Moves by Pimentel to take up land in the vicinity of Huehuetenango apparently did not influence other Spaniards to do likewise, for there is a lengthy hiatus in land acquisition between the 1560s and the end of the sixteenth century. The start of the seventeenth century, however, marked the beginning of a spate of Spanish interest in Cuchumatán landholding, which continued for the next century and a half.

Between 1607 and 1759, land was claimed through *composición*, a policy whereby an impecunious treasury either sold Crown property (*tierras realengas*) or legalized an irregular title on the payment of a fee. The proclivity of the Crown toward the latter option meant, in effect, that Spaniards could usurp Indian holdings knowing that token payment to the royal treasury was all that was needed to legalize the seizure. At least thirty-eight awards, amounting to over two hundred *caballerías* of land, can be documented (see table 14). The chronology of these titles coincides with what MacLeod believes to be a period of economic contraction throughout Central America, reflecting a retreat to modest, rural-based self-sufficiency on the part of Spaniards and criollos facing the limited opportunities of seventeenth-century life.[21]

In the century or so between 1635 and 1720, Spaniards were drawn more to lands south and east of Santiago de Guatemala, where

---

17 AGCA, A3, leg. 2863, exp. 41698. A *caballería* is a unit of land measuring approximately 42 hectares.

18 AGCA, A3, leg. 2863, exp. 41698.

19 Ibid.

20 AGCA, A3, leg. 2863, exp. 41696.

21 MacLeod ([1973]) 2008, 222–4 and 310–29).

(besides staple foods) indigo could be produced as a cash item and cattle raised as a source of hides and meat. Although the highlands to the north and west of the capital – rugged, cold, isolated, certainly amenable to subsistence agriculture but with little or no potential for cash cropping – were less encroached upon, some favoured pockets did arouse Spanish interest. Excellent grazing land in particular was abundant, the availability of pasture related directly to diminished resource use because of native depopulation. Furthermore, the absence of livestock in the pre-Columbian economy meant that the alpine meadows of the *páramo* could be turned to for this purpose for the first time in history. The Sierra de los Cuchumatanes, dismissed during the golden age of cacao as next to worthless, became more appealing. Spaniards began to discern possibilities in the region, not so much in farming as in ranching, especially the raising of sheep.

Of all the areas that attracted Spanish attention, by far the most desirable was the grazing land of the Altos de Chiantla (see plates 2 and 4). A notable landholder in these parts was Baltasar de Herrera who, at the time he dictated his will in 1687, owned the *hacienda* known as Nuestra Señora del Rosario. A property then of some fifteen *caballerías*, El Rosario supported over two thousand head of sheep in addition to some horses and cattle.[22] After Herrera's death, El Rosario was taken over by his son-in-law, Captain Domingo Moscoso Balmaior. The enterprising Moscoso sought to gain control over as much land on the Altos de Chiantla as possible. Early in the eighteenth century he acquired the property and livestock of José Alvarado Bracamonte and Melchor Rodríguez Mazariegos and by 1711 owned over sixty *caballerías* of prime pasture. The Moscoso holdings at that time supported some 14,000 head of sheep; the *hacendado* owned more land on the *páramo* and adjacent territory than all the other Spanish ranchers combined.[23]

When Moscoso died, he left his estate to his wife, Lucrecia de Herrera. When a notary penned her will on 9 September 1725, Doña Lucrecia listed as Moscoso property the three finest *haciendas* of the Altos de Chiantla: El Rosario, La Capellanía, and Chancol. El Rosario contained 10,600 sheep, five hundred mares, four hundred cows, three hundred horses, fifteen mules, and two donkeys, as well

22 AGCA, A1.20, leg. 1495, exp. 9974; Recinos (1954, 197).
23 Recinos (1954, 197).

as a number of houses for resident Indian workers, the *casa grande* of the *patrón*, and an elaborately decorated chapel. La Capellanía raised over five thousand sheep, three hundred mares, and several mules. Chancol comprised ten to twelve *caballerías* of quality pasture that had been purchased for six hundred *pesos* from Tomás García de Medina.[24]

On the death of Doña Lucrecia, the Moscoso holdings passed to her brother-in-law, Juan Martínez de la Vega. When he dictated his last will and testament on 27 February 1744, six Cuchumatán properties had been added to his estate:

Sajpojolá: A *hacienda* of thirteen and one-half *caballerías* that was purchased for 1,350 pesos from Doña Micaela de la Parra, widow of Sebastián Antonio de Aguayo.
San Antonio Musmul: A plot of land measuring nine *caballerías* bought from Pedro de Chávez.
Baco de Anco: A plot of land measuring five *caballerías* near Todos Santos Cuchumatán.
Xebuyugüitz: A *hacienda* of seventeen *caballerías* purchased from the heirs of Juan López de los Ríos.
Tuhuinimá: Five *caballerías* of land in the Río de las Vueltas.
Los Cheches: Five *caballerías* of land on the Altos de Chiantla overlooking Aguacatán.

These properties, along with the former Moscoso holdings, amounted to a sizable estate of some 137½ *caballerías*, supporting thirty thousand sheep, one thousand cattle, one thousand mares, 180 horses, four hundred pigs, forty-nine mules, and five pairs of oxen.[25]

Although Martínez de la Vega left some property to the church, his daughters Manuela and Juana received the bulk of the estate. Manuela, the wife of Manuel Francisco de Fuenlabrada, was left Hacienda El Rosario; Juana, the wife of Marcelo de Noriega, received Hacienda Chancol. She later sold Chancol to her brother-in-law, Fuenlabrada, for the sum of 7,287 pesos and four *reales*. The livestock component of the transaction was broken down as follows:

24 Ibid., 198.
25 AGCA, A1.43, leg. 2895, exp. 26738; Recinos (1954, 200).

7,900   sheep at three *reales* a head
1,315   rams at four *reales* a head
182   mares at two pesos a head
20   one-year-old colts at three pesos a head
20   stallions at five pesos a head
10   stallions at four pesos a head
18   goats at three *reales* a head
70   pigs at one peso a head
25   pigs at four *reales* a head
6   mules at eight pesos a head

The sale of Chancol also included a payment of 270 pesos by which Fuenlabrada assumed the debt of the Indian shepherds, farmers, and servants who worked on the *hacienda* and received money as an advance on wages; the right of the new owner to the labour of these people, and their offspring, was thus assured. Such arrangements were considered normal and routine, as indeed was peonage itself, the customary means of securing a workforce for the *haciendas* of the *páramo*.[26]

After Fuenlabrada's death in 1750 or 1751, his widow, Manuela, sold both Chancol and El Rosario (see plate 21) to Francisco Ignacio de Barrutia, a Spanish resident of Santiago de Guatemala.[27] The combined extent of the two *haciendas* was then almost two hundred *caballerías*, with the transaction negotiated as follows: 4,431 pesos for land; 1,017 pesos for the chapel of Nuestra Señora del Rosario, including all its jewels and ornaments; and 14,029 pesos for livestock, grain, wool, farm equipment, and houses. Like the ambitious Moscoso some forty years before, Barrutia then set out by aggressive and systematic buying to incorporate the fine pastures of the Altos de Chiantla into a single property. By the end of the eighteenth

---

26 AGCA, A.3, leg. 2775, exp. 49990; A1.24, leg. 6096, exp. 55491; Recinos 1954, 200–1.

27 Plate 21 is a black-and-white reproduction of a map that accompanies the general survey of late colonial life undertaken by Archbishop Pedro Cortés y Larraz in three dogged forays between 1768 and 1770. The *haciendas* known as El Rosario and Chancol, two of the finest ranching operations established on the rich pastures of the Altos de Chiantla, are numbered 5 and 6 respectively. Other places represented are Chiantla (1); Aguacatán and Chalchitán (2); Todos Santos Cuchumatán (3); and San Martín Cuchumatán (4). The original map, an attractive watercolour, may be found in AGI, Mapas y Planos (Guatemala 151).

century he had successfully acquired possession of some five hundred *caballerías* of land, an impressive estate by any standards.[28]

The seventeenth and eighteenth centuries marked the height of land acquisition throughout Central America. Resources available for exploitation were re-evaluated as expectations changed. Appraisals and perceptions formulated during the first hundred years of colonial rule were no longer appropriate or realistic. In the Sierra de los Cuchumatanes, agricultural expansion was somewhat delayed, but by the late seventeenth century Spaniards and criollos were present in the region in important numbers. They were especially lured by the ranching possibilities of the Altos de Chiantla. The majority of property owners were laymen, but the Church (individual priests or friars as well as convents and *cofradías*) also figured in the carving up of Cuchumatán pastures and farmland.[29] During the eighteenth century a handful of men emerged as wealthy owners of estates on the Altos de Chiantla, where sheep, cattle, horses, and mules were tended by resident Indian families bound to their *hacendados* by debt peonage. The creation of sizable Spanish holdings, however, was not undertaken entirely at the expense of native territorial integrity.

PATTERNS OF INDIAN LANDHOLDING

Under the policy of *congregación*, Indians who had been resettled at a new town site were legally entitled to an allotment of land from which to derive basic subsistence. Included in this allotment were both arable tracts and an area designated as *ejido*, uncultivated land held in common and used to cut firewood, graze livestock, hunt animals, and gather various products. In addition to the "new" lands held in the vicinity of *pueblos de indios*, Indian families continued

28 AGCA, AI, leg. 6001, exp. 52831; Recinos (1954, 201–2). The holdings of Barrutia were sold in 1830 to Joaquín Mont y Prats for 15,000 pesos. The estate was finally dismantled, with government intervention, toward the close of the nineteenth century.

29 See, for example, AGCA: ST (Sección de Tierras), Huehuetenango, *paquete 1*, exp. 8, and AI.24, leg. 1577, folio 3, which concern a title to seven *caballerías* of land on the Altos de Chiantla awarded in 1708 to the Mercedarian monastery of Jacaltenango; AGCA: ST, Huehuetenango, *paquete 1*, exp. 7, relating to land owned by *cofradías* in Aguacatán and Chalchitán in the early eighteenth century; AGCA: ST, *paquete 1*, exp. 17, dealing with land held by the parish priest of Cuilco, the Mercedarian friar Antonio González, in the mid-eighteenth century; and AGCA: ST, *paquete 2*, exp. 3, which pertains to land owned in the late eighteenth century by the parish priest of San Pedro Necta.

to cultivate the "old" lands surrounding their former homes in the mountains, though seldom with legal title or official sanction to do so. Not even the persistence of visiting bureaucrats or zealous local clergy prevented native farmers from returning to plant corn in the land of their forefathers. Despite concerted efforts, colonial policy never resulted in alienating Indians from their ancestral terrain, whether spiritually or materially. From the mid-sixteenth century on, then, a fundamental division existed in the pattern of native land tenure between "new" lands surrounding *pueblos de indios* and "old" lands some distance away.[30]

Indian towns held land under a communal title, and often successfully petitioned for territorial extensions beyond the standard one-league *ejido* allocation.[31] In order to maintain a firm legal standing, many communities wisely updated or "composed" their titles by making periodic payments to the Crown, thus lessening the risk of invasion and seizure by Spaniards, criollos, or (as time passed) land-hungry Ladinos. As late as 1789, for instance, the Indians of Sacapulas paid 143 pesos for a *composición de tierras*. The natives of Cunén adopted a similar strategy early in the nineteenth century to safeguard their land.[32] Certainly by the end of the colonial period, such recourse was common practice, but indigenous savvy in getting Hispanic legalism to work in their favour had developed much earlier.[33]

In many Cuchumatán towns, land was held not by the community as a whole but by *calpul* or *parcialidad*. Perhaps the best illustration of such an arrangement was at Sacapulas, where the distinct social groups making up the *pueblo de indios* were long associated with particular tracts of land, a situation never fully understood or sufficiently acknowledged by the Spaniards (see plate 19 and table 15). To the Indians of Sacapulas, however, this form of

30 See chapter 6, especially footnote 28, referring to the observations of Tovilla ([1635]) 1960, 218) and footnotes 53 and 55, referring to the comments of Dominican friars Tomás de Cárdenas and Juan de Torres, who wrote to the Crown on 6 January 1555 (AGI, Guatemala 168).

31 See, for example, AGCA, A1, leg. 6006, exp. 52897, the contents of which document formal title of 27 *caballerías* of land granted to San Andrés Cuilco on 25 May 1759.

32 AGCA: ST, El Quiché *paquete* 1, exp. 4; Solano (1977, 114–53).

33 See, among many examples, AGCA: ST, Huehuetenango, *paquete* 1, exp. 1 and *paquete* 2, exp. 8, both of which relate to a land dispute between Todos Santos Cuchumatán and Santiago Chimaltenango in the 1660s.

tenure enabled them to preserve a strong sense of autochthonous identity, despite the Christian nomenclature by which most *parcialidades* were known.[34] Some land was also set aside for the upkeep of *cofradías*, several Cuchumatán sodalities (in Aguacatán, Chiantla, Huehuetenango, Sacapulas, and Soloma) owning property on which cattle and sheep were raised with a view to financing religious celebrations and festivities.[35]

The most affluent members of native society were lineage heads known as *caciques* and *principales*. These Indian leaders were often awarded private grants of land in recognition of their elite status as well as for carrying out specific services – collecting tribute among them – for their Spanish masters (table 16). Although no *cacique*-owned estates, or *cacicazgos*, emerged in the Cuchumatanes to compare with those developed by high-ranking lineages in the Valley of Oaxaca, a number of native rulers were conspicuously better off than ordinary members of their community. One such individual was Pedro Hernández, an Indian leader of Santiago Chimaltenango who, when Fuentes y Guzmán was district governor, enjoyed an impressive personal estate comprising land, livestock, and "no small amount of money."[36]

An important feature of native landholding in communities adjacent to the Lacandón frontier was the cultivation of lowland areas to the west, north, and east of highland *pueblos de indios*. Seasonal migration down from the Cuchumatanes to work fertile, sparsely settled *tierra templada* or *tierra caliente* was a long-standing tradition at Santa Eulalia but also a habit among the Indians of San Sebastián Coatán, San Juan Cotzal, San Gaspar Chajul, and San Mateo Ixtatán.[37] Several leagues distant from lofty town centres, these lands, or *ranchos*, not only produced fine harvests of corn but also yielded cacao, chili peppers, cotton, sugar cane, and an abundance of fruits that could not be grown in the *tierra fría* of the highlands. They also provided Cuchumatán Indians with an opportunity to fish and to gather honey. Movement to and from these lowland

---

34 AGCA, A1, leg. 6042, exp. 53327.

35 AGCA, A1.11, exp. 6106, exp. 55864; A1.11, leg. 6106, exp. 55865; A1.11, leg. 6106, exp. 55802; A1.11, leg. 6106, exp. 55800; and AGCA: ST, Huehuetenango, *paquete* 1, exp. 7 and 12.

36 Fuentes y Guzmán ([1690–99] 1969–72, vol. 3, 24–5).

37 AGCA, A1, leg. 2, exp. 23; A1.17, leg. 210, exp. 5008; and A1.44, leg. 6115, exp. 56343.

fields was so well established that Fuentes y Guzmán, when composing his *Recordación florida* toward the end of the seventeenth century, showed their location in his sketch of the *corregimiento* of Totonicapán and Huehuetenango. The "Ranchos de Santa Eulalia," for example, he depicts as lying some four leagues to the north and west of the *congregación*, well beyond the limit of effective Spanish jurisdiction and control (see figure 2). One result of such seasonal migration was to blur or make meaningless property boundaries between neighbouring communities, which in these parts were fluid and ill-defined, on paper as well as on the ground. Another consequence was to place native families here in the enviable position of seldom having to be concerned, as were their counterparts elsewhere, about a shortage of cultivable land. The advantage, however, was offset by the problem of being vulnerable to attack by hostile Lacandones raiding from the Usumacinta rainforest to the north.[38]

Frontier farming was not an option for *pueblos de indios* along the southern edge of the Cuchumatanes. There good agricultural and grazing land was in shorter supply, a consequence of greater densities of native occupation and the closer proximity of Spanish, criollo, and Ladino settlers who could encroach on Indian holdings. Thus the townsfolk of San Sebastián Huehuetenango, in 1741 and again in 1811, petitioned the Crown for more land in view of the inability of existing resources to support their rising numbers.[39] The natives of Cuilco also asked the Crown for assistance, stating that hardship was upon them on account of land allocated as *ejido* being used by their parish priest to grow sugar cane and operate a *trapiche*, or sugar mill.[40] Similarly, in 1812 the Indians of Huehuetenango requested that they be awarded a sum of money in order to buy Crown land to supplement their present holdings, since much of the community *ejido* had been taken over by aggressive Ladinos. The Indians also complained bitterly about "the enormous animals owned by our Ladino neighbours, which invade our fields and destroy our crops."[41] Land was therefore at a greater premium along the southern border with Quetzaltenango, Totonicapán, and Sololá than in

38 See chapter 6 for further discussion of Lacandón raids and their consequences.

39 AGCA, A1, leg. 5983, exp. 52607; and A1, leg. 6051, exp. 53484.

40 AGCA: ST, Huehuetenango, *paquete* 1, exp. 17.

41 AGCA, A1.45.6, leg. 386, exp. 8058. The original reads "los enormes animales que tienen nuestros vecinos ladinos y que perjudican nuestras siembras."

remote northern reaches adjacent to uninhabited or lightly settled tropical lowlands. Not surprisingly, disputes over land ownership and property rights were more numerous and heated in the south than in the north.

LAND DISPUTES (1668–1822)

The surviving documentation indicates that conflict over land in the region was most significant during the eighteenth and early nineteenth centuries (tables 17 and 18). Land disputes certainly arose during earlier times, but likely were more pronounced between 1700 and 1821 for two reasons: first, in this period the native population began its slow recovery after the demographic collapse brought about by Spanish conquest, thus precipitating a need for more land to support growing numbers; and second, the years 1700 to 1821 saw Spaniards and Ladinos not only maintain but intensify their interest in the region, fuelling confrontation. Significantly, two of the earliest land disputes involved highly prized land on and adjacent to the Altos de Chiantla. The Spanish contestant in both cases was Juan Martínez de la Vega, a wealthy and influential *hacendado*. Indian communities fighting against the encroachment of the Spaniard's estate included Chiantla, Todos Santos, and San Martín Cuchumatán.

On 19 August 1705, Martínez de la Vega requested that he be assigned what he alleged were "tierras baldías" (vacant lands) one league north of Chiantla at a place known as Mamenguiché. His principal reason for wanting the land was to extend the amount of pasture available to him for the raising of sheep. The *hacendado's* request, however, was challenged by the Indians of Chiantla. Represented by their *alcaldes* and *regidores*, they claimed that the place in question was "the best land the community holds, for it is here that we grow corn and graze sheep so that we can pay the tribute required by His Majesty."[42]

In the legal entanglement that followed, seven individuals were called upon to furnish testimony to help bring about a settlement. Some Spaniards supported Martínez de la Vega. Among them was Manuel Martín, who stated that the Indians "have land in other parts

---

42 AGCA, A1, leg. 5960, exp. 52251. The original reads "los mejores pedazos que [tenemos] para [nuestras] sementeras y ovejas, de donde [sacamos] para pagar tributos a su Magestad y para otras cargas y pensiones."

that is both fertile and plentiful."[43] Other Spaniards testified in support of the Indians, among them Joseph Brillegar and Pedro de Chávez, the latter himself a local landholder and a rival of Martínez de la Vega. Arbitration by the *juez de tierras*, an official of the Crown responsible for the settlement of land disputes, eventually resulted in a new title to 178 *caballerías* being given to the Indians. Included in this allocation were four *caballerías* of land at Mamenguiché, suggesting that the conflict was settled in favour of the natives.[44]

Over thirty years later, in 1737, Martínez de la Vega, by then the owner of *haciendas* Chancol, El Rosario, and La Capellanía, was involved in another dispute. The Indian contestants on this occasion were the communities of Todos Santos and San Martín Cuchumatán. In a letter to the district governor, Martínez de la Vega bluntly states that "the Indians – without cause, without title, and without any reason whatsoever – have begun, most audaciously, to pasture their sheep on lands that are part of my *haciendas*."[45] The *hacendado* complained that the sheep, some 140 head, were overgrazing a certain pasture and thus causing damage to his property, all of which "has been composed and purchased from Your Majesty."[46] Two Indians, Francisco Pérez and Gaspar Chap, were singled out as the chief culprits.

For their part, the Indians of Todos Santos and San Martín Cuchumatán claimed that the stretch of land on which they grazed their sheep, known as Siquibilchas, was allocated to them as *ejido*. In a letter to the *juez de tierras*, they stated that the land was in fact recorded as belonging to them in community titles in their possession. They also mention that they had "no other land that can be used to graze our animals" and that Martínez de la Vega had "more than one hundred *caballerías* on which to raise his livestock, which is more than enough." Siquibilchas was needed, the Indians argued, "so that we can pay our tribute and clothe and feed our families."[47]

43 AGCA, A1, leg. 5960, exp. 52251. Martín's precise words are "los indios tienen otras tierras buenas y suficientes por otras partes."

44 See AGCA, A1, leg. 5960, exp. 52251 for further details of the arbitration.

45 AGCA, A1, leg. 5976, exp. 52505 and A1.45.8, exp. 3025, leg. 29183. Martínez de la Vega's precise words are "con gran audacia se han pasado introducir los indios sus ganados en mis haciendas, sin causa, sin título y sin razón alguna."

46 AGCA, A1, leg. 5976, exp. 52505; A1.45.8, leg. 3025, exp. 29183. The original reads "compuesta y pagada a su Magestad."

47 AGCA, A1, leg. 5976, exp. 52505. "Para la paga de los tributos y demás cargas," the original states, "y para vestir y sustentar nuestros hijos y mujeres."

Though they sent the appropriate authorities their community titles as proof of ownership, litigation this time went against them. Under threat of imprisonment and the confiscation of their sheep, they were told to withdraw their claim and to abandon the pasture. Francisco Pérez complied reluctantly with the order; Gaspar Chap did not, forcing the authorities to confiscate his sheep and prompting him to flee from justice.[48]

The two cases outlined above (see table 17 for further examples) may be considered more or less representative. Some conflicts were litigated in favour of Spaniards, criollos, or Ladinos, others in favour of the Indians. Not all disputes, however, were settled peacefully in a court of law, for tensions resulted on occasion in outbreaks of violence and damage to property. Such was the case when, sometime between 1768 and 1772, the Indians of San Sebastián Coatán, protesting against Spanish seizure of native territory in the *tierra caliente* to the north and west of the highland *congregación*, invaded the offending *hacienda* and burned houses, stole cattle and horses, and even kidnapped a Spanish administrator.[49] The Coatecos again took up arms between 1800 and 1810, in anger at further encroachment. They were joined on this occasion by about two hundred people from San Mateo Ixtatán, plundering the *hacienda* known as San Antonio Tierra Negra, stealing livestock, setting fire to a church, and kidnapping estate workers. Troops were dispatched from Comitán with orders to enter from Chiapas and restore order.[50] Another unpleasant incident took place at Huehuetenango in 1814, when the Indian farmer Tomás Moreno was attacked by a knife-bearing Ladino named Nolberto Zamallorga. The Ladino had driven his cattle onto Moreno's cornfield to graze, threatening the Indian with harm should they be removed.[51] Invasion of Indian lands by cattle owned by Spaniards and Ladinos was a common source of conflict.[52]

In addition to property disputes between Indian and non-Indian factions, conflict also arose between native groups (table 18). From 1730 until the early nineteenth century, the Indians of the Chalchitán *parcialidad* of Aguacatán clashed with the Indians of the Santo

48 AGCA, A1, leg. 5976, exp. 52505.
49 Davis (1997, 203).
50 Ibid., 203–4.
51 AGCA, A1.57, leg. 6117, exp. 56583.
52 See, for example, the contents of AGCA, A1.45.8, leg. 5329, exp. 44907; A1.45.9, leg. 2928, exp. 27452; and A1.45.8, leg. 2806, exp. 24672.

Tomás *parialidad* of Sacapulas over the ownership of a stretch of land known as Pichiquil, which lay midway between the two towns. According to the testimony of Fray Raymundo de Herrera, the parish priest of Sacapulas, Pichiquil belonged to the Indians of Santo Tomás by virtue of their being the descendants of the Lamaquib people, who were brought from a settlement called Solchum (Xolchun) to form part of the *congregación* of Sacapulas in the mid-sixteenth century. Pichiquil, the priest stated, had traditionally been worked by the Lamaquib of Xolchun. Their descendants, therefore, were the legitimate holders of the terrain. Since the Indians of Santo Tomás were now in need of more land, Herrera argued that they should be given legal title to their ancestral territory.[53] The Indians of Chalchitán, however, claimed that Pichiquil was originally held by their forefathers, the Bai'joon, and therefore belonged to them. Furthermore, they argued that the Indians of Sacapulas were considerably better off than they were, on account of owning "ten *haciendas* with both livestock and a plentiful amount of land, in addition to working salt deposits and not having, like our community, to provide the frequent users of the royal highway with food and lodging."[54]

A lengthy litigation ensued. Juan José Ordóñez, an official of the Crown, called for the complete remeasurement of the land boundaries between the towns of Aguacatán, Sacapulas, Cunén, and Nebaj. He was extremely sceptical of titles he believed were old and useless, and stated that Pichiquil was the property neither of Aguacatán nor Sacapulas but was *tierra realenga* that belonged to the Crown. Tempers flared as the dispute dragged on. Santo Tomás twice accused Chalchitán of robbing livestock from land near Pichiquil, grazed there by the *cofradías* of Sacapulas. By the end of the eighteenth century, arbitration by a royal surveyor gave legal ownership of the

53 AGCA, A1, leg. 5979, exp. 52536. According to the *Popol Vuh* – see Recinos (1950, 368–9) – the Lamaq or Lamaquib were one of the migrant groups that came from the East with the first K'iche' forefathers.

54 AGCA, A1, leg. 5978, exp. 52518. "Nosotros estamos en el camino real," declare the Indians of Chalchitán, "sujetos a estas pensiones, pobres y sin comodidad alguna." Their adversaries in Sacapulas, on the other hand, live "distante del camino real para estar libre de los tequios y habios," and are blessed not only with "salinas que hacen a los indios acomodados" but also are the owners of "diez haciendas de campo y en ellas una multitud grande de tierras." Towns that lay on the *camino real*, the "royal highway" that ran through parts of the Sierra de los Cuchumatanes and connected Guatemala with Mexico, were obliged to offer government officials and commercial travellers shelter for the night. Food and lodging, at the rate of two *reales* per night, should in theory have been paid for. See AGCA, A1.24, leg. 6091, exp. 55307, dated 1805, for elaboration.

disputed land to Santo Tomás, principally because their *parciali-dad* had a greater number of tribute payers, and hence more need of land, than their rivals in Aguacatán. The Indians of Chalchitán refused to recognize the decision and continued to occupy Pichiquil until their forceful eviction from the terrain in 1808 by the district governor, Prudencio de Cozar.[55] Some years later, however, the decision was reversed. Lobbying on the part of the Chalchitecos, in which a payment to the Crown proved particularly persuasive, resulted in another redrawing of boundaries, one that saw Pichiquil excluded from the territory allocated to Santo Tomás. The perseverance of Chalchitán, albeit with the assistance of a sum of money, had finally paid off.[56]

An equally complex dispute over land ownership occurred in the early nineteenth century between the Indian communities of Jacaltenango and Todos Santos Cuchumatán. Conflict again centred on land that formed a boundary between the two towns, the *todosanteros* believing that they had bought land from their Jacaltec neighbours, the latter viewing the exchange not as a sale but merely a temporary rental arrangement.[57]

The land under contest was in an area called Gechec, traditionally Jacaltec *ejido* but claimed by Todos Santos through "purchase" from Jacaltenango. In 1814, families from Todos Santos who worked plots of land at Gechec reported that Indians from Jacaltenango, Petatán, and Concepción had invaded and burned their homes, attacked and threatened innocent people, and made off with twelve sacks of corn.[58] The *todosanteros* retaliated, killing five people and severely beating many others. By 1817, after continuing attacks and counterattacks, the situation had deteriorated to such an extent that the parish priest of Jacaltenango, José León Faboada, warned Crown officials of the possibility of "a murderous riot with grave consequences."[59] In an attempt to resolve the feud, the *alcalde mayor*, Manuel José de Lara, arranged a meeting with parish repre-

---

55 AGCA, A1, leg. 5978, exp. 52518; A1, leg. 5979, exp. 52536; and A1, leg. 6051, exp. 53470.

56 AGCA: ST, El Quiché, *paquete* 1, exp. 5. Pichiquil remains today – see Morales Urrutia (1961, vol. 1, 663) – an *aldea* within the *municipio* of Aguacatán. The conflict is also examined by Hill and Monaghan (1987, 92–100).

57 AGCA, A1.45, leg. 6117, exp. 56588.

58 AGCA, A1. leg. 6055, exp. 53546; A1.45, leg. 6118, exp. 56709.

59 AGCA, A1.45.1, leg. 2806, exp. 24664. Faboada's precise words are "un motín sanguíneo y de muy fatales resultas." See also AGCA: ST, *paquete* 2, exp. 8, and A1.21, leg. 54800, exp. 47154.

sentatives and afterwards ordered a complete remeasurement of the land boundaries between the two communities. The solution put forward to resolve the dispute was either to divide the contested territory in two equal parts, or to offer Todos Santos an equivalent amount of land elsewhere, thus leaving Jacaltenango once again in sole control of Gechec. Both propositions, however, seem to have had little impact, for Jacaltenango and Todos Santos were still squabbling over land jurisdiction in the mid-nineteenth century.[60]

Conflict over property rights developed not only between neighbouring communities but also within them, between rival *parcialidades*. Nowhere was such internal bickering more endemic than at Sacapulas. Throughout the last quarter of the eighteenth century, the groups that collectively formed the *congregación* were in almost continual collision as each *parcialidad* sought to gain control over as much land as possible in the vicinity of the town site. The problem was compounded by rash Spanish attempts to impose a solution that ignored long-established divisions and practices. Particularly controversial was the proposal to redraw property boundaries so as to place the salt works owned by the *parcialidades* Santiago and San Sebastián within *ejido* limits (figure 7). Needless to say, the plan was not well received by the people of Santiago and San Sebastián, who waged a long legal battle (in the end, successfully) to defend the salt works against encroachment, especially from the *parcialidad* San Pedro (see plate 22).[61] Similarly, the *parcialidad* San

60 AGCA: ST, Huehuetenango, *paquete* 2, exp. 11, and B.100.1, leg. 1419, exp. 33408.

61 AGCA, A 1, leg. 6025, exp. 53126 and A 1, leg. 6037, exp. 53257. See also Hill and Monaghan (1987, 102–14). Plate 22 shows land in the vicinity of Sacapulas that became the focal point of bitter feuding in the late eighteenth century. The smaller square, inside of which the parish church and the *salinas* (salt works) are represented, is the area that Spanish authorities wished to see declared *ejido* or common land. The territory below (west) and to the right (south) of the *ejido*, bounded by the letters A, B, C, and D, was to be held by the *parcialidades* Santiago and San Sebastián, the age-old owners of the *salinas* and of the land surrounding them on both banks of the river. The territory below (west) and to the left (north) of the *ejido*, bounded by the letters G, H, K, and M, was to be held by the *parcialidad* San Pedro, an "immigrant" group resettled at Sacapulas in the mid-sixteenth century. Dispute arose when San Pedro attempted to gain access to the salt works depicted in the map as forming part of the *ejido*. Santiago and San Sebastián eventually regained control over the *salinas* and adjacent land on the south bank of the river close to the church, forcing the people of San Pedro to confine their activities to the north bank. The map once formed part of the litigation records contained in AGCA, A 1, leg. 6025, exp. 53126 but is now missing, the fate – see Kramer, Lovell, and Lutz (2013, 2014) for further discussion – of other important Guatemalan documents.

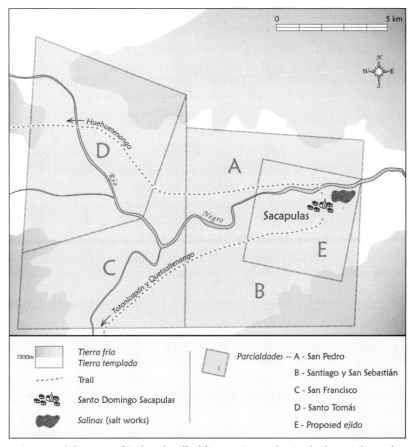

Parcialidades -- A - San Pedro
B - Santiago y San Sebastián
C - San Francisco
D - Santo Tomás
E - Proposed *ejido*

1500m — Tierra fría / Tierra templada

----- Trail

Santo Domingo Sacapulas

Salinas (salt works)

7 Proposed division of Indian landholding at Sacapulas in the late eighteenth century.

Francisco entered into litigation with the *parcialidad* Santo Tomás, chiefly over attempts by the Santo Tomás faction to restrict the access of their San Francisco neighbours to fertile irrigable land in the Río Negro valley.[62]

Feuds and antagonism over property ownership were therefore a prevalent feature of late colonial life. Conflict seems to have been most prolific along the more densely populated zone of Spanish-Indian contact stretching from Aguacatán and Sacapulas in the east

62 AGCA, A I, leg. 6021, exp. 53084; A I, leg. 6042, exp. 53327; and A I, leg. 6060, exp. 53305. A summary of the complex litigation may be found in Carmack (1973, 206–9).

to Chiantla and Huehuetenango in the centre-south and beyond to Jacaltenango and Santa Ana Huista in the north-west. Land was as highly prized during the eighteenth and early nineteenth centuries as it is today. We now turn to how the Cuchumatán earth was put to use.

THE AGRICULTURAL ECONOMY

By the introduction of new tools, new crops, and domesticated animals, the Spaniards radically and irrevocably altered patterns of land use throughout the Cuchumatanes. The conquerors had little success, however, in creating an agricultural economy that was of first-rank commercial significance, simply because most parts of the region were environmentally unsuitable for key cash crops such as cacao and the *xiquilite* plant from which indigo dye is made. One of the few market-oriented activities made possible by the physical geography of the region was the raising of livestock.

Several native communities are documented as supporting sizable herds, particularly of sheep. Fuentes y Guzmán, for instance, recorded "large and plentiful flocks of sheep, all with excellent meat" at Santiago Chimaltenango.[63] Joseph de Olvarrieta and Archbishop Cortés y Larraz noted the same at San Lorenzo, San Juan Ixcoy, San Pedro Soloma, San Miguel Acatán, San Sebastián Coatán, Santa Eulalia, and San Mateo Ixtatán.[64] Although most *pueblos de indios* kept some animals, whether sheep, goats, pigs, turkeys, chickens, or even a few head of cattle, Indian stock raising was far surpassed in the Spanish *haciendas* in the region.

According to Fuentes y Guzmán, the Spanish residents of Huehuetenango at the end of the seventeenth century depended for their livelihood "on *haciendas* that raise all kinds of livestock, because the countryside here is ideally suited for this type of activity."[65] When, a century later, Cortés y Larraz passed through the

63 Fuentes y Guzmán ([1690–99] 1969–72, vol. 3, 23). The chronicler's precise words are "grandes y pingües rebaños de ovejas y de escelentes carnes."
64 AGCA, A1.17.7, leg. 210, exp. 5008; Cortés y Larraz ([1768–70] 1958, vol. 2, 123).
65 Fuentes y Guzmán ([1690–99] 1969–72, vol. 3, 23). The chronicler's precise words are "viven de sus haciendas de campo de ganado mayor y menor, para que es propósito el país."

Malacatán area, a little to the south of Huehuetenango, he also recorded a landscape in which *haciendas* figured conspicuously (plate 23).[66] The largest ranches, as we already have documented, were found on the Altos de Chiantla where, in addition to horses, mules, and cattle, tens of thousands of sheep were grazed. On the Moscoso holdings alone, over twenty thousand sheep were raised "for the supply of wool and meat," chiefly to Huehuetenango, Quetzaltenango, and Santiago de Guatemala.[67] Although these three towns were the main focus of the trade in livestock, Cuchumatán *hacendados* also did business with the Spanish residents of Comitán and Ciudad Real in Chiapas.[68] The colonial space-economy was therefore oriented north and west toward Mexico as well as south and east toward central Guatemala. Wool production fostered the development of weaving, especially among the Indians of Chiantla, Huehuetenango, and Santa Isabel. Meat production and preservation were facilitated by the proximity of two local salt sources, one at Sacapulas, another at San Mateo Ixtatán.[69] Twice yearly the livestock business was given added vitality by agricultural fairs held at Chiantla, which coincided with religious ceremonies related to the cult of the Virgin.[70] These fairs attracted buyers and sellers of quality livestock from all over Mexico and Central America and, together with regular transactions, represented a noteworthy source of *alcabala* (sales tax) income for the Crown.[71]

66 Plate 23 shows the Spanish *haciendas* and *pueblos de indios* of Malacatán parish at the time of the tour of inspection undertaken by Cortés y Larraz between 1768 and 1770. The Spanish *haciendas* represented are La Cal (7); Michicil (8); Chiquibal (9); Eleca (10); Ischol (11); Quiahtzui (12); Salchil (13); Zuchil (14); Cancabal (15); and Malo (16). *The pueblos de indios* from which labour was drawn are Malacatán (1); Santa Bárbara (2); Colotenango (3); Ixtahuacán (4); San Gaspar Ixchil (5); and San Ramón (6). The original, painted in the same watercolour style as plate 21, is filed in AGI, Mapas y Planos (Guatemala 147).

67 AGCA, A1.24, leg. 6096, exp. 55491.

68 See, for example, AGCA, A1.1, leg. 6087, exp. 55071, concerning the passage of sheep driven overland from the Altos de Chiantla to Comitán in neigbouring Chiapas.

69 Fuentes y Guzmán ([1690–99] 1969–72, vol. 3, 23–4, 32, and 46–7).

70 Recinos (1954, 204). The agricultural fairs at Chiantla were held on 2 February and 8 September each year, in conjunction with feasts celebrating, respectively, the Purification and the Nativity of the Virgin.

71 AGCA, A1.24, leg. 6096, exp. 55491, records that the Moscoso holdings alone paid "crecidas cantidades de alcabalas" – large amounts of sales taxes – in

Though locally and, to a lesser extent, regionally important, the livestock economy must be viewed against the larger and more wide-spread backdrop of Indian subsistence and tribute-oriented agriculture. Native communities worked the land to live off of it and to pay their taxes. During years of good harvests, after subsistence needs had been met and tribute paid, there might be a surplus left that could either be stored or traded. In times of crisis, brought on by drought or excess rain, an outbreak of disease or an invasion of locusts, there was barely enough to survive on, even before tribute was due.[72]

Indians grew a variety of crops. Some were age-old Mesoamerican staples – corn, beans, chili peppers, and squash. Others, like wheat, sugar cane, onions, garlic, bananas, apples, and peaches, were introduced by the Spaniards. Native communities tended to specialize, then as now, in producing whatever was best suited to local conditions. Sugar cane was grown at San Ildefonso Ixtahuacán, San Pedro Necta, and San Andrés Cuilco, allowing not only sugar to be processed but *aguardiente* liquor to be distilled.[73] Salt was produced by the Indians of Sacapulas and San Mateo Ixtatán, and taken by itinerant merchants as far away as Chiapas, Quetzaltenango, and Suchitepéquez, where it was traded for cacao and cotton.[74] Todos Santos grew apples and made from them each year "more than two thousand jugs of cider, which sell for twenty-four *reales* a jug."[75] Wheat, its cultivation taught by missionaries in the sixteenth century, was grown as a cash crop at Cunén, Concepción, and San Sebastián Coatán; it was used to feed the Spanish residents of Ciudad Real,

addition to supporting "el gremio de los sombrereros de la ciudad de Guatemala" – a guild of hat-makers in the capital.

72 See, for outbreaks of disease especially, AGCA, A1, leg. 6940, exp. 57766; A3.16, leg. 249, exp. 5036; and A3.16, leg. 2899, exp. 43049. All three dossiers document the inability of the Indians of Soloma to feed themselves, let alone pay tribute, after they were struck by outbreaks of typhus and measles during the first quarter of the nineteenth century, a predicament discussed at length in the following chapter.

73 Fuentes y Guzmán ([1690–99] 1969–72, vol. 3, 28, 31, and 35).

74 AGCA, A1.17.7, leg. 210, exp. 5008; Fuentes y Guzmán ([1690–99] 1969–72, vol. 3, 46).

75 Fuentes y Guzmán ([1690–99] 1969–72, vol. 3, 33–4). I am indebted to the late Francis Gall, fond of refreshment himself, for bringing this detail to my attention.

Comitán, Chiantla, Huehuetenango, and Santiago de Guatemala, among other places.[76] Small amounts of cacao and *achiote* (a vegetable dye used to colour food) were produced at San Antonio and Santa Ana Huista, San Andrés Cuilco, and San Andrés Jacaltenango.[77] The dry scrubland around Toxoh, a small Mam community near Huehuetenango, lent itself to the growth of *nopal* cactus, which the locals exploited in the making of cochineal dye.[78] Honey was produced by the Indians of Petatán, and bananas and pineapples were grown at Purificación Jacaltenango.[79]

Land was therefore put to good use by Spaniards and Indians alike. Spanish interest in claiming title to land in the Cuchumatanes was at first negligible, with the exception of the area around Huehuetenango. Greater interest arose in the seventeenth century and, once initiated, continued and intensified throughout the eighteenth century and up until independence from Spain in 1821. Spanish acquisition of land began to have greater impact on native communities at the end of the seventeenth century as Indian numbers started to recover. Between 1700 and 1821, a growing Indian population coupled with Spanish desires to own land resulted in a spate of conflicts over property boundaries and territorial rights. Disputes developed not only between Spaniards and Indians but also between and within native communities.

The *hacienda*, with its orientation toward raising livestock tended by native peon labour, certainly emerged as a recognizable feature of the landscape, but Indians nonetheless managed to retain possession of much of their ancestral lands. Explanation of such a pattern lies intertwined in the region's physical geography, its limited economic potential, Spanish colonial ambitions, and the tenacity and willingness of Cuchumatán Indians to exercise their rights as subjects of the Crown by entering into lengthy and often complex litigation procedures. As Taylor correctly speculated, landholding in colonial

76 AGCA, A1.44, leg. 6115, exp. 56343, and A1.22, leg. 195, exp. 3947; Tovilla ([1635] 1960, 208); and Cortés y Larraz ([1768–70] 1958, vol. 2, 123).

77 AGCA, A1.44, leg. 6115, exp. 56343; Fuentes y Guzmán ([1690–99] 1969–72, vol. 3, 35).

78 Fuentes y Guzmán ([1690–99] 1969–72, vol. 3, 23).

79 AGCA, A1.44, leg. 6115, exp. 56343; Fuentes y Guzmán ([1690–99] 1969–72, vol. 3, 42).

Guatemala, at least judging from the Cuchumatán evidence, seems to bear little resemblance either to the north Mexican model or to the example of the Valley of Oaxaca. Rather, the Cuchumatán pattern straddles an intriguing middle ground. Future depredations were to erode the native estate with unprecedented ardour, confronting Maya peoples in Guatemala with a crisis as profound as conquest by Spain.[80] Yet so long as land remained within indigenous control, the survival of a distinctly Maya way of life was assured, not just in the Sierra de los Cuchumatanes but throughout highland Guatemala.

80 See Carmack (1983, 215–52), McCreery (1990, 96–115), and Lovell ([1995]) 2010, 120–31) for elaboration. C.A. Smith (1984, 204) reckons, broadly stated, that "by the first decade of the twentieth century Indian communities had lost about half of the lands they traditionally claimed during the colonial period."

9

Collapse and Recovery: Demographic Change in the Native Population

What causes the Indians to die and to diminish in number are secret judgments of God beyond the reach of man.

Pedro de Liévano (1582)

In many colonial societies, population size and economic performance tend to be related. Such a connection may be said to have prevailed in Spanish Central America: the economic history of the region, one of cyclical booms, setbacks, and readjustments, was tied closely to demographic trends and fluctuations. Thus, with a sizable native contingent from which to draw labour, economic prospects at first seemed encouraging. However, as Indian numbers withered in the course of the sixteenth and seventeenth centuries, economic activity languished and depression set in. When Indian populations stabilized by the close of the seventeenth century and began to grow, economic stagnation gave way to new initiatives and signs of revival.[1]

In colonial Guatemala, this crude, causal connection runs through a number of developments. Native depopulation was a major factor in the demise of the *encomienda* system. It also contributed to *hacienda* formation and the emergence of debt peonage as a means of securing a workforce.[2] Features such as these are thrown into sharper relief when viewed in relation to long-term population dynamics. This chapter pieces together a demographic profile for the Sierra de los Cuchumatanes, emphasizing the collapse and recovery (to this day) of its indigenous Maya majority.

1 MacLeod ([1973] 2008) convincingly documents this view throughout his magnum opus.
2 Ibid., 130, 224.

NATIVE POPULATION DYNAMICS (1520–1821)

Any attempt to reconstruct Cuchumatán population history is beset by a lack of consistent, representative data. The paucity of sources is acute for the sixteenth and most of the seventeenth century; the eighteenth, by comparison, is reasonably well documented. As with contact scenarios discussed in chapter 5, a prudent stand is to regard population estimates for colonial times as being equally speculative, scrutinizing them with caution before reaching any final conclusions.

The first records known thus far to contain demographic data on all important settlements are Indian tribute assessments (*tasaciones de tributos*) for the years 1664 to 1678; reliable and complete records prior to this period have yet to be found.[3] The problem is compounded by the fact that much extant material is either spatially indeterminate or relates to one of a number of surrogate categories: generating a population estimate inevitably entails statistical manipulation, which can be a risky procedure. Some problematic data are shown in table 19. Information upon which estimates can be made of sixteenth-century populations is especially scarce. Among available data are (1) reports of the size of Indian armies (table 4) encountered during battles of conquest, as recorded by the chronicler Fuentes y Guzmán; (2) Indian tributaries in a dozen or so towns (table 6) taxed by President Alonso López de Cerrato between February and August of 1549; and (3) a count of tribute payers in Huehuetenango, where Spanish authorities were based, assessed by President Diego García de Valverde between 1578 and 1582.[4] None of this information is remotely ideal to work with but is the best at hand.

Based on the size of Indian armies, a population estimate for the Cuchumatanes of around 150,000 can be generated for the years between 1525 and 1530 (see chapter 5). This figure may be indicative of a contact population of some 260,000, roughly the same size as the Cuchumatán population in the mid-twentieth century.[5]

3 AGCA, A3.16, leg. 1601, exp. 26391.

4 Fuentes y Guzmán ([1690–99] 1969–72, vol. 3, 18–22 and 51–71); AGI, Guatemala 128, "Tasaciones de los pueblos" (1549); and AGI, Guatemala 10, "Razón de las tasaciones" (1578–82). Sixteenth-century sources that relate to the native population of Guatemala are examined by Zamora (1983a, 291–328) and also, at some length, by Lovell and Lutz (2013, 173–223, 270–7).

5 A full discussion of how these estimates are arrived at may be found in chapter 5. See also Lovell and Lutz (2013, 173–83).

Of the two tribute assessments carried out in the sixteenth century, the one made by Valverde is considered more reliable than the Cerrato tally, for a number of reasons.[6] Foremost among these is that Cerrato leaned toward accepting the counsel of Indian *caciques* and *principales* rather than relying on data volunteered by *encomenderos* or – the most reliable procedure of all – on the basis of observations made on the ground; *visitas* (tours of inspection) like the one conducted by Alonso de Zorita in 1555 yielded much pertinent information.[7] Cerrato, apparently not wishing to subject himself to the rigours of a *visita*, overcompensated for the avarice of *encomenderos* by turning uncritically to local Indian leaders for assistance. In so doing, he almost certainly underestimated the tax-paying capacity of native communities: in order to reduce the amount of tribute demanded, *caciques* and *principales* furnished Cerrato with appraisals that, when acted upon, drew outrage from various secular interests and caused dismay even among the clergy.[8] By contrast, the Valverde *tasación*, undertaken personally by the president with the help of trusted Crown officials, enabled a more realistic appraisal of the Indian resource base. The Valverde *tasación* is especially useful because it contains two figures: the first an earlier tribute count, possibly that of Cerrato himself; the second the new Valverde count of

6 The tribute assessments carried out by Cerrato and Valverde are the subject of extensive critiques in Lovell and Lutz (2013, 184–95 and 212–23). For Cerrato, also see Carmack (1973, 138–40); for Valverde, also see Carmack (1973, 143) and MacLeod ([1973] 2008, 130–1).

7 Carmack (1973, 138–40); Veblen (1977, 494–5); and Zorita ([1585] 1963, 35–6, 271–3).

8 Lovell and Lutz (2013, 189–91). See also two items of correspondence in AGI, Guatemala 41, "Cabildo de Santiago de Guatemala al Rey," one dated 30 April 1549, the other 6 May 1549. In the first letter, the city council complains bitterly to the Crown that Cerrato "cut tribute by half, leaving Spanish residents so poor that they can no longer maintain themselves." The second letter has members of the city council again pleading poverty, alleging that "the tribute assessments are such that Indian towns scoff while we Spaniards weep." In a letter dated 27 April 1556 (see AGI, Guatemala 45) the treasurer Francisco de Castellanos and one of his associates, Francisco de Ovalle, estimate that the Crown received only 8,000 pesos from Indian tribute when it could in fact get two or three times as much. They mention specifically that Cerrato went about reassessing tribute-paying capacity without arranging tours of inspection beforehand. In AGI, Guatemala 128, "Tasaciones de los pueblos" (1548–51), folio 130 verso, the text for "Cochumatlan" (the present-day Todos Santos Cuchumatán) below the tribute assessment actually states that the two Spaniards designated as recipients – "estaban agraviados de esta tasación" – were offended by this levy.

1578–82.[9] Cerrato was content with statistical approximations: almost all his figures are rounded off in units of ten or twenty. Valverde, on the other hand, was an administrative perfectionist, assessing tribute-paying capacity down to individual family units.[10]

One of the towns assessed by Valverde was Huehuetenango. Because it was an important seat of officialdom – the *corregidor* at the time of the *tasación* was Francisco Díaz del Castillo, son of the conqueror and chronicler Bernal Díaz del Castillo – it seems reasonable to assume that Spanish bureaucrats had a fairly good idea of the number of Indians who could be expected to pay tribute. Huehuetenango, formerly assessed at 570 *tributarios*, was adjusted downwards by Valverde to 367 *tributarios*.[11] Tributaries at this time, judging from detailed evidence that exists for eight *pueblos de indios* elsewhere in Guatemala, were indigenous heads of households constituting roughly one-fifth of the total native population.[12] Applying this same ratio to the Valverde statistics for Huehuetenango suggests that the town and surrounding countryside in the mid-sixteenth century may have supported an Indian population of around 2,850, a figure that by 1580 might have fallen to around 1,835. In the *tasaciones* for 1664–78, the earliest extant documentation with tribute data for every significant Cuchumatán town, Huehuetenango accounts for 3.9 per cent of the total number of *tributarios*.[13] If we assume that Huehuetenango represented this same proportion in the sixteenth century, then the total number of Cuchumatán *tributarios* in 1550 would have been some 14,615 and in 1580 would have been in the order of 9,410. Applying to these figures a population-to-tributary ratio of five to one, the same conversion factor employed in at least three other studies of sixteenth-century Guatemala, generates a population estimate for the region of 73,000 in 1550 and 47,000 thirty years later.[14]

9 See Carmack (1973, 143); Lovell and Lutz (2013, 218–21).

10 AGI, Guatemala 10, "Razón de las tasaciones" (1578–82); Lovell and Lutz (2013, 217–23).

11 AGI, Guatemala 10, "Razón de las tasaciones" (1578–82), folio 15.

12 AGI, Guatemala 45, "Tasaciones de Chimaltenango, Comalapa, Petapa, San Juan y San Pedro Sacatepéquez, San Juan Amatitlán, Santa Inés y Zumpango" (1562). The tribute assessments of all eight of these towns are subjected to scrutiny in Lovell and Lutz (2013, 197–9).

13 AGCA, A3.16, leg. 1601, exp. 26391. The number of Cuchumatán *tributarios* adds up to 4,040½. Huehuetenango was assessed at 156½ tribute payers.

14 Carmack (1982, 139–40); Miles (1957, 766); Veblen (1977, 495).

Viewed on their own, these two estimates are merely suggestive, computed with a wide margin of error. They assume greater credibility, however, when measured against independent frames of reference provided by the research findings of Murdo MacLeod and Thomas Veblen. According to these scholars, the native population of Guatemala in the mid-sixteenth century numbered only about one-half the size it was between 1524 and 1548, primarily because of catastrophic mortality from outbreaks of disease.[15] Particularly destructive was a plague known as *gucumatz* (or *cocoliztli*) that raged from 1545 to 1548.[16] Similarly, the number of Indians alive in 1580 is thought to have been about one-half that of the mid-sixteenth century, on account of the equally devastating impact of a malady known as *matlazáhuatl*, which struck between 1576 and 1581.[17] If MacLeod and Veblen are correct, then a population of 150,000 between the years 1525 and 1530 (the Cuchumatán estimate based on the size of Indian armies) would have fallen to around 75,000 after *gucumatz* had runs its course. This figure coincides well with the estimate of 73,000 derived from the Valverde *tasación*. By the same reasoning, a population of 75,000 at mid-century would by 1580 have numbered around 37,500 because of mortality caused by *matlazáhuatl*. Once again, this figure lines up reasonably well to the estimate of 47,000 also derived from the Valverde assessment. The data available are scant, but at least they converge.

For almost a century after the Valverde *tasación*, little useful information has come to light concerning Cuchumatán demography. Data available, moreover, are difficult to interpret or break down with any degree of spatial or statistical accuracy. Sources include figures of the *servicio del tostón* for the *corregimiento* of Totonicapán and Huehuetenango in 1595 and an ecclesiastical census of the towns (and souls) under the spiritual charge of the Dominican monastery at Sacapulas in 1604.[18] Both sets of data, especially the former, deal

15 MacLeod ([1973] 2008, 19); Veblen (1977, 496).

16 Descriptions of *gucumatz* or *cocoliztli* are ones that MacLeod ([1973] 2008, 19) believes resemble the symptoms of pulmonary plague. Dobyns (1983, 264–5) diagnoses bubonic plague.

17 MacLeod ([1973] 2008, 19); Veblen (1977, 496). *Matlazáhuatl* is a disease of disputed diagnosis that some scholars – see S.F. Cook (1946, 321) and Gerhard (1972, 23) – consider to be typhus.

18 For the *servicio del tostón*, see AGI, Contaduría 969 (1595). The ecclesiatical census, the "Suma y memoria de los conventos, religiosos, pueblos, visitas y indios

with suspiciously round numbers, undermining their credibility in generating population estimates.[19]

The *tasaciones* of 1664–78 are the next records after the Valverde assessment that contain detailed data. This valuable set of documents gives a complete breakdown, by town and occasionally by *parcialidad*, of the entire tribute-paying population of the region. The total number of *tributarios* at the time was 4,040½.[20] Fuentes y Guzmán, during the second half of the seventeenth century, reckoned on a population to tributary ratio of four to one.[21] Using this same ratio, 4,040½ *tributarios* would be indicative of a native population of 16,162 around the year 1670.

For the remainder of the colonial period there is no shortage of reliable and comprehensive sources, chiefly in the form of unpublished documents housed in the Archivo General de Centro América and the Archivo General de Indias, upon which the population history of the Sierra de los Cuchumatanes may be reconstructed with greater confidence. These sources include tribute lists, reports compiled by officers of the Crown or servants of the Church, and meticulous censuses that register details by age, sex, class, and race. This information is synthesized in table 20 and rendered graphically in figure 8.

The most dramatic feature of Cuchumatán population history is the catastrophic decline in numbers that followed conquest by Spain. Massive demographic collapse probably began in the years immediately preceding Spanish arrival and continued throughout the sixteenth and for most of the seventeenth century. Reaching its nadir around 1680, native population began to recover and grow throughout the eighteenth century, though downturns still occurred. By the start of the nineteenth century, Indian numbers embarked on an uninterrupted upward trend.

---

que hay en Guatemala y Chiapa de la Orden de Santo Domingo" (1604), is housed in the Biblioteca del Palacio Real in Madrid, filed there as manuscript number 1756.

19 The figure for the *corregimiento* of Totonicapán and Huehuetenango is 5,000 *tostones*. Being the only figure among a dozen others that is rendered in such a conveniently round figure, it is best considered a rough estimate.

20 AGCA, A3.16, leg. 1601, exp. 26391.

21 Fuentes y Guzmán ([1690–99]) 1969–72, vol. 3, 15–18, 22–44).

EPIDEMIC DISEASE AND DEMOGRAPHIC CRISIS

The factors most responsible for the dynamic of population collapse and recovery are complex. Though controversy still surrounds the numbers involved, it is now recognized that parts of the Americas were densely settled at the time of the Columbus landfall and that indigenous populations declined precipitously in size thereafter.[22] Depopulation has traditionally been attributed to unmitigated carnage, ruthless enslavement, and harsh exploitation by Spanish colonists – the thesis of the infamous Leyenda Negra, or Black Legend.[23] It is not difficult to find references in the literature to support it. According to Bartolomé de las Casas, for example, between four and five million Indian lives were lost in Guatemala and neighbouring regions alone because of the tyranny of the conquistador Pedro de Alvarado. In the *Brevísima relación de la destrucción de las Indias* (1552), Las Casas singled out Alvarado and his next of kin as being among the most rapacious *conquistadores* of all. "The atrocities perpetrated by him and his brothers," Las Casas writes, "are enough to fill a particular volume, so many were the slaughters, crimes, injuries, butcheries, and beastly desolations."[24] Writing to King Charles V in the mid-sixteenth century, Las Casas declared that "Your Highness can be sure that of all ... the Indies where there have been the most excesses and disorder in committing injustices and iniquities ... there are, and have been, so many and such grave and evil

22 See Lovell and Lutz (2013, 173–248, 270–83) not only for estimates of the indigenous population of Guatemala throughout the colonial period but also for discussion of the sources, and rationale, upon which the estimates are based.

23 Gibson (1971) oversees an even-handed treatment of the issues, having already (1964, 403) made his own position clear. "The Black Legend," he writes, "provides a gross but essentially accurate interpretation of relations between Spaniards and Indians. The legend builds upon the record of deliberate sadism. It flourishes in an atmosphere of indignation, which removes the issue from the category of objective understanding. It is insufficient in its awareness of the institutions of colonial history. But the substantive content of the Black Legend asserts that Indians were exploited by Spaniards, and in empirical fact they were."

24 Rendered in translation from Las Casas ([1552] 1977, 45–50). The good friar calculated loss of life at "mas de quarto y de cinco cuentos de animas en quinze diez y seys años desde el año veynte y quatro hasta el quarenta" – "four to five million souls in the span of fifteen to sixteen years, from 1524 to 1540." For good measure, Las Casas adds: "They kill and destroy those [Indians] who remain, and will keep on killing."

vexations ... made against the Indians ... of the province of Guatemala [that] one cannot imagine the ways and cunning manner ... used to secure them."[25]

While the allegations of Las Casas and the moral position that he and others represented must be taken into consideration, the principal cause of native depopulation was not massacre and mistreatment at the hands of marauding Spaniards but the inadvertent introduction by them of Old World diseases to which indigenous peoples, the Maya of Guatemala among them, were immunologically defenseless.[26]

From the submergence of the Bering land bridge millennia ago, until the arrival of Europeans in the wake of Columbus, the inhabitants of the New World lived in virtual isolation from those of the Old. The separation resulted in Native Americans, upon first exposure, being fatally vulnerable to diseases with which Europeans and Africans had a long association and to which they had developed immunity. Possibly because of the harsh climate characteristic of Siberia, the Bering land bridge, and Alaska, early migrants never carried over diseases from the Old World to the New; sub-zero, Arctic conditions either killed off disease organisms or those humans laid low by sickness and ill health. Alternative explanations may be that the migrations across the Bering Strait occurred so long ago that many diseases had not yet evolved in the Old World before the forays of avant-garde ancestors; or that the original group of migrants was so small that immunity was lost due to some kind of genetic drift.[27] Whatever the reasons, the inhabitants of the New World developed resistance only to a few ailments: in pre-Columbian times, they suffered primarily from gastro-intestinal and respiratory disorders.[28] Prior to the arrival of Europeans, therefore, Native Americans enjoyed an existence relatively free of acute infectious disease. Woes such as measles, mumps, smallpox, and typhus – all endemic to the Old World – were unknown. When these diseases were introduced under "virgin soil" conditions, their combined impact, in the words

25 Las Casas, as rendered in translation in Sherman (1979, 182–4).
26 See Crosby (1972, 35–58; 1976, 289–99) and McNeill (1976, 176–207), among a now voluminous body of work discussed also by Alchon (2003); N.D. Cook (1998); and Cook and Lovell ([1992] 2001).
27 Crosby (1972, 30–1).
28 S.F. Cook (1946, 324); Dobyns (1983, 34–6); Alchon (2003, 32–59).

of one authority, "may well have caused the greatest destruction of lives in history."[29]

The first disease to arrive is now considered to be smallpox.[30] MacLeod reckons that its impact was at least as cataclysmic as that of the Black Death of 1346–50 on Europe: one-third to one-half of New World inhabitants afflicted by smallpox in the fifteenth and sixteenth centuries would have perished.[31] From the testimony of Toribio de Benavente, a Franciscan friar better known by his adopted name Motolinía, we know that smallpox swept through central Mexico with horrendous devastation.[32] It continued its lethal passage south toward Guatemala, accompanied perhaps by pulmonary plague or typhus.[33] As 1520 drew to a close, four years before the arrival of forces led by Pedro de Alvarado, Maya peoples in Guatemala were reeling from their initial exposure to what MacLeod aptly calls "the shock troops of the conquest."[34] Kaqchikel chroniclers lament that it was "in truth terrible, the number of dead among the people ... in that period ... when the plague raged."[35] This initial bout of pestilence was followed some twelve years later by an outbreak of measles. Thereafter, the ravages of epidemic disease were a common feature of native life, resulting in high mortality (table 21) during widespread outbreaks. As well as being struck by diseases of far-flung proportion, Cuchumatán communities also had to contend with more localized outbreaks (table 22).

Demographic collapse, therefore, is most critically linked to the incidence, and impact, of epidemic disease. Subjugation by imperial Spain was not achieved, nor colonial rule maintained, without brutality and exploitation often contributing to loss of life. Old World

29 MacLeod ([1973]) 2008, 20). For the concept of "virgin soil" epidemics, and the destruction they wrought, see Crosby (1976).

30 Crosby (1967) deserves credit for galvanizing debate, N.D. Cook (1998, 15–59; 2002, 349–86) for clarifying it, the timing of the first outbreaks of smallpox above all.

31 MacLeod ([1973] 2008, 5–17).

32 Motolinía ([1541] 1979, 13–140).

33 Shattuck (1938, 40–1); MacLeod ([1973] 2008, 19, 98).

34 MacLeod ([1973] 2008, 40). Shattuck (1938, 41), on the advice of France V. Scholes, dates the epidemic to 1521. McBryde (1946, 301–2) suggests that the date should be 1523 and contends that the disease in question was a strain of influenza.

35 Recinos and Goetz (1953, 115). Shattuck (1938, 42) quotes Fuentes y Guzmán (1690–99) as stating that, before Spanish intrusion, Guatemala was densely settled until smallpox and measles spread among the native population "like fire in dry grass, destroying entire cities of thousands of inhabitants."

pathogens, however, consumed far more native lives than did Hispanic depravity and greed. From the 1520s until the end of Spanish rule in 1821, Cuchumatán Indians were exposed to unrelenting waves of pestilence. Mortality rates varied but were consistently high. Between 1520 and 1683, indigenous numbers in the region fell by more than 90 per cent, from perhaps 260,000 to a low of about 16,000. That downward spiral abated by the end of the seventeenth century, when the first signs of recovery are manifest. Several fluctuations in the course of the eighteenth century, however, indicate continued vulnerability, to smallpox and typhus in particular. Only at the very end of the colonial period are there signs of a sustained increase in native numbers across the region as a whole (table 20 and figure 8).

Guatemalan and Spanish archives house a bounty of documents that describe, often in lugubrious detail, the devastation that was wrought. In an attempt to convey a nuanced sense of it, we now turn to examining outbreaks of smallpox and typhus between 1780 and 1810. While a focus on these three decades, and these two maladies, is dictated by the availability of data, by all accounts the events and circumstances described apply also to earlier episodes and crisis situations.

"DESTROYING GENERATION AFTER GENERATION": SMALLPOX, 1780–1810

After reaching its nadir of 16,000 around 1680, the Cuchumatán population increased in size, albeit slowly, for the next one hundred years. By 1779, it had risen about 75 per cent above the estimate calculated for 1683, numbering slightly over 28,000. The vast majority was indigenous; Ladinos and Spaniards accounted for only 5 per cent of the regional total at the end of the colonial period, and constituted an even smaller percentage during earlier times. Demographic recovery between 1683 and 1779, therefore, was an overwhelmingly native phenomenon, though *castas* (people of mixed race) were by then certainly present.[36] With the onset in 1780 of a virulent outbreak of

---

36 For insightful discussion of the emergence of *casta* populations in the region, their numbers, places of residence, and livelihoods, see Schwartzkopf (2013). Only in Cuilco, Chiantla, Huehuetenango, and Santa Ana Malacatán did Spaniards and Ladinos become notable elements of the local population. For the year 1779, see

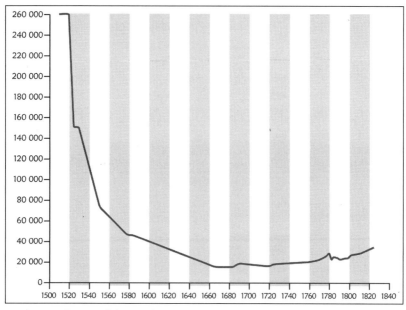

8 The population of the Cuchumatán highlands, 1520–1825.

smallpox, one that can be considered but a regional manifestation of a hemispheric pandemic, the upward trend was abruptly arrested.[37]

Smallpox is documented as having been in existence on 28 March 1780 in San Martín Mazapa and San Francisco Motozintla, communities in the westernmost part of the parish of Cuilco close to the *alcaldía mayor* of Chiapas. A priest named Manuel Ordóñez noted the date, the earliest recorded occurrence.[38] The epidemic persisted in the region, in San Lorenzo Mazatenango for instance, at least until January 1781, nine months later. In some communities (at San Martín Mazapa and San Francisco Motozintla, for example) smallpox raged for four months; others (for example, Santiago Chimaltenango and San Sebastián Huehuetenango) endured the pestilence one or two months longer. In Colotenango, smallpox lingered for fully seven months (see figure 9). The chronology of recorded

AGCA, leg. 6097, exp. 55507, folio 51; for the year 1803, when some five hundred *casta* families are documented, see A 1.44, leg. 6106, exps. 55866, 55867, and 55892.

37 AGCA, A 1, leg. 6112, exp. 56104 and A 1, leg. 6112, exp. 56108. For the hemispheric dimension of this outbreak of smallpox, see Fenn (2001), whose tracking of the disease and the devastation it wrought is without equal.

38 AGCA, A 1.44, leg.6097, exp. 55507, folio 27 verso.

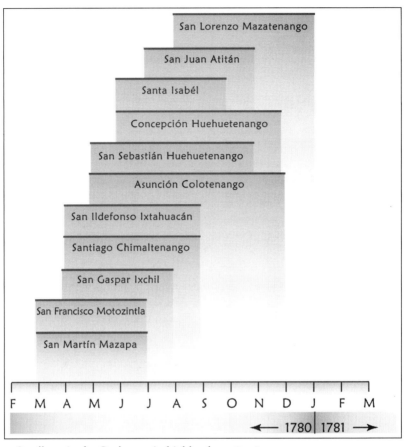

9 Smallpox in the Cuchumatán highlands, 1780–81.

incidence suggests a rapid spread of infection east from a location in Chiapas along the southern edge of the Cuchumatanes (possibly by way of the Cuilco valley) with a slower diffusion north into higher and more remote parts of the region.[39]

In response to his request, Francisco Geraldino, the *alcalde mayor* of Totonicapán and Huehuetenango, was supplied by priests like Ordóñez with data concerning the number of deaths that could be

39 AGCA, A I.44, leg. 6097, exp. 55507. Hopkins (1983, 8–9) notes that smallpox tends to spread "more rapidly in the winter months in temperate climates and during the dry season in tropical climates." His observation applies to some extent to the Cuchumatán chronology, which indicates a more rapid diffusion of infection west to east in the dry season and a slower diffusion north into higher elevations once the annual rains had begun.

attributed to smallpox.[40] Geraldino, acting on royal orders, then gathered parish statistics together, completing the task on 2 May 1781. His responsibility appears to have been twofold: first, he was to determine how many of the dead were tribute payers, an exercise undertaken to assess how taxes levied on stricken communities would in the immediate future be affected; second, he was to determine which towns were most in need of assistance, and act accordingly. Geraldino synthesized the information relayed to him – some priests were more conscientious in furnishing data than others – in a table he called a "general summary showing mortality related to the smallpox epidemic of 1780, with a listing of the number of dead tributaries and the amount [of money] with which communities were assisted."[41] A detailed town-by-town breakdown of the impact of the epidemic, based on Geraldino's summary, is shown in table 23.

Over 4,000 Indians of all ages perished, with almost 60 per cent of the total number of recorded deaths (see figure 10) occurring among children.[42] Of those who died, 259 were reported by Geraldino to have been tribute payers. Only one priest, Fray Juan Ramón Solís of the parish of Nebaj, provided Geraldino with specific details about the number of people who not only died from smallpox but who fell sick with fever and were nursed back to health.[43] This information enables some assessment to be made of the degree of infection and the rate of survival or recovery. The data are shown in table 24 and relate to the three Ixil communities of San Gaspar Chajul, San Juan Cotzal, and Santa María Nebaj. Some idea of how disruptive the epidemic must have been of such routine chores as tending fields, fetching water, or preparing food is indicated by Solís reporting that, in San Gaspar Chajul, three out of every five people became ill. Of those stricken with fever, one in four perished, a pattern that holds also for the neighbouring communities of San Juan Cotzal and Santa María Nebaj.

40 AGCA, A I.44, leg. 6097, exp. 55507, folio 34.
41 AGCA, A I.44, leg. 6097, exp. 55507, folio 49, "Estado general que manifiesta los que fallecieron durante la epidemia de viruelas en los pueblos de la alcaldía mayor de Totonicapán y Huehuetenango durante el año 1780" (1781).
42 Such high mortality among children is not surprising, as they constituted the majority of the non-immune population. Regeneration of non-immune populations allowed smallpox to occur in cycles of seven or eight years. See Swann (1980, 105) for elaboration.
43 AGCA, A I.44, leg. 6097, exp. 55507, folio 26.

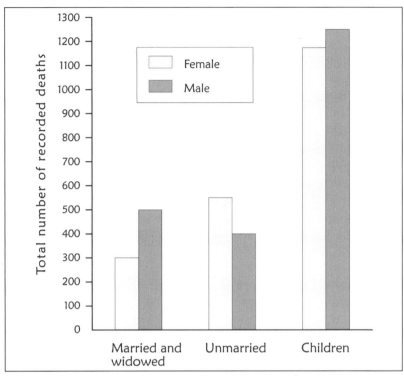

10 Smallpox mortality by family category, 1780–81.

Mortality rates varied considerably, from 8 per cent in San Gaspar Ixchil to 38 per cent in San Miguel Acatán, indicating that there was a significant spatial variation (figure 11) in the impact of the epidemic, some *pueblos de indios* being much harder hit than others (table 23). Assuming it was the same strain of smallpox that was involved, differences in disease impact were likely caused by a combination of factors, including demographic composition; population density; degree of settlement nucleation or dispersal; extent of previously acquired immunity; level of pre-contagion health and nutrition; effectiveness of quarantine procedures; proximity to routes of trade and communication; and numerous cultural and environmental characteristics relating to habit and habitat.[44] In other words, variable local conditions that changed in myriad, subtle, and complex ways from valley to valley, from town to town, best account for

44 For discussion of these same variables operating in a Mexican context, see Swann (1980, 97–109).

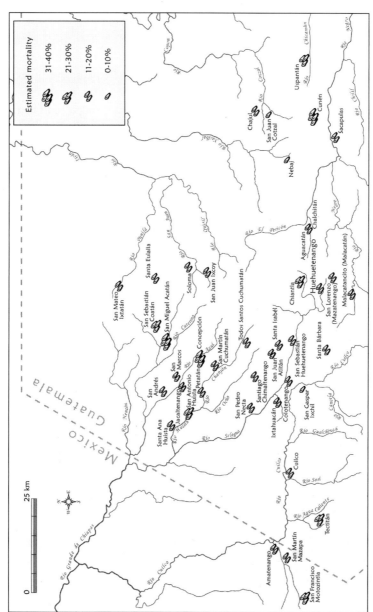

11 Estimated mortality by *pueblo de indios* caused by the smallpox outbreak of 1780–81.

172 The Colonial Experience

differences in mortality. Within a year the epidemic had reduced the population of the region, after a century or so of gradual recovery, from 28,000 to around 24,000, a drop of almost 15 per cent.

On 29 August 1780, authorities began to respond to the crisis. Geraldino issued a rather vague precautionary order stating that "the Indians should be cared for and assisted by drawing upon the resources of their communities."[45] Following an inspection of several stricken towns, officials made recommendations about what could be done to alleviate the situation, above all to halt the spread of disease. Most of these amounted to little more than allocating certain towns a sum of money drawn from their own *cajas de comunidad* or local *cofradías*. This money was then spent on bedding, clothing, and food and in administering the holy sacraments to the dead.[46] Parish priests were responsible for distributing goods and provisions, dispatched from Huehuetenango, among those families considered most in need. In Aguacatán and Chalchitán the sum of ten pesos bought an *arroba* of sugar and thirty-eight *petates*; in Todos Santos, twenty pesos purchased two *arrobas* of sugar, ten *petates*, and a quantity of cloth used for making blankets.[47] Financial assistance seems only to have been extended to eleven towns, with the majority of afflicted communities simply left to fight the sickness with their own limited resources. Though Francisco Asturias, in his history of Guatemalan medicine, records inoculation as having been carried out during this epidemic, just how extensive the practice was in the Sierra de los Cuchumatanes is a matter of conjecture.[48]

By early 1781 the epidemic that had begun a year or so before had run its course. Within ten years the tribute payers in the province of Totonicapán and Huehuetenango attained pre-contagion numbers.

45 AGCA, A1.44, leg. 6097, exp. 55507, folios 46 verso and 47. The original states "por punto general se mandó cuidar y socorrer a los indios de los fondos de sus comunidades."

46 Ibid., folios 46 and 47.

47 Ibid., folios 35 and 36.

48 Asturias (1958, 88); see also Shattuck (1938, 42). Few (2010) documents the practice of inoculation in meticulous detail during the 1780 epidemic, noting the prominent role played in it by José Flores, a "medical physician" who "later became head of the Audiencia de Guatemala's Royal Protomedicato and chair of medicine at the Universidad de San Carlos." Flores and a team of assistants trained in the art of injecting a person with live smallpox matter, which successfully undertaken, induced immunity to the disease, concentrated their activities to notable effect in and around the new colonial capital (the present-day Guatemala City) founded only a few years before the outbreak.

Total population, however, did not reach pre-contagion levels for another decade.[49] A less fatal, more localized outbreak of smallpox flared up again in 1795 and 1796.[50] Joseph Domingo Hidalgo, a Crown official and a contributor to the *Gazeta de Guatemala*, wrote positively about efforts to control the spread of infection:

> In 1795 and 1796 the towns that border the province of
> Chiapas ... were overrun by a terrible outbreak of smallpox,
> an all-consuming pestilence that has plagued this Kingdom
> of Guatemala throughout the 275 years it has been conquered
> by Spain, destroying generation after generation, leaving barely
> one-tenth of the [contact] population alive. On this occasion,
> however, due to the efforts of Don José Domás y Valle, president
> and captain general of the Kingdom, the outbreak was isolated,
> procedures of inoculation were set up, and the pestilence was
> stamped out at the peak of its virulence.[51]

About a dozen towns were affected by this outbreak, all of them lying to the north and west of Huehuetenango, with the eastern Cuchumatanes apparently left untouched and unharmed. Specific reference is made about the coldness, remoteness, and general environmental inhospitality of the region being among the "physical causes" of the resurgence and virulence of the outbreak, with the authorities admitting that rugged terrain would hamper relief operations, even if they were attempted in the first place.[52]

The epidemic of 1795–96 was followed seven years later by yet another appearance of smallpox, once again focused on the border area with Chiapas.[53] Although these renewed outbreaks were far less serious than the epidemics of 1780–81 or 1795–96, the authorities reacted (perhaps because of the impact of the earlier visitations) with stronger emergency measures, including inoculation and quarantine.[54] Since many of the towns where smallpox reappeared were located on the *camino real* between Mexico and Guatemala (Chiapas was the actual or perceived origin of many diseases that struck Cuchumatán

49 Hidalgo (1797), writing in the *Gazeta de Guatemala* of 31 July.
50 AGCA, A1.47, leg. 385, exp. 8012.
51 Hidalgo (1797), writing in the *Gazeta de Guatemala* of 31 July.
52 AGCA, A1.47, leg. 385, exp. 8012, folios 2 to 3 verso.
53 AGCA, A1.47, leg. 192, exp. 3922; A1.4, leg. 61105, exp. 55836.
54 AGCA, A1.47, leg. 192, exp. 3922.

Indians throughout the colonial period), this main artery was ordered closed.[55] A *garita* or control point at either San Antonio or Santa Ana Huista was set up to ensure that trade and journeys originating in neighbouring Mexico with an eventual Guatemalan destination be strictly monitored. Theoretically, restrictions were placed on the movement of people and goods early in December 1802, but enforcement was lax; one official charged that the watch was anything but vigilant, remarking that "people have come and still come increasingly from all parts."[56] Commerce and the exercise of personal convenience often made quarantine an impractical charade, at the Huistas and elsewhere.

By the early nineteenth century, however, a development had taken place that was to alter irrevocably the relationship between smallpox and humankind, with considerable potential benefits for native communities like those of the Sierra de los Cuchumatanes. In 1798 Edward Jenner, an English country doctor, published his findings concerning inoculation against smallpox, documenting his observation that milkmaids seemed never to succumb to smallpox because, as he correctly hypothesized, they had developed an immunity to the disease by first contracting cowpox. Subsequent inoculation of human patients with cowpox matter, the medical risks of which were negligible, demonstrated that immunity to smallpox did in fact occur, thus establishing "vaccination" as the definitive preventative measure against the disease.[57]

Word of Jenner's breakthrough spread throughout Europe, and in Spain was responsible for the setting up of a medical mission to circulate news of "the fortunate English discovery"[58] throughout Spanish America. Headed by Doctor Francisco Xavier de Balmis, the mission set sail from the port of La Coruña on 30 November 1803, bound for Mexico (and the Philippines beyond) with the enlightened objective

55 AGCA, A1.4, leg. 6105, exp. 55836.
56 AGCA, A1.47. leg. 192, exp. 3922. "Han venido y vienen sin cesar," the official noted, "gentes de todas partes."
57 Baxby (1981, 38–88, 179–96); Razzell (1977, ix).
58 The designation, "feliz descubrimiento inglés" in the original, comes from a document in AGCA, A1.47, leg. 4027, exp. 31012. For extensive discussion of the Spanish medical mission, see S.F. Cook (1941, 1942) and M.M. Smith (1974). Both researchers worked with sources housed in the Archivo General de la Nación in Mexico City. Smith, however, also had microfilm access to two voluminous *legajos* (Indiferente General 1558A and 1558B) housed in the Archivo General de Indias in Seville. Their contents have more recently attracted the attention of Martha Few (2010), who mines them most assiduously.

of informing local doctors of Jenner's successful experiments in establishing immunity against smallpox by means of vaccination.[59]

Francisco Pastor, a member of the Balmis mission, is recorded as having arrived in Totonicapán from Chiapas and the Yucatán on 4 November 1804.[60] Much to the chagrin of the *alcalde mayor*, Colonel Prudencio de Cozar, Pastor did not leave behind a supply of vaccine, but proceeded instead directly to Guatemala City, from where both vaccine and instructions on how to use it were later disseminated.[61] The arrival of Pastor in Guatemala made it possible, from late 1804 on, for colonial authorities to initiate campaigns of vaccination against smallpox, campaigns in which the Indian population, because of its acknowledged vulnerability, was identified as the most important target group.

Regional committees were set up throughout Guatemala to supervise vaccination procedures, with medical personnel trained in the application of the new techniques paid as much as four pesos a day for their services.[62] One doctor active in the Sierra de los Cuchumatanes was Ignacio Ruiz, recorded in a document dated 12 May 1806 as having "a pleasant manner and style with the Indians, one that has resulted in the vaccination, by himself alone, of 10,127 persons in over fifty towns in the province of Totonicapán and Huehuetenango."[63] By 1807, thanks to the efforts of Ruiz and others, over 3,400 Indians had been vaccinated, the majority of them children aged fourteen years and under (table 25). While this figure, in an era not noted for its prompt response to medical innovations or progressive ideas, at first seem impressive, subsequent events did much to erode the beneficial impact of vaccination on indigenous welfare. Resistance from wary sectors of the native population was always a problem, as was lack of cooperation among Spanish residents, some of whom were threatened with prison sentences for neglecting to arrange for the vaccination of Indians.[64] Fear of procedure, apathy among the non-native elite, and problems related to vaccine supply and availability all contributed to periodic outbreaks of smallpox in Guatemala long

59 S.F. Cook (1941, 545–6).
60 AGCA, A1.4, leg. 6091, exp. 55306, folio 160.
61 AGCA, A1.4, leg. 6091, exp. 55306.
62 AGCA, A1.47, leg. 193, exp. 3939.
63 Ibid. The original attributes to Ruiz "buen modo y estilo con los indios, de que resulto haber vacunado por su mano 10,127 personas."
64 AGCA, A1.47, leg. 2162, exp. 15558; A1.47, leg. 385, exp. 8012; and A1.47, leg. 191, exp. 3905.

after the Balmis-Pastor initiatives.[65] None of these outbreaks, however, had the profound impact of earlier epidemics, and the result was sustained growth of the native population, despite local fluctuations. If Indian survival was not quite guaranteed, at least the intensity of one of its most lethal constraints had been significantly tempered.

"REDUCED TO A LIFE OF MISERY": TYPHUS (1796–1809)

Shortly after the smallpox epidemic of 1795–96, many towns in the Cuchumatanes were struck by an outbreak of typhus, another infectious disease long recognized in Guatemala as a first-rank killer of Indians.[66] Incidence is first documented for 21 November 1796, when the *alcalde mayor* of Totonicapán and Huehuetenango, Colonel Francisco Xavier de Aguirre, informed his superiors in Guatemala City that a feverish epidemic was raging in his district.[67] Aguirre singled out the community of Jacaltenango, stating that "many Indians in the town are dying."[68] He reported that the disease had already claimed the lives of over five hundred Jacaltekos, among them sixty-one tribute payers.[69] Of the survivors, Aguirre mentions that "many of these unfortunate people will die because of a lack of food and assistance."[70]

From Jacaltenango, typhus spread to the nearby town of Concepción where, between 7 September 1796 and 27 September

---

65 See, for example, AGCA, B.82.3, leg. 1095, exp. 24046; B.82.3, leg. 1095, exp. 24048; B.82.3, leg. 1095, exp. 24050; and B.82.3, leg. 1095, exp. 24069, all of which concern an outbreak of smallpox throughout Guatemala between 1829 and 1831. The Kaqchikel región was particularly hard hit, especially San Juan Comalapa and surrounding communities. More isolated outbreaks are recorded for San Miguel Totonicapán in 1824 (AGCA, B.68, leg. 98, exp. 2694); San Antonio and Santa Ana Huista in 1825 (AGCA, B.99.2, leg. 1412, exp. 32999); and the Verapaz in 1826 (AGCA, B82.3, leg. 3587, exp. 81954). Dunn (1829, 151–3) also comments on problems related to the eradication of smallpox in Guatemala.

66 Zinsser (1935, 253–64) and Martínez Durán (1940, 5–33). See MacLeod (1986, 7–15) for eighteenth-century data on Mexico.

67 AGCA, A1.24, leg. 6106, exp. 55666.

68 Ibid.

69 AGCA, A3.16, leg. 255, exp. 5719.

70 AGCA, A1.24, leg. 6106, exp. 55666, folio 1, the *alcalde mayor's* precise words being "muchos de los infelices naturales moririan por falta de alimentos y remedios." Aguirre later arranged for a doctor, Vicente Bolinaga, to spend over three months attending to the sick throughout the region. Bolinaga received for his services six pesos a day.

1797, another 500 Indians succumbed – and this in a community that only twelve years earlier had a total population of 608 people.[71] Only fifty-six tribute payers were left among those who survived.[72] To prevent the infection spreading further, over one hundred homes were ordered to be burned to the ground. Even such drastic measures, however, proved futile, because the disease soon appeared some fifteen kilometres to the south and east of Concepción in the Mam community of Todos Santos. There it carried off 488 people, over half the town's population, among them ninety-six tributaries. Todos Santos was left with a total population of around 380 people, fifty-five of whom were tribute payers.[73] Here, too, dwellings and properties were razed, over sixty in all. The neighbouring community of San Martín Cuchumatán was also affected. There, eighty-seven Indians perished, among them thirty-six tributaries, leaving only ninety-one sickly survivors, nineteen of whom were tribute payers.[74]

By 16 October 1798, the epidemic had spread east to Ixil country.[75] Two hundred victims were reported buried in the churchyard at San Gaspar Chajul, where the pestilence at its height caused the deaths of ten to twelve people each day.[76] San Juan Cotzal and Santa María Nebaj suffered equally high mortality; in the latter, as at Chajul, Indians rioted against some of the measures that were imposed in order to halt the spread of disease, specifically attempts by officials to have the dead buried not in the local churchyard but in consecrated ground some distance away.[77] Perhaps the greatest absolute loss of life in a single town occurred at San Sebastián Huehuetenango, a Mam community that in 1795 supported a population of 2,878 people. There, a total of 1,070 Indians were reported dead, 245 of them registered as tribute payers. The neighbouring settlements of San Juan Atitán and Santa Isabel were also badly hit.[78]

Because of the high incidence of death among the tribute-paying population at San Sebastián Huehuetenango and elsewhere, the authorities were forced to adjust downward the tax assessments of

71 Ibid., folio 28 and A 1.44, leg. 6097, exp. 55507.
72 AGCA, A 1.24, leg. 6106, exp. 55666, folio 28.
73 Ibid.
74 Ibid., folio 27.
75 Ibid.
76 AGCA, A 1.49, leg. 192, exp. 3911.
77 AGCA A 1.24, leg. 6101, exp. 55668 and A 1.49, leg. 6102, exp. 55699.
78 AGCA, A 1.49, leg. 192, exp. 3911, folio 51, and Hidalgo (1797), writing in the *Gazeta de Guatemala* of 13 November.

most afflicted towns. By the end of the eighteenth century, the number of tributaries registered as residents of Jacaltenango, San Martín Cuchumatán, Todos Santos, San Gaspar Chajul, and San Miguel Uspantán had been significantly lowered.[79] In the case of Concepción, Petatán, and Nebaj, the *alcalde mayor* went so far as to suggest that the Indians be relieved outright of the burden of tribute, so considerable was the mortality in these three towns.[80]

No records have come to light for the typhus outbreaks of 1796–99 that are comparable in detail to those that exist for the smallpox epidemic of 1780–81. However, data available for eight towns again indicate a marked spatial variation in the degree of mortality, suggesting that the differential impact of disease once more be viewed in relation to local conditions and circumstances (table 26). Lower mortality in Huehuetenango likely reflects the existence in the district capital of better care facilities and medical expertise, as well as the desire of the city's Spanish and Ladino inhabitants (who at the time comprised about 60 per cent of the town's population) to combat the contagion among Indian residents for fear that they themselves might be affected. Higher mortality in Concepción, by contrast, is indicative of an impoverished community composed entirely of Indians who lived on an isolated, inaccessible mountainside at an elevation approaching 2,500 metres, beyond the reach of any kind of remedial assistance. And while Huehuetenango, and even Jacaltenango, recovered numbers fairly soon after typhus struck, attaining their pre-contagion size within a decade, in other communities (for example, Todos Santos and San Martín Cuchumatán) population levels remained significantly lower for many more years (table 26).

The turn of the century saw a lull in sickness; from 1799 to 1802 few occurrences of typhus are documented. Then, in 1803, there was another dramatic outbreak, accompanied (in the *pueblos de indios* of Soloma parish) by measles, smallpox, and an invasion of locusts.[81]

Typhus seems first to have reappeared in Santa Eulalia and San Juan Ixcoy, wreaking considerable havoc.[82] According to Mariano

79 AGCA, A1.24, leg. 6102, exp. 55697; A3.1, leg. 2894, exp. 42486; A3.16, leg. 242, exp. 4814; and A3.16, leg. 244, exp. 4869.

80 AGCA, A1.24, leg. 6102, exp. 55697; A3.1, leg. 2894, exp. 42486; and A3.16, leg. 424, exp. 4814.

81 AGCA, A1, leg. 249, exp. 5036; A3.16, leg. 245, exp. 4909, folio 2; and Claxton (1986, 143 and 146–8).

82 AGCA, A1.4, leg. 6107, exp. 55898 and A1.4, leg. 6107, exp. 55899.

Larrave, a doctor tending the sick throughout the parish, 325 Indians had perished at Santa Eulalia by 29 February 1804, with countless others suffering from pains and fever.[83] Unlike smallpox, which resulted in consistently high mortality among children, typhus struck severely at the adult population; of the 325 victims Larrave reported, 103 were children and 222 were adults.[84] Since prior to the outbreak of typhus the population of Santa Eulalia numbered 2,531, these deaths already represent a mortality rate of 13 percent.[85] At San Juan Ixcoy, with a population half the size of Santa Eulalia, over 250 people had died by 11 August 1804, a mortality rate closer to 20 per cent.[86]

The most detailed information at hand comes from priests who served in the towns of Soloma parish, and from the reports compiled by medical personnel who were sent to help fight the spread of infection. Of the priests, Fray José María Orellana was particularly attentive. On 30 April 1804, he wrote to *alcalde mayor* Cozar, describing the situation in Santa Eulalia:

Though the pestilence continues with the same virulence, I will be unable to estimate how many Indians perish, because only an elder and one or two families remain in town. A large number has already fled to the coast. Others have settled on a tract of land called Payconó [Paiconop], which belongs to the Indians of San Miguel Acatán. Some [have taken refuge] in the warmer lowlands that belong to their own community. These people bring the bodies of victims, who die with no spiritual comfort whatsoever, back to their home town for burial.[87]

Largely because of Orellana's appeals to the *alcalde mayor*, arrangements were made for another doctor to be dispatched to care for those afflicted, Mariano Larrave apparently having left Soloma shortly after compiling his report on the sickness at Santa Eulalia, dated 29 February 1804. The task fell to an inexperienced young doctor named Mariano Francisco Lenteno, who arrived in Huehuetenango

83 AGCA, A1.4, leg. 6107, exp. 55899 and A1.4, leg. 6107, exp. 55900.
84 AGCA, A1.4, leg. 6107, exp. 55899.
85 AGCA, A1.16, leg. 243, exp. 4853.
86 Ibid.
87 AGCA, A1.4, leg. 6107, exp. 55898. Orellana may have erred when stating that Payconó [Paiconop] "corresponde al pueblo de San Miguel" since it was formerly where Santa Eulalia was once located. See chapter 6, footnote 37.

on 13 May 1804, after a short visit to Quetzaltenango to purchase medicines, provisions, and a mule team (both animals and a muleteer, or *mozo*) for the journey high into the Cuchumatanes.[88] From letters and reports Lenteno later wrote, it is obvious that he had doubts and misgivings about where he was travelling to, the sort of people he would be attending to, and what in general was expected of him. His trip was preceded by an unsettling incident in Huehuetenango, where he fell into conversation with an opinionated Spaniard, a certain Señor Aguayo, who painted a grim picture of what lay ahead. Lenteno records in his journal that "a dreadful description has been given me of the character of the Indians, their savageness, and the risks to my life, as well as the lack of proper relief work even to the extent of people starving to death."[89] Such snippets of information could hardly have calmed the doctor for a mission he clearly regarded with trepidation from the outset.

Lenteno arrived on 15 May 1804 at San Juan Ixcoy, where he found Father Orellana prostrate with fever.[90] The priest would later write that the doctor's arrival "has been a great consolation to me," adding "though my fever still rages, may by God's will I be not one of many."[91] On 16 May, Lenteno wrote to the *alcalde mayor*, telling him "there are indeed many sick" and requesting that a woman helper be sent to San Juan Ixcoy to prepare food and assist in tending the needy.[92] His request was granted, and along with the *cocinera* came a supply of flour, rice, sugar, and vinegar.[93] With that meagre but important assistance, Lenteno set about his work, which included a trip from San Juan Ixcoy seven kilometres north to San Pedro Soloma, and another journey ten kilometres farther north, over a difficult, rocky trail, to Santa Eulalia. On 24 May he confirmed Orellana's earlier report of Santa Eulalia's mass abandonment, stating that "left behind are but three or four families," the townsfolk having fled to the perceived refuge of the mountains, "where they

88 AGCA, A.14, leg. 6107, exp. 55898.

89 Ibid. Lenteno's precise words are: "Me ha hecho una pintura horrible del carácter de los indios, su ferocidad y los riesgos de mi vida, la falta de auxilios hasta el caso de morir de hambre."

90 Ibid.

91 Ibid. "De gran consuelo" Orellana says of Lenteno's arrival. And though "siguen mis calenturas," his faith allows him to believe in salvation, that "Dios quiera no sea yo uno de tantos."

92 Ibid.

93 Ibid. Vinegar was deployed as both a domestic and personal disinfectant.

die, evidently in even greater misery."[94] He estimated that, each day, four to six people succumbed. "Under these circumstances," Lenteno went on to say, "in order to help as best as conditions permit, I go from one dwelling to the next, carrying antiseptic potions and other medicines."[95] Houses were aired each day with a combination of vinegar and ammonia vapour. A vinegar solution was used to wash and rub the bodies of the sick, particularly their faces and arms.

Even with the woman cook and a male muleteer to help him, Lenteno was soon exhausted. Mentally, he adapted to the "fear and panic" with which the Indians invariably viewed his medical ministrations, holding himself back if he found them terrorized at the thought of being treated with unknown cures and remedies.[96] The image of the people and the place first given Lenteno by the Spanish resident of Huehuetenango remained unaltered, if not reinforced, by his experiences during the four months he spent in Soloma. In a summary of his work to the *alcalde mayor*, dated 6 August 1804, he stated that he found the Indians sadly negligent in matters of personal hygiene. "These people never clean themselves," Lenteno wrote, "nor their clothes or dwellings, which are just like those where chickens and other domestic animals are kept."[97] He added, revealingly, that the Indians recognized no Spanish authority whatsoever, not even that of the parish priest, whom Lenteno claimed had no influence over his charges.[98]

The havoc and destruction wrought by typhus persisted in Soloma for the rest of 1804 and all the following year. On 8 May 1806, Fray Juan José Juárez, who replaced or assisted José María Orellana as parish priest, wrote to the *alcalde mayor* requesting that, on account of disease-related poverty, the Indians of Santa Eulalia be granted a pardon from their tributary obligations for the years 1804 and 1805, the people of San Miguel Acatán likewise for the year 1805.[99] Juárez points out the "miserable situation" in which Indians of Santa

94 Ibid.
95 Ibid. Lenteno's precise words are: "En estas circunstancias para socorrerles del modo que lo permiten, voy a sus casas llevando pociones antisépticas, tisanas y otras medicinas."
96 Ibid.
97 AGCA, A1.4, leg. 6107, exp. 55940. "Nunca limpian sus personas," the original reads, "vestidos ni habitaciones, que son igualmente de las gallinas y otros animales domésticos."
98 Ibid.
99 AGCA, A3.16, leg. 249, exp. 5036.

Eulalia and San Miguel Acatán had existed "since the first attacks of fever struck in 1803."[100] Citing local death registers for Santa Eulalia for the years 1803 to 1806, Juárez reported 1,039 typhus victims, which indicates a mortality rate of over 40 per cent.[101]

A request for tribute exemption was also submitted by the Indian leaders of San Pedro Soloma. The appeal once again was made on the grounds of impoverishment arising directly from the impact of contagion. Native representatives sought pardon from the *alcalde mayor* by mentioning specifically that "because we gave refuge in our homes to those who came from Santa Eulalia, fleeing the pestilence, our town was contaminated also, and many tribute payers died. Now, because we gave them corn so that they might eat, perhaps we will all go hungry this year [1806] and the next."[102]

When typhus broke out in Santa Eulalia, Indians from there not only fled south to San Pedro Soloma but also scattered west towards Concepción, a distance of some twenty-two kilometres. This piece of evidence comes from Francisco de Paula López, a Mercedarian friar who served as the parish priest of Jacaltenango. Paula López reports having come across, in November 1804, many people from Santa Eulalia who now lived in the mountains around Concepción.[103] In response to his inquiry as to how they came to be there, Paula López was told that "since the previous year they have fled, in great numbers, a feverish pestilence in their own community," and that many of the destitute and hungry "roamed the hills for eleven months" before arriving at Concepción.[104] Having seen the sorry state of the survivors, some lying sick and unclad, Paula López persuaded the Indians of Concepción, who themselves had suffered horrendously from typhus only eight years before, to provide the hapless refugees with land on which to grow corn, lest they starve to death.[105] Such desperate circumstances were later recounted by Juan José Juárez in his plea to the *alcalde mayor* that Santa Eulalia be granted a tribute

100 Ibid., folio 4.
101 Ibid., folio 4 verso.
102 Ibid., folio 1. "Por dar posada en nuestras casas a los que vinieron de Santa Eulalia," the native leaders state, "se enfermó nuestro pueblo y se murió mucha gente tributarios de Soloma que por darles maíz para que coma, tal vez vamos a tener hambre con ellos en este y en el año que entra de 1807."
103 Ibid., folio 3.
104 Ibid. "Desde el año anterior," the original reads, "andavan huyendo de una peste de calenturas."
105 Ibid.

exemption for 1804 and 1805.[106] In describing the wretched condition of his parishioners, Juárez likens them to "birds without a nest, flying aimlessly all over the countryside, without belongings, without parents, without children, and naked – oh, what suffering!"[107] The plight of those afflicted, however, is nowhere more poignantly conveyed than in a letter written on 5 May 1806 by the Ladino *comisionado*, or constable, of Soloma parish, Marcos Castañeda. His words, addressed to the *alcalde mayor*, capture a vivid sense of the tragedy in the way only an attentive eyewitness could:

> For four years now in the towns of Soloma there has been great distress due to the deaths caused by the typhus epidemic, which kills the Indians without relief or remedy, leaving them only in dire hardship. Through fear of death, we [the Ladino residents Marcos and Santiago Castañeda] fled with our families to the solitude of the mountains and the rocky wastes of Chemal, suffering there from the extremity of the climate, leaving our houses and possessions abandoned in Soloma. But God having seen fit to end this terrible affliction, we have returned once again to our homes.
>
> We find that the majority of the Indians of Santa Eulalia have perished and are lying unburied all over the place, their decaying corpses eaten by the animals that stalk the countryside. Because of this and the fact that countless sheep also perished, neglected in their pens, the pestilence raged even more. What grieves us most, however, as it would any pious heart, is to see the great number of orphaned children crying for the laps of their parents, asking for bread without having anyone to receive it from; to behold many widows and widowers mourning the loss of their consorts; and to watch old people lament the death of their offspring. After so much hard work, these unfortunate Indians have been reduced to a life of misery. Having come back to town [the Indians who survived] are without homes to live in, without resources to pay their expenses and tribute, and without corn to feed themselves and their families. If no measures are taken to assist these wretched people, they will without doubt starve to

106 Ibid., folios 4 and 5.

107 Ibid., folio 4 verso. The priest's precise words are "pájaros sin nido, errantes de monte en monte, de alero a alero, sin casas, sin bienes, sin padres, sin hijos y desnudos. ¡Que dolor!"

death, because they did not plant corn in the places where they sought refuge and so have nothing to live on, both for this year and for next, since it is now too late to plant their fields. It is a common thing in this parish to encounter Indians from Santa Eulalia, old and young alike, walking from town to town, from house to house, begging and searching for corn or charity. Others seek loans, leaving as security one of their children, for they have nothing else to offer.

Señor Alcalde Mayor, because I witness these setbacks from such close quarters, for the sake of God and a sign of His mercy, inform the President that help should be extended to the towns of this parish. At the very least, the people of Santa Eulalia and San Miguel Acatán could be exempted from paying tribute for the years during which they have suffered such great misfortune.[108]

Castañeda, writing three years later, reckoned that the typhus outbreak took the lives "of three-quarters of the Indians of San Miguel Acatán and Santa Eulalia," and stated that most survivors were rendered "destitute and homeless because their houses were burned to rid them of the contagion."[109] Assistance in the form of food, medicine, and a medical team was eventually forthcoming. Appeals that the Indians be given a full reprieve from paying tribute, however, met with no success. Prudencio de Cozar, the *alcalde mayor* to whom much of the above correspondence was directed, was able to secure only a temporary respite.[110] Inability on Cozar's part to gain a complete pardon incensed Father Juárez. "It seems to me that what is more important to you is that the Indians pay their tribute [so that] you receive your salary," he wrote scornfully to Cozar. "But I doubt if the Indians will be able to deliver, either this year or later, for they are sick and hungry and have nothing to pay with, since their crops are already lost."[111]

108 Ibid., folio 2.

109 AGCA, A3.14, leg. 386, exp. 8037, folio 8. "Tres cuartas partes de la población indígena," the original states, with those who survived "pobrísimos, sin ningunos bienes [y] sin casas, porque se quemaron para liberarlos de contagio."

110 AGCA, A.1.47, leg. 2162, exp. 15559; A3.16, leg. 249, exp. 5036; and A1.14, leg. 386, exp. 8037.

111 AGCA, A3.16, leg. 2899, exp. 43049. "Me parece que lo que importa más a Usted es el sueldo" are the priest's scathing words. So disgusted was Father Juárez

The bitter resignation in Father Juárez's address hints at the apathy, ineptitude, and lack of responsibility that bureaucrats in distant seats of authority showed in times of crisis. Such woeful disregard must have numbed the few Spanish priests and Ladino officials who managed to conduct their duties with some sense of obligation toward their native charges. In Soloma parish typhus lingered, with brutal devastation, for many years after its appearance in 1803, spreading sickness and death from San Juan Ixcoy in the south to San Mateo Ixtatán in the north, from Santa Eulalia in the east to San Miguel Acatán (and beyond) in the west.[112] Even during an epidemic involving great loss of life and appalling human suffering, an appropriate course of action, such as the suspension of all tributary obligations, proved too much for government bureaucracy to arrange.

"BEYOND THE REACH OF MAN"

Though the grief and despair of those affected command our most immediate attention, the episodes discussed above are also revealing from a demographic and epidemiological perspective. Of particular interest is the notable variation in the fate of *pueblos de indios* when exposed to epidemic disease. Thus, while the smallpox epidemic of 1780–81 resulted in the loss of approximately 4,200 lives, or 15 per cent mortality over the Cuchumatán region as a whole, death rates fluctuated significantly at the community level, from 8 per cent to 38 per cent. Variable local conditions best explain this complex pattern of differential mortality. Although smallpox was virulent and widespread enough in 1780–81 to reduce the size of the regional population, such a decline did not occur during a renewed outbreak of the disease fifteen years later. Nor did the regional population plummet in the wake of typhus epidemics in 1796–69 and 1803–09, even though these two outbreaks caused high mortality in the parishes of both Jacaltenango and Soloma. It was therefore possible for the spatial impact of outbreaks of pestilence to be quite localized – that is, for sickness to affect some communities without necessarily reaching (and devastating) adjoining or surrounding ones. In fact, a regional population profile like that pieced together for the Sierra de los Cuchumatanes, with downward and upward trends over time,

that he offered to pay Cozar's salary himself – "sí gusta se lo cobraré y se lo remitiré" – as it was beyond the means of the Indians to do so.

112 AGCA, A1.47, leg. 2162, exp. 15559 and A1.4, leg. 6107, exp. 55898.

is likely to conceal considerable fluctuation at the sub-regional (community or parish) level.[113] Such a dynamic suggests that, while studies in historical demography may be of assistance in the formulation of general principles governing the relationship between population movement and epidemic disease, they must also be cognizant of nuances of time and place.

Not by "secret judgments of God," then, but the spread of disease among vulnerable native populations did the Spanish conquest of America cause a demographic collapse that, in all probability, was the most catastrophic the world has ever known. In the Cuchumatán highlands, the magnitude and rapidity of native depopulation following first contact conforms to a pattern already well established for other parts of Latin America.[114] A population of perhaps 260,000 on the eve of conquest, roughly the same size as the mid-twentieth-century population of the region, had by 1680 declined to around 16,000, a fall of more than 90 per cent over a period of 160 years. While disease-related mortality was most massive and widespread in the century and a half immediately following European intrusion, death due to Old World contagion was a characteristic feature of late colonial times as well. By the last quarter of the seventeenth century, however, a process of demographic recovery had begun that continued throughout the eighteenth and nineteenth centuries. For most of this time, population increase was slow and sporadic because of the persistent outbreak of diseases to which Indians only gradually acquired immunities. Not until the beginning of the twentieth century did the native population of Guatemala begin to increase sharply, thanks to the impact of modern medical technology in substantially reducing rates of human mortality. By 1950, after a process of decline, recovery, and growth lasting over four hundred years, the population of the Cuchumatán highlands reached a level equivalent to that which it may have been before the arrival of the Spaniards and their pestilential allies.

113 For an illustration of this tendency, see Collins (1980, 48–58), which indicates that data for Jacaltenango do not fit the general Cuchumatán pattern.

114 See chapter 5 and Lovell and Lutz (2013, 173–83).

10

Conclusion: Refuge in the Mountains

Between the idea
And the reality
Between the motion
And the act
Falls the shadow
T.S. Eliot, *The Hollow Men* (1925)

By the opening years of the sixteenth century, the native peoples of the Cuchumatán highlands had broken away, after two or three generations of subjugation, from the hegemony of the K'iche' of Gumarcaah. Their newly won autonomy was not to last for long. Between 1525 and 1530, Maya communities in the Sierra de los Cuchumatanes came face to face with an outside force far more formidable than anything they had ever before confronted: the might and vision of imperial Spain. The Spanish conquest of the region was sustained and bloody, advanced considerably by Indian allies fighting on the side of the invaders. Military opposition was widespread, but particularly marked among the Mam, the Ixil, and the K'iche'an peoples of Uspantán. By 1530, however, overt physical resistance had come to an end, and the region entered an era of Spanish domination that was to last almost three hundred years.

Throughout the colonial period, Spaniards who sought fame and fortune found that other parts of Central America had more to offer them than did the Cuchumatán highlands. The Indian slave trade in Nicaragua and Honduras; silver mining in the hills around Tegucigalpa; the cultivation of cacao in Soconusco, Suchitepéquez, Guazacapán, and Izalcos; cattle raising and the indigo dye industry in the *tierra templada* to the south and east of Santiago de Guatemala – all these activities were more alluring for materially minded Spaniards than the few exploitable resources of the remote, rugged

Sierra de los Cuchumatanes. Furthermore, beyond supplying much-needed labour to the cacao plantations of the Pacific coast, the region had little direct participation in the great economic cycles that had such a dramatic and long-lasting impact elsewhere in the isthmus.[1] If, in terms of its colonial status and fiscal relationship with the mother country, Central America was indeed "the richest of the poor, or the poorest of the rich," then the Cuchumatán region must surely have ranked among imperial Spain's least prized possessions.[2] Diego de Garcés, the *alcalde mayor* of Zapotitlán, certainly believed that little was to be gained by establishing oneself there. When, in 1570, he declared it "tierra pobre y estéril, salvo de maíz y gallinas que hay en abundancia," Garcés was voicing a majority opinion.[3] A "poor and unfruitful land" where the "only plentiful things to be had are corn and chickens" could hardly capture the imagination of an enterprising Spaniard.

The Garcés appraisal is difficult to refute, for the Cuchumatán highlands were (and in many ways are still) a backwater, a periphery within a periphery.[4] The region's isolation and limited economic potential, however, did not mean that its lands and peoples went unnoticed and untouched. Given the nature of the Hispanic quest for empire, and the operation of certain processes initiated merely by European presence, no such outcome was possible. The colonial experience in the Cuchumatanes was marked by differences of degree, not of kind, from that in the rest of Central America.

In the middle years of the sixteenth century, Cuchumatán Indians were persuaded or forced to leave their old homes in the mountains and relocate in new church-dominated *congregaciones*. Spanish authorities undertook the creation of these *pueblos de indios* not only to facilitate native conversion to Christianity but also to form centralized pools of exploitable labour. In so doing, *congregación* produced a more orderly pattern of settlement that contrasted (at least in the eyes of the conquerors) with the scattered arrangements of pre-Hispanic times. Although its imprint persists to this day, *congregación* was not without its failures and frustrations. From the outset, rugged and

1 MacLeod ([1973] 2008).

2 The designation is that of Pierre and Huguette Chaunu, as rendered in MacLeod ([1973] 2008, lvii).

3 AGI, Guatemala 52, "Diego de Garcés to the Council of the Indies" (ca. 1560), a transcription of which may be found in Carmack (1973, 379–83).

4 See C.A. Smith (1978) and Lovell and Lutz (2013, 77–95) for a theorization of core-periphery schema in Guatemala.

inaccessible terrain hampered effective Spanish penetration beyond the immediate environs of *pueblos de indios*, leaving scores of native families well outside the reach of civil and religious authority. Moreover, deep-rooted cultural preferences for more dispersed ways of living, ones that did not sever the bond between Indian communities and the lands of their ancestors, eroded the effectiveness of *congregación*. This was especially the case during the seventeenth and eighteenth centuries when, with Spanish precepts of law and order seemingly ever more difficult to enforce, increasing numbers of families abandoned *congregaciones* for outlying rural areas. Flight was also triggered by the desire to escape the exploitation and oppression that came in various legal and extra-legal forms as long as native families stayed put in *congregaciones*. The centrifugal movement away from *pueblos de indios* was accompanied by a revival of pre-Christian rites and rituals, a development that was just as distasteful to officialdom as the fact that the fugitive Indians no longer contributed to the support of the colony or the enrichment of the Crown.

During early colonial times, the key factor in generating wealth for Spaniards was control of native labour, not native land. Drawn to Central America first and foremost as entrepreneurs who sought to profit from the work of others, Spanish conquerors and colonists turned to the acquisition of land only after their search for gold, silver, or a successful cash crop – a *produit moteur* – proved fruitless.[5] Apart from a few early titles in the Huehuetenango area, the taking up of land in the Sierra de los Cuchumatanes on the part of Spaniards began significantly only during the seventeenth century, when a sluggish economy meant that frugal self-sufficiency was not without advantage. The trend continued throughout the eighteenth century as Spaniards who acquired land in the region, particularly on the alpine meadows of the Altos de Chiantla, recognized the benefits of raising livestock, especially sheep. Though sizable *haciendas* were created, precipitating conflict between Spaniards and Indians over land rights and boundaries, the emergence of such estates did not erode the indigenous land base entirely. Some *pueblos de indios*, particularly in the south, may have found their holdings insufficient to pay their tribute and to feed their populations, but they held on tenaciously to what they had. Other Indian communities, especially those

---

5 MacLeod ([1973] 2008, 374–5) makes the case most convincingly, his notion of a *produit moteur* again inspired by the work of Pierre and Huguette Chaunu.

along the northern Lacandón frontier bordering fertile and sparsely settled *tierra caliente*, were never troubled by a shortage of land.

Under Spanish rule, the native population was introduced not only to a new religion, language, and set of customs; it was also exposed, as occurred throughout the Americas, to diseases brought by the invaders from the Old World. The effects of this inadvertent transfer were devastating. Ravaged time and again by epidemic outbreaks, Indian populations in the region between 1520 and about 1680 fell from possibly 260,000 to around 16,000, a drop of over 90 per cent in a century and a half. Although, by the end of the colonial era, native numbers had doubled in size from their nadir, demographic recovery was both sporadic and intermittent; Cuchumatán Indians only slowly acquired immunities to contagions long endemic to the Spaniards. Repeated outbreaks of sickness were debilitating, their impact on Indian life profound. When disease broke out, it invariably precipitated a chain of events, including catastrophic mortality, the inability of stricken towns to pay tribute, and the failure to plant fields for the year ahead. Famine, misery, and a wretched existence were then never far off, and only increased susceptibility to renewed outbreaks of pestilence. With the recurrence of such unforeseen setbacks, imperial expectations soon proved naïve and unattainable. The motion of conquest carried within it, hidden in blood and breath, disastrous acts that were a people's scourge and the ruin of an empire. More than any other single factor, the unleashing of Old World diseases on a vulnerable native population caused a shadow to fall between the idea and the reality of Spanish colonial rule, not only in the Cuchumatán highlands of Guatemala but throughout the entire Hispanic American realm.

Epilogue

They are an introverted people, consumed by internal fires which they
cannot or dare not express, eternally chafing under the yoke of conquest,
and never for a moment forgetting that they are a conquered people.

Oliver La Farge, *Santa Eulalia:*
The Religion of Cuchumatán Indian Town (1947)

Why, four decades after I started out, do I continue to write about
colonial Guatemala? I get asked that question often enough to be
able to answer it directly: I write about colonial Guatemala in order
to understand the country as it exists today.

Despite theoretical literature that lays claim to the contrary, for
me there is little "postcolonial" about how present-day Guatemala
operates. How Guatemala is run, how its resources are appropri-
ated, exploited, and profited from, how its ethnic groups relate and
coexist in a troubled nation state, how its Maya peoples (those of
the Cuchumatán highlands a dozen or so among twenty) endured
further assaults on their land and their lives in the nineteenth and
twentieth centuries to sustain a presence in the twenty-first – these
elemental features register fully only when viewed in colonial perspective. Guatemalan historian Severo Martínez Peláez insists on
this point. "The detailed picture of colonial life I have lavished upon
readers," he states when summing up *La Patria del Criollo*, "furnishes them with all the information they need to assess its *current*
significance." The word in italics, faithful to the original, is his, not
mine. "Colonial reality," Martínez Peláez concludes, "is our everyday reality."[1] Guatemalans of all stripes – Ladino or Indian, rich or
poor, urban or rural – live and die in the shadow of a colonial past
that haunts them still.

---

1 Martínez Peláez ([1970] 2009, 274). For an incisive critique of his work, an
enduring frame of reference for generations of Central American students and scholars, see Mallon (2011).

Let me begin, then, by commenting on recent works that have advanced our knowledge of Mesoamerica in general, Guatemala and Central America more specifically. There have been several notable developments, indeed some exciting new discoveries that reinforce the connections between the past and the present, indicating that though profound changes have occurred in Guatemala between the sixteenth century and the twenty-first, visceral traits persist.

CONTEXT AND PERSPECTIVE

In terms of English-language historiography, two projects long in the making stand out as landmark contributions. The first is the three-volume *Oxford Encyclopedia of Mesoamerican Cultures*, for which David Carrasco (2001) served as editor-in-chief; the second is the three-volume *Cambridge History of the Native Peoples of the Americas*, volume 2 of which, edited by Richard E.W. Adams and Murdo J. MacLeod (2000), deals with Mesoamerica.

Assembling the *Oxford Encyclopedia*, Carrasco informs us, called for him to work with a team of ten editors, sixteen advisors, and more than three hundred scholars to put together a grand total of 617 entries, each with an annotated bibliography referring readers to key sources. The whole, an elaborate gestalt, is considerably more than the sum of its parts. Carrasco reminds us at the outset that Mesoamerica is "the site of two major cultural transformations in Western Hemisphere history." The first involved "the complex evolution from the social world of the village to urbanized cultures," aspects of which are sketched out in chapter 3. A second transformation entailed "the encounter between Europe and the Americas," one that "fundamentally changed the course of human history," the core of this book. Rather than dwell on the disruptive and far-reaching effects of that encounter, Carrasco emphasizes that "natives, European settlers, and slaves from sub-Saharan Africa formed distinctive ... social, religious, and political relationships" that led to "new ways of being and constructing culture." He acknowledges that "colonial patterns are also periodically brought back to our contemporary consciousness, as demonstrated in the attention given to the Zapatista insurrection in Chiapas," which occurred on 1 January 1994, the very day that the North American Free Trade Agreement struck between Canada, Mexico, and the United States came into being. Grim civil strife in Guatemala between 1962 and 1996 is another case in point of "colonial patterns" jolting "our contemporary consciousness."[2]

If Carrasco downplays the destructive, in certain areas obliterating consequences of conquest, he is more trenchant when identifying three crucial developments behind his decision to orchestrate such an ambitious project. He singles out (1) innovative archaeological excavations; (2) remarkable progress in linguistics and in the decipherment of Maya hieroglyphic writing; and (3) sophisticated analyses of colonial and modern predicaments, which he attributes in large measure to the unearthing of "inventories and descriptions ... that were written by Indians, *mestizos*, and Euro-Americans." These records complement or run counter to "conquest narratives" produced by European protagonists, imperial bureaucracy, and traditional historiographical perspectives. Carrasco stresses, most importantly, that "Mesoamerica is not to be understood only in pre-Hispanic terms,"[3] the temporal frame of such influential researchers as William T. Sanders and Barbara J. Price (1968) and, more recently, Michael E. Smith and Frances F. Berdan (2003).

Critical discussions of historiography are found throughout the *Oxford Encyclopedia*. Carrasco points out how the intellectual labours he oversees differ from, but build on, the *Handbook of Middle American Indians* (HMAI), which appeared in sixteen volumes between 1964 and 1976, with Robert Wauchope (1964–76) serving as general editor. Six further volumes of the HMAI were published subsequently, under the general editorship of Victoria R. Bricker (1981–92). Bricker's HMAI volumes, in which epigraphy, ethnohistory, linguistics, and native texts figure prominently, offset what Carrasco considers the "anthropological perspective"[4] of their predecessors, though four volumes edited by Howard F. Cline (1972–75) serve as an admirable survey of ethnohistorical sources.

It is in matters relating to ethnohistory that Carrasco sees the *Oxford Encyclopedia* as differing most from the HMAI. The latter, he states, functions as an inventory of a "substantial body of written materials"; the former, more reflective of changing research interests, reports on investigations devoted to "politics and states, religion and

2 Carrasco (2001, vol. 1, ix).
3 Ibid., x.
4 Ibid., xi.

symbolism, social history and economic institutions, and missionaries and lay societies." What Carrasco terms "new disciplinary orientations" receive special attention in the *Oxford Encyclopedia*, among them gender studies and native textual production.[5] Some of these novel approaches, we will see, characterize recent research on Guatemala.

In shaping the *Cambridge History*, Adams and MacLeod worked with a score or so colleagues to steer to completion twenty-one essays that, like those in the *Oxford Encyclopedia*, trace the cultural evolution of Mesoamerica from earliest times to the close of the twentieth century. Part 1 of volume 2, edited by Adams, deals with archaeology; part 2 of volume 2, edited by MacLeod, focuses on history. Whereas many entries in the *Oxford Encyclopedia* are no more than a few pages, the chapters of the *Cambridge History* mostly run between forty and fifty pages, with bibliographical synopses complementing substantive narrative expositions. Adams prefers archaeology that is field-driven; his contributors generally eschew theory and deliver the goods in the form of minute findings, not lofty ruminations. MacLeod likes his history culled from the archives, but with the fine grain of documentary evidence throwing light on the big picture and the *long durée*. Adams believes that "Marxist models" do no justice at all to archeological inquiry and leans heavily on Anglo-American viewpoints when relaying information to the reader.[6] MacLeod handles the writing of Mesoamerican history more ecumenically.

Not everyone appreciates the results, and Adams, MacLeod, and their contributors have come in for stern criticism not only for what is in the *Cambridge History* but also for what is not. Robert W. Patch, for instance, finds the pedagogic principles upon which Adams operates "not only inaccurate but patronizing," and chastises MacLeod for having secured the services of but one Mexican scholar, María Ángeles Romero Frizzi, and no Guatemalans.[7] Patch, however, recognizes that sources of information other than those available in English are well represented, an opinion not shared by Serge Gruzinski (2002), who faults Adams and MacLeod both for the actual content of their solicitations and what he considers lamentable omissions. The slighting of French-language scholarship in

5 Ibid., xii.
6 Adams, in Adams and MacLeod (2000, vol. 2, part 1, 12). Arroyo and Salinas (2013) sum up the state of archaeological research in Guatemala most diligently.
7 Patch (2002).

particular pains him. In the final analysis, Adams, MacLeod, and the investigators with whom they corresponded over a period of ten years have much to show for their collective endeavour.

In terms of Spanish-language historiography, two general histories now exist, one for Guatemala, another for Central America. The former, coordinated by Jorge Luján Muñoz (1993–99), is a lavish enterprise that draws on international expertise as well as the talents of Guatemalan researchers; the latter, a less extravagant undertaking under the editorship of Edelberto Torres-Rivas (1994), also features the joint efforts of Central Americans and non-Central Americans. Ideologically, the six volumes of the *Historia General de Guatemala* tend to be more conservative than the six volumes of the *Historia General de Centroamérica*. No single enterprise better distils what we know about Central America than the historical atlas of Carolyn Hall and Héctor Peréz-Brignoli (2003), in which the creative cartography of John V. Cotter is a major asset. Of similar import, and impact, in relation to Guatemala alone is a historical atlas for which the indefatigable Jorge Luján Muñoz (2011) again assumed editorial control. Temporal coverage in all four of these projects spans the entire period of human settlement. The pages of *Mesoamérica*, three and a half decades after the journal first appeared, continue to function as a premier forum for debate and the dissemination of research findings, with an *Índice General* (2008) serving as an inventory of its contents between 1980 and 2008.

THE QUINCENTENNIAL IMPACT

In Mesoamerican studies, the years immediately prior to the Columbus Quincentennial in 1992 saw more and more researchers focus attention on geographical regions other than central Mexico, a trend that has continued. The cultural core, with its rich source materials and intriguing complexity, still dominates the literature, but neglected areas like the Cuchumatán highlands are now better represented. Such a development indicates a healthy process of maturation, although much remains to be done.

This book, then, occupies less of a vacuum than before. In the Central American context, two exceptional monographs by Linda A. Newson (1986, 1987) examine the historical geography of Honduras and Nicaragua, whose colonial experiences were markedly different from those of Guatemala, especially in terms of indigenous survival.

This is true also of El Salvador and Costa Rica, as shown by the investigations of William R. Fowler (1989) and Carolyn Hall (1985). For Yucatán, the work of Nancy Farriss (1984) stresses the theme of Maya resistance to Spanish rule, as do studies by Inga Clendinnen (1987) and Grant D. Jones (1989), the latter dealing with a frontier zone straddling what is today the northern half of Belize, part of the Guatemalan department of El Petén, and a portion of Mexico's Quintana Roo. For other areas of southern Mexico, inquiries by Jan Gasco (1987) and Rodney Watson (1990) scrutinize aspects of native life in Soconusco and highland Chiapas, which in colonial times were administered as part of the Audiencia of Guatemala. Further north, in Oaxaca, John K. Chance (1989) reconstructs relations between Spaniards and Indians in the isolated Sierra Zapoteca, in many respects a Mexican equivalent of the Sierra de los Cuchumatanes.

Our knowledge of colonial Guatemala has profited in recent years from the research of several scholars. The role of the Catholic Church in forging an Indian "west" and a Ladino "east" is explored by Adriaan C. van Oss (1986). Lawrence H. Feldman (1986) has analyzed production systems and distribution patterns in the much-overlooked Oriente. A similar concern with economic geography pervades the study by Jorge Luján Muñoz (1988) of the valley and environs of Santiago de Guatemala, which functioned for most of the colonial period as the capital city of a jurisdiction stretching from Chiapas and Soconusco in the north to the border between Costa Rica and Panama in the south. Ralph H. Vigil (1987) charts the life and times of Alonso de Zorita, a Crown official who, like President Alonso López de Cerrato, tried around the middle of the sixteenth century to impose royal authority by enforcing the New Laws in Guatemala. The tumultuous first years of conquest and colonization, we noted in chapter 6, are expertly handled by Wendy Kramer (1994), whose reconstruction of the early operation of *encomienda* breaks scholarly ground. Long overshadowed in the literature by their K'ich'e neighbours, the Kaqchikel Maya engage the interest of Barbara E. Borg (1986) and Robert M. Hill (1989, 1991), with the former coordinating with C. Roger Nance and Stephen L. Whittington (2003) a volume that also features contributions by George Guillemin and Sergio Rodas Manrique. The ethnohistory of the Tzutuhil Maya is likewise now better known, Sandra Orellana (1984) having devoted an entire volume to the study of their communities. Orellana (1987) has also written about native medical practices before and after Spanish intrusion. Discontent erupting into localized rebellion is touched on by María del Carmen León Cázares (1988) and Severo Martínez Peláez (1985), but receives the rigorous attention of Aaron Pollack (2005, 2008), who focuses on the Totonicapán uprising that took place in 1820 and had a "spillover effect" on the Cuchumatanes (see chapter 7). Music as a vehicle for acculturating the Maya is discussed insightfully by Dieter Lehnhoff (1986). Issues of acculturation in general figure prominently in Elías Zamora's depiction of continuity and change in the province of Suchitepéquez and Zapotitlán (1985). His regional perspective is mirrored by Michel Bertrand's portrayal of land and society in Rabinal and the Baja Verapaz (1987). The community studies of Sajcabajá by Jean Piel (1989) and of Sacapulas by Robert M. Hill and John Monaghan (1987) may best be described as historically informed ethnography. The latter is the more ambitiously executed of the two and, apart from *Conquest and Survival in Colonial Guatemala*, is the only book-length publication to date that seeks to illuminate what happened to Maya peoples in the Cuchumatán highlands under Spanish rule.

With the literature mentioned above furnishing a general Mesoamerican backdrop, we now turn to further details about the colonial and post-colonial experiences of Maya peoples in the Sierra de los Cuchumatanes.

INNOVATION AND CONSOLIDATION

Research on Guatemala is being enriched not only by the continued productivity of established scholars but by a new generation of investigators often inspired by a notably different agenda than that of their predecessors. This development holds true as much for what is being written about the colonial period as for the nineteenth and twentieth centuries. Native participation in academic work is also growing.

Indigenous perspectives on the conquest, and representation of their roles in it, have been furthered admirably by the work of Florine Asselbergs on the magnificent *Lienzo de Quauhquechollan* (see chapter 4). So rich is this remarkable source that one pictorial sequence alone has been scrutinized by Ruud van Akkeren (2002) to reconstruct hitherto undocumented Spanish forays into the Verapaz region in the early sixteenth century. Van Akkeren (2007) has since synthesized other important findings on what he explicitly calls "the indigenous vision of the conquest," very much how Laura E.

Matthew (2012) frames her work on the Nahua, Mixtec, and Zapotec auxiliaries who came from Mexico to fight alongside the Spaniards in subduing Guatemala. Matthew teams up with Michel J. Oudijk (2007) to showcase a number of studies of indigenous agency throughout Mesoamerica, adroitly articulated for the Sierra Norte of Oaxaca by Yanna Yannakakis (2008).

Collaborative synergy is also apparent in the production of a new edition of the sixteenth-century Kaqchikel manuscript *Memorial de Sololá*. Unlike the *Lienzo de Quauhquechollan*, the *Memorial de Sololá* has been a well-known indigenous source ever since Daniel Brinton (1885) in the nineteenth century and Adrián Recinos in the twentieth published their celebrated translations, Brinton directly into English, Recinos first into Spanish (1950) and then into English (1953) in partnership with Delia Goetz. Neither Brinton nor Recinos, however, were native speakers of Kaqchikel. Gifted though both men were, having the *Memorial de Sololá* translated by a group in which native speakers of the language have their say is most advantageous. With Simón Otzoy (1999) at the helm, ably assisted by fellow Kaqchikel linguists Martin Chacach and Narciso Cojtí, as well as historians Jorge Luján Muñoz and J. Daniel Contreras, the appearance of a facsimile version of the *Memorial de Sololá*, complete with an annotated translation in Spanish, represents another major step forward. The results are subjected to critical scrutiny by Christopher H. Lutz and James Mondloch (2002), the former from an ethnohistorical perspective, the latter from a linguistic one. Judith M. Maxwell and Robert M. Hill II (2006) have rendered the *Memorial de Sololá* into free-flowing English along with another Kaqchikel text, the *Xpantzay Cartulary*, once again aided in their labours by native speakers. Working with Karen Dakin, Lutz (1996) has furnished us with commentary on the plaintive accounts left by Indians living near Santiago de Guatemala on the tyranny that was their lot around the year 1572, when the judge Valdés de Cárcomo not only turned a blind eye to blatant excesses but indulged in them himself.

In addition to unprecedented levels of Maya involvement, younger scholars are leaving their mark by moving beyond traditional historiographical concerns (land, labour, tribute, settlement, colonization, demography, religion, trade, and commerce) to discuss matters related to race, gender, ethnicity, and identity. Among these are Alvis Dunn (1999), Greg Grandin (2000), Leonardo Hernández (1999), Robinson Herrera (2003), Catherine Komisaruk (2013), Paul Lokken

(2000, 2008, 2013), and Ruud van Akkeren (2000a, 2000b). By establishing that women, not just men, played influential roles, by weaving their stories into the fabric of colonial life, Martha Few (1995, 1999, 2002) has begun to fill a void. Although on first inspection Few's examination of Inquisition records would appear to have limited resonance – she concentrates on *mujeres de mal vivir*, women who lead evil lives, allegedly as "sorcerers, witches, magical healers, and leaders of clandestine devotions"[8] – her study is in fact socially diverse, allowing us to glimpse gender dynamics in a variety of settings.

Few's analyses revolve around the capital city of Santiago de Guatemala, for which Lutz (1994, 2005) provides elaborate socio-demographic particulars. Like Lutz, other established researchers have continued to publish. Grant D. Jones (1998), for instance, assiduously reconstructs the conquest of the Itzaj Maya, which did not occur until the late seventeenth century, and Sandra L. Orellana (1995) has written an ethnohistorical synthesis of the Pacific coast. Julio Martín Blasco and Jesús María García Añoveros have collaborated on a new edition of the tour of inspection undertaken by Pedro Cortés y Larraz (2001 [1768–1770]) in the late eighteenth century, during which the archbishop and his entourage logged an impressive 5,245 kilometres, riding or walking the length and breadth of the Diocese of Guatemala over a fourteen-month period. Having privileged access to the original manuscript housed in the Archivo General de Indias in Seville, Blasco and García Añoveros include in their edition 113 of the parish maps with which Cortés y Larraz adorned his "Moral-Geographic Description" (see plates 21 and 23). The archbishop's watercolour maps, in truth, are one of the jewels of colonial textual production, but their dismal reproduction mars an otherwise commendable exercise. Also commendable is the initiative on the part of colleagues of Adriaan C. van Oss (2003) to edit and translate nine of the late historian's essays, giving them thematic coherence in a posthumous collection that emphasizes ecclesiastical history. Kudos too for the labours of Stephen A. Webre, whose dedication either on his own (Webre 1989) or in collaboration (Herrera and Webre 2014) has resulted in two edited collections that synthesize admirably research inquiries on colonial Guatemala.

8 Few (2002, 129).

For Chiapas, adjacent to the Sierra de los Cuchumatanes and so invariably a useful base of comparison, Gudrun Lenkersdorff (1993, 2001) grapples with sixteenth-century conditions, while Jan de Vos (1997) moves on from there to modern times, as do Juan Pedro Viqueira and Mario Humberto Ruz ([1995] 1998). Focusing on Momostenango, Robert M. Carmack (1995) relates the history of the community from pre-Hispanic times to the present. In a dazzling piece of scholarship, Matthew Restall (2003) debunks what he considers "seven myths of the Spanish conquest," examining how key misrepresentations originated, why they have been perpetuated, and how lucid revisionist thinking can set the record straight. Several of Restall's arguments are echoed by Stephanie Wood, whose evocation of Nahua views of colonial Mexico portrays Indians "as individuals and groups who negotiated, mediated, and exchanged with the invading cultures in complex and sometimes subtle ways, but always as equally important actors on the stage."[9]

Studies of how Maya peoples in Guatemala were affected by the transition from late colonial times into the republican era have been advanced by the work of Jorge H. González (1994), David J. McCreery (1994), and René Reeves (2006). Ralph Lee Woodward, Jr. (1993) situates the Conservative presidency of Rafael Carrera in the context of Guatemala's first half-century of embattled nationhood, also discussed by Danielle Pompejano (1997) and Arturo Taracena (2000). Taracena (2002, 2003), fronting a team of researchers from the Centro de Investigaciones Regionales de Mesoamérica (CIRMA), has edited two volumes that cover the entire sweep of the nineteenth and twentieth centuries, exploring the complex interface of ethnicity, state, and nation in grounded case studies.

Debate about the place of Maya culture in a country forged upon its simultaneous exploitation and exclusion has, if anything, become even more charged since the heightened sensibilities of the Columbus Quincentennial. Another CIRMA initiative has seen Richard Adams and Santiago Bastos (2003) tackle the thorny issue of ethnic relations. Bastos and Manuela Camus (1993, 1995, 2003) chart the emergence of Maya organizations that pursue all sorts of objectives, from recognition of official language status to a fairer distribution of resources.

Addressing the latter issue, I once heard a Maya representative, Raxche', point out decades ago that improving the Maya lot could

9 Wood (2003, x).

more readily be attained if the government of Guatemala allocated resources in conformity with the findings of national censuses. "According to the government's own statistics," Raxche' commented wryly, "in 1994 Mayas constituted 42.8 per cent of Guatemala's population. When can we expect to have access to 42.8 percent of the country's resources?"

As the clamour for native rights grows, so does the number of groups lobbying to be heard. In 1994 the Consejo del Pueblo Maya (Council of Maya Peoples) was formed, functioning as one of thirteen umbrella organizations established to address the claims of over three hundred associations. Maya activism is discussed by Edward P. Fischer (2001), Fischer and R. McKenna Brown (1996), Kay B. Warren (1998), and Richard Wilson (1995). While the research of these scholars and other non-Maya investigators (Camus 2002; Carey 2001; G.W. Cook 2001; Falla 2001; Nelson 1999) adds to our knowledge, most noteworthy is the extent to which Maya intellectuals have appeared on the scene and become politically engaged. Those at the forefront include Demetrio Cojtí Cuxil (1984, 1996, 1997), Edgar Esquit Choy (2002), Víctor Gálvez Borrell and Edgar Esquit Choy (1997), Víctor Montejo (2005), Irma Otzoy and Enrique Sam Colop (1990), Demetrio Rodríguez Guaján (1992), Emilio del Valle Escalante (2009), and Irma Alicia Velásquez Nimatuj (2002). Montejo (1999) perhaps best represents voices raised in exile, a crucial perspective, given that over one million Guatemalans (the majority of them Maya Indians) are estimated to be working residents – some legal, most not – of the United States and Canada (Loucky and Moors 2000; Nolin 2002; Fink 2003; Foxen 2008). Though memories of past injustices linger, and thus tinge any expectations of realistic political solutions, a Maya agenda is being advocated in Guatemala as never before.

TERROR IN THE MOUNTAINS

The reverberating consequences of past injustices Maya peoples in the Cuchumatán highlands know only too well. Martínez Peláez again cuts to the quick: "The colonial regime was a regime of terror."[10] His hefty tome abounds with descriptions of incidents that unfolded in

10 Martínez Peláez ([1970] 2009, 264). "If we fail to take account of terror in all its different guises," he insists, "we cannot explain key elements of colonial life that have had such a profound impact on subsequent eras."

the mountains north of Huehuetenango. Indians resisted Spanish rule throughout the colonial period in a variety of ways, but fear of reprisal conditioned the norms of everyday life. Native agency, therefore, was strategic, measured to avoid a backlash. Even those groups who sided with the Spaniards and fought for them in anticipation of preferential treatment – the Kaqchikels are perhaps the best example – complained bitterly of the wrath and heavy-handedness of their erstwhile allies after native exertions had ensured Spanish hegemony. In the Kaqchikel case, an alliance of a mere six months triggered a revolt that lasted six years.

Relations between Spaniards and Indians, then, bred mutual feelings of suspicion, mistrust, scorn, and apprehension. These emotions, in turn, shaped attitudes, values, and patterns of behaviour that transcended Guatemala's formal independence from Spain in 1821. In the Cuchumatán case, some Maya communities fared even worse in the era of Liberal Reform than under Spanish rule, at least with respect to demands made on land and labour. Similarly, Maya communities in the region suffered dreadfully as a result of counter-insurgency operations in the early 1980s (McAllister and Nelson 2013; Carmack 1988; Falla 1994, 2011; Kobrak 2003, 2013; Lovell [1995] 2010). It was the colonial experience, however, that established parameters within which ethnic relations played themselves out (Lovell and Lutz 2013). Much like the Spaniards who ruled before them, the criollos and Ladinos who forged modern Guatemala believed themselves superior in every regard to Indians, and behaved accordingly (Taracena 2000). Details are called for.

Anthropologists have conducted fieldwork in the Cuchumatanes to such a degree that a distinctive genre has emerged – the community re-study. A community is visited and written about, decades apart, by two different anthropologists, with the earlier inquiry serving as a benchmark against which change may be gauged. Three good examples focus on Santiago Chimaltenango, Nebaj, and Santa Eulalia: pioneering research by Charles Wagley (1941), Jackson Steward Lincoln (1945), and Oliver La Farge (1947) has been followed up (respectively) by John M. Watanabe (1992), David Stoll (1993), and Shelton H. Davis ([1970] 1997). The latter three scholars afford us, in particular, valuable observations about the transformation of native land and labour under the modernizing initiatives of Justo Rufino Barrios and his Liberal successors (see Cambranes 1985) in the late nineteenth century.

Chimbal, the name by which local residents refer to Santiago Chimaltenango, laid claim to formal title of its old communal holdings on 19 May 1879, in accordance with laws passed by the Liberal government that required all communities to do so or run the risk of forfeiting ancestral land. Chimbal's claim was disputed by three of its neighbours: first San Juan Atitán, next San Pedro Necta, and then San Martín Cuchumatán. A survey was arranged to resolve matters. It established that Chimbal's colonial *ejido*, a standard allotment of one square league (16.6 square kilometres) of common land around the town centre, in fact measured 17.4 square kilometres. Chimbal's *ejido* was complemented by 54 square kilometres of *baldío*, or public land. When, on 10 September 1891, formal title was issued, it recognized as community holdings the 17.4 square kilometres of the *ejido* but included only 29 square kilometres of *baldío*, a little more than half of Chimbal's previous allotment.

Compared to what took place elsewhere, Chimbal cannot be said to have lost out unduly. Transactions concerning its property, though, are instructive. "In seeking legal title to safeguard their lands," Watanabe writes, "Chimaltecos in effect abdicated sovereignty over that land by appealing to state authority to validate their claims."[11] Liberal ways of thinking had arrived, been engaged, and been asserted.

Over to the east, in Nebaj, Stoll reinforces Lincoln's findings by documenting how Guatemala's expanding coffee economy penetrated and reconfigured land-labour relations there. Access to labour, not appropriation of land, was the initial attraction. In the early 1890s, a Spaniard named Isaías Palacios arrived in Nebaj to assume the post of town secretary. Palacios became adept at recruiting Indians by advancing them loans, which they were then obliged to repay by working on coffee plantations on the Pacific coast. He and his cronies secured contracts by offering Indians drink and then ensnaring them in booze-induced debt and dependency. Lincoln notes that "Indians drank on all ceremonial occasions" but records that it was Ladinos who were responsible "for increasing the amount and

11 Watanabe (1992, 170–1). He adds: "Town sovereignty fell increasingly to the mercy of Ladino bureaucrats and their lackeys, as evidenced by the loss of nearly half the town's *baldíos* in the 1891 land title."

the strength of the liquor for the purpose of enriching themselves."[12] A group of Ladinos who moved to Nebaj from Malacatán, Stoll discloses, manipulated the situation to their advantage, "selling liquor and loaning the cash needed to go on binges." Their duplicity, he states, "separated Ixils from much of their best arable land," for after a deal had been struck, "anything less than prompt repayment meant that the house or land put up for collateral could change hands."[13]

The titling process also eroded the native estate. In 1903 Nebaj was granted municipal title to 1,237 *caballerías*, 87 less than it previously enjoyed. Nebaj's neighbours, Chajul and San Juan Cotzal, were awarded 2,424 *caballerías* and 388 *caballerías*, 157 and 180 *caballerías* less than before. The land that was usurped, in lower-lying *tierra templada* at elevations suitable for growing coffee or raising sugar cane, was ceded to private individuals for commercial use. Farther north in Ixil country, Sotzil and Ilom received title to little more than land that lay close to residential compounds. Chel, Ixtupil, and Sacsiguan were deprived of their most prized tracts. Lisandro Gordillo Galán, a Mexican who served as town secretary for Chajul in 1895, did well for himself, for his name shows up regularly on property deeds there.

"Titling land may not seem the most obvious way to lose it," Stoll observes wryly, "but such has been the experience of indigenous people, for what can be titled can be alienated."[14] Stoll's words certainly apply to what happened at Santa Eulalia. There, La Farge observed, a government survey of native holdings "resulted in the passing of much land into the hands of Ladinos and a considerable reduction in the extent of the *ejidos*."[15] Davis diligently provides the

12 Lincoln (1945, 75–6). He observes: "The Indians in those days drank *comiteco* from Comitán, Mexico, a milder drink than the present-day *aguardiente*, and did not drink half as much as they did later when the Ladinos came and introduced the latter drink. At one time there were nearly eighty bars or drink shops in town. That was in the days when coffee prices were high, much Indian labor went to the *fincas*, and large sums of money were advanced to them, which was mostly spent on drink and ceremony."

13 Stoll (1993, 33).

14 Ibid., 34. He reflects further: "In theory, land already occupied by Indians could not be privatized, but in practice it often was. Owing to the expense of titling, most Ixils continued to hold their land under the authority of the town and its municipal title, not through the national land registry, which meant that they could be invaded by an outsider with a private title and enough money to sway the courts in his favor." The situation that Stoll and others document is comparable to how land was usurped in colonial times (see chapter 8) under the ruse of *composición*.

15 La Farge (1947, 4).

details. He reckons that 70 per cent of Santa Eulalia's land was taken over by Ladinos, especially land in Santa Cruz Yalmux and in the Ixcán, "zones of greatest ecological and economic potential." Of fifty-five lots titled in these two areas, only nine were granted to native claimants; of 1,520 *caballerías* allocated, Indians received 183. Championed by the Liberal government, Ladinos laid claim to land as private individuals, not as a corporate entity, the traditional Maya practice. Several Ladinos who belonged to Huehuetenango's militia, Davis reveals, lobbied for title to 200 *caballerías* on the grounds that (1) the holdings of Santa Eulalia were "large and sufficient" for native needs; (2) the claimants would use the land to which they sought title "for the development of capitalistic agriculture"; (3) during "the rise to power of Justo Rufino Barrios," Huehuetenango had played a "military role" worthy of government recognition; and (4) land ceded would foster the creation of a new *municipio* to the north of Santa Eulalia, one that would function "as a military outpost for the protection of the frontier between Mexico and Guatemala."[16] In July 1888, Ladino claimants received title to all 200 *caballerías* they had requested. Three months later the *municipio* of Barillas was founded, named after General Manuel Lisandro Barillas, the Liberal president who had personally welcomed the Huehuetenango militiamen when they travelled to Guatemala City to promote their case.

In the three scenarios taken from the work of Watanabe, Stoll, and Davis, the tensions generated by the titling process caused grievance and alarm but did not result in violence. Sadly, this was not the case at San Juan Ixcoy, a Q'anjoba'l community that has yet to attract the anthropological attention devoted to its neighbours. Historian David McCreery, however, has combed the archives to reconstruct a tragic episode of ethnic confrontation.

The story begins in 1893, when Ladino militiamen who were residents of Chiantla filed for title to land that lay between their community and San Juan. Also involved in the proceedings were Ladino militiamen from Soloma. The Indians of San Juan claimed that the land in question was rightfully theirs, held on the basis of "ancient titles" and worked by them "since time immemorial."[17] They arranged for an engineer to conduct a survey, agreeing to pay for his services

16 Davis (1970, 54–7).
17 McCreery (1988, 241).

by signing a contract with the recruiting agent, Friedrich Koch. The contract, McCreery indicates, committed San Juan to send men to work on a plantation called Buenos Aires "in return for the plantation paying the costs of the land survey."[18] As collateral, Koch was entrusted with documents already in San Juan's possession. To the community's consternation, the engineer's survey did nothing to promote their case. Failing to appreciate the extent of native resentment, agents from Buenos Aires arrived in San Juan and insisted that the contract to work in Buenos Aires be honoured. For the Indians of San Juan, the terms upon which their labour had been pledged had yet to be satisfied. A stand-off ensued.

Nothing had been resolved by the time the agents turned in for the night on 18 July 1898, in sleeping quarters arranged for them in the town hall, which is where they were when the building was set on fire. As they fled the blaze, they were assaulted and killed. Believing that it would be possible "to eliminate hostile witnesses and conceal their crime," the assailants "spread through the village, killing Ladino men, women, and children" – some thirty in all – as well as "abusing and threatening" any Indian residents who had cooperated with the agents.[19] When it turned out that some agents or their hirelings had managed to escape, San Juan braced itself for reprisal.

"The retaliation of the Government was prompt," Raymond Stadelman informs us, with as many as "ten Indian lives exacted for each slain Ladino."[20] The militiamen who stood to gain most from the titling process, those stationed at Chiantla and Soloma, rounded up sixty individuals who were later put on trial in Huehuetenango. McCreery found no evidence to indicate that San Juan was penalized by having land taken away from it, but he does concede that "in the aftermath of the violence the inhabitants were in a weak position to defend their rights."[21] The Chiantla militiamen were awarded

18 Ibid., 242.
19 Ibid., 244.
20 Stadelman (1940, 96–7).
21 McCreery (1988, 243). Drawing on additional data, McCreery (1993, 289–90) states: "The years immediately following the uprising witnessed an orgy of land grabbing at the Indians' expense, mostly by Ladinos from nearby municipalities. In 1903, Aureliano Recinos [a Ladino from Soloma] acquired the 30-*caballería* tract called Quisil, and the next year another Recinos, Marcos, received 15 *caballerías*, bounded on one side by the properties of yet another Ladino, General Aurelio Recinos. Other Ladinos also bought land in the area. In each case, San Juan protested the sales and refused to sign the measurement documents, but its 'ancient

113 *caballerías*, with their counterparts in Soloma also given a share of the spoils. Not long after receiving title, however, recipients sold the land to plantation owners on the Pacific coast. The buyers then rented the land back to the Indians of San Juan, exacting payment not in money but in labour. By this manoeuvre, an adroit articulation of the means of production, property secured in the highlands was used to guarantee a seasonal supply of workers for the lowlands.

Wounds left to fester at San Juan Ixcoy burst open again when, assisted once more by local militias, state security forces unleashed a campaign of terror throughout the Cuchumatanes during the armed conflict that was waged off and on in Guatemala between 1962 and 1996. Two voluminous inquiries, one undertaken by the Human Rights Office of the Archdiocese of Guatemala (1999), the other by a United Nations Commission for Historical Clarification (1999), present evidence that attributes the worst atrocities to army troops in 1981 and 1982, when incursions ostensibly mounted to combat guerrilla insurgency instead targeted unarmed civilian populations. The numbing statistics for Guatemala as a whole – reportedly over 200,000 dead, 93 per cent of them killed by state security forces, 83.33 per cent of all victims Maya Indians – are thrown into sharp relief by Paul Kobrak (2003), who concentrates on the war years in Huehuetenango alone. Kobrak's regional analysis is sensitive to local nuance, including the role played by the Ejército Guerrillero de los Pobres, the Guerrilla Army of the Poor, in exposing native communities to government repression. An investigation coordinated by Cultural Survival and the Anthropology Resource Center (1983) documents the carnage perpetrated on 17 July 1982 at Finca San Francisco, where more than three hundred people lost their lives. One eyewitness, whose testimony is corroborated by that of fellow survivors, told the investigation:

> The soldiers took our wives out of the church in groups of ten or twenty. Then twelve or thirteen soldiers went into our houses to rape our wives. After they were finished raping them, they shot our wives and burned the houses down ... All of our children had been left locked up in the church. They were crying, our poor children were screaming. They were calling us. Some of the

---

titles' remained in the hands of the *finca* Buenos Aires, its survey was incomplete, and it had no funds with which to pursue its case."

bigger ones were aware that their mothers were being killed and were shouting and calling out to us ... They took the children outside. The soldiers killed them with knife stabs. We could see them. They killed them in a house in front of the church. They yanked them by the hair and stabbed them in their bellies; then they disemboweled our poor little children. Still they cried. When they finished disemboweling them, they threw them into the house, and then brought out more. Then they started with the old people. "What fault is it of ours?" the old people asked. "Outside!" a soldier said. They took the poor old people out and stabbed them as if they were animals. It made the soldiers laugh. Poor old people, they were crying and suffering. They killed them with dull machetes. They took them outside and put them on top of a board; then they started to hack at them with a rusty machete. It was pitiful how they broke the poor old people's necks ... They began to take out the adults, the grown men of working age. They took us out by groups of ten. Soldiers were standing there waiting to throw the prisoners down in the patio of the courthouse. Then they shot them. When they finished shooting, they piled them up and other soldiers came and carried the bodies into the church.[22]

Kobrak provides chilling particulars of another sixteen massacres committed in Huehuetenango during the month he calls "Black July."[23] Massacres of non-combatants were carried out purposefully, Kobrak argues, to undermine any challenge to the status quo, real or imagined, on the part of the Guerrilla Army of the Poor. Any popular support the insurgents enjoyed soon vanished in the face of such calculated terror.

One massacre is the subject of the documentary film *Haunted Land*. Directed by Mary Ellen Davis (2002), *Haunted Land* follows a Chuj Maya named Mateo Pablo on his return to Guatemala after a life of exile, first in Mexico and then in Canada, where he now

22 Cultural Survival and Anthropology Resource Center (1983, 36–7). See also Kobrak (2003, 85–7), who refers to a register of 302 "identified victims," though "the total number may be more than 350." Falla (2011) contextualizes the tragic episode in a narrative reconstruction that begins in 1871 and runs to 2010.

23 Kobrak (2003, 81–9). He maps the march of destruction headed "by a captain named Castillo" and furnishes a table listing 41 "massacres and massive disappearances" that occurred in the Department of Huehuetenango between 23 March (Todos Santos Cuchumatán) and 24 October 1982 (El Granadillo, Ixtahuacán).

lives. Mateo is one of thirteen survivors of the slaughter that took place on 14 July 1982 in Petanac, a village perched in the mountains above Finca San Francisco. In the film, we see forensic scientists exhume the bodies of Petanac's inhabitants, Mateo's wife and their two small children among them. In one scene, a man identifies what is left of his father, thrown in a heap with three other murdered villagers, by the colour of his shirt and trousers, and by the make of his shoes.

"That's him," the man says. "I know that's him. That's my father."

Another man tells how he lost his entire family – his wife, his children, his parents, his brothers. "I was left alone, with nobody. I was an orphan, with no place to go. So I sought refuge in Mexico. I still feel this pain, which has never gone away."

Haunted Land closes with a Chuj Maya prayer-maker asking that the dead forgive the living for disturbing them and moving them to a final place of rest. Mateo helps carry dozens of wooden coffins to a nearby cemetery, where they are sealed in narrow tombs.

The man who was president of Guatemala in Black July, one horrific month in a reign of seventeen, himself hails from the Cuchumatán highlands: General Efraín Ríos Montt, born in Huehuetenango on 16 June 1926. Proud and unrepentant, steadfast and sure in the God-fearing faith by which he claims to have ruled, Ríos Montt was ordered on 28 January 2013 to stand trial for acts of genocide and crimes against humanity in Guatemala's Supreme Court, the first such tribunal anywhere in the world in which a one-time head of state was held to account in the country he governed. On 10 May he was found guilty and sentenced to eighty years in prison, where he was dispatched directly from the courtroom. For ten days, the ruling held. But impunity in Guatemala runs deep: on 20 May, citing lack of due legal diligence, the Constitutional Court overturned the verdict and ordered a retrial. Rios Montt, an octogenarian, frail of health but defiant of spirit, was released from captivity and placed once again under house arrest, heir to a conquest that has yet to end.

Glossary

adelantado Recipient of a royal contract to explore and conquer hostile territory, which carried with it entitlement to govern and to enjoy certain rights and privileges. In Guatemala, a title associated with Pedro de Alvarado.

aguardiente Locally made liquor usually distilled from sugar cane, often produced clandestinely to avoid government controls and taxes.

alcabala Sales tax placed on certain goods and commodities.

alcalde Officer given administrative and judicial duties by the *ayuntamiento* or *cabildo* on which he served. Applies to men in charge of both Spanish towns and *pueblos de indios*.

alcalde mayor Chief district officer, either a Spaniard or a criollo charged with governing an *alcaldía mayor*, a jurisdiction of comparable size as a *corregimiento* or *provincia*.

alcalde ordinario Ordinary member of a town council.

alcaldía mayor Administrative unit governed by an *alcalde mayor*.

aldea Village, a smaller unit of settlement than a *pueblo*, to which it was (or is) subordinate.

almud Unit of dry measure, one-twelfth of a *fanega*.

anejo or *anexo* Settlement with a church that was subordinate to a parish centre or *cabecera*. The term *pueblo de visita* has the same meaning as *anejo* or *anexo*, implying a dependent status.

Antigua Guatemala Literally, "ancient" or "old" Guatemala; the name given to Santiago de Guatemala after earthquakes in 1773 caused serious damage, prompting civil and ecclesiastical authorities to relocate the capital in what is today Guatemala City.

arroba   Unit or measurement of weight equivalent to eleven kilograms or twenty-five pounds.

audiencia   High court or governing body of a region and, by extension, the name given to the territory of jurisdiction itself. The Audiencia de Guatemala, based in Santiago de Guatemala, governed all of Central America from the present-day Mexican state of Chiapas to Costa Rica.

ayuntamiento   Town or city council. See *cabildo*.

barrio   Usually an urban or semi-urban neighbourhood whose residents shared a common identity, place of origin, or linguistic unity.

caballería   Measure of land, approximately 104 acres or 42 hectares.

cabecera   Principal town or city of a *municipio* or *departamento*, the seat of local government.

cabecera de doctrina   Indian town with a resident parish priest.

cabildo   Town or city council composed of various officials elected annually by outgoing members.

cacique   Hereditary Indian ruler considered a member of the native nobility, afforded certain privileges not enjoyed by commoners under Spanish rule.

calpul   Indigenous, clan-like social and territorial unit; a corruption of the Nahuatl term *calpulli*. Synonymous with the Spanish term *parcialidad*. Also referred to as *chinamit*, plural *chinamitales*.

camino real   Literally, "royal road," a main overland trail or highway.

canícula   Short dry spell that usually occurs midway through the rainy season in July or August.

carga   Load of indeterminate size, legally not to exceed fifty pounds but often weighing more, carried by Indian porters.

casa   Literally, house; in colonial parlance, a household.

casada/o   Married person: woman (*casada*) or man (*casado*). In terms of tributary status, a married Indian couple (husband and wife) usually paid full tribute.

caserío   Hamlet, a grouping of houses in a rural area, smaller in size and more dispersed than an *aldea*.

casta   Term applied to all persons of mixed racial descent.

cédula de encomienda   Title or certificate that formally registered the date and terms of an *encomienda* grant, the Indians granted in *encomienda*, and the name of the *encomendero* or recipient.

chinamit See *calpul* above. A socio-territorial unit associated with certain native lineages.

choza Hut; rudimentary dwelling.

cofradía Religious fraternity or sodality. Criollos, Indians, blacks, and certain persons of the middle strata had their own *cofradías*.

comisionado Constable or deputy; a low-ranking official, often Ladino, who represented government authority in a town or district with a predominantly indigenous population.

composición de tierra A way to make legal, through payment to the Crown, the acquisition of land often obtained by irregular or unlawful means.

congregación Policy of forced native resettlement, and by extension, a settlement thus created. Under *congregación*, previously dispersed Indian populations were "congregated" to live in nucleated centres under the watchful eyes of a parish priest and colonial officials. Also referred to as *reducción*.

corregidor Government official who administered a *corregimiento*, a position often sought and held by *criollos*.

corregimiento Administrative unit governed by a *corregidor*.

costumbre Traditional native ceremony, esoteric and strongly individualized.

criollo In Guatemala, a term used to denote the offspring of Spanish parents. More generally, the designation applies to all persons born in Americas of European ancestry.

crónica Narration of events written either by a layperson or, often the case in Guatemala, by members of a religious order or a secular cleric.

cuadrilla Gang of workers, often in the sixteenth century Indian slaves used in mining activities run by their Spanish masters/ owners.

cuerda Measure of land, about 0.04 hectares.

departamento Administrative and territorial term adopted in the 1820s after Guatemala's independence from Spain. At first there were seven departments; today Guatemala has twenty-two.

doctrinero Parish priest, who might also belong to a religious order, responsible for attending to Christian duties in the *doctrina* or jurisdiction assigned him.

ejido Area of common or communal land ceded by the Crown to Indian towns and to Spanish urban centres, used to grow crops, graze livestock, and gather or cut firewood.

encomendero   Privileged Spaniard or criollo awarded Indian tribute in the form of an *encomienda*.

encomienda   Award of Indian tribute in the form of goods and commodities and, especially early on in the colonial period, the provision of native labour.

entrada   Military expedition into unconquered territory.

estancia   Ranch or rural estate dedicated to the raising of livestock, most often cattle; smaller in size than a *hacienda*.

fanega   Unit of dry measure of about 1.5 bushels, weighing approximately 116 pounds or 53 kilograms.

finca   Large farm, in Guatemala usually a coffee plantation.

finquero   Owner of a *finca*.

fiscal   Judge or *oidor* in charge of the financial affairs of an *audiencia*.

gallinas de Castilla   European chickens, introduced with the arrival of Spaniards in the New World.

gallinas de la tierra   Turkeys, fowl domesticated and bred in the Americas.

ganado mayor   Larger livestock, i.e., cattle, horses, and mules.

ganado menor   Smaller livestock, i.e., goats, pigs, and sheep.

gucumatz   Indigenous term for a devastating outbreak of sickness that took many native lives in the mid-sixteenth century, an epidemic that may have been a form of bubonic or pulmonary plague.

hacendado   Owner of a large, rural estate or *hacienda*.

hacienda   Large, rural estate devoted to raising crops and/or livestock; a term used to denote Spanish- or criollo-owned properties.

huipil   Indian woman's handwoven blouse.

Indio or *yndio*   "Indian," a term that some today consider disrespectful or demeaning, but in colonial times (and parlance) used to describe individual members of Guatemala's indigenous population, commoners and nobility alike.

Indios or *yndios amigos*   Term used to denote various groups of Indian allies who, in the sixteenth century, assisted the Spaniards in large numbers as soldiers and auxiliaries in campaigns of conquest. Sizable contingents of *yndios amigos* who were indigenous to Mexico opted to remain in Guatemala after their military services were no longer required.

Indios de servicio   Indians who were an integral part of an *encomienda* award, obliged to provide personal service on a fixed schedule to their *encomendero*. The practice was formally abolished in the mid-sixteenth century.

invierno Winter, the rainy season in Guatemala, usually May to November.

jornalero Day labourer.

juez de milpa Official appointed to ensure that Indians planted and harvested their corn crop or *milpa*, not only in order to feed themselves but also to pay tribute.

juez repartidor Official charged under the *repartimiento* system with ensuring the distribution of Indians for forced labour on agricultural estates.

Ladino In Guatemala, a term referring to persons of mixed descent, usually some combination of Indian, African, and Spanish. A distinct ethnic category from Indian, Spaniard, or criollo, used today in national censuses to denote all persons not considered indigenous Maya.

las dos repúblicas Theoretical division of colonial society into one republic of Spaniards and another of Indians; an exclusionary construct that did not take into account the presence of African slaves, free blacks, mulattoes, *mestizos*, and Ladinos.

latifundia Large agricultural estates.

league Distance of about 4.2 kilometres.

legajo Bundle of archival documents, often covering a specific subject.

libros de cabildo Books of city or town council minutes recording official meetings held by members of council; a document of matters discussed, decisions reached, and appointments made.

licenciado Judge or lawyer.

manta A standard-sized square of woven cloth, usually of cotton; common item of tribute.

matlazáhuatl Disputed kind of pestilence, possibly typhus.

medida Measurement of land.

mestiza/o Person of mixed Indian and Spanish descent, female or male.

mestizaje Race mixture.

méritos y servicios Literally, "merits and services," usually recorded as a court document detailing the plaintiff's case, highlighting his loyalty and dedication to the Crown and corroborated by witnesses testifying on his behalf.

milpas Plots of lands, usually planted with corn and worked by Indians.

minifundia Small and often fragmented agricultural holdings.

minifundista Owner of a *minifuindia*, a peasant smallholder.

monte Land covered with scrub, not useful for agriculture but containing items like herbs, firewood, and small game.

municipio Post-independence successor to colonial-era *pueblos de indios*; a township, usually comprising a *cabecera* and several *aldeas* and *caseríos*.

mulato Strictly speaking, a man or woman (*mulata*) of mixed black-Spanish descent. In Guatemala, *mulato* also included in almost all cases those of black-Indian descent.

negro Black; a person allegedly of full African descent, slave or free.

oidor Judge who served as a member of an *audiencia*.

páramo In Guatemala, lofty plain or plateau surface upward of 3,000 metres in elevation.

parcialidad Term used by Spaniards to define social units often divided and resettled as separate entities in the process of *congregación*. Also used to describe ethnic groups that formed part of the same *pueblo*.

peninsular Spaniard born in Spain.

peso Gold or, more commonly, silver coin divided into eight *reales*; hence "pieces of eight."

peste Epidemic of unspecified nature.

petate Mat woven from reeds, used for sleeping on.

pleito Formal complaint made by one person or group against another, invariably contentious in nature and related to some kind of dispute or grudge.

principal Member of the Indian elite; a village elder.

provincia Literally, "province," a territorial division of similar areal extent as an *alcaldía mayor* and presided over by a governor.

pueblo de indios Indian town created by the process of *congregación*.

pueblo de visita Smaller Indian town unable to support a resident priest and so visited by one only occasionally.

rancho Hut (*choza*) or dwelling of a poor person; traditionally, a primitive house with a thatched roof. When *ranchos* are grouped together, they are called a *ranchería*.

real   Spanish silver coin, worth one-eighth of a *peso*; known in English as a piece of eight.

real cédula   Royal order or decree.

real servicio   Tax of one-half a *peso* levied on full Indian tributaries, beginning in 1592, paid to the Crown.

reducción   See *congregación*.

regidor   Alderman who served on an *ayuntamiento* or *cabildo* either in a Spanish city or in a *pueblo de indios*.

región andina   In the Sierra de los Cuchumatanes, land over 3,000 metres in elevation.

remedida   Remeasurement of land.

repartimiento   Draft of forced native labour.

repartimiento de algodón   Distribution by *corregidores* of raw cotton to women in *pueblos de indios*, to be cleaned and spun into thread and the finished product returned to local officials for compensation below market value.

repartimiento de mercancías   Forced sale of items to Indians (often unwanted and unneeded and involving payment in cash) by Spanish and criollo officials, undertaken to augment their regular salaries.

república de españoles   Policy supposedly grouping Spaniards into their own towns and cities, designed to protect Indian welfare. The policy failed for many reasons, primarily because of Spanish dependency on Indian labour. See *república de indios*.

república de indios   Obverse of *república de españoles*: a policy establishing *pueblos de indios* with the goal of protecting Indians from the abuses of Spaniards. See *república de españoles*.

requerimiento   Literally, "Requirement," a document read aloud in Spanish or a native language prior to military engagement, warning Indians to submit to Crown authority or face attack and certain defeat. Resistance to Spanish presence – in effect, failure to comprehend the terms of *Requerimiento* – resulted in enslavement of the Indian population and their being branded as *esclavos de guerra*, "slaves of war."

reservado   Indian exempt from tributary obligations because of advanced age, poor health, church service, *cabildo* membership, and (in some cases) military service alongside Spaniards in campaigns of conquest. This privilege was often ignored by Spanish authorities intent on generating revenue.

salinas Salt deposits.

Santiago de Guatemala Capital city founded in the Valley of Panchoy after the destruction in September 1541 of an earlier Spanish nucleus, today Ciudad Vieja, in the nearby Valley of Almolonga. Known as Antigua Guatemala after it was badly damaged by earthquakes in 1773, after which the capital was relocated in Guatemala City.

sarampión Measles.

servicio del tostón Head tax on top of normal tribute obligations imposed on all eligible Indian tributaries. See *real servicio*.

servicio ordinario Literally, "ordinary service"; all manner of obligations imposed on Indians who lived close to Spanish settlements, requiring work to be done for little or no compensation.

servicio personal Literally, "personal service"; the labour component of Indian tributary duties for Spanish *encomenderos*. The obligation was formally abolished under reforms enacted by President Alonso López de Cerrato in the mid-sixteenth century.

tabardillo Fever, usually thought to be typhus.

tasación de tributo Tribute assessment. Head count of an Indian *pueblo* undertaken to determine the amount of tribute deemed payable to an *encomendero* or the Crown.

tercio de Navidad Day around Christmas, six months after the *tercio de San Juan*, 24 June, when the second half of the annual levy of Indian tribute was due.

tierra caliente Literally, "warm land," located at elevations below 800 metres, along the Pacific coast or in low-lying parts of the interior.

tierra de comunidad Community land.

tierra fría Literally, "cold land," located at elevations upward of 1,600 metres.

tierra realenga Land belonging to the Crown.

tierra templada Literally, "temperate land," located at elevations between 800 and 1,600 metres.

tinamit In K'iche' and Kaqchikel, the name given to nucleated, military strongholds where the indigenous elite lived in late preconquest times.

título Literally, "title"; more specifically, a term used by Spaniards to describe indigenous documents that were created, often decades after first contact and conquest, to furnish details, often mythic, regarding places of origin, migrations, wars, and land boundaries.

tostón   Four *reales* or one-half of a *peso*.

trapiche   Rudimentary sugar mill that used animal rather than water power to grind cane.

tributario   Male Indian, between sixteen and fifty years of age, who paid tribute in goods and commodities twice a year to his Spanish master or to the Crown. Before the mid-sixteenth century, *tributarios* also had to provide labour services.

tributo   Quantity of goods, and also money, paid by Indian adults to individual *encomenderos* and to the Crown.

vecino   Resident of settled, well-established towns and cities.

verano   Summer, the dry season in Guatemala, from November until May.

visita   Formal tour of inspection of an ecclesiastical or civil jurisdiction by a high-ranking Crown official.

xiquilite   Grass-like plant; the leaves, picked and processed, yield the blue dyestuff *añil*, or indigo.

xiquipil   Of Nahuatl origin, a measure of 8,000 cacao beans.

Appendix: Tables

Table 1
Population of the Cuchumatán highlands (from the *Censo Nacional XI de Población*, 2002)

Municipio	Indian population	Non-Indian population	Total population
Aguacatán	36,812	4,859	41,671
Barillas	65,418	10,569	75,987
Colotenango	21,467	367	21,834
Concepción	15,321	1,640	16,961
Cuilco	10,362	36,045	46,407
Chiantla	5,239	69,739	74,978
Huehuetenango	4,047	77,247	81,294
Ixtahuacán	28,469	1,997	30,466
Jacaltenango	33,961	436	34,397
La Democracia	16,679	19,605	36,284
La Libertad	4,290	24,273	28,563
Malacatancito	5,024	10,516	15,540
Nentón	22,603	6,380	28,983
San Antonio Huista	3,499	9,176	12,675
San Gaspar Ixchil	5,801	8	5,809
San Juan Atitán	13,327	38	13,365
San Juan Ixcoy	18,670	697	19,367
San Mateo Ixtatán	28,803	1,190	29,993
San Miguel Acatán	21,769	36	21,805
San Pedro Necta	20,895	5,130	26,025
San Rafael la Independencia	10,810	20	10,830
San Rafael Petzal	6,247	173	6,420
San Sebastián Coatán	18,007	15	18,022
San Sebastián Huehuetenango	20,154	1,044	21,198
Santa Ana Huista	2,097	5,271	7,368
Santa Bárbara	15,214	104	15,318
Santa Eulalia	29,895	207	30,102
Santiago Chimaltenango	5,715	96	5,811
Soloma	34,656	1,108	35,764
Tectitán	2,163	5,026	7,189
Todos Santos Cuchumatán	23,881	2,237	26,118
Cunén	23,130	2,465	25,595
Chajul	29,398	2,382	31,780
Nebaj	50,766	2,851	53,617
Sacapulas	34,475	1,231	35,706
San Juan Cotzal	19,520	530	20,050
Uspantán	33,680	8,212	41,892
Total	742,264	312,920	1,055,184

Source: *Características de la población y de los locales de habitación censados* (Guatemala: Instituto Nacional de Estadística, 2003).
Note: For statistical convenience, the Cuchumatán highlands are considered to comprise the corporate area of the entire thirty-one *municipios* of the Department of Huehuetenango plus six *municipios* of the Department of Quiché: Cunén, Chajul, Nebaj, Sacapulas, San Juan Cotzal, and Uspantán.

Table 2
Pre-Hispanic settlements in the Cuchumatán highlands

	Site	Topographic location	Classification	Occupational sequence
(1)	Achitz	Valley	ND	Late Post-classic
(2)	Agua Blanca	Intermediate	–	Early Classic (?)
(3)	Baschuc	Valley	ND	Post-classic
(4)	Bijux	Valley	ND	Late Post-classic
(5)	Buena Vista	Valley	PD	–
(6)	Cambote	Intermediate	ND	Late Pre-classic to Early Classic
(7)	Caquixay	Valley	ND	Late Classic and Late Post-classic
(8)	Carvao	Spur	PD	Classic (?)
(9)	Cerro Pueblo Viejo	Hilltop	PD	–
(10)	Cucal	Valley	ND	Pre-classic (?)
(11)	Cujá	Valley	PD	–
(12)	Cu Manchón	Intermediate	PD	–
(13)	Chaculá	Valley	–	Classic
(14)	Chalchitán	Valley	ND	Pre-classic (?) to Early Post-classic
(15)	Chanquejelvé	Intermediate	PD	–
(16)	Chichel	Intermediate	–	–
(17)	Chichoche	Intermediate	ND	–
(18)	Chicol	Intermediate	PD	Classic
(19)	Chipal	Intermediate	PD	Post-classic
(20)	Chuchun	Valley	ND	Classic
(21)	Chutinamit	Intermediate	D	Post-classic
(22)	Chutixtiox	Hilltop	D	Late Post-classic
(23)	El Bosque	Spur	PD	–
(24)	El Caballero	Hilltop	D	Late Post-classic
(25)	El Cedro	Intermediate	–	Classic (?)
(26)	El Tigre	Hilltop	PD	–
(27)	Huil	Intermediate	ND	–
(28)	Huitchun	Hilltop	PD	Classic (?) and Late Post-classic
(29)	Lamak	Valley	–	Late Post-classic
(30)	Malacatancito	Top of ridge	D	Late Post-classic
(31)	Mutchil	Hilltop	ND	–
(32)	Nebaj	Valley	ND	Early Classic to Late Post-classic (?)
(33)	Oncap	Intermediate	ND	Late Post-classic
(34)	Pacot	Hilltop	D	Late Post-classic
(35)	Piol	Intermediate	ND	–
(36)	Pucal	Hilltop	PD	–
(37)	Pulai	Valley	ND	–
(38)	Quen Santo	Inclined plain	–	Classic

Table 2

Pre-Hispanic settlements in the Cuchumatán highlands (*continued*)

Site	Topographic location	Classification	Occupational sequence
(39) Río Blanco	Valley	ND	Late Pre-classic and Early Classic; possibly also Late Post-classic
(40) San Francisco	Intermediate	PD	–
(41) Tenam	Hilltop	D	–
(42) Tilayjón	Spur	–	–
(43) Tixchun	Valley	ND	Post-classic
(44) Tuchoc	Valley	ND	–
(45) Tzicuay	Intermediate	PD	Classic and Post-classic
(46) Uaxac Canal	Valley	–	Classic
(47) Vicaveval	Hilltop	D	Late Post-classic
(48) Vitenam	Intermediate	ND	–
(49) Xetenam	Hilltop	PD	–
(50) Xecataloj	Valley	ND	–
(51) Xoch	Valley	–	–
(52) Xolchun (Huehuetenango)	Intermediate	D	Late Post-classic
(53) Xolchun (Quiché)	Intermediate	PD	Classic and Post-classic
(54) Xolpacol	Hilltop	D	Late Post-classic
(55) Yalambojoch	Flat lowland	–	Classic
Zaculeu	Intermediate	D	Early Classic to Late Post-classic

Note: The topographic location "intermediate" means that the site is on the slope of a hill. Site classifications are D (defensive); PD (potentially defensive); and ND (non-defensive). Sites numbered 1 to 55 are plotted on figure 4, p. 37. For sources, see chapter 3, footnote 22.

Table 3
Archaeological sites and settlement chronology in the Cuchumatán highlands

Pre-classic (1500 BC–AD 300)	Classic (AD 300–1000)	Early Post-classic (AD 1000–1200)	Late Post-classic (AD 1200–1524)
			Acihtz
	Agua Blanca (?)		
		Baschuc	Baschuc
			Bijux
Cambote	Cambote		
	Caquixay		Caquixay
	Carvao (?)		
Cucal (?)			
	Chaculá		
Chalchitán (?)	Chalchitán (?)	Chalchitán (?)	
	Chicol		
		Chipal	Chipal*
		Chutinamit	Chutinamit*
			Chutixtiox*
			El Caballero*
	El Cedro (?)		
	Huitchun (?)		Huitchun*
			Lamak
			Malacatancito*
	Nebaj	Nebaj	Nebaj (?)
			Oncap
			Pacot*
	Quen Santo		
Río Blanco	Río Blanco		Río Blanco (?)
		Tixchun	
	Tzicuay	Tzicuay	Txicuay (?)
	Uaxac Canal		
			Vicaveval*
			Xolchun (Huehuetenango)
	Xolchun (Quiché)	Xolchun (Quiché)	Xolchun (Quiché)
			Xolpacol*
	Yalambojoch		
	Zaculeu	Zaculeu	Zaculeu*

* Indicates defensive or potentially defensive site. For sources, see chapter 3, footnote 22.

Table 4
Indian army sizes recorded during major battles of conquest, 1525–30

Date	Place of battle	Estimated Indian army size	Native communities supplying warriors
1525	Mazatenango (San Lorenzo)	–	Mazatenango
1525	near Mazatenango	5,000	Malacatán
1525	Zaculeu	6,000	Cuilco, Huehuetenango, Ixtahuacán, and Zaculeu
1525	Zaculeu	8,000	Various Cuchumatán communities affiliated with the Mam of Zaculeu
1530	Nebaj	5,000	Nebaj and other towns
1530	Uspantán	10,000	Cunén, Sacapulas, San Juan Cotzal, Uspantán, and some communities from the Verapaz region

Source: Fuentes y Guzmán, *Recordación florida* ([1690–99] 1969–72).

Table 5
Pueblos de indios in the Cuchumatán highlands (by parish)

Parish	Pueblos de indios *forming parish*
Chiantla	Chiantla, Aguacatán, Chalchitán, San Martín Cuchumatán, and Todos Santos Cuchumatán
Cuilco	Cuilco, Amatenango, San Francisco Motozintla, San Martín Mazapa, and Tectitán
Huehuetenango	Huehuetenango, San Juan Atitán, San Lorenzo, San Pedro Necta, San Sebastián Huehuetenango, Santa Isabel, and Santiago Chimaltenango
Jacaltenango	Jacaltenango, Concepción, Petatán, San Andrés, San Marcos, San Antonio Huista, and Santa Ana Huista
Malacatán	Malacatán, Colotenango, Ixtahuacán, San Gaspar Ixchil, and Santa Bárbara
Nebaj	Nebaj, Chajul, and San Juan Cotzal
Soloma	Soloma, San Juan Ixcoy, San Mateo Ixtatán, San Miguel Acatán, San Sebastián Coatán, and Santa Eulalia
Uspantán	Uspantán, Cunén, and Sacapulas

Sources: AGCA, A3.16, leg. 246, exp. 4912; Cortés y Larraz, *Descripción geográfico-moral de la diócesis de Goathemala* ([1768–70] 1958).

Table 6
Cuchumatán settlements listed in the tribute assessment prepared between
February and August 1549 by President Alonso López de Cerrato

Name of settlement	Number of tributaries	Name of encomendero(s)	Annual amount of tribute
Aguacatlán (Aguacatán)	200	Juan de Celada	6 *fanegas*[a] of corn 1 *fanega* of beans 600 feathers 220 *mantas*[b] 8 dozen chickens 2 *fanegas* of salt 2 dozen *petates*[c] 2 *arrobas*[d] of honey 10 *indios de servicio*[e] 4 *indios para ganado*[f]
Chalchuytlán (Chalchitán)	60	Hernán Pérez Peñate and the sons of Alonso de Pulgar	2 *fanegas* of cotton 80 *mantas* 10 dozen chickens 20 *cargas*[g] of salt 4 *indios de servicio*
Chimaltenango y Atitlán (Santiago Chimaltenango and San Juan Atitán)	35	Leonór de Castellanos	4 *fanegas* of corn 0.5 *fanega* of beans 150 *mantas*
Cochumatlán (Todos Santos Cuchumatán)	–	"Menores hijos" of Marcos Ruiz and García de Aguilar	6 *fanegas* of corn 200 *mantas* 8 dozen chickens
Cuylco (Cuilco)	290	Hernán Gutiérrez de Gibaja and Hernán Méndez de Sotomayor	6 *fanegas* of corn 1 *fanega* of beans 300 *mantas* 150 small *petates* 30 large *petates* 8 *cántaros*[h] of honey 6 dozen chickens 50 *fardos*[i] of chili peppers 6 *indios de servicio* 6 *indios para ganado*
Guevetenango (Huehuetenango)	500	Juan de Espinar	15 *fanegas* of corn 4 *fanegas* of cotton 5 *fanegas* of beans 300 *mantas* 100 cakes of salt 12 dozen chickens 100 *cargas* of chili peppers 6 *indios de servicio*

Table 6
Cuchumatán settlements listed in the tribute assessment prepared between
February and August 1549 by President Alonso López de Cerrato (*continued*)

Name of settlement	Number of tributaries	Name of encomendero(s)	Annual amount of tribute
Motolcintla (Motozintla)	138	Hernán Gutiérrez de Gibaja and Hernán Méndez de Sotomayor	6 *fanegas* of corn 100 *güipiles*ʲ 100 *petates y pares de cótaras*ᵏ 8 *cántaros* of honey 12 deer skins 8 dozen chickens
Nemá (Nebaj)	35	Francisco Sánchez Tamborino	2 *fanegas* of corn 3 dozen chickens 4 *indios de servicio*
Petatán (part of present-day Concepción)	–	Diego Sánchez Santiago	2 *fanegas* of corn 0.5 *fanega* of beans 30 *mantas* 100 small *petates* 3 *cargas* of chili peppers 4 dozen chickens 2 *indios de servicio*
Uzumacintla (part of present-day San Pedro Necta)	60	Melchor de Velasco	2 *fanegas* of corn 30 small *petates* and *mantas* 4 *indios de servicio* 1 *indio para ganado*
Vspantlán (Uspantán)	–	Santos de Figueroa	2 *fanegas* of corn 80 *mantas* 5 dozen chickens 0.5 *arroba* of wax 2 *cargas* of chili peppers 6 *indios de servicio* 2 *muchachos* (boy helpers)
Vyztlán (San Antonio and/or Santa Ana Huista)	45	Francisco López	4 dozen chickens 100 small *petates.* 2 *arrobas* of honey 4 *cargas* of chili peppers 4 *fanegas* of beans 4 *indios de servicio*

Table 6
Cuchumatán settlements listed in the tribute assessment prepared between
February and August 1549 by President Alonso López de Cerrato (*continued*)

Name of settlement	Number of tributaries	Name of encomendero(s)	Annual amount of tribute
Xacaltenango (Jacaltenango)	500	Son of Gonzalo de Ovalle	12 *fanegas* of corn 1.5 *fanegas* of beans 4 *fanegas* of cotton 400 *mantas* 10 dozen chickens 80 small *petates* 4 large *petates* 3 *fanegas* of wheat 6 *fanegas* of salt 2 *arrobas* of honey 25 *cargas* of chili peppers 6 *indios de servicio*
Ystatán (San Mateo Ixtatán)	30	Diego Sánchez Santiago	2 *fanegas* of corn 12 *fanegas* of salt 35 *mantas* 3 dozen chickens 2 *indios de servicio*
Zacapula (Sacapulas)	160	Cristóbal Salvatierra and "el menor hijo" of Juan Páez	96 *fanegas* of salt 18 dozen chickens 16 *indios de servicio*
Zoloma (Soloma)	140	Diego de Alvarado and Juan de Astroqui	4 *fanegas* of corn 100 *mantas* 150 chickens 8 *indios de servicio*

Source: AGI, Guatemala 128 ("Tasaciones de los pueblos de los términos y jurisdicción de la ciudad de Guatemala," 1548–51).

a A *fanega* is a unit of dry measure of roughly 1.5 bushels. The area planted with this amount of seed was known as the *fanega de sembradura*.
b A *manta* was a standard square of cotton cloth.
c A *petate* is a woven reed mat used for bedding and flooring.
d An *arroba* is a unit of weight equal to about eleven kilograms.
e *Indios de servicio* were Indians granted as an integral part of *encomienda* who could be employed at a number of tasks involving "servicio personal," personal service. Labour from the stipulated number of Indians was provided on a regular basis to the *encomendero*.
f *Indios para ganado* were Indians whose personal services to the *encomendero* involved looking after livestock.
g A *carga* was a load roughly equivalent to two *fanegas*.
h A *cántaro* is a jug or pitcher.
i A *fardo* is a bundle or bale.
j A *güipil* or *huipil* is traditionally the name given to a woman's blouse. In this case it may simply mean a unit of woven cotton cloth.
k *Pares de cótaras*: pairs of sandals.

Table 7
Awards of *encomienda* in Guatemala, 1524–48

Governors, lieutenant governors, and interim governors	Tenure in office	Number of awards	Number of encomenderos
Pedro de Alvarado	1524–26	25	21
Jorge de Alvarado	1527–29	86	56
Francisco de Orduña	1529–30	12	11
Pedro de Alvarado	1530–33	77	45
Jorge de Alvarado	1534–35	7	6
Pedro de Alvarado	1535–36	18	10
Alonso de Maldonado	1536–39	12	8
Pedro de Alvarado	1539–40	7	3
Francisco de la Cueva	1540–41	13	5
Bishop Marroquín and Francisco de la Cueva	1541–42	16	16
Alonso de Maldonado	1542–48	30	20

Source: Kramer (1994, 245); Lovell and Lutz (2013, 259).

Table 8
Encomienda in the Cuchumatán highlands, 1524–40

Date of first title	Community granted	Recipient
17/10/1524	Tecpán Puyumatlán (Santa Eulalia)	Gonzalo de Ovalle
3/10/1525	Huehuetenango	Juan de Espinar
20/2/1526	Uspantlán (Uspantán)	Diego de Rojas
1524–26	Ozumacintlán (San Pedro Necta)	Diego Cancino
1527–29	Tetechan (Tectitán)	Alonso Larios
1528	Cochumatlán (Todos Santos)	Marcos Ruiz
1528	Ayllón (Ilom)	Hernando de Yllescas
29/3/1528	Chalcuytlán (Chalchitán)	Diego de Rojas
29/3/1528	Petatlán (Petatán)	Gonzalo de Ovalle
10/8/1529	Cacalutlán or Colutla (Colotenango?)	Gonzalo de Ovalle
10/8/1529	Ystapalapán (San Mateo Ixtatán?)	Gonzalo de Ovalle
19/8/1529	Xacaltenango (Jacaltenango)	Gonzalo de Ovalle
1528–29	Zacapula (Sacapulas)	Antón de Morales y Juan Páez
1528–29	Nemá (Nebaj)	Francisco Sánchez
1528–29	Vyztlán (San Antonio and Santa Ana Huista)	Francisco López

Table 8
Encomienda in the Cuchumatán highlands, 1524–40 *(continued)*

Date of first title	Community granted	Recipient
1528–29	Cuilco	Rodrigo de Benavides
1528–29	Motocintla (San Francisco Motozintla)	Rodrigo de Benavides
16/10/1530	Aguacatán	Cristóbal de la Cueva
20/8/1531	Yscos (San Juan Ixcoy)	Marcos Ruiz
1540	Zoloma (Soloma)	Francisco de la Cueva

Source: Kramer (1994).

Table 9
Population of Huehuetenango and subject towns, 1530–31 and 1549

Head/subject town	1530–1531	1549[1]
Huehuetenango (includes Chiantla)	2,000–2,500 tributaries	500 tributaries
Santiago Chimaltenango (Chimbal, Chinbal)	500 *casas*[2]	125 tributaries[3]
San Juan Atitán (Atitán)	–	–
San Pedro Necta (Niquitlán, Niquetla)	200 *casas*[4]	20 tributaries

Sources: Kramer (1994, 222); Lovell and Lutz (2013, 260).
[1] All 1549 figures are from AGI, Guatemala 128 ("Tasaciones de los pueblos," 1548–51).
[2] Two hundred houses in the town centre, or *cabecera*, and three hundred in outlying settlements, or *estancias*. See AGI, Justicia 1031 ("Juan de Espinar con Pedro de Alvarado sobre el pueblo de Huehuetenango, 1537–40).
[3] Santiago Chimaltenango and San Juan Atitán together had 125 tributaries in 1549.
[4] AGI, Justicia 1031 ("Juan de Espinar con Pedro de Alvarado sobre Huehuetenango," 1537–40).

Table 10
Encomienda obligations in Huehuetenango, 1530–31 and 1549

Commodity or service	1530–31	1549
Clothing	800 lengths of cotton cloth 400 loincloths 400 jackets 400 blouses 400 skirts 400 sandals	300 lengths of cotton cloth
Foodstuffs	Unspecified amounts of corn, beans, chili peppers, and salt 108–126 large jugs of honey	Harvest from planting 22.5 bushels of corn Harvest from planting 7.5 bushels of black beans 100 loads of chili peppers 100 cakes of salt
Fowl	2,268 turkeys	Twelve dozen chickens
Other Items	400 reed mats	Harvest from planting six bushels of cotton
Labour	40 Indian men sent to work in and around Santiago de Guatemala in 20-day shifts all year 120–200 Indian men sent to work in the gold mines in 20-day shifts all year 30 Indian women sent to the gold mines each day in order to make tortillas and prepare food	Six Indian men to act as general servants
Slaves	80 male and 40 female slaves who worked in the gold mines	

Sources: AGI, Justicia 1031 ("Juan de Espinar con Pedro de Alvarado sobre Huehuetenango," 1537–40); AGI, Guatemala 128 ("Tasaciones de los pueblos," 1548–51); Lovell and Lutz (2013, 261).

Table 11
Repartimientos de mercancías, 1561–1813

Year	Place	Activity and comments	Source
1561	Huehuetenango	Forced sale of various goods at high prices among Tlaxcalan Indians resident in the district. Clergy as well as secular Crown officials implicated in the extortion.	AGI, AG 52
1641	Cuilco	Father Juan de Mata complains that the governor of Chiapas distributes *efectos de comercio* among his parish charges, an illegal and harmful activity in the eyes of the priest.	AGCA, A1.14, leg. 4064, exp. 31664
ca 1690	Cuilco and elsewhere	Widespread use by *corregidores* of *repartimientos de algodón*, whereby Indians are given raw cotton and expected to work it into finished form. While Cuilco is mentioned specifically, the source states that the practice is common "en todos los demás pueblos de esta jurisdicción [Totonicapán and Huehuetenango] y la de Quezaltenango."	Fuentes y Guzmán, *Recordación florida*, vol. 3, p.35
1703	Sacapulas	Describing themselves as "pobres miserables tributarios," native representatives petition against *repartimientos de algodón* being distributed among the womenfolk of their community. An order is passed in which the *alcalde mayor* responsible is told to desist from molesting the Indians in this way.	AGCA, A1.24, leg. 1573, exp. 10217
1716	Totonicapán and Huehuetenango	An inquiry into the conduct of the *alcalde mayor* of Totonicapán and Huehuetenango is to be undertaken by the captain general of Chiapas. The *alcalde mayor* is accused of numerous misdemeanours and abuses of office, including excessive demands, embezzlement of funds, and the non-payment of proper sums for services rendered by (and goods received from) various Indian communities.	AGCA, A1.24, leg. 4649, exp. 39688
1759	Santa Eulalia	A complaint is lodged by the men and women of the community, especially the latter, that excessive *repartimientos de algodón* make them "captives" and "slaves" of the *alcalde mayor*. The women claim they have to work all year round to fulfill the demands placed upon them.	Recinos, *Huehuetenango*, p. 215

Date	Place	Description	Source
1760s	Parishes of Huehuetenango, Nebaj, and Soloma	Rampant manipulation of *repartimientos de mercancías* by *alcalde mayor* Juan Bácaro, described by the source as one whose exploitation of the Indians has earned him "muy mala fama." Bácaro's treatment of natives is so ruthless that Cortés y Larraz claims some of them abandon town life for a fugitive existence in the hills in order to escape his oppression.	Cortés y Larraz, *Descripción geográfico-moral*, vol. 2, pp. 48–9, 118, and 124
1774	Parish of Soloma	Indian leaders protest, through their parish priest, against the overbearing demands placed upon them, particularly *repartimientos de algodón*, by the *alcalde mayor* Matías de Manzanares. In his defence, Manzanares claims native families accept the *repartimientos* voluntarily. The *alcalde mayor* is ordered by the *audiencia* not to persist with the practice.	AGCA, A1.14, leg. 190, exp. 3864
1776	Aguacatán	Complaints are lodged by the Indians that *alcalde mayor* Josef González Cosío insists they buy unnecessary goods from him at elevated prices. Native families are also forced to sell raw wool to Cosío at prices well below market value, thus ensuring that he (and others engaged in the practice) derive from it "una mina de oro." The *alcalde mayor* is fined 100 pesos by the *audiencia* for abuse of office.	Recinos, *Huehuetenango*, pp. 215–16
1779	Parish of Soloma	*Repartimientos de efectos* are once again being carried out, despite orders prohibiting the practice.	AGCA, A3.12, leg. 2897, exp. 43013
1813	Parishes of Cuilco, Nebaj, and Soloma	The *alcalde mayor* of Totonicapán and Huehuetenango, Narciso Mallol, is accused of procuring, by means of *repartimientos*, items such as salt, wheat, corn, and incense, all of which (once sold) contribute significantly to his enrichment. Despite attempts by Captain General José de Bustamante to prosecute Mallol, the *audiencia* intervenes on the latter's behalf. The *alcalde mayor* is eventually re-posted to Tegucigalpa.	Recinos, *Huehuetenango*, p. 216

Table 12
Alleged abuses committed by Spanish clergy, 1681–1819

Year	Place	Complaint	Source
1681	San Juan Ixcoy	Indians from the community claim that the parish priest is excessive in his demands for food and provisions.	AGCA A1.24, leg. 1566, exp. 10210
1759	Parish of Soloma	The parish priest, Fray Santiago Arriola, is said by his native charges to be unrelenting and excessive in his request for payment of such routine services as celebrating mass and administering the holy sacraments.	AGCA A1.16, leg. 5802, exp. 48989; Recinos, *Huehuetenango*, pp. 467–8
1759	San Ildefonso Ixtahuacán	The parish priest of Malacatán, Fray Simón José Collado, is accused by natives of the community of embezzling funds meant for reconstruction of the local church.	AGCA A1.11, leg. 5799, exp. 48925
1771	Todos Santos and San Martín Cuchumatán	Indians lodge complaints with the *audiencia* concerning "malos tratamientos" and extortions perpetrated by their parish priest, Father Miguel Hermenegildo Muñoz.	Recinos, *Huehuetenango*, p. 469
1773	Cunén	Native townspeople allege that Father Andrés Henríquez, their parish priest, does not pay them for looking after the livestock belonging to the church. They further assert that Henríquez sold six of their cows without consulting the owners beforehand.	AGCA A1.11, leg. 190, exp. 3868
1773	San Juan Ixcoy and San Pedro Soloma	The Indians accuse their parish priest, Father Tomás de Clavería, of expecting contributions far in excess of what available resources permit.	Recinos, *Huehuetenango*, p. 469
1773	San Gaspar Ixchil	Natives from the community petition against the unreasonable demands placed upon them, yet again, by Fray Simón José Collado. His greed, the Indians claim, is the principal cause of their continual impoverishment.	AGCA A1.11, leg. 2801, exp. 24609

Year	Place	Description	Source
1774	Aguacatán, Chiantla, and Todos Santos	The Indians state that their parish priest compels them to work as unpaid shepherds and porters. In addition to having to serve as involuntary labour, they complain of the sizable contributions they must make toward the upkeep of their local churches.	AGCA A1.11, leg. 2801, exp. 24613
1803	San Mateo Ixtatán	Natives from the community seek a reduction in the amount of money they are expected to contribute for the saying of mass and the organization of religious celebrations.	AGCA A1.11, leg. 2804, exp. 24642
1819	Huehuetenango	Indian representatives accuse their parish priest, Father Bernardino Lemus, of excessive demands and harsh treatment.	AGCA A1.11, leg. 2806, exp. 24669

Table 13
Cofradía assets of Cuchumatán parishes, 1770 and 1803

| | 1770 | | 1803 | |
Parish	Number of cofradías	Liquid capital (in pesos)	Number of cofradías	Liquid capital (in pesos)
Chiantla[a]	37	2,416	38	3,382
Huehuetenango[a]	29	2,746	67	Data incomplete
Cuilco[b]	13	1,157	24	2,124
Malacatán[b]	25	2,080	24	3,488
Jacaltenango[c]	20	1,529	18	1,360
Nebaj[c]	19	2,454	18	Data incomplete
Soloma[c]	31	3,100	37	3,472
Uspantán[c]	21	1,713	26	1,248

Sources: AGI, Guatemala 948, Archbishop Pedro Cortés y Larraz to the Crown (1768–70); AGCA, A1.11, leg. 6105, exps. 55798, 55799, 55800, 55802, and 55803; AGCA, A1.11, leg. 6106, exps. 55864, 55865, and 55893 (1803).
[a] Includes a sizable contribution from cofradías organized by Spaniards and Ladinos.
[b] Includes a small contribution from cofradías organized by Spaniards and Ladinos.
[c] Cofradía funds composed entirely or overwhelmingly of contributions by Indians.

Table 14
Spanish landholding (composiciones, denuncias, medidas, and remedidas) in the Cuchumatán highlands, 1607–1759

Year	Location	Amount (caballerías)	Recipient	AGCA source
1607	Altos de Chiantla	–	Francisco Rodríguez	A1, leg. 5937, exp. 51931
1623	Two leagues from Cuilco	12	Sebastián Montes de Oca	A1, leg. 5939, exp. 51953
1628	Altos de Chiantla	18	Bartolomé Ponce	A1, leg. 5939, exp. 51964
1652	Vicinity of Malacatán	2	Melchor González de Mazariegos	A1, leg. 5943, exp. 52010
1670	Between Aguacatán and Chiantla	2	José Pérez de la Plata	A1, leg. 5946, exp. 52054
1670	Altos de Chiantla	9.5	José de Alvarado	A1, leg. 5946, exp. 52055

Table 14
Spanish landholding (*composiciones, denuncias, medidas,* and *remedidas*)
in the Cuchumatán highlands, 1607–1759 (*continued*)

Year	Location	Amount (caballerías)	Recipient	AGCA source
1670	Altos de Chiantla	10.5	Juan López de Mata	A1, leg. 5946, exp. 52056
1676	Vicinity of San Juan Ixcoy	7	Melchor de Rodríguez	A1, leg. 5948, exp. 52087
1683	Altos de Chiantla	8.5	Pedro Chávez	A1, leg. 5949, exp. 52106
1684	Altos de Chiantla	2	Pedro Nolasco	A1.57, leg. 6095, exp. 55405
1685	Five leagues from Todos Santos Cuchumatán and San Juan Ixcoy	5.5	Melchor de Mencos	A1, leg. 5949, exp. 52111
1704	Vicinity of Huehuetenango	16	Tomás García de Medina	A1.80, leg. 5959, exp. 52241
1704	Altos de Chiantla	3.5	Nicolás de Mata	ST, Huehuetenango, 1:10
1705	Vicinity of Chiantla	11.5	Juan Salvador de Mata	ST, Huehuetenango, 1:3
1705	Vicinity of Huehuetenango	3	Antonia de León	A1.24, leg. 1574, exp. 10218
1705	Vicinity of Huehuetenango	6	Andrés de León	A1, leg. 5960, exp. 52252
1706	Vicinity of Chiantla	2	Tomás García de Medina	ST, Huehuetenango, 1:3
1706	Vicinity of Chiantla	4	Tomás García de Medina	ST, Huehuetenango, 1:3
1706	Vicinity of Huehuetenango	5.5	Ana María de Mazariegos	A1.24, leg. 1575, exp. 10219
1706	Vicinity of Huehuetenango	6.5	Tomás García de Medina	ST, Huehuetenango, 1:19
1706	Vicinity of Huehuetenango	3	Antonio Cifuentes	A1.24, leg. 1575, exp. 10219
1706	Vicinity of Huehuetenango	19	María de Vides	A1.24, leg. 1575, exp. 10219
1706	Vicinity of Huehuetenango	6	Tomás García de Medina	A1.24, leg. 1575, exp. 10219

Table 14
Spanish landholding (*composiciones, denuncias, medidas,* and *remedidas*)
in the Cuchumatán highlands, 1607–1759 (*continued*)

Year	Location	Amount (caballerías)	Recipient	AGCA source
1707	Vicinity of Chiantla	5	Domingo García Moscoso	A 1, leg. 1576, exp. 10220
1708	Altos de Chiantla	7	Convento de Jacaltenango	ST, Huehuetenango, 1:8
1708	Vicinity of Malacatán	4	Tomasa de Solís	ST, Huehuetenango, 1:16
1711	Between Aguacatán and Chiantla	4	Domingo García Moscoso	A 1.24, leg. 1578, exp. 10222
1714	Vicinity of Huehuetenango	2	Duarte Fernández de Hidalgo	A 1.57, leg. 5757, exp. 48171
1715	Altos de Chiantla	3.5	Nicolás de Mara	ST, Huehuetenango, 1:19
1717	Vicinity of Huehuetenango	10	Antonia de León	A 1.24, leg. 1582, exp. 10226
1723	Vicinity of Malacatán	1	Pedro Monzón	ST, Huehuetenango, 1:18
1726	Between Amatenango and Cuilco	2	Domingo Ramírez	ST, Huehuetenango, 1:13
1737	Vicinity of Malacatán	2	Martín Sánchez	ST, Huehuetenango, 1:16
1740	Vicinity of Cuilco	7.5	Pascual de León	ST, Huehuetenango, 1:14
1741	Vicinity of Cuilco	12	Nicolás de Barrios	ST, Huehuetenango, 1:2
1759	Vicinity of Malacatán	–	Antonio Santiago	ST, Huehuetenango, 1:16
1759	Vicinity of Malacatán	–	Juana Barrios	ST, Huehuetenango, 1:16
1759	Vicinity of Malacatán	–	Juan de Soto	ST, Huehuetenango, 1:16

Table 15
Proposed allocation of land at Sacapulas, ca. 1775–1800

Parcialidad	Location of holdings	Approximate extent of holdings	Indian tributaries (1794)
San Pedro	North bank of the Río Negro, across the river from the town centre.	81 caballerías*	67
Santiago and San Sebastián	South bank of the Río Negro (including salt works) adjacent to the town centre.	72 caballerías	141
San Francisco	To the west of land held by Santiago and San Sebastián, predominantly on the south side of the Río Negro.	78 caballerías	98
Santo Tomás	To the west of land held by San Pedro, predominantly on the north side of Río Negro and along both banks of the Río Blanco.	121 caballerías	60

Source: AGCA, A1, leg. 6025, exp. 53126; A1, leg 6040, exp. 53305; Lovell and Lutz (2013, 258).
* A caballería of land measures about 104 acres or 42 hectares.

Table 16
Land grants to Indian caciques and principales in the Cuchumatán highlands, 1600–1711

Year	Location	Amount (in caballerías)	Recipient(s)	AGCA source
1600	Vicinity of Chiantla	19.5	Antonio, Francisco, and Luís de Mendoza	A1, leg. 5935, exp. 51906
1628	Vicinity of Todos Santos Cuchumatán	6	Juan de Herrera	A1, leg. 5940, exp. 51969
1705	Vicinity of Chiantla	4	Baltasar Jiménez Celajú	A1, leg. 5940, exp. 51969
1711	Vicinity of Aguacatán	14	Pedro and Sebastián de Escobar	ST, Huehuetenango, 1:9

Table 17
Land disputes between Indian communities and non-Indian individuals
in the Cuchumatán highlands, 1705–1822

Year	Contestants	AGCA source
1705	Juan Martínez de la Vega against Chiantla	A 1, leg. 5960, exp. 52251
1737	Juan Martínez de la Vega against Todos Santos Cuchumatán	A 1, leg. 5935, exp. 51906; A 1, leg. 5976, exp. 52505
1748–59	Fray Juan Antonio González against Cuilco	ST, Huehuetenango, 1:17
1772–79	Mateo Morales and Juan José Franco against San Pedro Necta	A 1, leg. 6018, exp. 53040; A 1, leg. 6102, exp. 55702; A 1, leg. 2899, exp. 26827
1775	Nicolás Recinos against San Sebastián	A 1, leg. 6021, exp. 53075
1777	Pedro Henríquez against Santa María Cunén	A 1, leg. 6022, exp. 53093
1793	Parish priest of Huehuetenango against San Pedro Necta	A 1, leg. 6040, exp. 53302
1803	Ladino community against Indian community in Huehuetenango	A 1, leg. 6092, exp. 55333
1808	Luis Aguilar against the Indian communities of Jacaltenango parish	A 1, leg. 2919, exp. 27230; ST, Huehuetenango, 2:14
1810	Luis Aguilar against Jacaltenango	ST, Huehuetenango, 2:5
1813	José Domingo Franco against San Sebastián Coatán	A 1, leg. 6052, exp. 53498
1814	Nolberto Zamallorga against Indian community of Huehuetenango	A 1, leg. 6117, exp. 56583
1815	Ladino community against Indian community in Huehuetenango	ST, Huehuetenango, 2:13
1816	Hacienda San Lucas y San Antonio "Tierra Negra" against San Mateo Ixtatán and San Sebastián Coatán	A 1, leg. 6118, exp. 56683; A 1, leg. 5329, exp. 44907
1820	José and Joaquín Montejo against Jacaltenango	A 1, leg. 2806, exp. 27672; ST, Huehuetenango, 2:15, 18
1822	Vicente Gómez against Tectitán	ST, Huehuetenango, 2:17

Table 18
Land Disputes between Indian communities in the Cuchumatán highlands,
1668–1822

Year	Contestants	AGCA source
1668	Santiago Chimaltenango against Todos Santos Cuchumatán	ST, Huehuetenango, 1:1
1689	Jacaltenango against Santa Ana Huista	ST, Huehuetenango, 2:8
1711–12	San Antonio Huista, Santa Ana Huista, and Jacaltenango	A 1.24, leg. 1579, exp. 10223
1730– mid- 1800s	Aguacatán against Sacapulas	ST, Quiché, 1:5; A 1, leg. 5978, exp. 52518; leg. 5979, exp. 52536; leg. 5982, exp. 52582; leg. 6051, exp. 53470
1742–43	Jacaltenango against Santa Ana Huista	ST, Huehuetenango, 2:8; A 1, leg. 5985, exp. 52635
1743	San Antonio Huista against Santa Ana Huista	ST, Huehuetenango, 1:15
1810	Cunén against Sacapulas	ST, Huehuetenango, 2:13
1812	Jacaltenango against San Miguel Acatán	ST, Huehuetenango, 2:11
1813	Santiago Chimaltenango against Todos Santos Cuchumatán	ST, Huehuetenango, 2:12
1814– mid- 1840s	Jacaltenango against Todos Santos Cuchumatán	A 1, leg. 2806, exp. 24664; leg. 2857, exp. 25791; leg. 2927, exp. 27474; leg. 6055, exp. 53546; leg. 6117, exp. 56588; leg. 6118, exp. 56680; leg. 6118, exp. 56696; leg. 6118, exp. 56709; ST, Huehuetenango, 2:11
1817	San Miguel Acatán against San Marcos Jacaltenango	A 1, leg. 2929, exp. 27463
1819	Jacaltenango, San Miguel Acatán, and Todos Santos Cuchumatán	ST, Huehuetenango, 2:14
1821	San Martín Cuchumatán, Todos Santos Cuchumatán, and Jacaltenango	B 3.6, leg. 47, exp. 983
1822	Tectitán against Tacaná	ST, Huehuetenango, 2:17

Table 19
Selected Cuchumatán populations, 1570–1604

Date	Spatial category	Population
1570[a]	Amatenango	1,000 *vecinos*
1570[a]	Huehuetenango	1,000 *vecinos*
1570[a]	Los Mames	1,000 *vecinos*
1570[a]	Sacapulas y su visita	1,500 *vecinos*
1572[b]	Cuilco, Motozintla y sus estancias	1,000 *vecinos*
1572[b]	Huehuetenango y sus sujetos y estancias	1,000 *vecinos*
1572[b]	Jacaltenango y sus estancias	1,000 *vecinos*
1572[b]	Sacapulas y los pueblos en su comarca	1,600 *vecinos*
1595[c]	Corregimiento de Totonicapán	5,000 *tostones* (5,000 *tributarios*)
1604[d]	14 pueblos de Sacapulas	3,340 *indios*

Sources:
[a] "Memoria de los partidos que hay de clérigos en el obispado de Guatimala" (AGI, Guatemala 394).
[b] "Relación de los caciques y número de yndios que hay en Guatemala" (J. Garcia Icazbalceta Collection, vol. 20, no. 1, Latin American Collection, University of Texas at Austin).
[c] "Servicio del tostón año de 1595" (AGI, Contaduría 969).
[d] "Suma y memoria de los conventos, religiosos, pueblos, visitas y indios que hay en toda esta provincia del Guatemala y Chiapa de la orden de Santo Domingo" (Biblioteca del Palacio Real, Madrid, Ms. 175).

Table 20
Population of the Cuchumatán highlands, 1520–1825

Year	Population	Comments and source
1520	260,000	Extrapolation from the size of Indian armies recorded by Fuentes y Guzmán in the *Recordación florida* (1690–99).
1525–30	150,000	Estimate based on the size of Indian armies recorded by Fuentes y Guzmán in the *Recordación florida* (1690–99).
1550	73,000	Estimate based on figures for Huehuetenango in AGI, AG 10 and AGCA, A3.16, leg. 1601, exp. 26391.
1578–82	47,000	Estimate based on figures for Huehuetenango in AGI, AG10 and AGCA, A3.16, leg. 1601, exp. 26391.
1664–78	16,162	Based on comprehensive tribute assessments in AGCA, A3.16, leg. 1601, exp. 26391.
1683	16,000	Estimate based on partially destroyed regional census in AGI, Contaduría 815.
1690	19,258	Based on tribute data compiled by Fuentes y Guzmán in the *Recordación florida* (1690–99).

Table 20
Population of the Cuchumatán highlands, 1520–1825 (continued)

Year	Population	Comments and source
1710	18,000	Estimate based on figures of the *servicio del tostón* for Totonicapán and Huehuetenango in AGI, Contaduría 973.
1719	17,500	Estimate based on figures of the *servicio del tostón* for Totonicapán and Huehuetenango in AGI, Contaduría 977.
1724	18,500	Estimate based on figures of the *servicio del tostón* for Totonicapán and Huehuetenango in AGI, Contaduría 976.
1760	21,176	Based on comprehensive tribute assessments in AGCA, A3.16, leg. 950, exp. 17715.
1768–70	23,418	Based on a head count recorded by Cortés y Larraz in his *Descripción geográfico-moral de la diócesis de Goathemala* (1768–70).
1778	27,505	Based on head count in AGCA, A1.44, leg. 6097, exp. 55507.
1779	28,047	Based on head count in AGCA, A1.44, leg. 6097, exp. 55507.
1782	23,021	Based on head count in AGCA, A1.44, leg. 6097, exp. 55507.
1783	25,027	Based on head count in AGCA, A1.44, leg. 6097, exp. 55507.
1784	24,828	Based on head count in AGCA, A1.44, leg. 6097, exp. 55507.
1788	24,678	Based on comprehensive tribute assessments in AGCA, A3.16, leg. 246, exp. 4912.
1790	23,623	Based on detailed population and tribute data in AGCA, A3.16, leg. 237, exp. 4706.
1797–98	24,129	Based on population and tribute data recorded by Joseph Domingo Hidalgo in the *Gazeta de Guatemala*.
1801	27,477	Based on detailed population and tribute data in AGCA, A3.16, leg. 243, exp. 4853.
1811	29,571	Based on comprehensive tribute assessments in AGCA, A3.16, leg. 953, exp. 17773.
1825	34,691	Based on population data in AGCA, B84.3, leg. 1135 and 1136, exps. 26030, 26031, 26032, and 26034.

Table 21
Widespread outbreaks of disease in highland Guatemala, 1519–1746

Year	Disease	Impact
1519–20	Smallpox and perhaps also pulmonary plague or typhus	Very high mortality; at least one-third of the Indian population would have perished
1532–34	*Sarampión* (measles)	High mortality among Indians
1545–48	*Gucumatz* (a type of plague); *peste* (unspecified sickness)	Very high mortality among Indians
1563–65	Unspecified epidemic preceded by drought and famine	–
1571	*Peste* (unspecified sickness)	–
1576–77	*Peste, viruela* (smallpox), *matlazáhuatl* (typhus?), and *gucumatz*	High mortality among Indians; several more settlements entirely depopulated
1600–01	Smallpox (?)	–
1607–08	*Tabardillo* (typhus and/or a type of plague)	Disease only affected Indians; Spaniards untouched
1614	Unspecified epidemic	Illness confined to Indians
1631	*Tabardillo* (typhus)	Many deaths among Indians
1650	*Gucumatz*, bubonic plague	Many deaths; villages depopulated
1666	*Peste, tabardillo*	Many deaths
1686	Typhus and/or pneumonic plague	High mortality among Indians and the poor
1693–94	*Sarampión, viruela, tabardillo*	High mortality
1695	Smallpox	–
1704-05	*Peste*	–
1708–09	*Peste*	Only Indians affected
1710–11	*Peste*	Some villages completely depopulated
1733	*Peste*, smallpox, typhoid	Many deaths
1741	*Tabardillo*	–
1746	*Tabardillo*	–

Source: MacLeod ([1973] 2008, 98–100).

Table 22
Local outbreaks of disease in the Cuchumatán highlands, ca. 1550–1819

Year	Disease	Communities affected	Comments	Source
ca. 1550–ca. 1615	Pestes (unspecified sickness)	Aguacatán and other settlements in the "sierra de Cuchumatán"	The source records specifically that "con las pestes han venido [los pueblos] en diminución." Bishop Marroquín, in November 1553, suggested to the Dominicans that their order establish a monastery at Aguacatán. The friars chose to locate in Sacapulas instead, possibly because outbreaks of disease had already reduced Indian numbers at Aguacatán.	Remesal, *Historia General* (1619)
1552	Unspecified	Aguacatán and other towns	The source states that "los pueblos han venido en gran descrecimiento y disminución" and that "se han muerto e ido de ellos otra mucha más cantidad."	AGI, Justicia 286
1568	Unspecified	Aguacatán, Sacapulas, and two other towns held in *encomienda* by Alonso Páez	Because of Indian population decline, the income accruing to the *encomendero* is expected to total less than 100 pesos.	AGI, Patronato 68-2-3
1571	Unspecified	Sacapulas region	The same disease struck communities in the Verapaz, with considerable mortality.	AGCA, A1, leg. 5942, exp. 51995
ca. 1582	Unspecified	Chiantla, Huehuetenango "y sus estancias"	The source records that "los indios han venido en diminución, la encomienda ha venido a menos."	AGI, Patronato 61-2-4
1613	Unspecified	Todos Santos Cuchumatán	The tribute assessment has been lowered "por falta de tributarios." Mention is made of "indios viejos y enfermos."	AGI, Patronato 58-1-4

Table 22
Local outbreaks of disease in the Cuchumatán highlands, ca. 1550–1819 (*continued*)

Year	Disease	Communities affected	Comments	Source
1617	Unspecified	San Martín Cuchumatán	The source mentions "indios enfermos."	AGI, Patronato 58-1-5
ca. 1639	*Peste* (unspecified sickness)	La Magdalena, near Cunén, and Sacapulas	The source refers to "una formidable peste." The people who survived the epidemic were resettled in Cunén and Sacapulas, forming in the latter the *parcialidad* Magdalena.	AGCA, A1, leg. 6037, exp. 53258
1666	*Tabardillo* (typhus)	Huehuetenango	Indian tribute lowered after epidemic carried off 45 adults.	AGCA, A3.16, leg. 1600, exp. 26390
1733	*Viruela* (smallpox)	Cunén and Sacapulas	Many tributaries died. The Indians, unable to pay tribute, request an exemption.	AGCA, A3.16, leg. 2819, exp. 40918
1774	*Peste* (unspecified sickness)	Various towns in Totonicapán and Huehuetenango	The *alcalde mayor* informs treasury officials that, because of the pestilence, certain communities are unable to pay tribute.	AGCA, A3.16, leg. 943, exp. 17608
1780–81	*Viruela*	Every major settlement in the Cuchumatán region	Over 4,000 deaths among the Indians. Children were particularly hard hit by the epidemic, thought to have originated in Chiapas.	AGCA, A1.44, leg. 6097, exp. 55507
1786	*Tabardillo*	Concepción and Petatán	The sickness is recorded as having broken out on September 2.	AGCA, A1.4, leg. 6101, exp. 55666
1795	*Viruela*	Towns along the *camino real* and throughout Soloma parish	The disease is thought to have spread east and south from Chiapas.	AGCA, A1.47, leg. 385, exp. 8012

Date	Disease	Location	Description	Source
1796–99	*Tabardillo*	Various towns, especially those in the parishes of Huehuetenango, Jacaltenango, and Nebaj	Very high mortality. In San Sebastián Huehuetenango, over 1,000 Indians perished. An equal number died in Concepción and Jacaltenango.	AGCA, A1.24, leg. 6101, exp. 55666-9; AGCA, A1.49, leg. 192, exp. 3911; AGCA, A3, leg. 2894, exp. 42846; AGCA, A3.16, leg. 244, exp. 4869; AGCA, A3.16, leg. 255, exp. 5719
1802–07	*Tabardillo*	Towns throughout Soloma parish	Considerable mortality. Settlements abandoned, fields neglected, and normal life totally disrupted. Locust invasion exacerbates crisis. Great misery.	AGCA, A1, leg. 6105, exp. 55795; AGCA, A1, leg. 6107, exp. 55836; AGCA, A1.24, leg. 6091, exp. 55306; AGCA, A1.47, leg. 2162, exp. 15558; AGCA, A3.16, leg. 245, exp. 4909
1803–07	*Viruela*	Numerous towns, including Soloma, Santa Eulalia, and San Juan Ixcoy	Smallpox prevails, despite efforts by Spanish authorities to vaccinate the Indians.	AGCA, A1.4, leg. 6091, exp. 55307; AGCA, A1.47, leg. 2162, exp. 15558-9; AGCA, A1.47, leg. 192, exp. 3922
1804–05	*Sarampión* (measles)	Chiantla and the towns of Soloma parish	Disease probably originated in Chiapas.	AGCA, A1, leg. 6091, exp. 55307; AGCA, A3.16, leg. 2899, exp. 43063
1811	*Fiebre putrida* (a type of fever)	Various communities throughout Totonicapán and Huehuetenango	Doctors request permission to draw money from community funds to help fight the spread of sickness.	AGCA, A1, leg. 394, exp. 8238

Table 22
Local outbreaks of disease in the Cuchumatán highlands, ca. 1550–1819 (continued)

Year	Disease	Communities affected	Comments	Source
1812	Peste (unspecified)	Chajul and San Juan Cotzal	The Indians are unable to pay tribute because of disease-related mortality.	AGCA, A3.16, leg. 2900, exp. 43154 and 43178
1812–14	Tabardillo	Chiantla, San Juan Cotzal, and the towns of Soloma parish	Roads into the infected communities are ordered closed and a "cordón sanitario" is set up.	AGCA, A1.4, leg. 386, exp. 8055; AGCA, A1.4, leg. 6114, exp. 56316; AGCA, A1.4, leg. 6116, exp. 56424
1818–19	Tabardillo	Chiantla and Jacaltenango	Religious festivities are to be cancelled because of the prevailing sickness.	AGCA, A1.4, leg. 388, exp. 8099; AGCA, A1.4, leg. 6118, exp. 56743

Table 23
Mortality in Cuchumatán towns during the smallpox epidemic of 1780–81

Community	Married males	Married females	Widowers	Widows	Single males	Single females	Boys	Girls	Total no. of dead	No. of dead tributaries	Indian population in 1779	Mortality, in %
Aguacatán and Chalchitán	5	10	–	–	18	12	49	43	137	5	904	15
Amatenango	2	2	4	–	3	4	9	12	36	2	186	19
Colotenango	10	15	3	4	27	8	31	42	140	15	1,042	13
Concepción	7	17	–	2	22	14	44	41	147	7	480	31
Chajul	5	15	–	–	10	–	86	77	195	5	1,358	14
Chiantla	6	8	–	2	13	7	20	7	63	5	225	28
Cuilco	1	2	–	1	7	7	23	14	55	3	304	18
Cunén	16	20	7	1	3	2	12	16	77	10	244	32
Huehuetenango	5	6	1	1	15	17	20	15	80	6	602	13
Ixtahuacán	9	30	4	4	15	23	45	43	173	12	947	18
Jacaltenango	13	28	4	1	32	29	80	86	273	15	1,728	16
Malacatán	2	4	2	3	2	4	9	9	35	2	180	19
Nebaj	6	11	–	–	19	15	58	56	165	7	1,428	12
Sacapulas	14	42	11	9	21	24	78	101	300	10	1,906	16
San Andres Jacaltenango	1	8	–	–	8	5	19	13	49	1	294	17
San Antonio Huista	10	1	–	–	1	6	3	11	32	6	136	24

Table 23
Mortality in Cuchumatán towns during the smallpox epidemic of 1780–81 (continued)

Community	Married males	Married females	Widowers	Widows	Single males	Single females	Boys	Girls	Total no. of dead	No. of dead tributaries	Indian population in 1779	Mortality, in %
San Francisco Motozintla	–	3	–	2	3	3	7	12	30	1	125	24
San Gaspar Ixchil	–	–	1	1	3	3	5	8	21	1	273	8
San Juan Atitán	1	13	1	3	10	4	29	35	96	2	473	17
San Juan Cotzal	11	17	–	–	8	3	48	47	138	11	1,707	8
San Juan Ixcoy	5	9	–	1	21	24	35	39	154	6	934	16
San Lorenzo	4	7	–	–	2	2	11	11	37	4	330	11
San Marcos Jacaltenango	8	6	–	–	7	–	11	21	53	8	228	18
San Martín Cuchumatán	–	1	–	–	1	3	10	9	24	–	118	20
San Martín Mazapa	1	1	–	3	10	4	4	19	42	3	208	26
San Mateo Ixtatán	10	26	20	6	32	10	55	72	231	12	1,132	20
San Miguel Acatán	5	12	1	5	31	18	24	33	129	5	338	38
San Pedro Necta	3	8	1	–	11	5	26	13	67	3	527	13
San Sebastián Coatán	8	11	–	–	13	14	26	51	123	8	463	27

San Sebastián Huehuetenango	6	16	–	2	43	43	74	68	252	6	2,275	11
Santa Ana Huista	8	10	–	2	11	7	11	4	53	7	395	13
Santa Bárbara	3	2	–	–	10	3	15	17	50	3	386	13
Santa Eulalia	19	37	3	3	31	28	84	92	297	17	1,577	19
Santa Isabel	2	3	1	–	12	16	11	11	56	3	532	11
Santiago Chimaltenango	2	1	–	3	7	14	28	24	79	2	484	16
Petatán	9	–	2	1	1	–	4	–	17	9	94	18
Soloma	5	5	2	1	2	3	7	17	42	5	285	15
Tectitán	5	6	–	1	12	8	30	13	75	4	275	27
Todos Santos Cuchumatán	1	8	–	1	12	10	36	38	106	–	721	15
Uspantán	11	22	5	2	22	3	10	11	86	22	361	24
									4,215	253		

Source: AGCA, A1.44, leg. 6097, exp. 55507.
Note: All the above deaths occurred among the Indian population. In addition, there were 181 deaths among the Ladino and Spanish population of the region, mostly residents of Chiantla, Cuilco, Huehuetenango, and Malacatán.

Table 24
Extent of infection, recovery, and fatality during the smallpox epidemic of 1780 in
Ixil Country

A Community	B Population in 1779	C No. of people afflicted by smallpox in 1780	D C as % of B	E No. of smallpox deaths in 1780	F E as % of C (fatality rate)
San Gaspar Chajul	1358	836	62	195	23
San Juan Cotzal	1707	503	29	138	27
Santa María Nebaj	1428	614	43	165	27

Source: AGCA, A1.24, leg. 6097, exp. 55507.

Table 25
Vaccination against smallpox among Cuchumatán Indians, 1807

Parish	Number of Indians vaccinated	Cost of vaccination
Chiantla	515	64 pesos 3 *reales*
Jacaltenango	762	95 pesos 2 *reales*
Malacatán	621	77 pesos 5 *reales*
Nebaj	348	43 pesos 4 *reales*
Soloma	1,186	148 pesos 2 *reales*

Source: AGCA, A1.47, leg. 2162, exp. 15558.

Table 26
Population and mortality levels around the time of the typhus epidemic of 1796–99

A Community	B Population in 1784	C Population in 1795	D Indian deaths due to typhus	E D as % of B or C	F Population in 1801	E Population in 1811
Huehuetenango	509	786	97	12	857	1,115
Concepción	608	–	561	92	309	340
Jacaltenango	1,443	–	528	37	1,463	1,840
San Juan Atitán	543	687	351	51	392	430
San Martín Cuchumatán	144	–	87	60	99	95
San Sebastián Huehuetenango	2,067	2,878	1,070	37	2,059	2,300
Santa Isabel	461	300	82	27	345	435
Todos Santos Cuchumatán	704	827	488	59	415	440

Sources: AGCA, A1.44, leg. 6097, exp. 55507; Gazeta de Guatemala, 6 and 9 November 1797; AGCA, A1.24, leg. 6101, exp. 55666; A3.16, leg. 255, exp. 5719; A2.16, leg. 243, exp. 4853; and A3.16, leg. 953, exp. 17773.

Bibliography

This book is based on familiarity gained over the past forty years with a variety of unpublished and published materials housed in academic repositories in Canada, Guatemala, Scotland, Spain, and the United States. In addition to mentioning the archives and libraries visited in connection with the investigation, and before listing a number of titles that may be considered fundamental research aids, it is perhaps useful to comment briefly on what sources proved most fruitful for the purpose of this study. Several suggestions regarding topics that demand future inquiry can also be made.

PRIMARY ARCHIVAL SOURCES

Unpublished documents covering the entire colonial period were consulted in the Archivo General de Centro América (AGCA) in Guatemala City and in the Archivo General de Indias (AGI) in Seville. The AGCA, where *legajos* (document bundles) are made up of numerous *expedientes*, or files, was used more heavily than the AGI because the AGCA's unusual but functional catalogue facilitates a more efficient extraction of data than the AGI's rather unwieldy organization. When referred to in footnotes, *legajo* call numbers are abbreviated as "leg." and *expediente* call numbers as "exp.", the former designation always preceding the latter.

In the AGCA, the *fichero* (card index) of the following subjects yielded the highest return: Agricultura; Ayuntamiento; Epidemias; Esclavitud; Estadística; Encomienda; Fundación y Traslación de Poblaciones; Indígenas; Legislación; Minas; Patronato; Peticiones; Planos y Mapas; Provincia de Guatemala; Relaciones Geográficas; Tierras; Tasaciones; and Tributos. The AGCA also houses a land registry called the Sección de Tierras (ST), another bountiful source. Anyone who has worked in this archive cannot help but be impressed by the Herculean labour that went into its organization by José Joaquín Pardo (1905–64), the man responsible for classifying much of the documentation extant for the colonial period. The colonial contents of the AGCA have been microfilmed and may be consulted in this form at McMaster University Library in Hamilton, Canada. A guide to the AGCA has been published by Jorge Luján Muñoz (1982). When read in conjunction with the bibliographic essay of Christopher H. Lutz and Stephen A. Webre (1980), along with the "informe" of Pedro López Gómez (1991), it provides the basic orientation that every researcher who works in the AGCA needs at the outset. The archive's website also facilitates familiarity with its holdings and provides access for off-site consultation, though this is no substitute for in-situ investigation. Sadly, however, despite heightened security and increased professionalism in running the AGCA, its contents have been subjected repeatedly to mismanagement and looting – see Sulllivan (1995) and Kramer, Lovell, and Lutz (2013, 2014) – and so some documents consulted in the mid to late 1970s may no longer be extant.

At the AGI, because of the far greater volume of documentation and the more subtle complexity of the archive's inner logic, perseverance is the key. Research here focused primarily on sixteenth-century *encomienda*, tribute, and population data, all of which are scarce (for the Cuchumatán region at any rate) in the AGCA. The section of the AGI known as the Audiencia de Guatemala, comprising some 973 *legajos*, is marvellously rich but poorly classified. Work in the AGI, while always exciting, tends to proceed at a slower pace, particularly if a local or regional study is being undertaken. Other sections of the AGI in which relevant information was located include Contaduría, Indiferente General, Justicia, and Patronato. For orientation purposes, the reference section of the main reading room at the AGI contains an unpublished guide to the archive's sixteenth-century Guatemalan materials. This guide, bearing the call number Salón 127, was prepared by E.M. O'Flaherty as part of a microfilm project funded by the American Philosophical Society, an institution that now has copies of some seventy thousand documents relating to early colonial Guatemala. Like those of the AGCA, the AGI's vast holdings can now be accessed online.

In Spain, visits were made to the Archivo General de Simancas, the Biblioteca del Palacio Real, and the Real Academia de la Historia in order to determine whether or not these repositories hold pertinent Cuchumatán data. Though nothing of great substance materialized, it was important nonetheless to look. Trips to the Newberry Library in Chicago, to the University of Texas at Austin, and to the University of California at Berkeley proved more productive. Research at the Newberry meant (among other things) a unique opportunity to look at the *Popol Vuh*. Likewise in Austin, a spell at the Nettie Lee Benson Library allowed perusal of the J. García Icazbalceta Collection. In addition to providing an opportunity to consult rare books and manuscripts housed in the Bancroft Library, trips to Berkeley afforded the pleasure of discovering pertinent items of correspondence in the Sauer Collection and the papers of Sherburne F. Cook. My Scottish alma mater, the University of Glasgow, contains in its Special Collections a manuscript copy of Diego Muñoz Camargo's *Historia de Tlaxcala* (1584–85). Its graphic battle scenes leave no doubt as to how brutal and prolonged the conquest of Guatemala truly was, and how pivotal in it was the Tlaxcalan role.

Two regrets must be recorded. The first concerns the frustration, felt by other scholars also, at not having had ready access to the Archivo Histórico Arquidiocesano (AHA) in Guatemala City, an archive in the metropolitan cathedral known to contain a wealth of material relating to the affairs of the colonial church (Feldman 1985). Mario Humberto Ruz (2002) has embarked on the ambitious task of having data-laden *visitas pastorales* (spiritual tours of inspection) housed in the AHA transcribed and published. The second regret involves not having made use of parish records. The latter oversight may now seem inexcusable, but at the time when information was first being gathered, it made more sense, given the regional dimension of the study, to concentrate on the AGCA rather than work through individual parish holdings in the countryside. Not until I spent a few days in Jacaltenango, where the late Dorothy (Madre Rosa) Erickson, a medical doctor and Maryknoll sister, established a small archive and museum, did I realize the extent to which orders calling for historical records to be sent to Guatemala City were not always acted upon (Lovell 1991). Thus, despite my attempts to locate and scrutinize as many colonial-period documents as possible, a significant number were undoubtedly overlooked. When these sources are unearthed by future research, it can only be hoped that they elucidate rather than obfuscate the content of this study.

PUBLISHED SECONDARY SOURCES

With respect to the published literature, mention has been made in the preface of the outstanding work of the Berkeley School, perhaps best represented in the Ibero-Americana monographs, and of the exceptional contribution of Murdo MacLeod ([1973] 2008). To these enduring benchmarks must be added *La Patria del Criollo* ([1970] 2009), Severo Martínez Peláez's elegy for a Guatemalan homeland, and Robert M. Carmack's *Quichean*

Civilization (1973), which provides a critical analysis of the major documentary sources relating to past and present-day Guatemala. A tour-de-force of incisive reading and reflection, Carmack's critique remains indispensable. Key titles published since the time of his labours are flagged in the epilogue.

Until detailed archaeological and ethnohistorical investigations with an explicitly Cuchumatán focus are conducted, an understanding of the pre-conquest experience of the region and its peoples must be framed, in large part, by extrapolating from the work of Carmack and his associates in the K'iche'an area. Some scholars, however, disagree with what they view as Carmack's literal interpretation of certain sources, particularly the *Popol Vuh*, and point out that, contrary to the ethnohistorical account of Toltec invasion from the north, the archaeological record of the Quiché basin shows a strong continuity from Classic to Post-classic times (Gruhn and Bryan 1976; Van Akkeren 2008, 2012). Carmack has synthesized decades of work in the field in his magnum opus, *The Quiché Mayas of Utatlán* (1981). Anthropological work in the Cuchumatanes similarly necessitates speculating that the findings of fieldwork undertaken elsewhere in highland Guatemala, or even in parts of Mexico, may apply also to Cuchumatán communities. There is an urgent need, for example, for diachronic community studies that examine Indian social units so as to discern, among other things, whether or not they have continued in association with specific territory since pre-conquest or colonial times. In the context of Chiapas, as noted in chapter 2, George Collier (1975) argues for such continuity, while the research of Robert Wasserstrom (1983) suggests otherwise. The study of land tenure and inheritance conducted by Shelton Davis (1970, 1997) for Santa Eulalia serves as a model for the historically oriented anthropology that is sorely required. Such an orientation by Anne Collins (1980) has produced a fine reconstruction of how the colonial experience in Jacaltenango resulted in the formation, along lines first suggested by Fernando Cámara (1952) and Eric Wolf (1957), of a classic "closed corporate peasant community." The research of Robert Hill II and John Monaghan (1987) indicates a similar process at work in Sacapulas. The apparent contradiction in the evidence for Chiapas suggests that Mesoamericanists, while striving for a longer view and an amplified context, must be more aware of the spatial and temporal limitations of their findings. As the volume of essays edited by Murdo MacLeod and Robert Wasserstrom (1983) underscores, matters of geographical and historical specificity must always be borne in mind.

For the three centuries of Spanish rule in Central America, Lesley Byrd Simpson's *Studies in the Administration of the Indians of New Spain* (1934–40) and the work of Howard Cline (1949, 1972a, b), Peter Gerhard (1972,

1977), and Adriaan van Oss (1986) are crucial to an understanding of *congregación* and the day-to-day administration of empire. William Sherman's *Forced Native Labor in Sixteenth-Century Central America* (1979) fills a large gap in our awareness of how Spaniards controlled and exploited the Indian population during the first century of colonial rule. The role that government played in shaping Central American colonial society has been addressed by Miles Wortman (1982). Our knowledge of colonial life in and around the capital city of Santiago de Guatemala owes much to the labours of Sidney D. Markman (1966) and Verle L. Annis (1968), and has been considerably enhanced by the more recent work of Christopher H. Lutz (1994, 2005). Before an accurate picture emerges of Indian and Spanish landholding in colonial Central America, regional studies similar to the ones undertaken for parts of Mexico by Charles Gibson (1952, 1964), William B. Taylor (1972), David Brading (1978), Herman Konrad (1980), and Eric Van Young (1981) will have to be initiated. An edited volume by Carmack, Early, and Lutz (1982), in which a dozen or so population profiles are offered at the local or regional level, provides a thorough overview of highland Guatemalan historical demography. This particular issue was the subject of a memorable panel at the twenty-seventh meeting of the American Society of Ethnohistory, held at Albany, New York, back in October 1979. Sessions similar to that one, organized as part of a larger learned forum or convened with a more specialized constituency as its core, advance communication between scholars and serve to review current states of the art and suggest future directions.

Two of the great chroniclers of the sixteenth and seventeenth centuries, Antonio de Remesal ([1619] 1964–66) and Francisco Antonio de Fuentes y Guzmán ([1690–99] 1932–33, 1967–72), have left behind valuable data on the Cuchumatanes. Remesal's work contains exceptionally detailed information on the operation of *congregación* and is one of the few early published sources that explicitly mention a decline in the size of the Indian population owing to the ravages of epidemic disease. Remesal may have been inspired to write the first colonial history of Guatemala by the example of his fellow Dominican, Fray Bartolomé de las Casas, but he was in many ways more meticulous and analytical in his work than was his mentor. The writings of Fuentes y Guzmán are marvellously rich, probably because the chronicler served in 1672 and 1673 as *corregidor* of Totonicapán and Huehuetenango, a charge that enabled him to become personally acquainted with the Cuchumatán terrain. Of the twenty-seven chapters that form Book Eight of the *Recordación florida*, twenty-one are devoted to a discussion of the history and geography of the Cuchumatanes. Fuentes y

Guzmán's first-hand knowledge of the Cuchumatán region lends his account greater credibility than certain other parts of the *Recordación florida* that deal with subjects beyond the chronicler's ken. The dossier of Pedro Cortés y Larraz ([1768-70] 1958) is the best eighteenth-century account of the region, the original replies to his queries written by parish priests (AGI, Guatemala 948) containing significantly more data than the archbishop's at times acerbic summary. His watercolour maps, eight in all for "curatos" in the Sierra de los Cuchumatanes, are a joy to behold. Large documentary collections such as the *Colección de documentos inéditos, relativos al descubrimiento, conquista y organización de las antiguas posesiones españolas de América y Oceanía* (Madrid, 1864–84, 42 vols.) and the *Colección de Ultramar* (Madrid, 1864–84; 1885–1932) are rather daunting to work with. These tomes are probably most useful for projects on a larger and more complex scale than this study.

Acuña, René. 1968. "Título de los señores de Sacapulas." *Folklore Americas* 28, no. 1: 1–37.

Adams, Richard E.W., and Murdo J. MacLeod, eds. 2000. *The Cambridge History of the Native Peoples of the Americas*. Vol. 2, *Mesoamerica*, Parts 1 and 2. New York: Cambridge University Press.

Adams, Richard N., and Santiago Bastos, eds. 2003. *Las relaciones étnicas en Guatemala, 1944–2000*. Antigua Guatemala: Centro de Investigaciones Regionales de Mesoamérica (CIRMA).

Agencia Española de la Cooperación Internacional para el Desarrollo. 2010. *Arquitectura de remesas*. Guatemala: Centro Cultural de España en Guatemala.

Alchon, Suzanne A. 2003. *A Pest in the Land: New World Epidemics in Global Perspective*. Albuquerque: University of New Mexico Press.

Alvarado, Pedro de. (1524) 1944. "Dos cartas de Pedro de Alvarado a Hernán Cortés." *Anales de la Sociedad de Geografía e Historia de Guatemala* 19, no. 5: 386–96.

Anderson, Thomas H. 1969. "Geology of the San Sebastián Huehuetenango Quadrangle, Guatemala." Ph.D dissertation, University of Texas.

Anderson, Thomas H., Burke Burkart, Russell E. Clemons, Otto H. Bohnenberger, and Don N. Blout. 1973. "Geology of the Western Altos Cuchumatanes, Northwestern Guatemala." *Bulletin of the Geological Society of America* 84: 805–26.

Anna, Timothy E. 1983. *Spain and the Loss of America*. Lincoln and London: University of Nebraska Press.

Annis, Verle Lincoln. 1968. *The Architecture of Antigua Guatemala, 1543–1773*. Guatemala: Editorial Universitaria, Universidad de San Carlos de Guatemala.

Aragón Cabrera, Daniel, and Benjamín Ruíz Escobar. 1975. "Consideraciones sobre producción de lana y su aplicación artesanal en el municipio de San Miguel Acatán, del departamento de Huehuetenango." *Guatemala Indígena* 10, nos. 3–4: 98–105.

Arriola, Jorge Luis. 1973. *El libro de las geonímias de Guatemala: Diccionario etimológico*. Guatemala: Seminario de Integración Social Guatemalteca.

Arroyo, Bárbara, José Cal Montoya, Leticia González S., Ricardo Sáenz de Tejada, and Luis Pedro Taracena, eds. 2013. *Nuestra historia, debates y propuestas*. Guatemala: Editorial Cara Parens.

Arroyo, Bárbara, and Luis Méndez Salinas. 2013. "La historia antigua y la evaluación de Preclásico al Postclásico, 1800 a.C–1521 d.C." In *Nuestra historia, debates y propuestas*, edited by Bárbara Arroyo et al., 1–99. Guatemala: Editorial Cara Parens.

Asselbergs, Florine. 2002. "La conquista de Guatemala: Nuevas perspectivas del *Lienzo de Quauhquechollan*." *Mesoamérica* 44: 1–53.

– 2004. *Conquered Conquistadors*: The Lienzo de Quauhquechollan – A Nahua Vision of the Conquest of Guatemala. Leiden: CNWS.

– 2008. *Conquered Conquistadors*: The Lienzo de Quauhquechollan – A Nahua Vision of the Conquest of Guatemala. Boulder, Colorado: University Press of Colorado.

– 2009. "*Lienzo de Quauhquechollan*: Crónica pictográfica nahua sobre la conquista española de Guatemala." *Crónicas Mesoamericanas* 2, 163–81. Guatemala: Universidad Mesoamericana.

– 2010. *Los conquistadores conquistados*: El Lienzo de Quauhquechollan – Una visión nahua de la conquista de Guatemala. Translated by Eddy H. Gaytán. Antigua Guatemala and South Woodstock, VT: Centro de Investigaciones Regionales de Mesoamérica and Plumsock Mesoamerican Studies.

Asturias, Francisco. 1958. *Historia de la medicina en Guatemala*. Guatemala: Editorial Universitaria, Universidad de San Carlos de Guatemala.

Baker, Alan R.H., Robin A. Butlin, A.D.M. Phillips, and Hugh C. Prince. 1969. "The Future of the Past." *Area* 1: 46–51.

Bakewell, Peter J. 1971. *Silver Mining and Society in Colonial Mexico: Zacatecas, 1546–1700.* Cambridge: Cambridge University Press.

Bancroft, Hubert H. 1890. *History of Central America.* 3 vols. San Francisco: The History Company.

Bastos, Santiago, and Manuela Camus. 1993. *Quebrando el silencio: Organizaciones del pueblo maya y sus demandas, 1986–1992.* Guatemala City: Facultad Latinoamericana de Ciencias Sociales.

– 1995. *Abriendo caminos: Las organizaciones mayas desde el Nobel hasta el Acuerdo de derechos indígenas.* Guatemala City: Facultad Latinoamericana de Ciencias Sociales.

– 2003. *Entre el mecapal y el cielo: Desarrollo del movimiento maya en Guatemala.* Guatemala City: Facultad Latinoamericana de Ciencias Sociales.

Baxby, Derrick. 1981. *Jenner's Smallpox Vaccine: The Riddle of Vaccinia Virus and Its Origin.* London: Heinemann Educational.

Becquelin, Pierre. 1969. *Arquéologie de la Région de Nebaj, Guatemala.* Mémoires de L'Institut d'Ethnologie 2. Paris: Institut d'Ethnologie, Musée de l'homme.

Beezley, William H., and Judith Ewell, eds. 1989. *The Human Tradition in Latin America: The Nineteenth Century.* Wilmington, DE: SR Books.

Bergmann, John F. 1969. "The Distribution of Cacao Cultivation in Pre-Columbian America." *Annals of the Association of American Geographers* 59, no. 1: 85–96.

Bertrand, Michel. 1982. "Les mecanismes de la revolte indigenne en Verapaz du XVIe siècle." In *Rabinal et la vallée moyenne du Río Chixoy, Baja Verapaz, Guatemala.* Cahiers de la RCP 500 Publicación 4, 107–40. Paris: CNRS, Institut d'Ethnologie.

– 1987. *Terre et societé coloniale: les communantes Maya-Quiché de la région de Rabinal du XVIe au XIXe siécle.* Mexico: Centre d'Etudes Mexicaines et Centroamericaines.

Blom, Frans, and Oliver La Farge. 1926–27. *Tribes and Temples.* 2 vols. New Orleans: Tulane University Press.

Borah, Woodrow. 1951. *New Spain's Century of Depression.* Ibero-Americana series no. 35. Berkeley and Los Angeles: University of California Press.

Borg, Barbara E. 1986. "Ethnohistory of the Sacatepéquez Cakchiquel, Maya, ca. 1450–1600 A.D." Ph.D. dissertation, University of Missouri.

Borhegyi, Stephan F. de. 1965. "Archaeological Synthesis of the Guatemalan Highlands." *Handbook of Middle American Indians* 2: 3–58. Austin: University of Texas Press.

Boyer, Richard. 1977. "Mexico in the Seventeenth Century: Transition of a Colonial Society." *Hispanic American Historical Review* 57, no. 3: 455–78.

Brading, David A. 1971. *Miners and Merchants in Bourbon Mexico, 1763–1810.* Cambridge: Cambridge University Press.

– 1978. *Haciendas and Ranchos in the Mexican Bajío: León, 1700–1860.* Cambridge: Cambridge University Press.

Brading, David A., and Harry E. Cross. 1972. "Colonial Silver Mining: Mexico and Peru." *Hispanic American Historical Review* 52, no. 4: 545–79.

Breton, Alain, ed. and trans. (1994) 1999. *Rabinal Achí: Un drama dinástico maya del siglo XV.* Mexico-Guatemala: Centro Francés de Estudios Mexicanos y Centroamericanos.

Bricker, Victoria R. 1981. *The Indian Christ, the Indian King: The Historical Substrate of Maya Myth and Ritual.* Austin: University of Texas Press.

– vol. ed. 1981–92. *Handbook of Middle American Indians.* 6 vols. Austin: University of Texas Press.

Brintnall, Douglas E. 1979. *Revolt against the Dead: The Modernization of a Mayan Community in the Highlands of Guatemala.* New York: Gordon and Breach.

Brinton, Daniel G., ed. and trans. 1885. *The Annals of the Cakchiquels.* Philadelphia: Library of Aboriginal American Literature.

Burkitt, Robert. 1924. "A Journey in Northern Guatemala." *Museum Journal* 15, no. 2: 115–45. Philadelphia: University of Pennsylvania.

– 1930. "Explorations in the Highlands of Western Guatemala." *Museum Journal* 21, no. 1: 41–72. Philadelphia: University of Pennsylvania.

Cabezas Carcache, Horacio, ed. 2005. *Mesoamérica.* Guatemala: Universidad Mesoamericana.

– 2009. "Introducción." *Crónicas mesoamericanas* 2, 11–14. Guatemala: Universidad Mesoamericana.

Cambranes, Julio C. 1985. *Café y campesinos: Los orígenes de la economía de plantación moderna en Guatemala.* Guatemala: Editorial Universitaria, Universidad de San Carlos de Guatemala.

Camus, Manuela. 2002. *Ser indígena en la Ciudad de Guatemala.* Guatemala City: Facultad Latinoamericana de Ciencias Sociales.

– ed. 2007. *Comunidades en movimiento: La migración internacional en el norte de Huehuetenango.* Guatemala: Instituto Centroamericano de Desarrollo y Estudios Sociales and Centro de Documentación de la Frontera Occidental de Guatemala.

– 2008. *La sorpresita del norte: Migración internacional y comunidad en Huehuetenango.* Guatemala: Instituto Centroamericano de Desarrollo y

Estudios Sociales and Centro de Documentación de la Frontera
Occidental de Guatemala.

Cardoza y Aragón, Luis, ed. and trans. (1929) 1972. *Rabinal Achí: Ballet-drama de los indios quichés de Guatemala*. Mexico: Editorial Porrúa.

Carey, David. 2001. *Our Elders Teach Us: Maya-Kaqchikel Historical Perspectives*. Tuscaloosa and London: University of Alabama Press.

Carmack, Robert M. 1965. "The Documentary Sources, Ecology, and Culture History of the Prehispanic Quiché Maya of Guatemala." Ph.D. dissertation, University of California at Los Angeles.

– 1968. *Toltec Influence on the Postclassic Culture History of Highland Guatemala*. Middle American Research Institute Publication 26. New Orleans: Tulane University Press.

– 1973. *Quichean Civilization: The Ethnohistoric, Ethnographic, and Archaeological Sources*. Berkeley and Los Angeles: University of California Press.

– 1977. "Ethnohistory of the Central Quiché: The Community of Utatlán." In *Archaeology and Ethnohistory of the Central Quiché*, edited by Dwight T. Wallace and Robert M. Carmack, 1–19. Institute for Mesoamerican Studies Publication 1. Albany: State University of New York.

– 1981. *The Quiché Mayas of Utatlán: The Evolution of a Highland Guatemalan Kingdom*. Norman and London: University of Oklahoma Press.

– 1982. "Social and Demographic Patterns in an Eighteenth-Century Census from Tecpanaco, Guatemala." In *The Historical Demography of Highland Guatemala*, edited by Robert M. Carmack, Christopher H. Lutz , and John D. Early, 137–50. Institute for Mesoamerican Studies Publication 6. Albany: State University of New York.

– 1983. "Spanish-Indian Relations in Highland Guatemala, 1800–1944." In *Spaniards and Indians in Southeastern Mesoamerica: Essays on the History of Ethnic Relations*, edited by Murdo J. MacLeod and Robert Wasserstrom, 215–52. Lincoln and London: University of Nebraska Press.

– ed. 1988. *Harvest of Violence: The Maya Indians and the Guatemalan Crisis*. Norman and London: University of Oklahoma Press.

– 1995. *Rebels of Highland Guatemala: The Quiché-Mayas of Momostenango*. Norman and London: University of Oklahoma Press.

– 2009. "Titulo Nijaíb I." *Crónicas Mesomericanas* 2: 97–123. Guatemala: Universidad Mesoamericana.

Carmack, Robert M., Christopher H. Lutz, and John D. Early, eds. 1982. *The Historical Demography of Highland Guatemala*. Institute for

Mesoamerican Studies Publication 6. Albany: State University of New York.

Carmack, Robert M., and James L. Mondloch. 2009. "Título K'oyoi." *Crónicas Mesoamericanas* 2: 14–67. Guatemala: Universidad Mesoamericana.

Carrasco, David, editor-in-chief. 2001. *The Oxford Encyclopedia of Mesoamerican Cultures: The Civilizations of Mexico and Central America.* 3 vols. New York: Oxford University Press.

Carrescia, Olivia L. 1982. *Todos Santos Cuchumatán: Report from a Guatemalan Village.* Brooklyn, NY: Icarus Films.

– 1989. *Todos Santos: The Survivors.* Brooklyn, NY: Icarus Films.

– 2011. *A Better Life.* Brooklyn, NY: Icarus Films.

Castañeda, César. 1998. *Lucha por la tierra, retornados y medio ambiente en Huehuetenango.* Guatemala: Facultad Latinoamericana de Ciencias Sociales.

Chance, John K. 1989. *Conquest of the Sierra: Spaniards and Indians in Colonial Oaxaca.* Norman and London: University of Oklahoma Press.

Chevalier, François. 1952. *La formation des grands domaines au Mexique: Terre et société aux XVI–XVIII siècles.* Paris: Université de Paris.

Chinchilla Aguilar, Ernesto. 1984. *Primer reparto de tierras para labranza: Guatemala, 1528–1538.* Guatemala: Unión Tipográfica.

Clark, Andrew H. 1954. "Historical Geography." In *American Geography: Inventory and Prospect,* edited by Preston E. James and Clarence F. Jones, 70–105. Syracuse: Syracuse University Press.

Claxton, Robert H., ed. 1986. *Investigating Natural Hazards in Latin American History.* Carrollton: West Georgia College.

Clendinnen, Inga. 1987. *Ambivalent Conquests: Maya and Spaniard in Yucatán, 1517–1570.* Cambridge: Cambridge University Press.

Cline, Howard F. 1949. "Civil Congregations of the Indians in New Spain, 1598–1606." *Hispanic American Historical Review* 29, no. 3: 349–69.

– 1972a. "Introductory Notes on Territorial Divisions of Middle America." In *Handbook of Middle American Indians* 7: 17–62. Austin: University of Texas Press.

– 1972b. "Viceroyalty to Republics, 1786–1952: Historical Notes on the Evolution of Middle American Political Units." In *Handbook of Middle American Indians* 7: 138–65. Austin: University of Texas Press.

– vol. ed. 1972–75. *Handbook of Middle American Indians: Guide to Ethnohistorical Sources.* 4 vols. Austin: University of Texas Press.

Cojtí Cuxil, Demetrio. 1984. "Problemas de la identidad nacional guatemalteca." *Revista Cultura de Guatemala* 5, no. 1: 17–21.

– 1996. "The Politics of Maya Re-vindication." In *Maya Cultural Activism in Guatemala,* edited by Edward F. Fischer and Robert McKenna Brown, 19–50. Austin: University of Texas Press.

– 1997. *Ri maya' moloj pa Iximulew: El movimiento maya en Guatemala.* Guatemala City: Editorial Cholsamaj.

Collier, George A. 1975. *Fields of the Tzotzil: The Ecological Bases of Tradition in Highland Chiapas.* Austin: University of Texas Press.

Collins, Anne C. 1980. "Colonial Jacaltenango, Guatemala: The Formation of a Corporate Community." Ph.D. dissertation, Tulane University.

Contreras, J. Daniel. 1951. *Una rebelión indígena en el partido de Totonicapán en 1820: El indio y la Independencia.* Guatemala: Imprenta Universitaria.

– 2008. "Historia Quiché de Don Juan de Torres." *Crónicas Mesoamericanas* 1: 107–28. Guatemala: Universidad Mesoamericana.

Cook, Garrett.W. 2001. *Renewing the Maya World: Expressive Culture in a Highland Town.* Austin: University of Texas Press.

Cook, Noble David. 1981. *Demographic Collapse: Indian Peru, 1520–1620.* Cambridge: Cambridge University Press.

– 1998. *Born to Die: Disease and New World Conquest.* New York: Cambridge University Press.

– 2002. "Sickness, Starvation, and Death in Early Hispaniola" *Journal of Interdisciplinary History* 32, no. 1: 349–86.

Cook, Noble David, and W. George Lovell, eds. (1992) 2001. *"Secret Judgments of God": Old World Disease in Colonial Spanish America.* Norman: University of Oklahoma Press.

Cook, Sherburne F. 1939. "Smallpox in Spanish and Mexican California, 1770–1845." *Bulletin of the History of Medicine* 7: 153–91.

– 1939. "The Smallpox Epidemic of 1797 in Mexico." *Bulletin of the History of Medicine* 7: 937–69.

– 1941–42. "Francisco Xavier Balmis and the Introduction of Vaccination to Latin America." *Bulletin of the History of Medicine* 11: 543–60; 12: 70–101.

– 1946. "The Incidence and Significance of Disease among the Aztecs and Related Tribes." *Hispanic American Historical Review* 26, no. 3: 320–35.

Cook, Sherburne F., and Woodrow Borah. 1971–79. *Essays in Population History.* 3 vols. Berkeley and Los Angeles: University of California Press.

Cooper, Donald B. 1965. *Epidemic Disease in Mexico City, 1761–1813: An Administrative, Social, and Medical Study.* Austin: University of Texas Press.

Cortés, Hernán. (1519–26) 1963. *Cartas y documentos*. Edited by Mario Hernández Sánchez-Barba. Mexico City: Editorial Porrúa.

Cortés y Larraz, Pedro. (1768–70) 1958. *Descripción geográfico-moral de la diócesis de Goathemala*. Edited by Adrián Recinos. 2 vols. Biblioteca "Goathemala" 20. Guatemala: Sociedad de Geografía e Historia de Guatemala.

– (1768–70) 2001. *Descripción geográfico-moral de la diócesis de Goathemala*. Edited by Julio Martín Blasco and Jesús María García Añoveros. Madrid: Consejo Superior de Investigaciones Científicas.

Crosby, Jr., Alfred W. 1967. "Conquistador y Pestilencia: The First New World Pandemic and the Fall of the Great Indian Empire." *Hispanic American Historical Review* 47, no. 3: 321–37.

– 1972. *The Columbian Exchange: Biological and Cultural Consequences of 1492*. Westport, CT: Greenwood Press.

– 1976. "Virgin Soil Epidemics as a Factor in the Aboriginal Depopulation in America." *William and Mary Quarterly* 33, no. 2: 289–99.

Cultural Survival and Anthropology Resource Center. 1983. *Voices of the Survivors: The Massacre at Finca San Francisco, Guatemala*. Peterborough, NH: Transcript Printing Co.

Cumberland, Charles C. 1968. *Mexico: The Struggle for Modernity*. New York: Oxford University Press.

Dakin, Karen, and Christopher H. Lutz. 1996. *Nuestro pesar, nuestra aflicción: Memorias en lengua náhuatl enviadas a Felipe II por indígenas del Valle de Guatemala hacia 1572*. Mexico City and South Woodstock, VT: Universidad Nacional Autónoma de México and Plumsock Mesoamerican Studies.

Darby, H. Clifford. 1953. "On the Relations of Geography and History." *Transactions of the Institute of British Geographers* 19: 1–11.

Davidson, William V., and James J. Parsons, eds. 1980. *Historical Geography of Latin America: Papers in Honor of Robert C. West*. Geoscience and Man 21. Baton Rouge: Louisiana State University Press.

Davis, Mary Ellen. 2002. *Haunted Land*. Montreal: Productions B'alba.

Davis, Shelton H. 1970. "Land of Our Ancestors: A Study of Land Tenure and Inheritance in the Highlands of Guatemala." Ph.D. dissertation, Harvard University.

– (1970) 1997. *La tierra de nuestros antepasados: Estudio de la herencia y la tenencia de la tierra en el altiplano de Guatemala*. Antigua, Guatemala: Centro de Investigaciones Regionales de Mesoamérica; South Woodstock, VT: Plumsock Mesoamerican Studies.

Denevan, William M. 1961. *The Upland Pine Forest of Nicaragua: A Study in Cultural Plant Geography*. Publications in Geography 12. Berkeley: University of California Press.

– 1971. *A Bibliography of Latin American Historical Geography*. Publication 6. Washington, DC: Panamerican Institute of Geography and History.

– ed. (1976) 1992. *The Native Population of the Americas in 1492*. 2nd ed. Madison: University of Wisconsin Press.

Denevan, William M., and Kent Mathewson, eds. 2009. *Carl Sauer on Culture and Landscape: Readings and Commentaries*. Baton Rouge: Louisiana State University Press.

Dessaint, Alain Y. 1962. "Effects of the Hacienda and Plantation Systems on Guatemala's Indians." *América Indígena* 22, no. 4: 323–54.

Deuss, Krystyna. 2007. *Shamans, Witches, and Maya Priests: Native Religion and Ritual in Highland Guatemala*. London: Guatemalan Maya Centre.

de Vos, Jan. (1980) 1993. *La paz de Dios y del rey: La conquista de la Selva Lacandona*. Mexico City: Fondo de Cultura Económica.

– 1997. *Vivir en frontera: La experiencia de los indios de Chiapas*. Mexico City: Centro de Investigaciones y Estudios Superiores en Antropología Social.

Díaz del Castillo, Bernal. (1632) 1970. *Historia verdadera de la conquista de la Nueva España*. Mexico City: Editorial Porrúa.

Dieseldorff, Erwin P., Eduard Seler, and Ernst Förstemann. 1904. "Two Vases from Chamá." In *Bulletin of the Bureau of American Ethnology* 28: 634–64. Washington, DC: Government Printing Office.

Dirección General de Estadística. 1969. *Censo Agropecuario 1964*. Guatemala: Dirección General de Estadística.

– 1975. *Octavo censo de población: Cifras difinitívas*. Guatemala: Dirección General de Estadística.

Dobyns, Henry F. 1966. "Estimating Aboriginal American Populations: An Appraisal of Techniques with a New Hemispheric Estimate." *Current Anthropology* 7: 395–416, 425–35, 440–4.

– 1983. *Their Number Become Thinned: Native American Populations Dynamics in Eastern North America*. Knoxville: University of Tennessee Press.

Dunn, Alvis E. 1999. "Aguardiente and Identity: The Holy Week Riot of 1786 in Quetzaltenango, Guatemala." Ph.D. dissertation, University of North Carolina.

Dunn, Henry. (1829) 1981. *Guatemala: or, the Republic of Central America, in 1827–1828*. London: James Nisbet.

Durham, William H. 1979. *Scarcity and Survival in Central America: Ecological Origins of the Soccer War.* Stanford: Stanford University Press.

Elliott, John H. 1976. *Imperial Spain, 1469–1716.* Harmondsworth, UK: Pelican Books.

Elliott, Raymond, and Helen Elliott. 1966. "Ixil." In *The Languages of Guatemala,* edited by Marvin K. Mayers, 125–39. The Hague: Mouton and Co.

Esquit Choy, Edgar. 2002. *Otros poderes, nuevos desafíos: Relaciones interétnicos en Tecpán y su entorno departmental, 1871–1935.* Guatemala City: Instituto de Estudios Interétnicos.

Falla, Ricardo. 1994. *Massacres in the Jungle: Ixcán, Guatemala, 1975–1982.* Translated by Julia Howland. Boulder, San Francisco, and Oxford: Westview Press.

– 2001. *Quiché Rebelde: Religious Conversion, Politics, and Ethnic Identity in Guatemala.* Translated by Philip Berryman. Austin: University of Texas Press.

– 2011. *Negreaba de zopilotes: Masacre y sobrevivencia en la Finca San Francisco, Nentón, Huehuetenango, Guatemala.* Guatemala: Asociación para el Avance de Ciencias Sociales.

Falla, Ricardo, and Elena Yocjom. 2012. *El sueño del Norte en Yalambojoch: Facetas de migración retornada.* Guatemala: Asociación para el Avance de Ciencias Sociales.

Farriss, Nancy M. 1978. "Nucleation versus Dispersal: The Dynamics of Population Movement in Colonial Yucatán." *Hispanic American Historical Review* 58, no. 2: 187–216.

– 1983. "Indians in Colonial Yucatán: Three Perspectives." In *Spaniards and Indians in Southeastern Mesoamerica: Essays on the History of Ethnic Relations,* edited by Murdo J. MacLeod and Robert Wasserstrom, 1–39. Lincoln: University of Nebraska Press.

– 1984. *Maya Society under Colonial Rule: The Collective Enterprise of Survival.* Princeton: Princeton University Press.

Feldman, Lawrence H. 1985. "El Archivo Eclesiástico de Guatemala." *Mesoamérica* 9: 170–7.

– 1986. *A Tumpline Economy: Production and Distribution Systems in Sixteenth-Century Eastern Guatemala.* Culver City, CA: Labyrinthos.

Fenn, Elizabeth A. 2001. *Pox Americana: The Great Smallpox Epidemic of 1775–82.* New York: Hill & Wang.

Few, Martha. 1995. "Women, Religion, and Power: Gender and Resistance in Daily Life in Late Seventeenth-Century Santiago de Guatemala." *Ethnohistory* 42, no. 4: 627–37.

- 1999. "'No es la palabra de Dios': Acusaciones de enfermedad y las policías culturales de poder en la Guatemala colonial." *Mesoamérica* 38: 33–54.
- 2002. *Women Who Live Evil Lives: Gender, Religion, and the Politics of Power in Colonial Guatemala, 1650–1750.* Austin: University of Texas Press.
- 2010. "Circulating Smallpox Knowledge: Guatemalan Doctors, Maya Indians, and Designing Spain's Smallpox Vaccination Expedition, 1780–1803." *British Journal for the History of Science* 43, no. 4: 519–37.

Fink, Leon. 2003. *The Maya of Morganton: Work and Community in the Nuevo New South.* Chapel Hill: University of North Carolina Press.

Fischer, Edward. F. 2001. *Cultural Logics and Global Economies: Maya Identity in Thought and Practice.* Austin: University of Texas Press.

Fischer, Edward F., and Robert McKenna Brown, eds. 1996. *Maya Cultural Activism in Guatemala.* Austin: University of Texas Press.

Foster, George M. 1960. *Culture and Conquest: America's Spanish Heritage.* Viking Fund Publications in Anthropology 27. New York: Wenner-Gren Foundation for Anthropological Research.

Fowler, William R. 1988. "La población nativa de El Salvador al momento de la conquista española." *Mesoamérica* 15: 79–116.
- 1989. *The Evolution of Ancient Nahua Civilizations: The Pipil-Nicarao of Central America.* Norman: University of Oklahoma Press.

Fox, John W. 1977. "Quiché Expansion Processes: Differential Ecological Growth Bases within an Archaic State." In *Archaeology and Ethnohistory of the Central Quiché*, edited by Dwight T. Wallace and Robert M. Carmack, 82–97. Institute for Mesoamerican Studies Publication 1. Albany: State University of New York.
- 1978. *Quiche Conquest: Centralism and Regionalism in Highland Guatemalan State Development.* Albuquerque: University of New Mexico Press.

Foxen, Patricia. 2008. *In Search of Providence: Transnational Mayan Identities.* Nashville, TN: Vanderbilt University Press.

Fuentes, Carlos. 1985. *Latin America: At War with the Past.* Toronto: CBC Enterprises.

Fuentes y Guzmán, Francisco Antonio de. (1690–99) 1932–33. *Recordación florida: Discurso historial y demostración natural, material, militar y política del reyno de Guatemala.* Edited by J. Antonio Villacorta. 3 vols. Biblioteca "Goathemala" nos. 6–8. Guatemala: Tipografía Nacional.
- (1690–99) 1967–72. *Obras históricas de don Francisco Antonio de Fuentes y Guzmán.* Edited by Carmelo Sáenz de Santa María. 3 vols.

Biblioteca de Autores Españoles 230, 251, and 259. Madrid: Ediciones Atlas.

Gage, Thomas. (1648) 1958. *Thomas Gage's Travels in the New World.* Edited by J. Eric S. Thompson. Norman: University of Oklahoma Press.

Galeano, Eduardo. (1982) 1985. *Memory of Fire: Genesis.* Translated by Cedric Belfrage. New York: Pantheon Books.

Gall, Francis. 1978–83. *Diccionario geógrafico de Guatemala.* 2nd ed. 4 vols. Guatemala: Instituto Geográfico Nacional.

Gálvez Borrell, Víctor, and Edgar Esquit Choy. 1997. *The Mayan Movement Today: Issues of Indigenous Culture and Development in Guatemala.* Guatemala City: Facultad Latinoamericana de Ciencias Sociales.

García Añoveros, Jesús María. 1987. "Don Pedro de Alvarado: Las fuentes históricas, documentación, crónicas y bibliografía existente." *Mesoamérica* 13: 243–82.

García Bernal, Manuela Cristina. 1978. *Yucatán: Población y encomienda bajo los Austrias.* Seville: Escuela de Estudios Hispano-Americanos.

Gasco, Jan. 1987. "Cacao and the Economic Integration of Native Society in Colonial Soconusco, New Spain." Ph.D. dissertation, University of California at Santa Barbara.

Gerhard, Peter. 1972. *A Guide to the Historical Geography of New Spain.* Cambridge: Cambridge University Press.

– 1972. "Colonial New Spain, 1519–1786: Historical Notes on the Evolution of Minor Political Jurisdictions." In *Handbook of Middle American Indians,* vol. 12, 63–117. Austin: University of Texas Press.

– 1977. "Congregaciones de indios en la Nueva España antes de 1570." *Historia Mexicana* 26, no. 3: 347–95.

– 1979. *The Southeast Frontier of New Spain.* Princeton: Princeton University Press.

Gibson, Charles. 1952. *Tlaxcala in the Sixteenth Century.* New Haven: Yale University Press.

– 1966. *Spain in America.* New York: Harper & Row.

– 1967. *The Aztecs under Spanish Rule: A History of the Indians of the Valley of Mexico, 1519–1820.* Stanford: Stanford University Press.

– ed., 1971. *The Black Legend: Anti-Spanish Attitudes in the Old World and the New.* New York: Alfred Knopf.

– 1975. "Writings on Colonial Mexico." *Hispanic American Historical Review* 55, no. 2: 287–323.

Góngora, Mario. 1962. *Los grupos de conquistadores en tierra firme, 1509–1530: Fisonomía de un tipo de conquista.* Santiago: Universidad de Chile.

González, Jorge H. 1994. "A History of Los Altos, Guatemala: A Study of Regional Conflict and National Integration, 1750–1885." Ph.D. dissertation, Tulane University.

Grandin, Greg. 2000. *The Blood of Guatemala: A History of Race and Nation*. Durham, NC, and London: Duke University Press.

Gruhn, Ruth, and Alan L. Bryan. 1976. "An Archaeological Survey of the Chichicastenango Area of Highland Guatemala." *Cerámica de Cultura Maya* 9: 75–119.

– 1977. "Los Tapiales: A Paleo-Indian Campsite in the Guatemalan Highlands." *Proceedings of the American Philosophical Society* 121, no. 3: 235–73.

Gruzinski, Serge 2002. "Histoires indiennes: Avancées et lacunes d'une approche éclatée." *Annales* 57, no. 5: 1311–21.

Hall, Carolyn. 1985. *Costa Rica: A Geographical·Interpretation in Historical Perspective*. Boulder, CO, and London: Westview Press.

Hall, Carolyn, and Héctor Pérez-Brignoli. 2003. *Historical Atlas of Central America*. Cartography by John V. Cotter. Norman and London: University of Oklahoma Press.

Haring, Clarence H. 1963. *The Spanish Empire in America*. New York: Harcourt, Brace, Jovanovich.

Hartshorne, Richard. 1939. *The Nature of Geography*. Lancaster, PA: Association of American Geographers.

Harvey, David. 1967. "Models of the Evolution of Spatial Patterns in Human Geography." In *Models in Geography*, edited by Richard J. Chorley and Peter Haggett, 549–608. London: Methuen.

– 1969. *Explanation in Geography*. London: Edward Arnold.

– (1973) 2009. *Social Justice and the City*. Rev. ed. Athens, GA: University of Georgia Press.

Henige, David. 1998. *Numbers from Nowhere: The American Indian Contact Population Debate*. Norman: University of Oklahoma Press.

Hernández, Leonardo. 1999. "Implicated Spaces, Daily Struggles: Home and Street Life in Late Colonial Guatemala City, 1750–1824." Ph.D. dissertation, Brown University.

Herrera, Robinson A. 2003. *Natives, Europeans, and Africans in Sixteenth-Century Santiago de Guatemala*. Austin: University of Texas Press.

Herrera, Robinson A., and Stephen A. Webre, eds. 2014. *La época colonial en Guatemala: Estudios de historia cultural y social*. Guatemala: Editorial Universitaria, Universidad de San Carlos de Guatemala.

Hidalgo, Joseph Domingo. 1797. "Descripción de la provincia de Totonicapán." *Gazeta de Guatemala* (31 de julio, 6 de noviembre, 13 de noviembre).

Higbee, E.C. 1947. "The Agricultural Regions of Guatemala." *Geographical Review* 37, no. 2: 177–201.

Hill II, Robert M. 1989. *The Pirir Papers and Other Colonial-Period Cakchiquel Maya Testaments*. Nashville: Vanderbilt University Publications in Anthropology.

– 1991. *Colonial Cakchiquels: Highland Maya Adaptations to Spanish Rule, 1600–1700*. Fort Worth, TX: Harcourt, Brace, Jovanovich.

Hill II, Robert M., and John Monaghan. 1987. *Continuities in Highland Maya Social Organization: Ethnohistory in Sacapulas, Guatemala*. Philadelphia: University of Pennsylvania Press.

Hopkins, Donald R. 1983. *Princes and Peasants: Smallpox in History*. Chicago: University of Chicago Press.

Human Rights Office of the Archdiocese of Guatemala. 1999. *Guatemala: Never Again*. Maryknoll, NY: Orbis Books.

Instituto de Agricultura, Recursos Naturales y Ambiente. 2006. *Pérfil ambiental de Guatemala: Tendencias y reflexiones sobre la gestión ambiental*.

Instituto Geográfico Nacional. 1961–62. *Diccionario geográfico de Guatemala*. 1st ed. 2 vols. Guatemala: Instituto Geográfico Nacional.

Instituto Nacional de Estadística. 2003. *Características de la población y de los locales de habitación censados*. Guatemala: Instituto Nacional de Estadística.

Israel, Jonathan I. 1975. *Race, Class, and Politics in Colonial Mexico, 1610–1670*. Oxford: Oxford University Press.

Ivic de Monterroso, Matilde. 2008. "Testamento de los Xpantzay de Tecpán Guatemala." *Crónicas Mesoamericanas* 1: 129–40. Guatemala: Universidad Mesoamericana.

– 2009. "Historia de los Xpantzay de Tecpán Guatemala: Introducción." *Crónicas Mesoamericanas* 2: 87–96. Guatemala: Universidad Mesoamericana.

Johannessen, Carl L. 1963. *Savannas of Interior Honduras*. Ibero-Americana series no. 46. Berkeley: University of California Press.

Jones, Chester Lloyd. 1940. *Guatemala, Past and Present*. Minneapolis: University of Minnesota Press.

Jones, Grant D. 1983. "The Last Maya Frontiers of Colonial Yucatán." In *Spaniards and Indians in Southeastern Mesoamerica: Essays on the History of Ethnic Relations*, edited by Murdo J. MacLeod and Robert Wasserstrom, 64–91. Lincoln and London: University of Nebraska Press.

– 1989. *Maya Resistance to Spanish Rule: Time and History on a Colonial Frontier*. Albuquerque: University of New Mexico Press.

- 1998. *The Conquest of the Last Maya Kingdom*. Stanford: Stanford University Press.

Juarros, Domingo. (1808) 1981. *Compendio de la historia del Reino de Guatemala, 1500–1800*. Guatemala: Editorial Piedra Santa.

- 1823. *A Statistical and Commercial History of the Kingdom of Guatemala in Spanish America*. Translated by John Bailey. London: J. Hearne.

Kaufman, Terrence. 1976. "Archaeological and Linguistic Correlations in Mayaland and Associated Areas of Mesoamerica. *World Archaeology* 8, no.1: 101–08.

Keen, Benjamin. 1963. "Introduction." In *Life and Labor in Ancient Mexico: The Brief and Summary Relation of the Lords of New Spain*, by Alonso de Zorita, 3–77. New Brunswick, NJ: Rutgers University Press.

Kelly, John E. 1932. *Pedro de Alvarado: Conquistador*. Princeton: Princeton University Press.

Kidder, Alfred V., Jesse D. Jennings, and Edwin M. Shook. 1946. *Excavations at Kaminaljuyú, Guatemala*. Publication 561. Washington, DC: Carnegie Institution of Washington.

Kirchoff, Paul. 1942. "Mesoamérica." *Acta Americana* 1: 92–107.

Kirkpatrick, Frederick A. 1939. "Repartimiento – Encomienda." *Hispanic American Historical Review* 21, no. 3: 372–9.

Knapp, Gregory, ed. 2002. *Latin America in the Twenty-First Century: Challenges and Solutions*. Austin: Conference of Latin Americanist Geographers and University of Texas Press.

Kobrak, Paul. 2003. *Huehuetenango: Historia de una guerra*. Guatemala City: Magna Terra Editores.

- 2013. "The Long War in Colotenango." In *War by Other Means: Aftermath in Post-Genocide Guatemala*, edited by Carlota McAllister and Diane M. Nelson, 218–40. Durham and London: Duke University Press.

Komisaruk, Catherine. 2013. *Labor and Love in Guatemala: The Eve of Independence*. Stanford: Stanford University Press.

Konrad, Herman W. 1980. *A Jesuit Hacienda in Colonial Mexico: Santa Lucía, 1576–1767*. Stanford: Stanford University Press.

Kramer, Wendy. 1994. *The Politics of Encomienda Distribution in Early Spanish Guatemala, 1524–1544: Dividing the Spoils*. Boulder, CO: Westview Press.

Kramer, Wendy, W. George Lovell, and Christopher H. Lutz. 2013. "Pillage in the Archives: The Whereabouts of Guatemalan Documentary Treasures." *Latin American Research Review* 48, no. 3: 153–67.

– 2014. *Saqueo en el Archivo: El paradero de los tesoros documentales guatemaltecos*. Antigua Guatemala: Centro de Investigaciones Regionales de Mesoamérica.

La Farge, Oliver. 1940. "Maya Ethnology: The Sequence of Cultures." In *The Maya and Their Neighbors*, edited by Clarence L. Hay et al., 281–91. New York: D. Appleton Century.

– 1947. *Santa Eulalia: The Religion of a Cuchumatán Indian Town*. Chicago: University of Chicago Press.

La Farge, Oliver, and Douglas Byers. 1931. *The Year Bearer's People*. Middle American Research Institute Publication 3. New Orleans: Tulane University Press.

Lanning, John Tate. 1956. *The Eighteenth-Century Enlightenment in the University of San Carlos de Guatemala*. Ithaca, NY: Cornell University Press.

– 1985. *The Royal Protomedicato: The Regulation of the Medical Professions in the Spanish Empire*. Edited by John J. TePaske. Durham, NC, and London: Duke University Press.

Las Casas, Bartolomé de. (1555) 1977. *Brevísima relación de la destrucción de las Indias*. Edited and introduced by Manuel Ballesteros y Gaibrois. Madrid: Fundación Universitaria Español.

Lenkersdorf, Gudrun. 1993. *Génesis histórica de Chiapas, 1522–1532: El conflicto entre Portocarrero y Mazariegos*. Mexico City: Universidad Nacional Autónoma de México.

– 2001. *Repúblicas de indios: Pueblos mayas en Chiapas, siglo XVI*. Mexico City: Universidad Nacional Autónoma de México.

Lehnhoff, Dieter. 1986. *Espada y pentagrama: La música polifónica en la Guatemala del siglo XVI*. Guatemala: Universidad Rafael Landívar.

Leighly, John, ed. 1963. *Land and Life: A Selection from the Writings of Carl Ortwin Sauer*. Berkeley and Los Angeles: University of California Press.

León Cázares, María del Carmen. 1988. *Un levantamiento en nombre del Rey Nuestro Señor*. Centro de Estudios Mayas 18. Mexico City: Universidad Nacional Autónoma de México.

Lincoln, Jackson S. 1945. *An Ethnographic Study of the Ixil Indians of the Guatemalan Highlands*. Chicago: Microfilm Collection of Manuscripts on Middle American Cultural Anthropology, University of Chicago.

Lischka, Joseph J. 1979. "Reconocimiento arqueológico de algunos sitios de la Sierra de los Cuchumatanes." *Antropología e Historia de Guatemala* 1, época 2: 11–19.

Livi-Bacci, Massimo. (2005) 2008. *Conquest: The Destruction of the American Indios*. Translated by Carl Ipsen. Cambridge, UK: Polity Press.

Lockhart, James. 1969. "Encomienda and Hacienda: The Evolution of the Great Estate in the Spanish Indies." *Hispanic American Historical Review* 49, no. 3: 411–29.

Lokken, Paul. 2000. "From Black to Ladino: People of African Descent, Mestizaje, and Racial Hierarchy in Rural Colonial Guatemala, 1600–1700." Ph.D. dissertation, University of Florida.

– 2008. "Génesis de una comunidad afro-indígena en Guatemala: La Villa de San Diego de Gomera en el siglo XVII." *Mesoamérica* 50: 37–65.

– 2013. "From the 'Kingdom of Angola' to Santiago de Guatemala: The Portuguese Asientos and Spanish Central America, 1594–1640." *Hispanic American Historical Review* 93, no. 2: 171–203.

Long, Haniel. (1939) 1987. *The Marvellous Adventure of Cabeza de Vaca*. London: Picador.

López Gómez, Pedro. 1991. *El Archivo General de Centro América, Ciudad de Guatemala: Informe*. Madrid: ANABAD.

Loucky, James, and Marilyn Moors, eds. 2000. *The Maya Diaspora: Guatemalan Roots, New American Lives*. Philadelphia: Temple University Press.

Lovell, W. George. (1990) 2015. *Conquista y cambio cultural: La Sierra de los Cuchumatanes de Guatemala, 1500-1821*. Antigua Guatemala: Centro de Investigaciones Regionales de Mesoamérica.

Lovell, W. George. 1990. "Mayans, Missionaries, Evidence, and Truth: The Polemics of Native Resettlement in Sixteenth-Century Guatemala." *Journal of Historical Geography* 16, no. 3: 77–94.

– 1991. "Parish Registers in Jacaltenango, Guatemala." *Latin American Research Review* 26, no. 3: 171–8.

– 1992. "'Heavy Shadows and Black Night': Disease and Depopulation in Colonial Spanish America." *Annals of the Association of American Geographers* 82, no. 3: 426–43.

– (1995) 2010. *A Beauty That Hurts: Life and Death in Guatemala*. Rev. 2nd ed. Austin: University of Texas Press.

– 1998. "Disease and Empire." *Canadian Geographer* 42, no. 4: 397–400.

– 2002. Review of *Numbers from Nowhere* by David Henige. *Ethnohistory* 49, no. 2: 468–70.

– 2004. "A Measure of Maturity: Advances and Achievements in Mesoamerican Studies." *Journal of Historical Geography* 30, no. 1: 173–8.

– 2006. "Columbian Exchange: Disease." In *Iberia and the Americas: Culture, Politics, and History*, edited by J. Michael Francis, vol.1, 296–303. Santa Barbara, CA: ABC-CLIO.

Lovell, W. George, and Christopher H. Lutz, with Wendy Kramer and William R. Swezey. 2013. *"Strange Lands and Different Peoples": Spaniards and Indians in Colonial Guatemala*. Norman: University of Oklahoma Press.

Lovell, W. George, Christopher H. Lutz, and William R. Swezey. 1984. "The Indian Population of Southern Guatemala, 1549–1551: An Analysis of López de Cerrato's *Tasaciones de Tributos*." *The Americas* 40, no. 4: 459–77.

Lovell, W. George, and William R. Swezey. 1981. "La población del sur de Guatemala al momento de la conquista española." *Antropología e Historia de Guatemala* 2, época 3: 43–54.

– 1990. "Indian Migration and Community Formation: An Analysis of *Congregación* in Colonial Guatemala." In *Migration in Colonial Spanish America*, edited by David J. Robinson, 18–40. Cambridge: Cambridge University Press.

Luján Muñoz, Jorge. 1982. *Guía del Archivo General de Centro América*. Guatemala: Ministerio de Educación.

– 1988. *Agricultura, mercado y sociedad en el corregimiento del Valle de Guatemala, 1670–1680*. Guatemala: Imprenta y Fotograbado Llerana.

Luján Muñoz, Jorge, gen. ed. 1993–1999. *Historia general de Guatemala*. 6 vols. Guatemala City: Fundación para la Cultura y el Desarrollo.

– ed. 2011. *Atlas histórico de Guatemala*. Guatemala: Academia de Geografía e Historia de Guatemala.

Lutz, Christopher H. 1994. *Santiago de Guatemala, 1541–1773: City, Caste, and the Colonial Experience*. Norman and London: University of Oklahoma Press.

– "Introducción y notas históricas." 1996. In *Nuestro Pesar, Nuestra Aflicción – Tunetuliniliz, Tucucuca: Memorias en lengua náhuatl enviadas a Felipe II por Indígenas del Valle de Guatemala hacia 1572*, edited by Karen Dakin and Christopher H. Lutz, xi–xlvii. Facsímiles de lingüística y filología nahuas, 7. Mexico City and Antigua Guatemala: Universidad Nacional Autónoma de México and Centro de Investigaciones Regionales de Mesoamérica

– 2005. *Santiago de Guatemala: Historia social y económica, 1541–1773*. Guatemala: Editorial Universitaria, Universidad de San Carlos de Guatemala.

Lutz, Christopher H., and W. George Lovell. 1990. "Core and Periphery in Colonial Guatemala." In *Guatemalan Indians and the State, 1540–1988*, edited by Carol A. Smith, 35–51. Austin: University of Texas Press.

Lutz, Christopher H., and James Mondloch. 2002. "Una elegía kaqchikel: Evaluación del *Memorial de Sololá*." *Mesoamérica* 44: 151–73.

Lutz, Christopher H., and Stephen A. Webre. 1980. "El Archivo General de Centro América y otros recursos investigativos en Guatemala." *Mesoamérica* 1: 274–85.

Mackie, Sedley J., ed. and trans. 1924. *An Account of the Conquest of Guatemala in 1524 by Pedro de Alvarado*. New York: Cortés Society.

MacLeod, Murdo J. 1970. "Las Casas, Guatemala, and the Sad but Inevitable Case of Antonio de Remesal." *Topic: A Journal of the Liberal Arts* 20: 53–64.

– (1973) 2008. *Spanish Central America: A Socioeconomic History, 1520–1720*. With a new introduction. Austin: University of Texas Press.

– 1983. "Ethnic Relations and Indian Society in the Province of Guatemala, ca.1620 – ca. 1800." In *Spaniards and Indians in Southeastern Mesoamerica: Essays on the History of Ethnic Relations*, edited by Murdo J. Macleod and Robert Wasserstrom, 189–214. Lincoln and London: University of Nebraska Press.

– 1986. "The *Matlazáhuatl* of 1737–1738 in Some Villages in the Guadalajara Region." In *Investigating Natural Hazards in Latin American History*, edited by Robert H. Claxton, 7–15. Carrollton: West Georgia College.

MacLeod, Murdo J., and Robert Wasserstrom, eds. 1983. *Spaniards and Indians in Southeastern Mesoamerica: Essays on the History of Ethnic Relations*. Lincoln and London: University of Nebraska Press.

Madigan, Douglas G. 1976. "Santiago Atitlán, Guatemala: A Socio-economic and Demographic History." Ph.D. dissertation, University of Pittsburgh.

Mallon, Florencia E. 2011. Review of Severo Martínez Peláez, *La Patria del Criollo: An Interpretation of Colonial Guatemala* (2009). *American Historical Review* 116, no. 1: 135–7.

Mann, Charles C. 2005. *1491: New Revelations of the Americas before Columbus*. New York: Alfred A. Knopf.

Markman, Sidney David. 1966. *Colonial Architecture of Antigua Guatemala*. Memoirs of the American Philosophical Society 64. Philadelphia: American Philosophical Society.

Martin, Cheryl E. 1985. *Rural Society in Colonial Morelos*. Albuquerque: University of New Mexico Press.

Martínez Durán, Carlos. 1940. *Las epidemias de tifus en Guatemala*. Guatemala: Tipografía Sánchez y de Guise.

Martínez Peláez, Severo. (1970) 1975. *La patria del criollo: Ensayo de interpretación de la realidad colonial guatemalteca*. San José: Editorial Universitaria Centroamericana.

– (1970) 1998. *La patria del criollo: Ensayo de interpretación de la realidad colonial guatemalteca*. Mexico City: Fondo de Cultura Económica.

– (1970) 2009. *La Patria del Criollo: An Interpretation of Colonial Guatemala*. Translated by Susan M. Neve and W. George Lovell. Edited and introduced by W. George Lovell and Christopher H. Lutz. Durham, NC, and London: Duke University Press.

– 1985. *Motines de indios: La violencia colonial en Centroamérica y Chiapas*. Cuadernos de la Casa Presno 3. Puebla: Centro de Investigaciones Históricas y Sociales.

Martinson, Tom L., ed. 1992. *Benchmark 1990*. Auburn, AL: Conference of Latin Americanist Geographer.

Mathewson, Kent, and Martin B. Kenzer, eds. 2004. *Culture, Land, and Legacy: Carl O. Sauer and the Berkeley School of Geography*. Baton Rouge: Louisiana State Univesity Press.

Matthew, Laura E. 2000. "El nahuatl y la identidad mexicana en la Guatemala colonial." *Mesoamérica* 40: 41–68.

– 2012. *Memories of Conquest: Becoming Mexicano in Colonial Guatemala*. Chapel Hill: University of North Carolina Press.

Matthew, Laura E., and Michel R. Oudijk, eds. 2007. *Indian Conquistadors: Indigenous Allies in the Conquest of Mesoamerica*. Norman and London: University of Oklahoma Press.

Maxwell, Judith M., and Robert M. Hill II. 2006. *Kaqchikel Chronicles: The Definitive Edition*. Austin: University of Texas Press.

May, J.M., and D.L. McLellan. 1972. *The Ecology of Malnutrition in Mexico and Central America*. New York: Hafner Publishing.

Mayers, Marvin K., ed. 1966. *The Language of Guatemala*. The Hague: Mouton & Co.

McAllister, Carlota, and Diane M. Nelson, eds. 2013. *War by Other Means: Aftermath in Post-Genocide Guatemala*. Durham, NC, and London: Duke University Press.

McArthur, Harry, and Lucille McArthur. 1966. "Aguacatec." In *The Languages of Guatemala*, edited by Marvin K. Mayers, 140–65. The Hague: Mouton & Co.

McBryde, Felix Webster. 1946. "Influenza in America during the Sixteenth Century (Guatemala: 1523, 1559–1562, 1576)." *Bulletin of the History of Medicine* 8, no. 2: 296–302.

- 1947. *Cultural and Historical Geography of Southwest Guatemala*. Institute of Social Anthropology Publication 4. Washington, DC: Smithsonian Institution.

McCreery, David J. 1983. "Debt Servitude in Rural Guatemala, 1876–1936." *Hispanic American Historical Review* 63, no. 4: 735–59.

- 1988. "Land, Labor, and Violence in Highland Guatemala: San Juan Ixcoy (Huehuetenango), 1890–1940." *The Americas* 45, no. 2: 237–49.

- 1989. "Atanasio Tzul, Lucas Aguilar, and the Indian Kingdom of Totonicapán." In *The Human Tradition in Latin America: The Nineteenth Century*, edited by William H. Beezley and Judith Ewell, 39–58. Wilmington, DE: SR Books.

- 1994. *Rural Guatemala, 1760–1940*. Stanford: Stanford University Press.

McGovern-Bowen, Carolyn G. 1983. *Mortality and Crisis Mortality in Eighteenth-Century Mexico: The Case of Pátzcuaro, Michoacán*. Discussion Paper 83. Syracuse: Syracuse University.

McNeill, William H. *Plagues and Peoples*. 1976. New York: Anchor and Doubleday Press.

Miles, Suzanne W. 1957. "The Sixteenth-Century Pokom-Maya: A Documentary Analysis of Social Structure and Archaeological Setting." *Transactions of the American Philosophical Society* 47: 731–81.

Miranda, José. 1952. *El tributo indígena en la Nueva España durante el siglo XVI*. Mexico City: El Colegio de México.

Montejo, Victor. 1999. *Voices from Exile: Violence and Survival in Modern Maya History*. Norman and London: University of Oklahoma Press.

- 2005. *Maya Intellectual Renaissance: Identity, Representation, and Leadership*. Austin: University of Texas Press.

Morales Urrutia, Mateo. 1961. *La división política y administrativa de Guatemala*. 2 vols. Guatemala: Editorial Iberia-Gutenberg.

Mörner, Magnus. 1964. "La política de segregación y el mestizaje en la Audiencia de Guatemala." *Revista de Indias* 24, nos. 95–96: 137–51.

- 1973. "The Spanish American Hacienda: A Survey of Research and Debate." *Hispanic American Historical Review* 53, no. 3: 183–216.

Motolinía, Toribio de Benavente. (1541) 1941. *Historia de los indios de la Nueva España*. Mexico City: Editorial Salvador Chávez Hayhoe.

- (1541) 1979. *Historia de los indios de la Nueva España*. Mexico City: Editorial Porrúa.

Nance, C. Roger, Stephen L. Whittington, and Barbara E. Borg. 2003. *Archaeology and Ethnohistory of Iximché*. With contributions by George Guillemin and Sergio Rodas Manrique. Gainesville: University of Florida Press.

Navarrete, Carlos. 1979. *Las esculturas de Chaculá, Huehuetenango.* Instituto de Investigaciones Antropológicas Cuaderno 31. Mexico City: Universidad Nacional Autónoma de México.

– 1980. "Las rutas de comunicación prehispánica en los Altos Cuchumatanes: Un proyecto arqueológico-etnohistórico." *Antropología e Historia de Guatemala* 2: 7–19.

Nelson, Diane M. 1999. *A Finger in the Wound: Body Politics in Quincentennial Guatemala.* Berkeley and Los Angeles: University of California Press.

Newson, Linda A. 1982. "Labor in the Colonial Mining Industry of Honduras." *The Americas* 39, no. 2: 185–203.

– 1985. "Indian Population Patterns in Colonial Spanish America." *Latin American Research Review* 20, no. 3: 341–74.

– 1986. *The Cost of Conquest: Indian Decline in Honduras under Spanish Rule.* Boulder, CO: Westview Press.

– 1987. *Indian Survival in Colonial Nicaragua.* Norman: University of Oklahoma Press.

Nicholson, Henry B. 1975. "Middle American Ethnohistory: An Overview." In *Handbook of Middle American Indians* 15, 487–505. Austin: University of Texas Press.

Nolasco Pérez, Pedro. 1966. *Historia de las misiones mercedarias en América.* Madrid: Edición Revista "Estudios."

Nolin, Catherine L. 2002. "Transnational Ruptures and Sutures: Questions of Identity and Social Relations among Guatemalans in Canada." *GeoJournal* 56: 59–67.

Oakes, Maud. 1951a. *Beyond the Windy Place: Life in the Guatemalan Highlands.* New York: Farrar, Straus, & Young.

– 1951b. *The Two Crosses of Todos Santos: Survivals of Mayan Religious Rituals.* New York: Pantheon Books.

Orellana, Sandra. 1984. *The Tzutujil Mayas: Continuity and Change, 1250–1630.* Norman and London: University of Oklahoma Press.

– 1987. *Indian Medicine in Highland Guatemala: The Pre-Hispanic and Colonial Periods.* Albuquerque: University of New Mexico Press.

– 1995. *Ethnohistory of the Pacific Coast.* Lancaster, CA: Labyrinthos.

Otzoy, Irma, and Enrique Sam Colop. 1990. "Identidad étnica y modernización entre los mayas de Guatemala." *Mesoamérica* 19: 97–100.

Otzoy, Simón, et al. 1999. *Memorial de Sololá.* Guatemala City: Comisión Interuniversitaria de Conmemoración del Quinto Centenario del Descubrimiento de América.

Patch, Robert W. 1993. *Maya and Spaniard in Yucatan, 1648–1812.* Stanford: Stanford University Press.

– 2002. Review of *The Cambridge History of the Native Peoples of the Americas*, vol. 2, parts 1 and 2, *Mesoamerica*, edited by Richard E.W. Adams and Murdo J. MacLeod. *American Historical Review* 107, no. 5: 1602–3.

– 2013. *Indians and the Political Economy of Colonial Central America, 1670–1810*. Norman: University of Oklahoma Press.

Pettersen, Carmen L. 1976. *The Maya of Guatemala: Their Life and Dress*. Guatemala: Museo Ixchel del Traje Indígena.

Piedrasanta Herrera, Ruth. 2009. *Los chuj: Unidad y ruptura en su espacio*. Guatemala: Armar Editores.

Piel, Jean. 1989. *Sajcabajá: Muerte y resurrección de un pueblo de Guatemala, 1500–1970*. Guatemala: Seminario de Integración Social Guatemalteca.

Pollack, Aaron. 2005. "K'iche' Uprising in Totonicapán: The Places of Subaltern Politics." Ph.D. dissertation, Clark University.

– 2008. *Levantamiento K'iche' en Totonicapán: Los lugares de las políticas subalternas*. Guatemala: Asociación para el Avance de los Ciencias Sociales.

Pompejano, Danielle. 1997. *La crisis del antiguo régimen en Guatemala, 1839–1871*. Guatemala: Editorial Universitaria, Universidad de San Carlos de Guatemala.

Ponce, Alonso, Alonso de San Juan, and Antonio de Ciudad Real. (1586) 1966. "Relación breve y verdadera de algunas cosas de las muchas que sucedieron al padre fray Alonso Ponce en las provincias de Nueva España." *Anales de la Sociedad de Geografía e Historia de Guatemala* 39, nos. 1–4: 123–291.

Price, Robin. 1982. "State Church Charity and Smallpox: An Epidemic Crisis in the City of Mexico, 1797–1798." *Journal of the Royal Society of Medicine* 75: 354–67.

Proskouriakoff, Tatiana. (1946) 1963. *An Album of Maya Architecture*. Norman and London: University of Oklahoma Press.

Razzell, Peter. 1977. *The Conquest of Smallpox: The Impact of Inoculation on Smallpox Mortality in Eighteenth-Century Britain*. Firle, UK: Caliban Books.

Recinos, Adrián. 1952. *Pedro de Alvarado: Conquistador de México y Guatemala*. Mexico: Fondo de Cultura Económica.

– 1954. *Monografía del departamento de Huehuetenango*. 2nd ed. Guatemala: Ministerio de Educación Pública.

– 1957. *Crónicas indígenas de Guatemala*. Guatemala: Editorial Universitaria, Universidad de San Carlos de Guatemala.

– ed. and trans. (1947) 1950. *Popol Vuh: The Sacred Book of the Ancient Quiché Maya*. English version by Delia Goetz and Sylvanus G. Morley. Norman and London: University of Oklahoma Press.

– ed. and trans. 1950. *Memorial de Solalá: Anales de los Cakchiqueles.* Mexico: Fondo de Cultura Económica.

Recinos, Adrián, and Delia Goetz, eds. and trans. (1950) 1953. *The Annals of the Cakchiquels / Titles of the Lords of Totonicapán.* Norman and London: University of Oklahoma Press.

Recopilación de las leyes de los reynos de las Indias. 4 vols. 1973. Madrid: Ediciones Cultura Hispánica.

Reeves, René. 2006. *Ladinos with Ladinos, Indians with Indians: Land, Labor, and Regional Ethnic Conflict in the Making of Guatemala.* Stanford: Stanford University Press.

Reina, Rubén E., and John Monaghan. 1981. "The Ways of the Maya: Salt Production in Sacapulas, Guatemala." *Expedition* 23, no. 3: 13–33.

Remesal, Antonio de. (1619) 1964–66. *Historia general de las Indias occidentales y particular de la gobernación de Chiapa y Guatemala.* 2 vols. Biblioteca de Autores Españoles, nos. 175 and 183. Madrid: Ediciones Atlas.

Restall, Matthew. 2003. *Seven Myths of the Spanish Conquest.* New York: Oxford University Press.

Restall, Matthew, and Florine Asselbergs. 2007. *Invading Guatemala: Spanish, Nahua, and Maya Accounts of the Conquest Wars.* University Park: Penn State University Press.

Ricketson, Oliver G. 1940. "The Cuchumatanes Re-visited." *Scientific Monthly* 51: 341–57.

Robinson, David J. 1972. "Historical Geography in Latin America." In *Progress in Historical Geography*, edited by Alan R.H. Baker, 168–84, 260–73. Newton Abbot: David & Charles.

– 1979. "Introduction to Themes and Scales." In *Social Fabric and Spatial Structure in Colonial Latin America*, edited by David J. Robinson, 1–24. Ann Arbor, MI: University Microfilms International.

– ed. 1981. *Studies in Spanish American Population History.* Boulder, CO: Westview Press.

– ed. 1990. *Migration in Colonial Spanish America.* Cambridge: Cambridge University Press.

Rodríguez, Mario. 1978. *The Cádiz Experiment in Central America, 1808–1826.* Berkeley and Los Angeles: University of California Press.

Rodríguez Becerra, Salvador. 1977. *Encomienda y conquista: Los inicios de la colonización en Guatemala.* Seminario de Antropología Americana Publicación 14. Seville: Universidad de Sevilla.

Rodríguez Guaján, Demetrio. 1992. *Cultura maya y políticas de desarrollo.* Chimaltenango, Guatemala: Coordinadora Kaqchikel de Desarrollo Integral.

Rosenblat, Angel. 1954. *La población indígena y el mestizaje en América.* 2 vols. Buenos Aires: Editorial Nova.

Roy, Alex J., and Matthew S. Lachniet. 2010. "Late Quaternary Glaciation and Equilibrium-Line Altitudes of the Mayan Ice Cap, Guatemala, Central America." *Quaternary Research* 74: 1–7.

Ruz, Mario Humberto, ed. 2002. *Memoria eclesial guatemalteca: Visitas pastorales* 1. Mexico: Universidad Nacional Autónoma de México.

Sacor Q., Fidel Hugo. 2008. "Rabinal Achí o Danza del Tun." *Crónicas Mesoamericanas* 1: 141–53. Guatemala: Universidad Mesoamericana.

Sáenz de Santa María, Carmelo. 1969. "Estudio Preliminar." In *Obras históricas de Don Francisco Antonio de Fuentes y Guzmán*, vol. 1: v–lxxxii. Biblioteca de Autores Españoles, no. 230. Madrid: Ediciones Atlas.

– 1972. "La reducción a poblados en el siglo XVI en Guatemala." *Anuario de Estudios Americanos* 29: 187–228.

Saint-Lu, André. (1970) 1978. *Condición colonial y conciencia criolla en Guatemala, 1524–1821.* Translated by Pierrette de Villagrán. Guatemala: Editorial Universitaria, Universidad de San Carlos de Guatemala.

Sanchiz Ochoa, Pilar. 1976. *Los hidalgos de Guatemala: Realidad y apariencia en un sistema de valores.* Seminario de Antropología Americana Publicación 13. Seville: Universidad de Sevilla.

Sanders, William T., and Barbara J. Price. 1968. *Mesoamerica: The Evolution of a Civilization.* New York: Random House.

Sauer, Carl Ortwin. (1925) 1963. "The Morphology of Landscape." In *Land and Life: A Selection from the Writings of Carl Ortwin Sauer*, edited by John Leighly, 315–50. Berkeley and Los Angeles: University of California Press.

– (1941) 1963. "Foreword to Historical Geography." In *Land and Life: A Selection from the Writings of Carl Ortwin Sauer*, edited by John Leighly, 351–79. Berkeley and Los Angeles: University of California Press.

– 1948. *Colima of New Spain in the Sixteenth Century.* Ibero-Americana series no. 29. Berkeley and Los Angeles: University of California Press.

– *The Early Spanish Main.* 1966. Berkeley and Los Angeles: University of California Press.

Schávelzon, Daniel. 1990. "Arqueologia y política en Centroamérica: Las excavaciones de Zaculeu y su contexto histórico, 1946–1950." *Demócrito* 1, no. 1: 9–26.

Schmid, Lester. 1967. *The Role of Migratory Labor in the Economic Development of Guatemala.* Land Tenure Center Research Paper 22. Madison: University of Wisconsin.

Schwartzkopf, Stacey. 2008. "Maya Power and State Culture: Community, Indigenous Politics, and State Formation in Northern Huehuetenango, Guatemala, 1800–1871." Ph.D. dissertation, Tulane University.

― 2013. "Rural *Castas*, State Projects, and Ethnic Transformation in Western Guatemala, 1800–1821." *Ethnohistory* 60, no. 4: 721–47.

Seler, Eduard. 1901. *Die Alten Ansiedlungen von Chaculá im Distrikte Nentón des Departements Huehuetenango der Republik Guatemala* . Berlin: Verlag von Dietrich Reimer.

― (1901) 2003. *The Ancient Settlements of Chaculá in the Nentón District of the Department of Huehuetenango, Republic of Guatemala*. Edited by John M. Weeks. Lancaster, CA: Labyrinthos.

Seler-Sachs, Caecilie. 1900. *Auf alten Wegen in Mexiko und Guatemala: Reiseerrinnerungen und Eindrücke aus den Jahren 1895–1897*. Berlin: Dietrich Reimer (Ernst Vohsen).

Sellers-García, Sylvia. 2014. *Distance and Documents at the Spanish Empire's Periphery*. Stanford: Stanford University Press.

Shattuck, George C. 1938. *Medical Survey of the Republic of Guatemala*. Washington, DC: Carnegie Institution of Washington.

Sherman, William L. 1969. "A Conqueror's Wealth: Notes on the Estate of Don Pedro de Alvarado." *The Americas* 26, no. 2: 199–213.

― 1979. *Forced Native Labor in Sixteenth-Century Central America*. Lincoln and London: University of Nebraska Press.

― 1983. "Some Aspects of Change in Guatemalan Society, 1470–1620." In *Spaniards and Indians in Southeastern Mesoamerica: Essays on the History of Ethnic Relations*, edited by Murdo J. MacLeod and Robert Wasserstrom, 169–88. Lincoln and London: University of Nebraska Press.

Simpson, Lesley Byrd. 1934–40. *Studies in the Administration of the Indians in New Spain*. Ibero-Americana series nos. 7, 13, and 16. Berkeley and Los Angeles: University of California Press.

― 1966. *The Encomienda in New Spain: The Beginnings of Spanish Mexico*. Berkeley and Los Angeles: University of California Press.

Smith, A. Ledyard. 1955. *Archaeological Reconnaissance in Central Guatemala*. Carnegie Institution of Washington Publication 608. Washington, DC: Carnegie Institution of Washington.

Smith, A. Ledyard, and Alfred V. Kidder. 1951. *Excavations at Nebaj, Guatemala*. Carnegie Institution of Washington Publication 594. Washington, DC: Carnegie Institution of Washington.

Smith, Carol A. 1978. "Beyond Dependency Theory: National and Regional Patterns of Underdevelopment in Guatemala." *American Ethnologist* 5, no. 3: 574–617.

- 1984. "Local History in Global Context: Social and Economic Transitions in Western Guatemala." *Comparative Studies in Society and History* 26, no. 2: 193–228.
- ed. 1990. *Guatemalan Indians and the State, 1540–1988*. Austin: University of Texas Press.
Smith, Clifford T. 1965. "Historical Geography: Current Trends and Prospects." In *Frontiers in Geographical Teaching*, edited by Richard J. Chorley and Peter Haggett, 118–43. London: Methuen.
Smith, Mary E. 1973. *Picture Writing from Ancient Southern Mexico: Mixtec Place Signs and Maps*. Norman: University of Oklahoma Press.
Smith, Mary E., and Frances F. Berdan, eds. 2003. *The Postclassic Mesoamerican World*. Salt Lake City: University of Utah Press.
Smith, Michael M. 1974. "The *Real Expedición Marítima de la Vacuna* in New Spain and Guatemala." *Transactions of the American Philosophical Society*, new series 64, no. 1.
Solano y Pérez Lila, Francisco de. 1974. *Los mayas del siglo XVIII: Pervivencia y transformación de la sociedad indígena guatemalteca durante la administración borbónica*. Madrid: Ediciones Cultura Hispánica.
- 1977. *Tierra y sociedad en el Reino de Guatemala*. Guatemala: Editorial Universitaria, Universidad de San Carlos de Guatemala.
Stadelman, Raymond. 1940. "Maize Cultivation in Northwestern Guatemala." In *Contributions to American Anthropology and History* no. 6, 91–125. Washington, DC: Carnegie Institution of Washington.
Stanislawski, Dan. 1947. "Early Spanish Town Planning in the New World." *Geographical Review* 37, no. 1: 94–105.
Steinberg, Michael, and Matthew Taylor. 2008. "Guatemala's Altos de Chiantla: Changes on the High Frontier." *Mountain Research and Development* 28: 255–62.
Stephens, John Lloyd. (1841) 1949. *Incidents of Travel in Central America, Chiapas, and Yucatan*. New Brunswick, NJ: Rutgers University Press.
Stoll, David. 1993. *Between Two Armies in the Ixil Towns of Guatemala*. New York: Columbia University Press.
Stone, Doris Z. 1932. "Some Spanish Entradas, 1524–1695." In *Middle American Research Institute* publication 4, 208–96. New Orleans: Tulane University Press.
Sullivan, J. 1995. "Guatemalan Held in Document Sale in New York." *New York Times*, 28 June, B1–3.
Swann, Michael M. 1980. "The Demographic Impact of Disease and Famine in Late Colonial Northern Mexico." *Geoscience and Man* 21: 97–109.

Taracena Arriola, Arturo. 2000. *Invención criolla, sueño ladino, pesadilla indígena: Los Altos de Guatemala, de región a estado, 1740–1871.* Antigua Guatemala: Centro de Investigaciones Regionales de Mesoamérica.

– ed. 2002. *Etnicidad, estado y nación en Guatemala, 1808–1944.* Vol. 1. Antigua Guatemala: Centro de Investigaciones Regionales de Mesoamérica.

– ed. 2003. *Etnicidad, estado y nación en Guatemala, 1944–1996.* Vol. 2. Antigua Guatemala: Centro de Investigaciones Regionales de Mesoamérica.

Tax, Sol. 1937. "The Municipios of the Midwestern Highlands of Guatemala." *American Anthropologist* 39, no. 3: 423–44.

– ed. 1952. *Heritage of Conquest.* New York: Macmillan.

Tax, Sol, and Robert E. Hinshaw. 1969. "The Maya of the Midwestern Highlands." In *Handbook of Middle American Indians* 7, 69–100. Austin: University of Texas Press.

Taylor, William B. 1972. *Landlord and Peasant in Colonial Oaxaca.* Stanford, CA: Stanford University Press.

– 1974. "Landed Society in New Spain: A View from the South." *Hispanic American Historical Review* 54, no. 3: 387–413.

– 1980. Review of William L. Sherman, *Forced Native Labor in Sixteenth-Century Central America* (1979). *Hispanic American Historical Review* 60, no. 2: 324–25.

Tedlock, Dennis, ed. and trans. 2003. *Rabinal Achi: A Mayan Drama of War and Sacrifice.* New York: Oxford University Press.

Tejada Bouscayrol, Mario. (2002) 2010. *Historia social del norte de Huehuetenango.* 2nd ed. Guatemala: Centro de Estudios y Documentación de la Frontera Occidental de Guatemala.

TePaske, John J., and Herbert S. Klein. 1981. "The Seventeenth-Century Crisis in New Spain: Myth or Reality." *Past and Present* 90: 116–35.

Termer, Franz. 1927. "Observaciones geográficas en los Altos Cuchumatanes." *Anales de la Sociedad de Geografía e Historia de Guatemala* 4, no. 1: 7–13.

– 1933. "Paisajes geográficos del norte de América Central." *Anales de la Sociedad de Geografía e Historia de Guatemala* 10, no. 2: 148–66.

Torres-Rivas, Edelberto., gen. ed. 1994. *Historia general de Centroamérica.* 6 vols. San José: Facultad Latinoamericana de Ciencias Sociales.

Tovilla, Martín Alfonso. (ca.1635) 1960. *Relación histórica-descriptiva de las provincias de la Verapaz y de la del Manché.* Edited by France V. Scholes and Eleanor B. Adams. Guatemala: Editorial Universitaria, Universidad de San Carlos de Guatemala.

Tozzer, Alfred M. 1912. "A Spanish Manuscript Letter on the Lacandones in the Archive of the Indies at Seville." *Proceedings of the Eighteenth International Congress of Amercianists*, 497–09. London.

United Nations Commission for Historical Clarification. 1999. *Guatemala: Memory of Silence*. Guatemala City: Litoprint.

Universidad de San Carlos. 1971. *Tenencia de la tierra en Guatemala*. Guatemala: Editorial Universitaria, Universidad de San Carlos de Guatemala.

Urschel, Donna. 2009. "Love and War: Shell Pendant Reveals Clues to Ancient Toltec Culture." *Library of Congress Information Bulletin 68*, no. 2.

Valle Escalante, Emilio del. 2009. *Maya Nationalisms and Postcolonial Challenges in Guatemala*. Santa Fe, NM: School for Advanced Research.

Van Aken, Mark. 1981. "The Lingering Death of Indian Tribute in Ecuador." *Hispanic American Historical Review* 61, no. 3: 429–59.

Van Akkeren, Ruud. 2000a. *Place of the Lord's Daughter: Rab'inal, Its History and Dance Drama*. Leiden: Universiteit Leiden.

– 2000b. "El baile-drama Rab'inal Achi: Sus custodios y linajes de poder." *Mesoamérica* 40: 1–39.

– 2002. "Lugar del cangrejo o caracol: La fundación de Rab'inal-Tequicistlán, Guatemala." *Mesoamérica* 44: 54–81.

– 2007. *La visión indígena de la conquista*. Guatemala: Serviprensa.

– 2008. "Título de los señores de Sacapulas." In *Crónicas Mesoamericanas* 1: 59–92. Guatemala: Universidad Mesoamericana.

– 2009. "Título de los indios de Santa Clara la Laguna." In *Crónicas Mesoamericanas* 21: 69–91. Guatemala: Universidad Mesoamericana.

– 2012. *Xib'alb'a y el nacimiento del nuevo sol: Una visión posclásica del colapso maya*. Guatemala City: Editorial Piedra Santa.

Van Oss, Adriaan C. 1986. *Catholic Colonialism: A Parish History of Guatemala, 1524–1821*. Cambridge: Cambridge University Press.

– 2003. *Church and Society in Spanish America*. Amsterdam: Askant.

Van Young, Eric. 1981. *Hacienda and Market in Eighteenth-Century Mexico: The Rural Economy of the Guadalajara Region, 1675–1820*. Berkeley and Los Angeles: University of California Press.

– 1983. "Mexican Rural History since Chevalier: The Historiography of the Colonial Hacienda." *Latin American Research Review* 18, no. 3: 5–61.

Vázquez, Francisco. (1688) 1937–44. *Crónica de la Provincia del Santísimo Nombre de Jesús de Guatemala*. 4 vols. Biblioteca

"Goathemala" nos. 14–17. Guatemala: Sociedad de Geografía e Historia de Guatemala.

Veblen, Thomas T. 1975. "The Ecological, Cultural, and Historical Bases of Forest Preservation in Totonicapán, Guatemala." Ph.D. dissertation, University of California at Berkeley.

– 1977. "Native Population Decline in Totonicapán, Guatemala." *Annals of the Association of American Geographers* 67, no. 4: 484–99.

Velásquez Nimatuy, Irma A. 2002. *La pequeña burguesía indígena comercial de Guatemala: Desigualdades de clase, raza y género.* Guatemala: Asociación para el Avance de las Ciencias Sociales.

Vigil, Ralph H. 1987. *Alonso de Zorita: Royal Judge and Christian Humanist, 1512–1585.* Norman: University of Oklahoma Press.

Villamarín, Juan A., and Judith E. Villamarín. 1975. *Indian Labor in Mainland Colonial Spanish America.* Newark, DE: University of Delaware.

Viqueira, Juan Pedro, and Mario Humberto Ruz, eds. (1995) 1998. *Chiapas: Los rumbos de otra historia.* Mexico: Universidad Nacional Autónoma de México.

Wagley, Charles. 1941. *The Economics of a Guatemalan Village.* Menasha, WI: American Anthropological Association.

– 1969. "The Maya of Northwestern Guatemala." In *Handbook of Middle American Indians* 7, 46–68. Austin: University of Texas Press.

Wallace, Dwight T., and Robert M. Carmack, eds. 1977. *Archaeology and Ethnohistory of the Central Quiche.* Institute for Mesoamerican Studies Publication 1. Albany: State University of New York.

Warren, Kay B. 1998. *Indigenous Movements and Their Critics: Pan-Maya Activism in Guatemala.* Princeton: Princeton University Press.

Wasserstrom, Robert. 1983a. *Class and Society in Central Chiapas.* Berkeley and Los Angeles: University of California Press.

– 1983b. "Spaniards and Indians in Colonial Chiapas, 1528–1790." In *Spaniards and Indians in Southeastern Mesoamerica: Essays on the History of Ethnic Relations*, edited by Murdo J. MacLeod and Robert Wasserstrom, 92–126. Lincoln and London: University of Nebraska Press.

Watanabe, John M. 1981. "Cambios económicos en Santiago Chimaltenango, Guatemala." *Mesoamérica* 2: 20–41.

– 1990. "Enduring yet Ineffable Community in the Western Periphery of Guatemala." In *Guatemalan Indians and the State: 1540 to 1988*, edited by Carol A. Smith, 183–204. Austin: University of Texas Press.

– 1992. *Maya Saints and Souls in a Changing World*. Austin: University of Texas Press.

Watson, Rodney C. 1990. "Informal Settlement and Fugitive Migration amongst the Indians of Late-Colonial Chiapas." In *Migration in Colonial Spanish America*, edited by David J. Robinson, 238–78. New York: Cambridge University Press.

Wauchope, Robert, gen. ed. 1964–1976. *Handbook of Middle American Indians*. 16 vols. Austin: University of Texas Press.

Webre, Stephen A. 1980. "The Social and Economic Bases of Cabildo Membership in Seventeenth-Century Santiago de Guatemala." Ph.D. dissertation, Tulane University.

– ed. 1989. *La sociedad colonial en Guatemala: Estudios regionales y locales*. Antigua Guatemala and South Woodstock, VT: Centro de Investigaciones Regionales de Mesoamérica and Plumsock Mesoamerican Studies.

Weeks, John M. 2003. "Foreword" and "Notes" for *The Ancient Settlements of Chaculá*, by Eduard Seler, xi–xv and 16–19. Lancaster, CA: Labyrinthos.

Wheatley, Paul. 1971. *The Pivot of the Four Quarters*. Edinburgh: Edinburgh University Press.

Whetten, Nathan L. 1961. *Guatemala: The Land and the People*. New Haven: Yale University Press.

Williams, Michael, with David Lowenthal and William M. Denevan. 2014. *To Pass On a Good Earth: The Life and Work of Carl O. Sauer*. Charlottesville: University of Virginia Press.

Wilson, Richard. 1995. *Maya Resurgence in Guatemala: Q'eqchí Experiences*. Norman and London: University of Oklahoma Press.

Wolf, Eric R. 1957. "Closed Corporate Peasant Communities in Mesoamerica and Central Java." *Southwestern Journal of Anthropology* 13, no. 1: 1–18.

– 1959. *Sons of the Shaking Earth*. Chicago: University of Chicago Press.

– (1986) 2001. "The Vicissitudes of the Closed Corporate Peasant Community." In *Pathways of Power: Building an Anthropology of the Modern World*, edited by Eric R. Wolf, with Sydel Silverman, 160–5. Berkeley and Los Angeles: University of California Press.

Wood, Stephanie. 2003. *Transcending Conquest: Nahua Views of Spanish Colonial Mexico*. Norman and London: University of Oklahoma Press.

Woodbury, Natalie F.S. 1953. "The History of Zaculeu." In *The Ruins of Zaculeu, Guatemala*, edited by Richard B. Woodbury and Aubrey S. Trik, vol. 1, 9–20. Richmond: United Fruit Company.

Woodbury, Richard B., and Aubrey S. Trik, eds. 1953. *The Ruins of Zaculeu, Guatemala*. 2 vols. Richmond, VA: United Fruit Company.

Woodward, Ralph Lee. 1993. *Rafael Carrera and the Emergence of the Republic of Guatemala, 1821–1871*. Athens and London: University of Georgia Press.

Wortman, Miles L. 1975. "Bourbon Reforms in Central America, 1750–1786." *The Americas* 32, no. 2: 222–38.

– 1975. "Government Revenue and Economic Trends in Central America, 1787–1819." *Hispanic American Historical Review* 55, no. 2: 251–86.

– 1982. *Government and Society in Central America, 1680–1840*. New York: Columbia University Press.

Ximénez, Francisco. (1715–20) 1929–31. *Historia de la provincia de San Vicente de Chiapa y Guatemala*. 3 vols. Biblioteca "Goathemala" 1–3. Guatemala: Sociedad de Geografía e Historia de Guatemala.

Yannakakis, Yanna. 2008. *The Art of Being In-Between: Native Intermediaries, Indian Identity, and Local Rule in Colonial Oaxaca*. Durham and London: Duke University Press.

Zamora Acosta, Elías. 1983a. "Conquista y crisis demográfica: La población indígena del occidente de Guatemala en el siglo XVI." *Mesoamérica* 6: 291–328.

– 1983b. "La tenencia de la tierra entre los mayas de Guatemala en la época prehispánica: Planteamiento de la cuestión y proposición de una tipología." *Anuario de Estudios Americanos* 37: 443–64.

– 1985. *Los mayas de las tierras altas en el siglo XVI: Tradición y cambio en Guatemala*. Seville: Diputación Provincial de Sevilla.

Zavala, Silvio. 1935. *La encomienda indiana*. Centro de Estudios Históricos: Madrid.

– 1940. *De encomiendas y propiedad territorial en algunas regiones de la América española*. Mexico: José Porrúa.

Zinsser, Hans. 1935. *Rats, Lice and History*. Boston: Little, Brown.

Zorita, Alonso de. (1585) 1963. *Life and Labor in Ancient Mexico: The Brief and Summary Relation of the Lords of New Spain*. Edited and translated by Benjamin Keen. New Brunswick, NJ: Rutgers University Press.

Zúñiga Corres, Ignacio. 1968. "750 aniversario de la fundación de la orden militar de Nuestra Señora de la Merced." *Anales de la Sociedad de Geografía e Historia de Guatemala* 41, nos. 2–4: 423–572.

Index

Acuña, Jorge de, 59
Adams, Richard, 200
Adams, Richard E.W., 192, 194–5
Agaab (Sacapulas), 49
agricultural fairs, 153
agricultural specialization, 21–2, 154
agriculture, 21, 22, 143–4, 154. *See also* landholding
Aguacatán, 69, 87n21, 93n36, 143, 147–9, 172; *congregación* at, 88–93 passim; *encomienda* at, 111, 121; gold and silver in vicinity of, 45n50; Indian rebellion at, 69, 96n46; pre-conquest era at, 43–9 passim; Tlaxcalan Indians at, 73–4, 92n30
Aguayo, Sebastián Antonio de, 139
Aguazap, 89
Aguirre, Francisco Xavier de, 101, 176
Aguirre, Fray Sebastián de, 101
Akateko Maya (Jakalteco), 19
alcaldes, 103, 117, 119, 145
alcaldes mayores, 119, 122, 130, 149, 188; abuse of office by, 124–6; disease and, 168, 175, 176, 178–84 passim

Altos de Chiantla, 16–17, 123, 145, 153, 189; Spanish landholding on, 138–41, 189
Alvarado, Diego de, 230
Alvarado, Gonzalo de, 52, 53, 56, 57–64 passim, 65, 69, 72, 77
Alvarado, Jorge de, 56, 69–70, 71–3
Alvarado, Pedro de, 36, 50, 74, 111–13; excesses committed by, 163–4; as leader of conquest, 54–7 passim, 92n30; perceptions of Guatemala, 34, 80; wealth and power of, 85, 121
Alvarado Bracamonte, José, 138
Alvarado y Velasco, Mariana de, 115
amag, 51, 52
Angulo, Pedro de, 88, 89, 93n34
Annals of the Cakchiquels, 78–9, 86n12
Aragón, Pedro de, 59
Arévalo, Francisco de, 59
Arias, Gaspar, 66, 68
Army of the Poor, 207–8
Asantic (Asantih), 99
Asselbergs, Florine, 70–4, 197

Astroqui, Juan de, 230
Asturias, Francisco, 172
Awakateko Maya, 19, 57
Aztecs, 50, 72

Bácaro, Juan, 122, 235
Baco de Anco, 139
Bai'joon, 148
Bailey, John, 58
Balamiha (Aguacatán), 49
Balcárcel, Jose de, 115
Balmis, Francisco Xavier de, 174,
176
Bancroft, Hubert H., 59, 65, 67, 68
Barillas, 19, 22, 205
Barrios, Justo Rufino, 25, 203, 205
Barrutia, Francisco Ignacio de,
123–4, 140–1
Bastos, Santiago, 200
Bergmann, John F., xv
Black Legend, 163
Borah, Woodrow, 75, 124, 133,
134
Bourbon Reforms, 104n78, 117
Bravo, Francisco, 135n14
Bricker, Victoria, 55n6, 95n46, 193
Brinton, Daniel, 198
Burkitt, Robert, 12n3, 24–5, 32n5
Byers, Douglas 11, 49

cabecera de doctrina, 105
Cabezas, Alonzo, 70
Cabezas, Horacio, 33n7
cacao, 16, 45, 48, 96, 121, 135,
143, 152, 154, 155, 187, 188
caciques, 86, 143, 159
Caibil Balam, 44, 50, 53, 57–64
passim
caja de comunidad, 125
Cakchiquel Maya, 44, 78

calpul, 52, 91, 142
Cambote, 38
Canil, 74n70, 92n31
Canil Acab, 60
Caquilax , 90
Cárcomo, Valdés de 198
Cárdenas, Tomás de, 87n18, 97–9
passim
Carmack, Robert M., 7, 33n6,
35–6, 41n32, 43, 47–55 passim,
58n15, 65n32, 200, 259–61
Carrasco, David, 192–4
Carrera, Rafael, 200
Castañeda, César, 19n9, 23n30, 24
Castañeda, Marcos and Santiago,
183–4
Castellanos, Francisco de, 66–9,
159n8
Cerrato, Alonzo López de, 97, 109,
110, 113, 114, 121, 158–60,
196, 218
Chaculá, 32, 38
Chajul (San Gaspar), 51, 143, 169,
177–8, 204; congregación at, 88,
89, 90, 91, 94, 95, 99; conquest
of, 46, 66, 67; encomienda at,
111; fugitivism at, 99
Chalchitán (archaelogical site), 38,
38n23
Chalchitán (parcialidad), 93, 147–
9, 172
Chancol, 17
Chancol (hacienda), 123, 138–40,
146
Chap, Gaspar, 146–7
Chaunu, Pierre and Huguette,
188n2, 189n5
Chávez, Pedro de, 139, 146
Chaxá, 89, 90n23
Chel, 89, 90n23, 204

Chemal, 183
Chevalier, François, 133–5
Chiantla, 16, 17, 19, 22, 120, 127,
    128, 130, 137, 143, 145, 205,
    206; agricultural fairs at, 153;
    congregación at, 87, 88, 89, 106;
    encomienda at, 111, 121; silver
    mining at, 112, 122, 136
Chiapas, 11, 12, 16, 17n7, 20,
    38n23, 97, 102, 104, 122, 125,
    132, 153, 154, 168, 173, 192,
    196, 200
Chichicastenango, 66–7
Chicui, 90
Chigna Huiucelut, 57
Chimbal. See Santiago
    Chimaltenango
Chinabjul. See Huehuetenango
chinamit, 52
Ch'orti' Maya, 56
Chuj Maya, 19, 25n37, 208
Chutinamit, 39, 46, 51
Chutixtiox, 39, 46, 51
Ciudad Real, 153, 154
Ciudad Vieja, 65n32
civil administration, 102–5 passim
Classic culture, 35
clergy, 104, 107, 159; abuse of
    office by, 126–7
Cline, Howard, 193
cocoliztli. See gucumatz (disease)
cofradías, 127, 141, 143, 148, 172
Cojtí Cuxil, Demetrio, 201
Collier, George, 20
Collins, Ann, 20n14, 89n22,
    107n82, 125n62
Colotenango (Asunción), 22, 167
Comitán, 11, 69, 89, 93n35, 127,
    147, 153, 155, 204n12
composición, 137, 142, 204n14

Concepción, 22, 26, 101, 149, 154,
    176, 178, 182
congregación: operation and
    dynamics of, 84–93, 105; regional
    adjustments to, 93–9, 188–9
congregaciones. See pueblos de
    indios
conquistadores, 58, 60n22, 68, 77,
    83, 163
Constitution of 1812, 129
Cook, Noble David, xvi, 165n30
Cook, Sherburne, 76
Copán, 35, 38
corn cultivation, 16, 17, 21–2
corn yields, 21
corregidores, 117; abuse of office
    by, 116, 124–6
Cortés, Hérnan, 54, 56
Cortés y Larraz, Pedro, 45n50, 101,
    122, 126n63, 140n27, 152–3,
    199
Cotter, John, 195
Council of the Indies, 103
Cozar, Prudencio de, 149, 175, 184
Crosby, Alfred W., 165n30
Cuchumatán, etymology of, 12
Cuchumatánes. See Cuchumatán
    highlands
Cuchumatán highlands: archaeol-
    ogy of, 36–40; conquest of,
    57–74, 187; ethnohistory of,
    40–2; geology of, 16, 18; glacial
    history of, 16; physical geogra-
    phy of, 11, 16–18; precipitation
    patterns of, 17–18
Cuilco, 19, 22, 43, 61, 102, 125,
    144, 166n36
cultural landscape, 5–7
Cunén, 43, 46, 67, 142, 148, 154;
    congregación at, 88, 90, 91

Dakin, Karen, 198
Davis, Mary Ellen, 208
Davis, Shelton, 202, 204–5
debt peonage, 25, 123, 132, 133,
    134, 141, 157
Denevan, William M., xvi, 6n14,
    75n1, 75n4
depopulation, 75, 138, 157, 158–
    66 passim, 186
derrama, 131
Deuss, Krystyna, xvii, 27n43
Díaz del Castillo, Bernal, 58n15, 83
Díaz del Castillo, Francisco, 99, 160
Diéguez, Juan, 15
disease, 95, 118–19; New World
    diseases, 164; Old World dis-
    eases, 76, 79, 161, 164–6, 185–6.
    See also gucumatz; *matlazáhuatl*;
    measles; plague; smallpox;
    typhus
Dobyns, Henry, 163n16
Dominicans, 88–9, 97, 98, 105,
    107, 161
Dunn, Alvis, 198

ecclesiastical administration, 102–7
    passim
ejido, 87, 92n32, 141, 142, 144,
    146, 149, 150, 203, 204
El Caballero, 39
El Rosario (*hacienda*), 133, 138,
    139, 140, 146
encomenderos, 109, 110–15 pas-
    sim, 116, 118, 121, 131
encomienda, 116–17, 118, 121,
    131, 157; derivation of, 109n1;
    general operation of, 108–9; in
    Huehuetenango, 111–15;
    regional operation of, 110–11,
    196

epidemics. *See* disease
Escuytenango, 89
Espinar, Juan de, 108, 111–14, 115,
    121, 136, 137
ethnic relations, 127–32 passim
Exbalamquen, 66

Farriss, Nancy, 12n3, 102, 196
Fenn, Elizabeth, 167n37
Few, Martha, 172n48, 174n58, 199
Finca San Francisco, 207
Flores, José, 172n48
Foster, George, 83
Fox, John, 45n50, 49
Franciscans, 105, 165
Fuente, Francisco de la, 114
Fuentes y Guzmán, Francisco
    Antonio de, 94, 99, 117n31, 131,
    135n14, 143, 165n35; scholarly
    contribution of, 11n1, 57n12,
    58–69 passim, 77–8, 136n16,
    144, 152, 158, 162, 261–2
fugitivism, 95, 99–101, 127, 189

Gage, Thomas, 12, 23n27
Gall, Francis, 36
Garcés, Diego de, 96n45, 188
Garcia Bernal, Cristina, 102n71
Garcia de Medina, Tomás, 139
Gechec, 149–50
Geraldino, Francisco, 168–9, 172
Gerhard, Peter, 102, 161n17
Gibson, Charles, 78, 97n50,
    104n78, 131n79, 134, 163n23
goitre, 23
González, José Joaquín, 45n50
Grandin, Greg, 198
Guajiaquero, 111
Guatemala: *audiencia* of, 103–4,
    126, 172n48, 196; conquest of,

53–6; contemporary population of, 18

Guatemala City, 18, 35, 130, 172n48, 175, 205

Guazacapán, 187

gucumatz (disease), 161, 246

Gucumatz (K'iche' king), 42, 43, 47

Gumarcaah, 42–3, 45–50 passim, 52, 55, 187

Guzmán, Juana de, 114

haciendas, 115, 123–4, 133–4, 138–40, 146–8, 152–3, 155, 157, 189. *See also* agriculture; landholding

Hall, Carolyn, 195, 196

Haring, Clarence, 126

Hartshorne, Richard, 3, 4

Harvey, David, 3, 4, 5

Henríquez, Andrés, 91, 92n29

Hernández, Leonardo, 198

Hernández, Pedro, 143

Herrera, Antonio de, 65n32

Herrera, Baltasar de, 138

Herrera, Lucrecia de, 138

Herrera, Raymundo de, 148

Herrera, Robinson, 198

Hidalgo, Joseph Domingo, 92n32, 173

Higbee, E.C., 24n34

historical geography, nature of, 3–6

Honcab. *See* Oncap

Huehuetenango: Department of 11, 19n9, 23, 24n34, 26n42; *partido* of 12, 104

Huehuetenango, town of, 19, 22, 105, 97, 99n57, 101, 105, 122, 125, 126n63, 128, 130, 147, 152–3, 166n36, 172, 178,

205–9; *congregación* at, 87, 88; *encomeinda* at, 110–15, 121; landholding in vicinity of, 136, 137, 143, 144, 152, 155, 189; population history of, 158, 160, 161; Tlaxcalan Indians at, 73, 92n30

Huista valley, 48

Huiz, 89

Hyul. *See* Juil

idolatry, 98, 120

Ilom, 90, 91, 94, 95, 204; Indian rebellion at, 69, 96n46

Indian armies, 53–74 passim, 77, 78, 158, 161

Indian labour, 24–6, 108, 113, 119–24 passim, 131, 135, 140

Indian population, 18–19, 34, 35, 53, 74, 75–80, 133, 145, 157–62, 163, 166–7, 173, 176, 185–6, 190

Indian tribute, 69, 74, 77, 84, 91, 100, 108–19, 131, 143, 154, 158–60 passim; classification procedures, 116; Indian elites soliciting right, 41; legislation governing, 129; resistance toward payment of, 128–30

indigo, 96, 138, 152, 187

indios de servicio, 121–2

inoculation, 172–4

intendancy system, 104, 118

Ixtupil, 204

Ixil Maya, 19, 25, 43, 46, 57, 65–7, 78, 89, 94–5, 101n66, 117n31, 129, 169, 177, 187, 204

Ixtahuacán (San Ildefonso), 26, 43, 61, 154

Izalcos, 187

Jacaltec Maya, 49, 149
Jacaltenango, 20n14, 96, 107, 119, 141n29, 260; *congregación* at, 87, 88, 89; *encomienda* at, 110, 115n26, 121; land dispute at, 149–50; typhus at, 176, 178, 185, 186n113
Jenner, Edward, 174–5
Jones, Grant, 196, 199
Jorge, Gaspar, 100
Juárez, Juan José, 181–5
Juil, 90n23

Kaminaljuyú, 35
Kanter, Gustav, 32n5, 39n25
Kaqchikel Maya, 49, 50, 54, 56, 71n, 165, 176n65, 198, 202. *See also* Cakchiquel Maya
Kaufman, Terrence, 17n7
Kelly, John E., 34n9
K'iche' Maya, 19, 31–2, 33, 36, 40–2, 52, 54–5, 57, 187. *See also* Quiché Maya
Kirchoff, Paul, 33
Kobrak, Paul, 207, 208
Koch, Friedrich, 206
Komisaruk, Catherine, 198
Kramer, Wendy, 68, 110, 196

Lacandón Maya, 99n58, 143, 190; intrusions by, 93–5, 101, 144; Spanish attempts to subjugate, 88n19, 122
La Capellanía, 17
La Capellanía (*hacienda*), 138, 139, 146
La Democracía, 223
La Farge, Oliver, 11, 12, 20, 25n36, 31, 49, 87, 191, 202, 204
Lake Atitlán, 48

La Libertad, 19
Lamaquib, 92n31, 148
La Mesilla, ix
land, Indian attitudes towards, 15n4, 87, 90, 142
land disputes, 40, 145–52
landholding: contemporary patterns of, 23–4; historical evolution of, 87, 115, 135–45 passim, 155–6
land reform, 25
Lara, Manuel José de, 130, 149
Larrave, Mariano, 178–9
Las Ánimas, 128
Las Casas, Bartolomé de, 41, 48, 163–4, 261
latifundia, 133
Latin America: historical geography of, 6–7
Laws of Burgos, 84
lead mining, 122, 128, 136
Lenteno, Mariano Francisco, 179–81 passim
León, Alonso de 100, 127
León Cardona, Juan de, 64
León Faboada, José, 149
Leyenda Negra. See Black Legend
Liberal Reforms, 25, 202
Lienzo de Quauhquechollan, 12n2, 71–3, 197
Liévano, Pedro de, 157
Lincoln, Jackson Steward, 202, 203, 204n12
Lockhart, James, 115
locust invasion, 118, 131, 154, 178
Lokken, Paul, 198
López, Juan 128
López de los Ríos, Juan, 139
López de Palacios, Juan, 60n22
Los Cheches, 139

Los Tapiales, 34
Luján Muñoz, Jorge, 120n42, 195, 196, 198, 258
Lutz, Christopher H., 198, 199

Mackie, Sedley J., 58
MacLeod, Murdo, 79, 97, 124, 131n79, 133–5 passim, 137, 161, 165, 192, 194–5, 259, 260
Malacatán, 19, 59–60, 107, 121, 153, 204
Malacatancito. *See* Malacatán
Maldonado, Alonso de, 70
Maldonado de Paz, Juan, 135n14
Mamenguiché, 145–6
Mam Maya, 12, 19, 39, 40, 43, 44, 48, 49, 50, 57–65 passim, 69, 72, 77, 87, 155, 177, 187
Manzanares, Diego de, 74
Marroquín, Francisco, 85, 86, 231, 247
Martín, Manuel, 145
Martínez de la Vega, Juan, 127, 133, 139, 145–6
Martínez de la Vega, Juana, 139
Martínez de la Vega, Manuela, 139
Martínez Peláez, Severo, 191, 197, 201, 259
matlazáhuatl, 161
Matthew, Laura, 197–8
Maya culture: contemporary patterns of, 18–27 passim, 200; historical evolution of, 31, 96–7
Maya religion, 87, 97, 98, 99, 100, 101
Mazagua, 68
Mazatenango. *See* San Lorenzo
McBryde, Felix Webster, 18, 22, 165n34
McCreery, David, 25n37, 205–6

measles, 154n72, 164, 165, 178
Méndez, Gonzalo, 105
Mercedarians, 89, 104, 105, 107, 141n29, 182
Mesoamerican studies, xiii–xiv, 6, 195
minifundios, 24n34
Mixteca Alta, xi
Montejo, Victor, 201
Montes de Oca, Juan, 122n50
Montoya, Pedro de, 128
Mont y Prats, Joaquín, 141n28
Moreno, Tomás, 147
mortality, variation in rates of, 161, 166, 169, 170, 172, 178–9, 185, 186
Moscoso, Domingo Balmaior, 138
Motolinía (Toribio de Benavente), 165
Motozintla (San Francisco) 135, 167
municipios: origin and nature of, 19–21, 23, 205

Namá, 90
Navarrete, Carlos, 32n5
Nebaj (Santa Maria), 32, 90n23, 101, 107, 148, 202, 203–4; *congregación* at, 88, 89, 91; conquest of, 66, 67; *encomienda* at, 111; seasonal migration at, 24–5; smallpox and typhus at, 169, 177, 178
Nentón, 19
New Laws, 84, 98n54, 196
Nicholson, Henry, 7
Noriega, Marcelo de 139

Oaxaca, xi, xiv, 134, 143, 156, 196
Olmos, Pedro de, 66

Olvarrieta, Joseph, 152
Oncap (Onkap), 90, 91
Ordóñez, Juan José, 148
Ordóñez, Manuel, 167
Orduña, Francisco de, 66, 68,
111–12
Orellana, José María, 179, 180
Otzoy, Simón, 198
Ovalle, Francisco de, 159n8
Ovalle, Gonzalo de, 68
Oviedo, Bernardino de, 59

Pablo, Mateo, 208–9
Pacot, 39, 46
Páez, Juan, 121
Paiconop, 93–4, 179
Palenque, 35, 38
Paleo-Indian culture, 34
páramo. See Altos de Chiantla
parcialidades, 52, 90–1, 93, 94n41,
97, 150–1; at Sacapulas, 91–2,
142
Parra, Micaela de la, 139
Pastor, Francisco, 175
Patch, Robert W., 122n50, 125n60,
126n63, 194
Paula Lopez, Francisco de, 182
Pérez, Francisco, 146, 147
Pérez-Brignoli, Héctor, 195
Petanac, 209
Petatán, 88, 89, 149, 155, 178
Pichiquil, 45n50
Piedrasanta, Ruth, 17n7, 25n37,
27n43, 36n21
Piedras Negras, 35
Pimintel, Luis Manuel, 114, 115,
136–7
plague, 78–9, 161, 165
plantation agriculture, 25, 26, 188,
203, 206, 207

plant domestication, 12n3, 34
Pocomán Maya. *See* Poqomam
Maya
Ponce, Alonso, 105
Popol Vuh, 40–4 passim, 47,
148n53, 260
population. *See* Indian population;
Spanish population
population decline. *See*
depopulation
population history, 157–62
Poqomam Maya, 56
Post-classic culture, 35–6, 39, 42,
50, 55
Potosí, 136
Pre-classic culture, 34, 36
principales, 86, 119, 143, 159
Proskouriakoff, Tatiana, 38n23,
39n24
pueblos de indios, 84, 88, 90, 95,
102, 103, 105, 108, 111, 116,
118, 141–2, 144, 152, 188–9. *See
also congregación*
Puyumatlán (Santa Eulalia), 70,
73n66, 110

Q'anjob'al Maya, 19, 57, 110
Q'eqchi' Maya, 56
quarantine, 170, 173, 174
Quen Santo, 38
Quetzaltenango, city of, 54, 153,
154, 180
Quetzaltenango, Department of,
12
Quezaltenango. *See* Quetzaltenango
Quicab, 43, 44, 47, 49
Quiché conquest, 42–50
Quiché Maya, 19, 31–2, 33, 36,
40–2, 52, 54–5, 57, 187
Quiriguá, 38

Rabinal Achí, 40, 46
Ramírez de Quiñones, Pedro, 88, 89
Ramón Solís, Juan, 169
real servicio. See servicio del tostón
Recinos, Adrián, 41n32, 48, 198
reducción. See congregación
regidores, 103, 117, 145
región andina, 17
Remesal, Antonio de, 88–91, 93, 98n53, 107n82; scholarly contribution of, 88n20, 261
repartimiento, 119–20, 122, 135; *de mercancías*, 125–6; derivation of, 11n39
reparto de efectos. See repartimiento de mercancías
Requerimiento, 60–1
Ricketson, Oliver, 12n3
Río Blanco, 39; archaeological site, 38
Río Chixoy. *See* Río Negro
Río Cuilco, 11, 16
Río de las Vueltas, 139
Río Grande de Chiapas, 16
Río Hondo, 59
Río Ixcán, 94
Río Malacatán, 112, 135
Río Negro, 11, 18, 23, 39, 67, 97, 151
Río Selegua, 16, 43
Ríos Montt, Efraín, 209
Río Usumacinta, 16
Rodríguez Mazariegos, Melchor, 138
Rogel, Juan, 86
Rojas, Diego de, 69
Ruiz, Ignacio, 175
Ruiz, Marcos, 228, 231, 232

Sacapulas, 18, 39n24, 40, 43, 45, 46, 48, 49, 67, 107n82, 161, 197, 260; *congregación* at, 88, 89, 91–2, 97, 105; *encomienda* at, 110, 121; goitre at, 23n27; gold in the vicinity of, 45n50; Indian rebellion at, 129, 130; land disputes at, 148, 150–1; landholding at, 142–3; salt making at, 22–3, 45, 153, 154; Tlaxcalan Indians at, 74; Zorita's *visita* to, 98–9. *See also parcialiadades*
Sacchaná, 38, 39n23
Sacsiguan, 204
Sáenz de Santa María, Carmelo, 68
Sajpojolá, 139
Sakiulew. *See* Zaculeu
Salazar, Antonio de, 59, 63
Salquil, 90, 91
salt making, 22–3, 45–6, 154
salutación, 131
San Antonio Huista, 24
San Antonio Musmul, 139
San Antonio Tierra Negra (*hacienda*), 147
San Juan Atitán, 22, 63, 99, 177, 203
San Juan Cotzal, 90n23, 143, 204; *congregación* at 88, 89, 91; smallpox and typus at 169, 177
San Juan Ixcoy, 22, 23, 26n42, 38n23, 110, 152; massacre at, 205–7; typhus at, 178, 179, 180, 185
San Lorenzo (Mazatenango), 59, 78, 152, 167
San Martín Cuchumatán, 12, 48, 63, 89n22, 129; *congregación* at, 88, 89; land disputes at, 133, 145, 146, 203; typhus at, 177, 178

San Martín Mazapa, 167
San Mateo Ixtatán, 22, 23, 110, 143, 152; fugitivism at, 99, 127; Indian rebellion at, 94, 129n74, 147; salt making at, 22, 23, 153, 154; typhus at, 185
San Miguel Acatán, 22, 101, 152, 170, 179, 181-2, 184, 185
San Pedro Necta, 22, 141n29, 154, 203
San Sebastián Coatán, 22, 143, 147, 152, 154
San Sebastián Huehuetenango, 144, 167, 177
Santa Ana Huista, 19, 88, 89, 152, 155, 174, 176n65
Santa Bárbara, 22, 128
Santa Cruz Yalmux, 205
Santa Eulalia, 22, 23, 31n1, 70, 73n66, 110, 119, 143, 144, 152, 202, 204-5, 260; congregación at, 93-4; typhus at, 178-85 passim
Santa Isabel, 153, 177
Santa María Chiquimula, 130
Santa María de Jesús, 54
Santiago Chimaltenango, 20, 24, 63, 143, 152, 167, 202, 203
Santiago de Guatemala, 65, 78, 114, 120, 121, 123, 128, 135n14, 137, 140, 153, 155, 159n8, 187, 196, 198, 199, 261
Santo Tomás (parcialidad), 92, 105, 147-9, 151
Sauer, Carl, 3-6 passim, 83n3, 259
Schwartzkopf, Stacey, 25n37, 166n36
seasonal migration, 26, 143-4
Seler, Eduard, 31n1, 32, 38, 75
Sellers-García, Sylvia, 103n74

Sequechul, 57
Serquil, Indian rebellion at, 69, 96n46
servicio del tostón, 117, 118, 161
servicio personal, 121, 122
settlement patterns, 19-21, 31, 50-2, 102, 116
seventeenth-century economic depression, 95, 96, 110-11, 133, 134, 137, 157, 189
sheep-raising, 17, 22, 122-4, 138-40, 143, 145, 146-7, 152-3, 189
Sherman, William, 54, 85, 88n19, 113n13, 122, 261
Sierra de los Cuchumatanes. See Cuchumatán highlands
silver mining, 45n50, 112, 122, 136, 187
Siquibilchas, 146
slavery, 52, 64, 67, 69, 112, 121, 130-1, 163, 187, 217
smallpox, 78, 79, 164-71, 173-5, 176n65, 178, 185
Smith, Carol, 156n80
social organization, 51-2, 90-1, 93, 142
Soconusco, 47, 187, 196
Soloma, 22, 26, 110, 121, 143, 152, 180, 205-7; impact of typhus epidemic on, 119, 154n72, 178, 179, 181-3, 185
Sotzil, 204
Spanish population, 166; and encomienda, 109, 115
Stadelman, Raymond, 21, 23n29, 24, 26, 206
Stephens, John Lloyd, 15
Stoll, David, 203-4
Suchitepéquez, 121, 154, 187, 197

Taracena, Arturo, 200
tasaciones de tributes, 110, 114, 116, 118, 158–62, passim. *See also* Indian tribute
Taylor, William B., xiii, 134, 156, 261
Tecpán Guatemala, 49, 59, 80
Tecún Umán, 55
Tegucigalpa, 128, 187
Temal, 90
Tenam, 39
Tenochtitlán, 51
Teotihuacán, 35, 51
Tepancuapam, 38n23
tercio de Navidad, 117
tercio de San Juan, 117
Termer, Franz, xii, 12
tierra caliente, 16, 121, 143, 147, 190
tierra fría, 17, 45, 96, 143
tierra templada, 16, 22, 45, 48, 96, 143, 204
Tikal, 35
tinamit, 51, 52
Título C'oyoi, 40, 44, 45
Título de los Señores de Sacapulas, 40, 41
Tlaxcala, 71
Tlaxcalan Indians, 73–4, 78, 92n30, 259
Todos Santos Cuchumatán, 12, 21, 22, 26, 43, 48, 63, 72, 154, 159n8, 172; *congregación* at, 88–9; land disputes at, 133, 142n33, 145–6, 149–50; smallpox and typhus at, 177, 178
Torres, Juan de, 87n18, 88, 89, 97–9
Torres-Rivas, Edelberto, 195
Totonicapán: Department of, 12, 75–9, 90n25 passim; Indian

rebellion at, 128, 130, 197; *partido* of, 12; town of, 34, 59, 175
Totonicapán and Huehuetenango: *alcadía mayor* of, 11, 45n50, 104, 122, 125n62, 130, 168, 176; *corregimiento* of, 11, 13, 61n23, 104, 117, 144, 161, 162n19, 261; *provincia* of, 97, 172, 175
Tovilla, Martín Alfonso, 45, 91
tribute. *See* Indian tribute
Tuhuinimá, 139
typhus, 119, 154n72, 161n17, 164–6, 176–85
Tzeltal Maya, 122
Tzotzil Maya, 20
Tzutuhil Maya, 196
Tz'utujil Maya, 48, 54. *See also* Tzutuhil Maya

Uaxac Canal, 38
Uspantán: conquest of, 65n32, 66, 67, 68–9, 187; *encomienda* at, 110, 121; typhus at, 178
Uspanteko Maya, 19, 57, 65–7, 69, 78
Usumacinta basin, 11, 16
Utatlán. *See* Gumarcaah

Vacá, 89
vaccination, 174–5, 254
Valverde, Diego García de, 109, 114–15, 158, 159–62
Van Akkeren, Ruud, 39n24, 197, 199
Vázquez, Francisco, 105
Veblen, Thomas T., 75–6, 77, 78, 79, 161
Verapaz, 45, 47, 48, 67, 72, 73, 176n65, 197

Verastegui, Francisco de, 59
Vac Amag. *See* Wukamak

Wagley, Charles, 19–20, 202
Wasserstrom, Robert, 12n2, 20, 102, 125n62, 131, 260
Watanabe, John, 20, 25n37, 202, 203
Watson, Rodney, 102, 196
Wauchope, Robert, 193
Woodbury, Natalie, 31n1, 32, 56, 58, 59n18, 61n23, 61n24
Woodward, Ralph Lee, 200
Wolf, Eric, 19, 20n14, 21, 33n7, 260
wool production 22, 153
Wortman, Miles, 95n44, 104n78, 117n28, 118n35, 134, 261
Wukamak, 42

Xaclbal valley, 94
Xebuyugüitz (*hacienda*), 139
Xelahuh. *See* Quetzaltenango

Ximénez, Francisco, 41, 51, 95n42, 105
Xolchun (Huehuetenango), 46, 50, 148
Xolchun (Quiché), 39, 148
Xolpacol, 46

Yalambojoch, 32, 38, 39n23
Ylom. *See* Ilom
Yucatán, 12, 102, 196
Yximché, 49

Zacatecas, 136
Zacchaná. *See* Sacchaná
Zaculeu, 32, 39, 46, 49, 50, 51, 87; conquest of, 43–4, 48, 53, 60–4 passim, 111; etymology of, 43n42
Zalchil. *See* Salquil
Zamallorga, Nolberto, 147
Zamora, Elías, 158n4, 197
Zapotitlán, 96, 188, 197
Zorita, Alonso de, 98–9, 159, 196
Zurrilla, Francisco de 112, 113